D0889662

Schizophrenia

Exploring the
Spectrum of Psychosis

Schizophrenia
Exploring the Spectrum of Psychosis

Edited by

R.J. Ancill, S. Holliday *and* J. Higenbottam

Department of Psychiatry, St. Vincent's Hospital, Vancouver,
British Columbia, Canada

JOHN WILEY & SONS

Chichester · New York · Brisbane · Toronto · Singapore

Copyright © 1994 by John Wiley & Sons Ltd,
Baffins Lane, Chichester,
West Sussex PO19 1UD, England
Telephone National Chichester (0243) 779777
International (+44) 243 779777

All rights reserved.

No part of this book may be reproduced by any means,
or transmitted, or translated into a machine language
without the written permission of the publisher.

Other Wiley Editorial Offices

John Wiley & Sons, Inc., 605 Third Avenue,
New York, NY 10158-0012, USA

Jacaranda Wiley Ltd, 33 Park Road, Milton,
Queensland 4064, Australia

John Wiley & Sons (Canada) Ltd, 22 Worcester Road,
Rexdale, Ontario M9W 1L1, Canada

John Wiley & Sons (SEA) Pte Ltd, 37 Jalan Pemimpin #05-04,
Block B, Union Industrial Building, Singapore 2057

Library of Congress Cataloging-in-Publication Data

Schizophrenia : exploring the spectrum of psychosis / edited by R.J.
Ancill, S. Holliday, and J. Higenbottam.
p. cm.
Proceedings of the Schizophrenia 1994 Conference, held in
Vancouver, B.C.
Includes bibliographical references and index.
ISBN 0 471 95255 9
1. Schizophrenia—Congresses. I. Ancill, R. J. II. Holliday,
Stephen G. III. Higenbottam, J. IV. Schizophrenia Conference (1994
: Vancouver, B.C.)
[DNLM: 1. Schizophrenia—congresses. WM 203 S33777 1994]
RC514.S3354 1994
616.89'82—dc20
DNLM/DLC
for Library of Congress 94-21813
CIP

British Library Cataloguing in Publication Data

A catalogue record for this book is available from the British Library

ISBN 0 471 952559

Produced from camera-ready copy supplied by the author
Printed and bound in Great Britain by Bookcraft (Bath) Ltd, Midsomer Norton, Avon

In Memory of Dr. Ernest J. Runions
"Mentor, Friend and Colleague"

Contents

Contributors

Martha E. Adams, M.D.

Clinical Investigation Unit and Schizophrenia Research Program, Clarke Institute of Psychiatry, Toronto, Ontario, Canada

Raymond J. Ancill, M.A., M.B., FRCPysch (UK), FRCPC

Head, Department of Psychiatry, St Vincent's Hospital and Clinical Professor, Department of Psychiatry, University of British Columbia, Vancouver, British Columbia, Canada

Leona L. Bachrach, Ph.D.

Research Professor of Psychiatry, Maryland Psychiatric Research Center, University of Maryland School of Medicine, Baltimore, Maryland, United States

Gayla Blackwell, R.N., M.S.W.

Clinical Research Center for Schizophrenia and Psychiatric Rehabilitation, Camarillo State Hospital, Los Angeles, California, United States

Gary R. Bond

Professor, Department of Psychology, Indiana University - Purdue University at Indianapolis, Indianapolis, Indiana, United States

Graham Burrows, M.D., Ch.B., DPM, FRANZCP, FRCPsych

Professor Director of Psychiatry, Department of Psychiatry, University of Melbourne, Austin Hospital, Heidelberg, Australia

T.A. Carpenter, M.A., Ph.D.

Assistant Director of Research, Herchel Smith Laboratory for Medicinal Chemistry, University of Cambridge, Cambridge, United Kingdom

Thad A. Eckman, Ph.D

Clinical Research Center for Schizophrenia and Psychiatric Rehabilitation, Camarillo State Hospital, Los Angeles, California, United States

Laurie D. Hall, Ph.D.

Herchel Smith Professor of Medicinal Chemistry, School of Clinical Medicine, University of Cambridge, Cambridge, United Kingdom

J.J. Herrod, M.B., B.Chir, B.Sc., Ph.D.

Registrar in Psychiatry, Addenbrooke's N.H.S. Trust, Cambridge, United Kingdom

Ian Hindmarch, Ph.D., FB.Ps.S.

Professor of Human Psychopharmacology, and Head, Human Psychopharmacology Research Unit, University of Surrey, Godalming, Surrey, United Kingdom

Courtenay M. Harding, Ph.D.

Assistant Professor of Psychiatry and Associate Director, Program for Public Psychiatry, School of Medicine, University of Colorado, Denver, Colorado, United States

Robert Howard, M.D.

Section of Old Age Psychiatry, Institute of Psychiatry, De Crespigny Park, London, United Kingdom

Kathryn J. Kotrla, M.D.

Assistant Professor of Psychiatry, University of Texas, Houston, Texas, United States

Timothy G. Kuehnel, Ph.D. — Clinical Research Center for Schizophrenia & Psychiatric Rehabilitation, Camarillo State Hospital, Los Angeles, California, United States

Malcolm Lader, D.Sc., Ph.D., M.D., F.R.C.Psych — Professor of Clinical Psychopharmacology, Institute of Psychiatry, De Crespigny Park, London, United Kingdom

Raymond Levy, M.B., Ch.B., FRCP, Ph.D., DPM, FRCPsych — Professor of Old Age Psychiatry, Institute of Psychiatry, London, United Kingdom

Robert P. Liberman, M.D. — Professor, Department of Psychiatry, University of California at Los Angeles and Director, Clinical Research Centre for Schizophrenia and Psychiatric Rehabilitation, Camarillo State Hospital, Los Angeles, California, United States

G.W. MacEwan, M.D., FRCPC — Director, Adult Psychiatric Services, St Vincent's Hospital, and Clinical Assistant Professor, Department of Psychiatry, University of British Columbia, Vancouver, British Columbia, Canada

P.J. McKenna, M.B., Ch.B., MRCPsych., MA (Oxon) — Consultant in Psychiatry, Addenbrooke's N.H.S. Trust, Cambridge, United Kingdom

R.M. Murray, DSC, FRCPsych. — Professor and Chairman, Department of Psychological Medicine, Institute of Psychiatry and King's College Hospital, De Crespigny Park, London, United Kingdom

Trevor R. Norman

Department of Psychiatry, University of Melbourne, Austin Hospital, Heidelberg, Australia

Godfrey Pearlson, M.B., FAPA

Director, Division of Psychiatric Neuro-Imaging and Professor, Departments of Psychiatry and Mental Hygiene, Johns Hopkins University, Baltimore, Maryland, United States

Ann Pulver

Psychiatric Epidemiology and Genetics, Department of Psychiatry, Johns Hopkins University, Baltimore, Maryland, United States

Peter V. Rabins, M.D.

Professor, Department of Psychiatry, Johns Hopkins University, Baltimore, Maryland, United States

Gary Remington, M.D., Ph.D., FRCPC

Clinical Investigation Unit, Schizophrenia Program, Clarke Institute of Psychiatry, Toronto, Ontario, Canada

Ruth M. Ryan, M.D.

Assistant Professor, and Director, Mental Health Services for Persons with Developmental Disabilities, University of Colorado, Denver, Colorado, United States

Michael A. Simpson, M.D., M.B., B.Sc., MRCS, MRCPsych, DPM

Director, Centre for Psychosocial & Traumatic Stress, Pretoria, South Africa

Stephen M. Stahl, M.D., Ph.D.

Professor, Department of Psychiatry and Director, Clinical Neuroscience Research Center, University of California, San Diego, California, United States

John R. Steinberg, M.D.

Clinical Assistant Professor, Departments of Family Medicine and Psychiatry, University of Maryland, Baltimore, Maryland, United States

John A. Talbot, M.D.

Professor and Chairman, Department of Psychiatry, University of Maryland, Baltimore, Maryland, United States

Charles J. Wallace

Clinical Research Center for Schizophrenia and Psychiatric Rehabilitation, Camarillo State Hospital, Los Angeles, California, United States

Danial R. Weinberger, M.D.

Chief, Clinical Brain Disorders Branch, Division of Intramural Research Programs, National Institute of Mental Health, NIMH Neuroscience Centre at St Elizabeth's, Washington, District of Columbia, United States

Richard Williams, M.B., B.Sc., M. Phil., MRCPsych, FRCPC

Associate Professor, Department of Psychiatry, University of Calgary, Calgary, Alberta, Canada

P.W.R. Woodruff

Lecturer, Department of Psychological Medicine, Institute of Psychiatry, London, United Kingdom

Preface

No other physical or psychiatric disease causes as much suffering as Schizophrenia. People suffering from this illness are constantly hounded by hallucinations or delusions, or suffer from deficits which prevent them from being able to function psychologically or socially. Their families find the illness troubling in that they often do not understand its cause, nor have a clear idea of how to help. Society has the task of trying to provide care for individuals with schizophrenia who may suffer a long and arduous course of their illness.

Research and treatment into schizophrenia has had a difficult past. Too often patients were housed in institutions where little or no treatment was being applied. When treatments were given often they were with medications which caused serious short and long-term side effects, making the patient very uncomfortable. In terms of research dollars spent, there has been little funds available for research in schizophrenia compared with other illnesses such as cancer, multiple sclerosis or diabetes.

The last decade has brought about many improvements in the ways we understand and treat patients with schizophrenia. The areas of treatment have had the most impressive advances which have benefited patients with schizophrenia. The cornerstone of all treatment of the psychosis within schizophrenia is the use of an antipsychotic medication to improve the psychotic symptoms such as hallucinations and delusions. Medications such as clozapine and risperidone have shown that they can have significant benefits for patients with schizophrenia. Clozapine has been a breakthrough medication in the treatment of refractory schizophrenia and has shown that it can significantly improve schizophrenic patients who had long been given up as being untreatable. Risperidone has come on to the market recently with the promise that it will be as effective as traditional older antipsychotic medications but will not have as many short term side effects such as the stiffness and tremor seen in the extrapyramidal side effects. Overall the promise heralded by these two new medications has spurred significant interest in new psychopharmacological treatments of schizophrenia.

This clinical excitement has helped continue advances seen in other treatment areas of schizophrenia. One of example of this is the rehabilitative programs which are now being more widely offered to patients with schizophrenia. These rehabilitative programs, particularly when applied for patients who have been deinstitutionalized and placed in their home community, have shown significant benefits in the quality of life and overall functioning of patients with schizophrenia. New medications such as clozapine and risperidone have helped in that they allow patients to have significant benefits from their medications without being hampered by the side effects which have caused them great discomfort.

This excitement continues to build when you look at the research recently done in schizophrenia. Noninvasive functional and structural imaging techniques have allowed us to clearly see that there are changes in the brain's of people with schizophrenia. A clear consistency to all of these findings has not yet been achieved but it does help solidify with the general medical community the fact that schizophrenia is not a mere functional disorder but is rather a clear central nervous system disease. Genetic research showing relationships of specific dopamine genes to the functional abilities of medication such as clozapine are a good example of how the research and clinical spheres intersect and in this combined fashion bring together a better understanding of schizophrenia.

It is upon this recent exciting and fertile ground that the Schizophrenia 1994 Conference embarks. What the last decade of research in clinical treatment of schizophrenia has shown us is that there will not be a single method or approach that will provide all of the answers or treat all of the symptoms. It is with this in mind that the "Schizophrenia 1994: Exploring the Spectrum of Psychosis" Conference provides a broad focus for issues in the research and treatment of schizophrenia. This book is derived, in large part, from the plenary topics addressed at this conference. It appropriately explores the full realm of psychosis as it applies not only to schizophrenia but other psychotic disorders. This broad focus allows the reader to extract significant findings into psychosis and its treatment, and possibly apply them to schizophrenia in a way which has rarely been done previously.

The range of topics in this book is impressive. This includes looking at basic research such as Daniel Weinberger's chapter on brain development to Stephen Stahl's assessment of receptor activity and medication effects on them. Psychosocial rehabilitation issues as addressed in chapters by Gerald Hogarty and Robert Liberman show how expectations for patients with schizophrenia have improved. John Talbott and Leona Bachrach in their chapters provide an excellent social perspective for treatments that have occurred to patients with schizophrenia over the last few decades.

So whether your interest lies in looking at basic biological research, psychosocial rehabilitative therapies or medication treatments of the patient with schizophrenia, I think that you will find this book challenging and exciting. I think it captures the essence of the exciting Schizophrenia 1994 Conference.

Dr. Bill MacEwan
Director, Adult Psychiatric Services
Department of Psychiatry, St. Vincent's Hospital
Vancouver, BC   Canada

LESSONS LEARNED ABOUT THE CHRONIC MENTALLY ILL SINCE 1955

John A. Talbott

INTRODUCTION

I have chosen 1955 for two obvious reasons. First, it was the year in which the population housed in state and county psychiatric hospitals across the United States reached its height of almost 560,000 (Stroup and Manderscheid, 1988). Second, it was the year during which chlorpromazine was introduced into the formularies of most state hospital systems (Ayd, 1970). Since then, almost 40 years of deinstitutionalization has reduced this population to about 100000 individuals during which period we have seen the continuing introduction of new pharmacological agents, including imipramine and lithium (see Table 1).

My choice of starting this analysis in 1955 does not imply that nothing of consequence occurred regarding care and treatment of the chronic mentally prior to that date. Indeed, several critical developments were present that directly led to the current situation (Talbott, 1982; Talbott, 1983).

First, while the nation's first public psychiatric hospital, the "Publick Hospital" in Williamsburg, Virginia, was opened in 1773, and state mental hospitals blossomed in the nineteenth century, there were a host of "alternatives" to hospitals established in the United States beginning in 1855. The first of these was the Farm of St Anne in Illinois, followed by cottage plans and boarding out programs; aftercare, outpatient services, traveling and satellite clinics; crisis intervention programs; day hospitals, home care and halfway houses; and social

---

Schizophrenia: Exploring the Spectrum of Psychosis. Edited by R. Ancill. © 1994
John Wiley & Sons Ltd

and vocational rehabilitation. Indeed, by 1955, we had in place most of what we would now consider essential to the establishment of a community mental health center or community system of care; albeit not available in sufficient numbers or widely enough (see Figure 1).

Table 1. The Population in State and County Hospitals

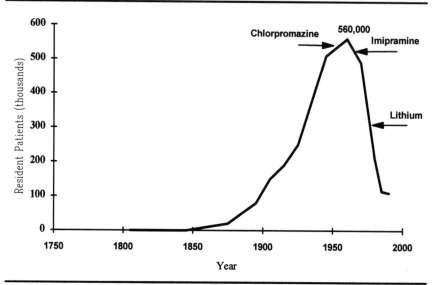

Source: Stroup, A.L. and Manderscheid, R.W. (1988). "The development of the state mental hospital system in the United States: 1840 - 1980", J. Wash. Acad. Sciences, 78, 59 - 68.

Second, in 1946, following World War II, the United States Congress enacted our first national Mental Health Act. This was prompted by the experience during the war of discovering that many inductees suffered from previously undetected mental illnesses and the public's shock at learning that during one month, more draftees were discharged for "medical reasons" than inducted; coupled with the horrible conditions in state psychiatric hospitals encountered by conscientious objectors performing alternate service there; plus a wish to upgrade the small federal "Division of Mental Hygiene" to a National Institute comparable to other parts of the National Institute of Health. This act stimulated research, demonstration projects, training and assistance to states. More important, though, it set in motion a process that resulted in a report from a "blue ribbon" Joint Commission on Mental Illness and Health entitled "Action For Mental Health," that called for an altered role for the large state hospitals, that in turn resulted in the community mental health center (CMHC) legislation of 1965, led by then-President John F. Kennedy.

Figure 1. Alternatives to Psychiatric Hospitals

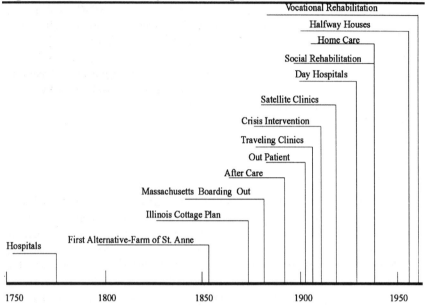

Source: Kales, A., Stefanis, C.N. and Talbott, J. A. (1990). Recent Advances in Schizophrenia, Springer-Verlag, New York.

Third, there was a sea change in American psychiatry concerning the philosophy in care and treatment of the mentally ill. This was prompted in part by the visit of a dozen or so leaders in American psychiatry to the UK in 1954 where they were profoundly impressed by the prevailing philosophy that regarded persons with psychiatric disorders like those with medical or surgical disorders. They also were impressed with innovations such as the "open door" and the "therapeutic milieu". Some of the same experts had also participated on a committee of the World Health Organization (WHO), that drafted a document during this same decade spelling out exactly what elements constituted what they termed a "community hospital"; e.g., outpatient services, partial hospitalization, community education, rehabilitation and research.

In 1954, New York State passed the first state Community Mental Center Services Act. The ingredients specified in this landmark legislation were: inpatient and outpatient services, consultation and education, and rehabilitation. Thus, by 1955, by adding together the different elements specified by New York State and WHO, the outlines emerged of the 1963 Kennedy CMHC bill (with the addition of 24-hour emergency care, diagnostic services, precare and aftercare). It is of note that the CMHC Amendments of 1975 were enacted to "pick-up" many of the pieces left in the wake of deinstitutionalization; e.g., screening mentally ill persons in the courts and community agencies prior to admission to state hospitals, follow-up care, and transitional housing as well as services for under-served populations such as persons suffering from alcoholism, drug abuse, children and the elderly.

The Survey

In order to ascertain what experiences and research since 1955 could shed light on what we have learned about the care and treatment of the mentally ill since deinstitutionalization began in 1955, I undertook a survey of over 20 experts in the field of chronic mental illness. This is a totally unscientific sample, consisting primarily of those doing research and writing on the subject, but includes most of the prominent names associated with the field. After receiving their answers to a broad request for developments in research and experience, I clustered them in groupings and had the experts rank-order them. What I will present in the remainder of the chapter represents the top ten areas, grouped under three headings: (I) Illness, (II) Treatment and (III) Programs. For each of the ten sub-areas, I have selected one or more important studies, which I will summarize, drawing from each a Lesson Learned. At the end of this presentation, I will try to tie these ten lessons together.

The three broad categories and ten sub-areas are:

I. Illness
    1. Course
    2. Relapse
    3. Length Of Stay

II. Treatment
    4. Therapy
    5. Behavior Modification
    6. Therapeutic Interaction
    7. Rehabilitation

III. Programs
      8. Community
      9. Alternatives
      10. Continuity of Care

Before starting, I think it is important to state that I utilized Leona Bachrach's (1976) definition of persons suffering from mental illness as "those individuals who are, have been, or might have been, but for the deinstitutionalization movement, on the rolls of long-term mental institutions, especially state hospitals".

I. ILLNESS

1. Course of illness. Prior to 1955, we had very little data on the courses of illness followed by persons suffering from chronic mental illnesses such as schizophrenia and little idea of their ultimate outcome. Now, however, we have a much better idea (see Tables 2 and 3).

Table 2. Long Term Follow-up Studies

date		author	locale	duration
1934	- 1970	Tsuang et al	Iowa	35 years (Av.)
1942	- 1966	Manfred Bleuler	Switzerland	23 years
1945	- 1975	Huber et al	West Germany	22 years (Av.)
	- 1976	Ciompi & Muller	Lausanne, Sw	37 years (Av.)
1950 ' 8 - 1980's		Brooks/Harding	Vermon	32 years

The first five studies published on the long term outcome of persons suffering from schizophrenia followed patients from 22 to 37 years, most starting long before the introduction of antipsychotic medications. They demonstrate strikingly similar results (Tsuang 1979, Bleuler 1968, Huber 1980, Ciompi 1980). This is surprising, since the studies were results (Harding 1987). conducted in two European countries and two American states.

Table 3: Long Term Outcome

	Recovered	Significantly Improved	Total better
Tsuang	20%	26%	46%
Bleuler	23%	43%	66%
Huber	26%	31%	57%
Ciompi	29%	24%	53%
Harding	34%	34%	68%

At a minimum, 20% of patients recover (with a range of 20-34%), at least 24% show significant improvement (range 24-43%) leading to a total percentage who are better off at follow-up at a minimum of 46% (range 46-68%).

Table 4. Course of Illness for Persons with Schizophrenia

	Onset	Course Type	End State	Percent (n=228)
1	Acute	Undulating	Recovery or mild	25.4
2	Chronic	Simple	Moderate or severe	24.1
3	Acute	Undulating	Moderate or severe	11.9
4	Chronic	Simple	Recovery or mild	10.1
5	Acute	Undulating	Recovery or mild	9.6
6	Chronic	Simple	Moderate or severe	8.3
7	Acute	Undulating	Moderate or severe	5.3
8	Chronic	Simple	Recovery or mild	5.3

Source: Ciompi, L. (1980). Catemnestic long-term study on the course of life and aging of schizophrenics, Schizophr. Bull., 6(4), 606 - 618.

We also understand much more today than we did in 1955 about the courses of illness of persons suffering from schizophrenia. Luc Ciompi (1980) identified eight different patterns; dividing them by onset (acute or chronic), course (simple or episodic) and end state (recovery/mild or moderate/severe). The largest group, constituting a quarter of the sample, had acute onsets, undulating courses and rather good outcomes. Almost the same number, however, had chronic onsets, simple (deteriorating) courses and poor outcomes (see Table 4).

What then can we learn from these long-term follow-up studies. First, that despite often stormy, dehabilitating and even deteriorating courses of severe illness, some individuals suffering from schizophrenia wind up rather alright. Second, that different persons have differing onsets, courses and outcomes.

As a result, any system of care for persons suffering from schizophrenia must not be unifocal; that is, it cannot focus only on hospital treatment or only on community care. Instead, it must accommodate persons who have sudden onsets of illness (e.g., with emergency and crisis services), chronic onsets (e.g., with monitoring and periodic reassessment); undulating courses (e.g., with acute crisis, hospital and outpatient services), simple courses (outpatient, partial hospital, supervised housing, community care teams, residential care, case management, etc.); poorer outcomes (ongoing long-term care) and better outcomes. The lesson to be learned here then, is that we need:

Lesson #1: Different Strokes For Different Folks.

2. Relapse. Relapse in persons suffering from schizophrenia and other chronic illnesses is another area in which we had little data prior to 1955. Now, due to the work of several investigators, however, we know much more than we did then.

Hogarty (1979) has established that even on medication, over 40% of persons suffering from schizophrenia will relapse in one year. In addition, Docherty (1978) and Herz (12) have identified non-psychotic prodromata of relapse; symptoms such as anxiety, irritability, parapraxes, decreased performance efficiency, distractibility, boredom, apathy and listlessness (see Figure 3).

Figure 3. Nonpsychotic Prodromata of Relapse

Anxiety
Irritability
Parapraxes
Decreased Performance Efficiency
Distractibility
Boredom
Apathy
Listlessness

This identification of such common symptoms has led to fruitful research on "low dose" and "no-dose" strategies (Marder 1987, Carpenter 1987). In addition, recognition of these common indicators of relapse, coupled with individual patients' own typical pre-psychotic behaviors such as calling the police, staying up all night, etc., enables clinicians to utilize low dose or no dose strategies, moving in with medication only when individuals are at risk for exacerbations in their illnesses.

Thus, we can conclude from these studies that while we are dealing with a difficult, often-relapsing illness (40% in a year), we can predict relapse in some patients and refine our treatment approaches. The lesson to be learned here then is that:

Lesson #2: Relapse Makes Some Sense.

3. Length of inpatient hospital stays.
Since 1955, several critical analyses of lengths of inpatient hospitals stays have been published (Glick 1979, Herz 1976, Mattes 1982). A major problem with studies on lengths of stay is that they have dropped dramatically since 1955; thus the standard of what is "short" vs what is "long" has changed (shortened) each year. For example, the study with the longest length of stay defines "short" as under 90 days and "long" as 179 days; the study with the shortest length of stay defines "short" as 8 days and "long" as 24 days.

Nonetheless, the results show a consistent pattern; that long-term hospitalization does not add anything for those suffering from chronic mental illnesses. It was previously believed that persons suffering from chronic illnesses required longer admissions and those suffering their first breaks, short stays. (Talbott and Glick 1986) Now, however, we must conclude that persons coming in for their 12th or 13th hospitalization do better with a rapid reevaluation, re-equilibration on medication and revision of the treatment plan, followed by discharge to a community program, and those having their first break, deserve a complete and thorough psychiatric, social and neuropsychological evaluation. The lesson here then, is that:

Lesson #3: More Is Not Better.

II. Treatment

4. Therapy. Several persons (May and Simpson 1980, Luborsky 1975, Mosher and Keith 1979) have been concerned with the few studies (for example, Herz 1974) that compare individual versus group therapy with persons suffering from schizophrenia. The two commonest methods of comparison use box scores or meta-analyses. I have attempted to summarize May and Simpson's careful analysis of these studies in Table 5.

Table 5. Studies Comparing the Superiority of Treatment in Inpatient vs. Outpatient Settings Group vs. Individual Treatment

Results	Group	Outpatient	InPatient	Individual
Positive	12	3	11	2
Negative	9	3	15	9
Neutral	5	1	4	0

There are more studies showing a positive than negative result from group treatment and more showing the superiority of therapy in outpatient settings. May and Simpson conclude that "...with schizophrenics, group therapy is more successful with outpatients after discharge than is group or individual therapy with inpatients..." In addition, Luborsky notes that one specific study (O'Brien 1972) clearly "showed an advantage for group treatment."

Therefore, contrary to the prevailing belief of patients, families, psychiatrists and even third-party reimbursers, group therapy would appear from the data to have the edge over individual treatment. The lesson then, is that:

Lesson #4: Group Therapy Is the Preferred Treatment, especially when conducted in outpatient settings.

5. Behavior Modification. Gordon Paul (1969) reviewed the research on treatment approaches for persons suffering from chronic mental illnesses and concluded that two showed special promise these were behavioral methods and milieu treatment. He then studied the outcomes of these two approaches versus controls in a state hospital population in Illinois. The results (Paul and Lentz

1977) were quite dramatic. All patients were randomly assigned to inpatient hospital treatment that consisted of one of three treatment programs: a behavioral approach emphasizing resocialization and social relearning techniques; milieu therapy; or "traditional state hospital treatment," which essentially consisted of medication and large group meetings. After discharge, all were followed with traditional aftercare, that is, the behavioral or milieu approaches were discontinued.

At 18 months, 92.5% in the Social Learning Program and 71% who had been exposed to the Milieu Program were still in the community, versus only 48.4% of the Controls. It is ironic, therefore, to note the absence of structured behavioral programs in psychiatric hospitals today, versus their popularity 20 years ago, despite such obvious success. Granted, lengths of stays have fallen, graduate psychology programs are now more interested in other areas, and many ward programs incorporate behavioral methods as "routine standard care," but their current absence cannot be attributed to lack of efficacy. My lesson here, therefore, is that:

Lesson #5: Behavior Therapy Is Effective.

6. Therapeutic Interaction. For a number of years there has been growing evidence for the increased efficacy of combinations of treatment interventions (see Table 6). Philip May (1968) compared the effectiveness of "ataraxic" medication, individual psychotherapy, milieu treatment and ECT alone and the combination of "ataraxic" medication and individual psychotherapy. He found that the worst outcomes were in two "alones": psychotherapy or milieu; and that while the combination was better, it was not statistically significantly better than drugs alone.

Table 6. Drug / Psychosocial Interaction

Affective Illness	Drugs +	Psychosocial	= Additive
	1 +	1	= 2
Schizophrenia	Drugs +	Psychosocial	= Interactive
	1 +	1	= 1.x

Source: Beitman, B.D. and Klerman, G.L. (1984). Combining Psychotherapy and Drug Therapy in Clinical Practice, Spectrum Publications Inc., New York.

Beitman and Klerman (1984), however, saw a definite effect; they concluded that with affective illness the two interventions were additive (that is, $1 + 1 = 2$), whereas with schizophrenia they were interactive (that is $1 + 1$ might equal 1.3 or 1.4). More recently, Gerald Hogarty (1986) demonstrated that (as stated previously) about 40% of persons suffering from schizophrenia experienced relapses in one year, even on medication; but the addition of either social skills training or family treatment cut that in half (to about 20%), and the provision of all three interventions resulted in no relapses. This powerful effect erodes over time. but its initial impact is impressive (see Figure 4).

Figure 4. Combined Treatment Effect in One Year

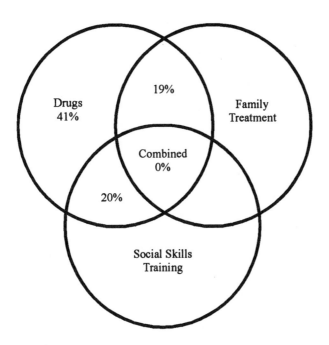

Source: Hogarty, G.E., Anderson, C.M., Reiss, D.J., Kornblith, S.J., Greenwald, D.P., Javna, C.D. and Madonia, (1986). Family psychoeducation, social skills training and maintenance chemotherapy in the aftercare treatment of schizophrenia, I. one-year effects of a controlled study on relapse and expressed emotion, Arch. Gen. Psychiatry, 43, 633-642.

The inevitable conclusion that I draw, then, from examination of these studies is that not only does treatment make a significant difference in persons suffering from schizophrenia, in combination it makes a very sizeable difference. Thus the lesson here, is that:

Lesson #6: **More Is Better.**

7. Rehabilitation. The field of psychiatric rehabilitation, like that of physical rehabilitation, almost did not exist in 1955. Since then, however, we have seen the steady growth of research, experience and expertise. To summarize all we have learned in the recent past from the research in psychiatric rehabilitation, William Anthony (1986) has expostulated a list of "myths" (see Figure 5).

Figure 5. Fifteen Historical Myths

1. Increasing drug treatment compliance can singularly effect rehabilitation outcome.
2. The majority of psychiatrically disabled persons are being successfully rehabilitated.
3. Traditional types of inpatient treatment, such as psychotherapy, group therapy, and drug therapy, positively effect rehabilitation outcome.
4. Total push inpatient therapies, such as milieu therapy, token economics and attitude therapy, positively effect rehabilitation outcome.
5. Hospital based work therapy positively effects employment outcome.
6. Time limited community based treatment is superior to hospital based treatment in terms of rehabilitation outcomes.
7. Community based treatment settings are well utilized by persons who are psychiatrically disabled.
8. Where a person is treated is more important than how a person is treated.
9. Psychiatric symptomatology is highly correlated with future rehabilitation outcome.
10. A person's diagnostic label provides significant information relevant to a person's future rehabilitation outcome.
11. There is a strong correlation between a person's symptomatology and a person's skills.
12. A person's ability to function in one particular environment (e.g., a community setting) is predictive of a person's ability to function in a different type of environment (e.g., a work setting).
13. Rehabilitation outcome can be accurately predicted by professionals.
14. A person's rehabilitation outcome is a function of the credentials of the mental health professional with whom the person interacts.
15. There is a positive relationship between rehabilitation outcome and the cost of the intervention
16.

Source: Anthony, W.A., Kennard, W.A., O'Brien, W.F. and Kornblith, S.J. (1986). Psychiatric rehabilitation: past myths and current realities, Community Mental Health Journal, 22(4), 249-264.

Another innovator in the field John Stares, followed several patients for extended periods of time and concluded that there was no one single index of disability, instead there were several indices, including work, social skills, symptomatology and general; all of which were independent of the others (Stares 1978, 1984). While clinically we have suspected that persons can have a great deal of symptomatology but little disability and vice-versa, it is useful to know this definitively. Because someone cannot function in one place, does not mean he or she cannot function in another.

Finally, Robert Liberman and colleagues (1980, 1982, 1984,1986a, 1986b, 1987) has pioneered in the development of rehabilitation training modules that can be easily understood, learned and communicated among professionals in the field. These are available in written and video formats and use very practical methods of improving social skills, such as Behavioral Rehearsal, Prompting, Modeling, Reinforcement, Shaping, In-vivid Exercises, and Homework. The modules include such areas as Conversation Skills, Personal Effectiveness, Social Problem-solving, Personal Finances, Grooming, Vocational Preparedness, Medication Management, and Recreation for Leisure.

Thus, I conclude from all these efforts that if patients have a disability in addition to a disease, they require both treatment and rehabilitation and that we now possess the knowledge as to how to effectively deliver rehabilitation. The lesson here, then, is that:

Lesson #7: Treatment Alone Is Not Enough.

III. PROGRAMS

8. Community Programs. Fountain House, which was founded shortly following World War II, pioneered in providing a community-based program that offered what I term the psycho-social triad of housing, vocational rehabilitation and social rehabilitation. Studies have shown that outcome for participants in this innovative program were strikingly better than those of controls (Beard 1978). Whereas 17% of Fountain House members were readmitted 6 months after discharge from the hospital, only 37% of controls were.

Leonard Stein and Mary Ann Test studied a group of patients randomly assigned to an assertive community treatment approach that provided individualized treatment and care from a comprehensive array of services (Stein and Test 1980, Test and Stein 1980). Their results showed that patients receiving this targeted approach showed subsequently lower rehospitalization and symptomatology and significantly increased employment, satisfaction and time spent with trusted friends.

The economic results (Weisbrod, Stein and Test 1980), however, revealed a problem many community programs face. For while the overall impact was a reduction in estimated total costs of 6% per patient, the costs of delivering these decentralized, individualized services was 11% more, offset, however, by increased benefits of 16%. Thus, if the cost side of personnel, etc., is financed by mental health resources, and the benefits accrued because of decreased police costs and family burden as well as increased tax revenues, etc., the mental health authorities and legislators do not see the investment paid back into the same account it was spent from.

With all the caveats about making generalizations about a diverse population, then, the lesson to be learned from this research is that:

Lesson #8: Community treatment is better.

9. Alternatives to Hospitals. As mentioned above and as displayed in Illustration 2, we have seen the innovation of and expansion in alternatives to hospitals for over a century. What is the scientific evidence of their efficacy or lack of it?

Interestingly, a decade ago two meta-analyses of various alternative treatment programs were published in the United States within months of each other (Braun 1981, Kiesler 1982). Their conclusions were astoundingly similar. Braun et al concluded that "...experimental alternatives...have led to psychiatric outcomes not different from and occasionally superior to those of patients in control groups." Kiesler stated that "In no case were the outcomes of hospitalization more positive than alternative treatment." These conclusions have led to the development of even more alternatives, such as the Inn at the Massachusetts Mental Health Center (Gudeman 1983). Here, again, the lesson seems clear, that:

Lesson #9: Alternatives To Hospitals Are Better.

10. Continuity of Care. The final area in my survey results, deals with what may be the most important issue of all when it comes to discussing treatment and care of individuals suffering from chronic mental illnesses; continuity of care. In looking at the entire body of research on what seems most effective in preventing or forestalling exacerbations of illness or rehospitalization, two items appear again and again; continuance on medication and continuance in some form of aftercare or outpatient program; both of which are so dependent on continuity of care. It is therefore not only discouraging to learn (Minkoff 1978) that fewer than 25% of persons continue to be seen in programs following discharge and fewer than 50% continue their prescribed medication but to realize that continuity of care is actually practiced so seldom with this population.

Confirmation of the importance of longitudinal involvement comes for the Veteran's Administration's Cooperative Day Hospital Study (Linn 1979) that concluded that "...high patient turnover and brief but more intensive treatment...may lead to relapse..."

My reading of all these results indicates to me that the lesson to be learned here is that, no matter how good the treatment, rehabilitation and care is, if patients are not involved on an on-going basis, it hardly matters. So I conclude that:

Lesson #10: Continuity of Care Is Critical.

IV. CONCLUSIONS

In this survey of what of significance has occurred regarding the chronic mentally ill since 1955, I do not want to give the impression that these ten areas are the only areas of importance. Certainly, we have experienced an explosion in the areas of basic science (e.g., genetics) and neuroscience (e.g., neurotransmitters) as well as more clinically-related research in areas such as epidemiology and imaging. In addition, the growth of the family movement has been an enormous help in the advocacy for research in and services for the chronic mentally ill in the United States. Unfortunately, during this 40 year period, another force has been that of the legal advocates, who have sponsored initiatives (such as the right to refuse treatment, attempts to end involuntary commitment, etc.) that have been well-intentioned but naive and have bedeviled our ability to provide service advocacy for afflicted patients.

Ironically, though, it is probably neither science nor advocacy that has shaped and will continue to shape services for the seriously mentally ill, but the economic forces psychiatry and all of medicine in the United States are currently facing. Just as services have been profoundly influenced in the recent past by cost-cutting and cost-controlling initiatives such as: prospective pricing, utilizing diagnostic related groups (DRG's); health maintenance organizations (HMO's); and managed care, future directions are certain to be directed by whatever shape the final American national health care reform takes.

As a footnote, it is disappointing to note that despite the federal government's vigorous efforts to promote CMHC's in the 1960's and 1970's to help states and localities share the burden of community care of the mentally ill, except for the inadequately-funded Community Support Program and the McKinney Program for the Homeless, federal leadership has been lacking.

Figure 6. Lessons Learned

I. Different strokes for different folks.
II. Relapse makes some sense.
III. More is not necessarily better.
IV. Group is the preferred therapy.
V. Behavioral methods are effective.
VI. More is better.
VII. Treatment alone is not enough.
VIII. Community treatment is better.
IX. Alternatives are better.
X. Continuity of care is conflict.

What are the bigger lessons to be learned from my list of ten lessons (see Figure 6)? At first blush it would appear that some lessons are contradictory; e.g., more is not better when it refers to inpatient hospitalization but more is better when it refers to modalities delivered in the community. However I think that there are certain themes that do emerge from these ten lessons.

First, multiple treatments and rehabilitation seem to provide better outcomes. Second, continuity of care seems to be critical. And third, comprehensive care must be provided.

None of these principles is new. But, we have yet to implement what our research findings demonstrate. To accomplish that, several things must be done. First, we must bring about changes in the system or non-system of care we have, addressing not merely the problems of individual patients but the "system" of care for them. Second, we must pay attention to policy issues, shaping it rather than letting it shape us. And third, we must perform more health services experiments such as (1) those sponsored by the Robert Wood Johnson Foundation, which is looking into making services for the chronic mentally ill work better in our large cities, (2) those stemming from the Institute of Medicine's study comparing generic services for the chronic mentally ill, frail elderly and mentally retarded over the age of 21, and (3) those that attempt to assess the clinical and fiscal impact of new funding and administrative efforts, such as capitation, etc.

The biggest lesson to be learned, however, from our almost 40 year old experiment with deinstitutionalization, is that we simply have not learned our lessons. While waiting for science to bring us a definitive answer regarding the causation and treatment of those suffering from chronic mental illness, we must still act. If we truly want to address the problems posed by this difficult population, we must first begin by implementing what we know and do it now.

REFERENCES

Anthony, W.A., Kennard, W.A., O'Brien, W.F. and Kornblith, S.J. (1986). "Psychiatric rehabilitation: past myths and current realities", Comm. Ment. Health J., 22(4), 249 - 264.

Ayd, F.J. (1970). Discoveries in Biological Psychiatry, Lippincott, Philadelphia.

Bachrach, L.L. (1976). "Deinstitutionalization: an analytical review and sociological perspective", NIMH, Rockville, MD.

Beard, J.H., Malamud, T.J., and Rossman, E. (1978). "Psychiatric rehabilitation and long-term rehospitalization rates: the findings of two research studies". Schizophr. Bull., 4(4), 622 - 635.

Beitman, B.D. and Klerman, G.L. (1984). Combinination Psychotherapy and Drug Therapy in Clinical Practice, Spectrum Publications, Inc., New York.

Bleuler, M. (1969). "A 23-year longitudinal study of 208 schizophrenics and impressions in regard to the nature of schizophrenia". In The Transmission of Schizophrenia (eds. D. Rosenthal and S.S. Ketty), Pergamon, Oxford.

Braun. P.. Kochansky W G., Shapiro, R., Greenberg, S., Gudeman, J.E., Johnson, S. and Shore, M.F. (1981). "Overview: deinstitutionalization of psychiatric patients, a critical review of outcome studies", Am. J. Psychiatry, 138(6), 736 - 749.

Carpenter, W.T., Heinrichs, D.W. and Hanlon, T.E. (1987). "A comparative trial of psychopharmacologic strategies in schizophrenia", Am. J. Psychiatry 144, 1466 - 1470.

Ciompi, L. (1980). "Catamnestic long-term study on the course of life and aging of schizophrenics", Schizophr. Bull., 6(4), 606 - 618.

Docherty, J.P., VanKammen, D.P., Siris, S.G. and Marder, S.R. (1978). "Stages of onset of schizophrenic psychosis", Am. J. Psychiatry, 135(4), 420 - 426.

Glick, I.D. and Hargreaves, W.A. (1979). Psychiatric Hospital Treatment for the 1980's, Lexington Books, Lexington, MA.

Gudeman, J.E., "Shore, hospitalization and an inn instead of inpatient care for psychiatric patients", The New Engl. J. of Med., 308(13), 749 - 753.

Harding, C.M., Zubin, J. and Strauss, J.S. (1987). "Chronicity in schizophrenia: fact, partial fact or artifact?", Hosp. Comm. Psychiatry, 38(5), 477 - 486.

Herz, M.I. (1984). "Recognizing and preventing relapse in patients with schizophrenia", Hosp. Comm. Psychiatry, 35(4), 344 - 349.

Herz, M.I., Endicott, J. and Spitzer, R.L. (1976). "Brief vs. standard hospitalization: the families", Am. J. Psychiatry, 133, 795 - 801.

Herz, M.I., Spitzer, R.L., Gibbon, M., Greenspan, K. and Reibel, S. (1974). "Individual vs. group aftercare treatment", Am. J. Psychiatry, 131(7), 808 - 812.

Hogarty, G.E., Anderson, C.M., Reiss, D.J., Kornblith, S.J., Greenwald, D.P., Javna, C.D. and Madonia, M.J. (1986). "Family psychoeducation, social skills training and maintenance chemotherapy in the aftercare treatment of schizophrenia, I. oneyear effects of a controlled study on relapse and expressed emotion", Arch. Gen. Psychiat, 43, 633 - 642.

Hogarty, G.E., Schooler, N.R., Ulrich, R., Mussare, F. and Ferro, P. (1979). "Fluphenazine and social therapy in the aftercare of schizophrenic patients", Arch. Gen. Psychiat, 36, 1283 - 1294.

Huber, G., Gross, G., Schuttler, R. and Linz, M. (1980). "Longitudinal studies of schizophrenic patients", Schizophr. Bull, 6(4), 592 - 605.

Kales, A., Stefanis, C.N. and Talbott, J.A. (1990). Recent Advances in Schizophrenia, Springer-Verlag, New York.

Kiesler, C.A. (1982). "Mental hospitals and alternative care, noninstitutionalization as potential public policy for mental patients", Am. Psychologist 37(4), 349 - 360.

Liberman, R.P. (1982). "Assessment of social skills", Schizophr. Bull, 8(1), 62 - 84.

Liberman, R.P., Falloon, I.R.H. and Wallace, C.J. (1984). "Drug-psychosocial interactions in the treatment of schizophrenia", in The Chronically Mentally Ill: Research and Services (Ed. M. Mirabi), Spectrum Publications, Inc., New York.

Liberman, R.P. (1986a). "Psychiatric rehabilitation of schizophrenia: editor's introduction", Schizophr. Bull, 12(4), 540 - 541.

Liberman, R.P., Mueser, K.T., Wallace, C.J., Jacobs, H.E., Eckman, T. and Massel, H.K. (1986b). "Training skills in the psychiatrically disabled: learning coping and competence", Schizophr. Bull., 12(4), 631 - 647.

Liberman, R.P. (1987). "Skills training for community adaptation of chronic mental patients", Comm. Psychiatrist, 2(3), 5 - 17.

Linn, M.W., Caffey, E.M., Klett, C.J., Hogarty, G.E. and Lamb, R. (1979). "Day treatment and psychotropic drugs in the aftercare of schizophrenic patients," Arch Gen Psychiatry, 36, 1055 - 1066.

Luborsky, L., Barton, S. and Luborsky, L. (1975). "Comparative Studies of Psychotherapies: is it true that "everyone has won and all must have prizes?",Arch. Gen. Psychiatry, 32, 995 - 1008.

Marder, S.R., Van Putten, T., Mintz, J., Lebell, M., McKenzie, J. and May, P.R. (1987). "Low-and conventional-dose maintenance therapy with fluphenazine decanoate, two year outcome", Arch. Gen. Psychiatry, 44, 518 - 521.

Mattes, J.A. (1982). "The optimal length of hospitalization for psychiatric patients: a review of the literature", Hosp. Comm. Psychiatry, 33(10), 824 - 828.

May, P.R.A. (1968). Treatment of Schizophrenia. A Comparative Study of Five Treatment Methods, Science House, New York. May, P.R.A. and Simpson, G.M. (1980). Schizophrenia: evaluation of treatment methods. In Comprehensive Textbook of Psychiatry. 3rd Edition (eds. H.I. Kaplan, K.M. Freedman and B.J. Sadock), APPI, Baltimore MD.

Minkoff, K (1978). "Map of the chronic mental patient". In The Chronic Mental Patient (ed. J.A. Talbott), APA, Washington, DC.

Mosher, L.R. and Keith, S.J. (1979). "Research on the psychosocial treatment of schizophrenia: a summary report", Am. J. Psychiatry, 136(5), 623 - 631.

O'Brien, C., Hamm, K., Ray, B., et al (1972). "Group vs individual psychotherapy with schizophrenics: a controlled outcome study", Arch. Gen. Psychiatry 27, 474 - 478.

Paul, G.L. (1969). "Chronic mental patient: current status-future directions", Psycho. Bull., 71, 81 - 94.

Paul, G.L. and Lentz, R.J. (1977). Psychosocial Treatment of Chronic Mental Patients, Harvard University Press, Cambridge, MA.

Stein, L.I. and Test, M.A. (1980). "Alternative of mental hospital treatment, I. conceptual model, treatment program, and clinical evaluation", Arch. Gen. Psychiatry 37, 392 - 397.

Strauss, J.S. (1984). "Assessment of treatment in outpatient settings". In The Chronically Mentalls Ill: Research and Services (ed. M. Mirabi), Spectrum Publications, Inc., New York.

Strauss, J.S. and Carpenter, W.T., Jr. (1978). "The prognosis of schizophrenia: rationale for a multidimensional concept", Schizophr. Bull. 4(1), 56 - 67.

Stroup, A.L. and Manderscheid, R.W. (1988). "The development of the state mental hospital system in the United States", 1840-1980, J. Wash. Acad. Sciences, 78, 59 - 68.

Talbott, J.A. (1982). "Twentieth-century developments in American Psychiatry", Psych Quarterly, 54(4), 207 - 219.

Talbott, J.A. & Kaplan, S.R. (1983). Psychiatric Administration: A Comprehensive Text for the Clinician-Executive, Grune & Stratton, Orlando FL.

Talbott, J.A. (1983). "Trends in the delivery of psychiatric services". In Psychiatric Administration (eds. J.A. Talbott and S.R. Kaplan), Grune & Stratton, New York.

Talbott, J.A. and Glick, I.D. (1986). "The inpatient care of the chronically mentally ill", Schizophr. Bull., 12(1), 129 - 140.

Test, M.A. and Stein, L.I. (1980). "Alternative to mental hospital treatment, III. social cost", Arch. Gen. Psychiatry, 37, 409 - 412.

Tsuang, M., Woolson, R. and Fleming, J. (1979). "Long-term outcome of major psychoses, I: schizophrenia and affective disorders compared with psychiatrically symptom-free surgical conditions", Arch. Gen. Psychiatry, 36, 1295 - 1301.

Wallace, C.J., Nelson, C.J., Liberman, R.P., Aitchison, R.A., Lukoff, D., Elder, J.P. and Ferris, C. (1980). "A review and critique of social skills training with schizophrenic patients", Schizophr. Bull., 6(1), 42 - 63.

Weisbrod, B.A., Test, M.A. and Stein, L.I. (1980). "Alternative to mental hospital treatment, II. economic benefit-cost analysis", Arch. Gen. Psychiatry, 37, 400 - 405.

2

DEINSTITUTIONALIZATION: WHAT DOES IT REALLY MEAN?

Leona L. Bachrach

Several broad statements may be made about the effects of deinstitutionalization on the lives of people who suffer from schizophrenia and other long-term mental illnesses.

First, until such time as the definition of deinstitutionalization becomes standardized, confusion over its meaning, and its impact, will continue.

Second, however defined, deinstitutionalization is not a *fait accompli;* it is a continuing process that currently influences the lives of mentally ill individuals profoundly.

Third, the outcomes of deinstitutionalization to date have been mixed: both problems and successes may be identified.

Fourth, the future success of deinstitutionalization efforts will depend upon our ability to adopt a new, more realistic understanding of what this complex phenomenon entails.

These propositions are discussed in the pages that follow.

Schizophrenia: Exploring the Spectrum of Psychosis. Edited by R. Ancill © 1994
John Wiley & Sons Ltd

DEFINITIONAL CONFUSION

The concept of deinstitutionalization is one of many that mental health planners and service providers use that lack consistency. It shares this fault with such other critical concepts as "chronic mental illness", "asylum", "homelessness", "intensive case management", "least restrictive environment", and even "community mental health" (Bachrach, 1989, 1994). Conceptual fuzziness is in fact sufficiently widespread in mental health circles that it behooves us to ask whether imprecision fulfills some purpose in the world of mental health service planning, or whether it is a chance occurrence. My own belief is that imprecision is no mere accident and that it serves important, if sometimes unrecognized, functions in health and human services policy development.

In the past I have likened the semantic issues surrounding deinstitutionalization to those related to a popular American debate: whether to stop awarding university scholarships to athletically gifted but academically unprepared students (Bachrach, 1989). The American journalist, William Raspberry (1989), asked to comment on whether limiting such awards is a "good idea", wrote that this question could not be answered "until we address its implied antecedent. *Good for what"?*

So it is with deinstitutionalization. Without a commonly accepted understanding of its purposes, discussions of its utility and outcomes are at best confusing, at worst futile.

COMPETING DEFINITIONS

That various meanings are imputed to the term "deinstitutionalization" is immediately apparent from even the most cursory review of the literature. One definition that focuses exclusively on geography views deinstitutionalization as "moving mental patients from enormous, remote hospitals into small community residences" (Anonymous, 1982). Other less neutral definitions carry distinct political overtones. One defines the term as a "22-letter mouthful that once referred to a reform of the mental health system [but should now] be read as a euphemism for official cruelty" (Anonymous, 1984). Another speaks of "dumping mental patients out of state mental hospitals onto local communities, with promises of community treatment that never came true" (Anonymous, 1986).

Some definitions convey value judgments. One accuses deinstitutionalization of being a euphemism for homelessness (Anonymous, 1986). Another, by Etzioni

(1976), calls deinstitutionalization a "policy fashion" that "romanticizes the benefits of community-based care". Still another, by Marlowe and Weinberg (1982), views deinstitutionalization as "a process and a system for helping the seriously emotionally disturbed person to achieve his or her right to as normal a life as possible."

Talbott (1975), a psychiatrist known for his initiatives on behalf of severely mentally ill individuals, views the term as a misnomer that should be replaced by "transinstitutionalization" to indicate that patients have had their "locus of living and care transferred from a single lousy institution to multiple wretched ones". Another psychiatrist, Dumont (1982), writes even more pointedly, "Let us stop the cant and quibbling. This thing, deinstitutionalization, is nothing more or less than a polite term for the cutting of mental health budgets."

There is a degree of inconsistency in people's understanding of the term, and these several examples, diverse as they are, only skim the surface (Bachrach, 1989). They do, however, suffice to demonstrate one of the major difficulties in evaluating the outcomes of pursuing deinstitutionalization policy: that because many constructions of this term contain implicit value judgments, it is, in the words of Jones and Fowles (1984), "often used as a criticism rather than a description".

DEFINING THE SCOPE

Intrusive value judgments and imprecision of this kind hardly provide a firm basis for successful deinstitutionalization programming. How, then, may we overcome these vexing problems?

As a first step, we must recognize that arguments over deinstitutionalization's meaning will not be easy to resolve, for they are intimately tied up with territorial concerns. Semantic disagreements frequently serve the purpose of diverting attention away from difficult substantive issues (Bachrach, 1994); and although such diversionary tactics may not be consciously promoted, they can be extremely useful to planners and policy-makers who seek to slow down the pace of system change and pursue their own agendas.

Nevertheless, we must continue our quest for definitional consensus. The term "deinstitutionalization" serves as the basis for service planning and policy development daily; and unless some agreement can be achieved about its meaning, those assessing its merits will continue to speak at cross-purposes.

What is needed, then, is a definition that is objective enough to minimize the intrusion of value judgments and broad enough to convey complexity. I propose this working definition as a first step toward that end:

- *Deinstitutionalization refers to the replacement of long-stay psychiatric hospitals with smaller, less isolated community-based service alternatives for the care of individuals with schizophrenia and other major mental illnesses.*

A CONTINUING PROCESS

This neutral definition permits us to convey the sense of early policy statements promoting deinstitutionalization. In the United States, deinstitutionalization, in theory, was to consist of three component processes: the release of patients residing in psychiatric hospitals to alternative facilities in the community; the diversion of potential new admissions into those alternative facilities; and the development of special community-based programs, combining psychiatric and support services, for the care of a noninstitutionalized patient population (Bachrach, 1976). The last of these processes was held to be particularly important, for it acknowledged that patients' altered life circumstances would inevitably result in new configurations of service need.

Although deinstitutionalization has proceeded somewhat differently in other countries, the American experience is sufficiently representative that it may serve to illustrate the policy's evolution (Bachrach, in press). Deinstitutionalization took root and grew during the 1960s, a time of vitality, humanism, and optimism in the United States (Romano, 1980). It stood alongside other civil rights protests of the day in supporting the rights of oppressed people, for there was widespread belief that community-based care would be more humane and more therapeutic than hospital-based care. Additionally, many early architects of deinstitutionalization anticipated that changing the major locus of service delivery would result in substantial cost savings.

So persuasive were these advocates that they were able to form a rare coalition of social reformers and fiscal reformers to support their cause. It became difficult-at times almost heretical-to find fault with an initiative with such broad-based appeal. Thus, in 1963, when John Kennedy challenged Congress to adopt a "bold new approach" in mental health service delivery, his ideas were enthusiastically received. The President's plea to downsize psychiatric hospitals provided substance and direction for a trend that, thanks to the advent of psychotropic medications, was already underway in some parts of the country (Romano, 1980). Congress responded with enabling legislation and generous financial support, and a federal plan to replace psychiatric hospitals with a nationwide network of some 1,500 community mental health centers was launched.

Changes in the Zeitgeist, however, as well as growing impatience over the lack of demonstrable evidence for the superiority of community-based care, weakened the deinstitutionalization movement and made it a vulnerable political target (Concannon, 1992). Only about half of the centers were funded and built before the federal program came to an end in the early 1980s. The individual states, not the federal government, then assumed major responsibility for deinstitutionalization; and today community mental health facilities in the private and the non-federal public sectors are among the most highly utilized psychiatric service sites in the country.

The effects of pursuing deinstitutionalization policy in the United States are partially reflected in service statistics. In 1955, the resident patient count in American state mental hospitals stood at a record high of 560,000. That number has declined in each successive year and stands today at 101,000, a reduction of 82%. Even more impressive is the drop of 88% in the resident patient rate, from 339 per 100,000 population in 1955 to 41 per 100,000 today (Manderscheid and Sonnenschein, 1992).

These data take on special meaning when we consider that there are, according to unpublished National Institute of Mental Health estimates, some 2.5 million long-term mentally ill people living in the United States. With only 101,000 enrolled in state hospitals on any given day, we may account for about 4% of the total. Of the remaining 96% there are substantial numbers whom we cannot locate, although many are surely in distress and in desperate need of help.

However, gross statistics tell us little about the subtleties of deinstitutionalization, for they fail to convey the dynamic nature of that policy. Deinstitutionalization consists of far more than this striking decline in hospital populations; it is also a vital process of social change - of movement away from one orientation in patient care to another that is radically different (Thornicroft and Bebbington, 1989). In this sense, it involves all of the elements of the service system in an ongoing series of accommodations and shifting boundaries, so that virtually no agency delivering mental health care is exempt.

Today deinstitutionalization affects those patients who continue to be admitted to psychiatric hospitals, by shortening their stays in those facilities, and sometimes by making discharge an end in itself that overrides clinical concerns. It also affects those individuals who do not use psychiatric hospitals, but who might have done so in another era -i.e., those people whose very admissions are prevented or diverted. Unfortunately, some of these people receive no mental health services whatever and sometimes end up homeless on the streets (Lamb et al., 1992). And it certainly affects the many "revolving door" patients and those who end up in correctional facilities because they have no established niche in a fragmented, unstable service system.

LINGERING PROBLEMS

That there is disequilibrium in today's systems of care is hardly surprising. For the past three decades many jurisdictions have officially supported the principle that the development of community programs and the depopulation of psychiatric hospitals must occur simultaneously (Bachrach, 1976; Bradley, 1976). In reality, however, hospital services have often been terminated long before replacements have been supplied in the community. This, in turn, has led to the creation of populations of severely underserved, inappropriately served, and sometimes totally unserved, mentally ill individuals (President's Commission, 1978).

We may, in short, conclude that the first two of the three component processes of deinstitutionalization noted above-releasing patients from, and reducing admissions to, psychiatric hospitals-have proceeded apace. However, the critical third process, that of developing a full array of services in the community to meet the unique needs of a noninstitutionalized patient population, has often lagged.

This situation has resulted in a variety of serious service delivery issues in many communities. Part of the difficulty should probably be attributed to the optimism and speed with which deinstitutionalization was originally pursued. Early advocates were so completely certain of the curative powers of community-based care that they sometimes elected to understate both the seriousness and the chronicity that are part of long-term mental illness. Indeed, they were sometimes so expansive in their optimism that they chose to think in terms of mental health, and effectively to ignore the existence of mental illness. It is probably no accident that the major American service initiative for mentally ill people in that era was called a "community mental health center"; words like "clinic" and "hospital" were dismissed as too pessimistic.

Such unchecked optimism and "positive thinking" led to problems. Had we been more realistic and less denying, we might have anticipated that there would inevitably be practical difficulties surrounding the transfer of care from a hospital-based system where services were centralized and easily accessed, to an essentially decentralized and fragmented community-based system. Either the patient would now have to seek care aggressively and put together the various bits and pieces of his or her own treatment plan, or the community would somehow have to do that for the patient. Very probably, both would be required to work together in this very complicated enterprise.

But the sad truth is, of course, that patients often encountered serious financial, psychological, geographical, and attitudinal barriers to their care. And, for its part, the community often did not know how to-or perhaps did not really want to act aggressively on behalf of mentally ill people.

In fact, the history of deinstitutionalization in much of the United States is one in which clear preference has been given to patients who are able to take the initiative in seeking their own care. The system seems to have had problems in serving those patients whose illnesses, or whose lack of motivation or ingenuity, makes them less functional or less assertive.

We might also have anticipated that, as deinstitutionalization progressed, the community would be charged with providing an extensive array of services for mentally ill individuals. The psychiatric hospital, for better or worse-and certainly not always as we would have wanted it-had been performing a variety of formal and informal functions that would now have to be duplicated in a new setting (Bachrach, 1976; Romano, 1980; Thornicroft and Bebbington, 1989). It had also been fulfilling a most important auxiliary function, that of providing respite and support for patients' families.

However, in contrast to the need for service comprehensiveness, planning in the early years of deinstitutionalization was often conceptualized along only one dimension. It frequently had a distinctly geographical focus and concentrated on where people would live-either inside or outside the hospital; and it underestimated the need for such basic nonresidential services as psychiatric care, medical care, and rehabilitative opportunities, to say nothing of social support, safety, and asylum. By way of illustration I would point to the first definition of deinstitutionalization cited above "moving mental patients from enormous, remote hospitals to small community residences". Definitions of this kind, even though they fail to acknowledge the treatment and support services that psychiatric hospitals provided and that would now have to be replaced in the community, were extremely popular in the early years of deinstitutionalization.

Moreover, in addition to providing a full array of services, the community would now have to integrate or link those services - something that was hardly necessary when virtually all programs were concentrated in a single physical setting and administered by one authority. Once again, however, the need for service integration was not fully appreciated.

Deinstitutionalization also suffered widely, and continues to do so, from the absence of sufficient capital for effecting new program strategies. While many communities strive conscientiously to serve patients in deinstitutionalized service systems, funds continue to flow into psychiatric hospitals in what many critics perceive as a maldistribution of resources. However, there is often no choice. So long as hospitals and community-based facilities must co-exist, a substantial amount of money must necessarily be spent on supporting the hospitals. It is expensive to keep these places open, functioning, and even minimally humane - but how could it be otherwise for facilities that are charged with providing total care for extremely disabled individuals?

Thus, we know today, from our accumulating experience with deinstitutionalization, that its architects often acted naively in overlooking its many subtleties. We are faced constantly with evidence that their idealistic expectations of community-based care, while they were noble and certainly consistent with civil rights ideology, were often not grounded in the realities of service need for mental patients who have multiple, severe, and persistent disabilities.

A POSITIVE LEGACY

It is because these problems are so critical and striking that assessments of deinstitutionalization often appear to be negative: these are circumstances that absolutely require remediation. Yet it is equally important to note the positive outcomes of pursuing this policy, for there are, in fact, a number of excellent community-based programs that have responded with success to the challenges of deinstitutionalization. I have seen examples of these "model" programs in every country I have visited, although within any country they tend to be rare, localized, and dependent upon the existence of aggressive and dedicated leadership.

Quite apart from these excellent programs, deinstitutionalization has also fostered a critical "paradigm shift" that now influences service planning in all kinds of service settings. People with schizophrenia and other major mental illnesses, no longer hidden and out of sight, have entered our visual field, and their presence has demonstrated the need for services that are person-focused and essentially positive in direction. Having these patients visible in the community has greatly sensitized us to the fact that they are not all alike: that each is a person who requires specialized programming and individualized treatments.

So widespread is this positive legacy of deinstitutionalization today (Bachrach, 1993) that we sometimes even forget about the "dumping" that occurred in some psychiatric hospitals in the past. It is a legacy that is illustrated in the United States in a growing insistence on integrating psychosocial rehabilitation and psychiatric treatment (Liberman, 1992) in patient care. It is reflected as well in newly developing outreach efforts that alter clinicians' traditional concepts of time and space by requiring them to go wherever patients are: to meet them on their own ground, both physically and psychologically (Cohen, 1990; Zealberg et al., 1993).

Deinstitutionalization's positive legacy is also manifested in a growing literature that underscores the necessity for professionals to respond to patients as people with uniquely personal hopes, fears, frustrations, and ambitions; and to involve those patients and their relatives in the treatment planning process to the fullest extent possible. And although these developments are in themselves not new, they have come into their own in this era of deinstitutionalization.

TOWARD A NEW UNDERSTANDING

How, then, may we summarize our experience with deinstitutionalization? What does it really mean? Have mental health services actually become, as anticipated, more therapeutic and more humane since this policy has been pursued? The answer is yes-but only at some times and only for certain patients. Has community-based care turned out to be less expensive than hospital-based care? The answer is probably not, when we consider all the hidden costs associated with simultaneously running what is, in essence, a two -tiered system covering both hospital- and community-based care (Okin, 1978, 1993). On a more positive note, however, many planners have begun to downplay the imputed cost savings of deinstitutionalization and now focus instead on the more humanistic elements of the policy. Thus, the "success" of deinstitutionalization depends largely upon what yardsticks are being used at which points in history.

Whatever assessment we are disposed to make, however, it can probably be said with some certainty that it is too early to evaluate deinstitutionalization as an entity; for, despite our decades of experience, the policy has not been given a fair chance to prove itself. In most places, deinstitutionalization has been, at best, only partially implemented, and it remains an incomplete process. We shall not know whether it can succeed until we have created a full array of community-based interventions to serve as de facto alternative services for the care of those individuals who, in an earlier era, would have been hospitalized, many for very long periods of time (Warner, 1989).

What is needed in the meantime is, to some extent, self-evident. Countries promoting deinstitutionalization must reconsider their responsibility to mentally ill people and grant them access to the psychiatric and support services they require (Boodman, 1994). Psychiatric care must be afforded equal status with other health services in insurance blueprints and government plans. Mental illness must be destigmatized, and adequate resources channeled into humane and relevant service programs. Research utilizing both quantitative and qualitative methodologies must be supported to expand our knowledge base about what kinds of programming are best suited for what patients under what specific circumstances.

A new understanding of deinstitutionalization is also needed-one that is based in reality and capitalizes on our accumulated experience. Deinstitutionalization can no longer be viewed as a panacea. We must acknowledge the difficulties of providing care in the community to people whom we once locked away because, in all candor, we did not wish to see them. We must openly admit the possibility of chronicity for persons afflicted with schizophrenia and other major mental illnesses and be prepared to provide comprehensive programming and continuity of care as needed. This in turn means that we must develop the means for integrating services in fragmented systems of care-a very difficult but absolutely essential requirement.

Beyond this, successful deinstitutionalization demands that we recognize and support the diversity of the patient population and the individuality of its members, some of whom fare well in community programs, but many of whom get lost in the cracks and require special attention and interventions (Cohen, 1990). The need for inpatient services for some members of the patient population, usually short term but sometimes of longer duration, must also be acknowledged, for we have seen that the community is not necessarily the most benign treatment site for all patients at all times.

That these conditions are far more easily described than accomplished makes them no less critical to the future success of deinstitutionalization.

The American philosopher, Santayana (1905), wrote at the beginning of this century that, "Those who cannot remember the past are condemned to repeat it". The past, as applied to deinstitutionalization, contains several important lessons (Lamb, 1993).

First, we must recognize that we have probably reached the point of no return with deinstitutionalization, for it is unlikely that we will ever go back totally to hospital-oriented systems of care.

Second, we must learn to view deinstitutionalization in all its complexity, not from the vantage point of our own ideologies and personal concerns.

Third, we must face the fact that service delivery problems will almost certainly be exacerbated in the future by a scarcity of funds and, in many places, a wavering dedication to serving those in need (Bragg, 1994; Robinson, 1993). The situation may, in short, get worse before it gets better, and agencies must be prepared to stretch their limits.

Finally, we must take heart from the past. That we can now identify and discuss the problems that surround deinstitutionalization places us one giant step ahead of where we were when the movement began. Today we have a knowledge base that did not exist in the 1960s, and we have several decades of experience to point us in the right direction. We must exploit these resources and seek ever more innovative ways to treat people with schizophrenia and other major mental illnesses.

REFERENCES

Anonymous (1982). "Willowbrook plan worked", New York Times 4 September, p. 20.

Anonymous (1984). "Suffering in the streets', New York Times, 15 September, p. A18.

Anonymous (1986). "Redeinstitutionalization", New York Times 25 August, p. A24.

Bachrach, L.L. (1976). Deinstitutionalization: An Analytical Review and Sociological Perspective, National Institute of Mental Health, Rockville, Maryland.

Bachrach, L.L. (1989). "Deinstitutionalization: a semantic analysis", J. Soc. Issues, 45, 161 - 171.

Bachrach, L.L. (1993). "The biopsychosocial legacy of deinstitutionalization", Hosp. Community Psychiatry, 44, 523 - 524, 546.

Bachrach, L.L. (1994). "The semantics of mental health service delivery", Presented at the 74th Annual Meeting of the Ontario Psychiatric Association, Toronto, 28 January.

Bachrach, L.L. (in press). "American deinstitutionalization revisited", Epidemiol. Psichiatr. Sociale, 3.

Boodman, S.G. (1994). "Closing a state mental hospital", Washington Post Health, 18 January, p. 8.

Bradley, V.J. (1976). "Policy termination in mental health: the hidden agenda", Policy Sci. 7, 215 - 224.

Bragg, R. (1994). "Homeless seeing less apathy, more anger", New York Times, 25 February, pp. Al, B2.

Cohen, N.L., ed. (1990). Psychiatry Takes to the Streets, Guilford Press, New York.

Concannon, K.W. (1992). "Dousing a point of light", Washington Post 9 August, p. C7.

Dumont, M.P. (1982). Review of Private Lives/Public Spaces by E. Baxter and K. Hopper, and Shopping Bag Ladies by A.M. Rousseau, Am. J. Orthopsychiatry, 52, 367 -369.

Etzioni, A. (1976). "Deinstitutionalization," a public policy fashion. Evaluation, 3, 9 -10.

Jones, K. and Fowles, A.J. (1984). Ideas on Institutions. Routledge & Kegan Paul, London.

Kennedy, J.F. (1963). Message from the President of the United States Relative to Mental Illness and Mental Retardation, 88th Congress, First Session. House of Representatives Document no. 58, 5 February. U.S. Congress, Washington.

Lamb, H.R. (1993). "Lessons learned from deinstitutionalization in the U.S"., British Journal of Psychiatry 162, 587-592.

Lamb, H.R., Bachrach, L.L., and Kass, F.I., eds (1992). Treating the Homeless Mentally Ill: A Report of the Task Force on the Homeless Mentally Ill APA, Washington.

Liberman, R.P., ed. (1992). "Effective Psychiatric Rehabilitation", New Directions for Mental Health Services, no. 53. Jossey-Bass, San Francisco.

Manderscheid, R.W. & Sonnenschein, M.A., eds (1992). Mental Health, United States, 1992, US Government Printing Office, Washington.

Marlowe, H.A., and Weinberg, R.B. (1982) Introduction. In The Management of Deinstitutionalization: Proceedings of the 1982 Florida Conference on Deinstitutionalization, ed. H.A. Marlowe and R.B. Weinberg, pp. i - v. University of South Florida, Tampa. psychiatry.

Okin, R.L. (1978). "The future of state mental health programs for chronic psychiatric patients in the community", Am. J. Psychiatry, 135, 1355 - 1358.

Okin, R.L. (1993). Brewster v. Dukakis. Presented at the Annual Meeting of the American Psychiatric Association, San Francisco, 25 May.

President's Commission on Mental Health (1978.) Report to the President from the President's Commission on Mental Health, US Government Printing Office, Washington.

Raspberry, W. (1989). "Prop 42: what is it good for?", Washington Post, 1 February, p. A24.

Robinson, E. (1993). "East and west, a gloomy forecast: Europeans see an end to long guaranteed social welfare "rights"., Washington Post, 12 April, pp. Al, A14.

Romano, J. (1980). "Twenty-five years later", Psychiatric Quarterly, 52, 7 - 21.

Santayana, G. (1905). Reason in Common Sense. Dover Publications edition, 1980, New York.

Talbott, J.A. (1975). "Current cliches and platitudes in vogue in psychiatric vocabularies", Hosp. Community Psychiatry, 26, 530.

Thornicroft, G. and Bebbington, G. (1989)."Deinstitutionalisation - from hospital closure to service development", Br. J. of Psychiatry, 155, 739 - 753.

Warner, R. (1989). "Deinstitutionalization: how did we get where we are?", J. Soc. Issues, 45, 17 - 30.

Zealberg, J.J., Santos, A.B., and Fisher, R.K. (1993). "Benefits of mobile crisis programs", Hosp. Community Psychiatry, 44, 16 - 1.

3

SKILLS TRAINING FOR THE SERIOUSLY MENTALLY ILL: MODULES IN THE UCLA SOCIAL AND INDEPENDENT LIVING SKILLS PROGRAM

Robert P. Liberman, Charles J. Wallace,
Gayla Blackwell, Thad A. Eckman., and Timothy G. Kuehnel

INTRODUCTION

Many treatment and rehabilitation programs claim to utilize methods for "social skills training" or "training in community living" (Test, 1992); however, most programs-at best-use implicit, unstructured and ad hoc methods for teaching mentally disabled persons the instrumental and affiliative skills needed for optimal community integration. Given the cognitive deficits and learning disabilities evidenced by many persons with schizophrenia, it is likely that only highly structured and carefully planned methods of training, in which principles of human learning are implanted, will result in durable and generalizable skills being acquired (Liberman, 1988; Liberman et al., 1989). In addition, to assure the quality and consistency of skills training, the procedures need to be well-specified so they are readily followed and used by a variety of practitioners with different education, clinical training, and experiences.

Thus, social skills training techniques should be designed to meet the specialized needs of the mentally ill in overcoming their learning disabilities and fit the unique resources and constraints of local programs. To allow reliable replication by a wide array of paraprofessionals and professionals who are delivering clinical services to the seriously mentally ill, *a modular approach* to training

Schizophrenia: Exploring the Spectrum of Psychosis. Edited by R. Ancill © 1994
John Wiley & Sons Ltd

social and independent living skills was developed by Wallace and Liberman and their colleagues at the UCLA Clinical Research Center for Schizophrenia and Psychiatric Rehabilitation.

A module is a delimited element of service that has an integrated theme, provides patients with information needed to acquire specific knowledge and skills, is streamlined for structured and prescriptive delivery by clinicians, and can fit as a component into a broader treatment and rehabilitation program (Gordon et al., 1980). Meeting these modular criteria, psychoeducational and social skills training techniques have been shown in controlled clinical trials to markedly reduce relapse and rehospitalization, improve social functioning, and reduce family stress and burden (Wallace and Liberman 1985; Falloon et al., 1985; Leff et al., 1985; Hogarty et al. 1986; Tarrier et al., 1988).

The educational content of the modules focused on the needs and deficits of schizophrenics that were key obstacles to successful management of their illness; for example, self-management of medication, coping with symptoms, and performing the instrumental and affiliative skills necessary for community tenure. The training activities of the modules were designed to compensate for the cognitive dysfunctions and learning disabilities of patients; for example, repetition and overlearning was accomplished through video-assisted models, behavioral rehearsal, and in vivo exercises. To achieve replicability for clinical and research purposes, the techniques were highly detailed in stepwise fashion; by following this prescriptive structure, clinicians can easily and accurately use the techniques irrespective of differences in their education or professional experience.

TRAINING MODULES: STRUCTURE AND PROCESS

The social skills training techniques were "packaged" as self-contained modules, each of which consists of a Trainer's Manual, Patient's Workbook, Demonstration Videocassette, and User's Guide (Wallace et al., 1985). Through the use of each module, clinicians can teach the instrumental, social, and problem-solving skills of a major area of independent living, such as self-management of medication, care of personal hygiene, and participation in recreation and leisure activities. The Trainer's Manual specifies what is to be said and done to teach these skills; the videocassette demonstrates the skills; the Patient's Workbook includes additional written materials, self-monitoring forms and homework exercises to help participants learn the skills; and the User's Guide provides technical assistance to administrators and practitioners in implementing the modules.

Each module is divided into skill areas, which are taught using the same instructional techniques. The *Medication Management Module*, for example, is divided into five skill areas: recognizing the benefits of antipsychotic medication, recognizing its side effects, monitoring these side effects, interacting with physicians and other caregivers about medication issues, and recognizing the benefits of long-acting, injectable medication. Each skill area, in turn, contains a specified range of competencies that serve as the educational objectives of the module.

Each of these skill areas is taught systematically using seven *learning activities*: that enable participants to acquire and practice the skills in the training sessions and in the "real world." The first learning activity, introduction to a skill area, describes the skills that will be taught and the benefits that participants might expect if they use them. Reading or paraphrasing a script form the Trainer's Manual, the trainer asks a set of prepared questions from the Trainer's Manual to assess a participants comprehension of the material. Appropriate answers are specified in the Trainer's Manual; incorrect or incomplete answers are corrected by the trainer's use of a standardized sequence of prompting, coaching, and reinforcement. Successful completion of this introduction promotes insight and motivation for the substantive learning tasks that follow.

The trainer then demonstrates the skills by conducting the second learning activity, video assisted modeling.. The trainer plays the module's videocassettes which shows peers, who are actors, performing each of the skills. The video has periodic "stops" that prompt the trainer to ask prepared questions from the Trainer's Manual to assess participants' understanding of the demonstration. As in the introduction, incorrect or incomplete answers are corrected with the sequence of prompting, coaching, and reinforcement.

After the skills have been demonstrated, the trainer conducts the third learning activity, *roleplaying*. Each participant is asked to roleplay the skills that have just been demonstrated, and the trainer uses a prepared checklist in the Trainer's Manual to assess the accuracy of the roleplay. An incorrect performance results in the trainer's use of a standardized sequence of prompting, modeling, and coaching.

The trainer then prepares participants to use the skills outside of the training session. The trainer conducts the fourth learning activity, *solving resource management problems*, by asking a set of prepared questions from the Trainer's Manual that teaches participants to actively consider how to obtain the resources they will need to perform the skills in the real world. Appropriate answers are also specified in *video-assisted modeling* the Trainer's Manual; incorrect or incomplete answers result in the trainer's use of the standardized sequence of prompting, coaching, and assistance. The trainer conducts the fifth learning activity, *solving outcome problems,* in much the same manner except that the problems involve unexpected obstacles to the implementation of the skills, rather than resources to be obtained. Because the problem-solving method of coping with challenges and disappointments is repeated in every skill area of every module, a general problem-solving approach to dealing with stressors is hopefully acquired by participants.

The trainer then has participants use the skills outside of the training session. The trainer conducts the sixth learning activity, *in-vivo exercises,* by supervising participants as they complete a prepared task from the Trainer's Manual and which involves use of the skills in the real world. The trainer accompanies the participants on the exercises, and provides encouragement, support, and positive feedback. The trainer conducts the seventh learning activity, homework assignments, in much the same manner except that the participants perform the skills on their own, and provide "permanent product" evidence that they have completed the assignments.

These seven learning activities are used for all skill areas in all modules. Although a module can be conducted with one participant, training is most efficient and effective when conducted in the group format with from four to eight participants and one trainer. More than eight participants reduces the opportunities for each to answer the prepared questions and engage in the roleplay and the problem-solving exercises. Fewer than four substantially increases the cost of conducting a module. Training is most efficient and effective when the sessions are conducted from two to three times per week for 1 - 1 1/2 hours each. More than 1 1/2 hours taxes most participants' attention span, and fewer than two sessions per week requires a lengthy training period, beyond the four month duration of twice-weekly sessions to complete.

CAN PATIENTS WITH SCHIZOPHRENIA ACQUIRE SKILLS?

Because the prevailing view of schizophrenia as a brain disorder to be treated with biological, not psychosocial, treatments has many psychiatric practitioners doubting the value and efficacy of behavioral rehabilitation, it is necessary to produce empirical evidence to document that persons with schizophrenia can learn, sustain, and generalize to real life the skills taught in the modules. Further, the modules would be more convincing as clinical innovations to administrators and service providers if it could be demonstrated that they are effectively utilized by paraprofessionals as well as professional mental health specialists.

Two independent studies were conducted to determine whether patients with schizophrenia could learn and retain the knowledge and skills offered by four different modules (Medication Management, Symptom Management, Recreation for Leisure, and Grooming & Personal Hygiene). In one study, 41 outpatient male veterans, who met the DSM III-R criteria for schizophrenia and had been ill for an average of 14 years, were randomly assigned to twice weekly skills training in the Medication and Symptom Management Modules or to equally frequent supportive group therapy for a total of six months (Eckman et al., 1992). Skill attainment was assessed before and after the six month training program, and again at 6 months and 12 months following the end of training, through a series of standardized interview and performance tests. Assessors, trained to satisfactory levels of interrater reliability, rated each patient's performance on a 4-point scale from "poor" to "excellent" for verbal content and nonverbal and paralinguistic skills relevant to each of the skills that were taught in the modules.

The patients exposed to the skills training improved *Medication Management Module*, their performance from 55% to 90% of possible skill attainment in the while the contrast group receiving supportive group therapy increased minimally from 55% to 60%. Similar acquisition of skills was noted for the Symptom Management Module. Acquisition of skills by those receiving the modular program was statistically significant, in contrast to the supportive therapy patients. Furthermore, the patients who received skills training performed well on the post-treatment assessments of knowledge and skills regardless of their initial level of psychopathology, indicating that the modular procedures were indeed successful in compensating for any learning disabilities attributable to cognitive deficits or symptoms.

In a second study, 200 long-term mentally ill persons (90% of whom were diagnosed as having schizophrenia or schizoaffective disorder) received modular skills training in their residential treatment facilities or day hospital (Wallace et al., 1992). The subjects spanned a wide range of functional and symptomatic status; for example, participants who were living at the state hospital were far more regressed and symptomatic than others who were functioning semi-independently in supervised board and care homes in the community. The baseline ratings of the interview and performance-based test that was administered before and after training reflected the marked differences in functional level of the various patient cohorts. The average age of the subjects was 33; they had been ill on average for 12 years, and 74% were male.

In the state hospital unit and the two larger community residential care sites, a two-group, random assignment, experimental research design was used, with the control group patients in a waiting list, holding pattern. Given the smaller number of patients available in the day hospital and three smaller residences, a one-group, pre/post, quasi-experimental research design was used. The modules used in this study included *Recreation for Leisure, Grooming and Personal Hygiene, and Medication Management.*

The skills acquired by the patients exposed to the modules in the state hospital and three larger homes were analyzed using pre/post test scores in a two-way (Group; Site) factorial analysis of co-variance. The results revealed significant differences between the experimental and control groups for each module, with no differences between the sites. To analyze the replicability of the modules' effects, scores for all sites with a treatment group were analyzed separately for each module with a two-way (Site; Pre vs Post) split-plot factorial analysis of variance. The results revealed highly significant pre-post test differences. It is worth noting that these favorable results were achieved mostly by line level paraprofessional staff who received only limited training and supervision by professionals in psychology.

ARE THE SKILLS LEARNED THROUGH THE MODULES DURABLE?

To justify the labor-intensive requirements of social skills training, the skills acquired by patients in training sessions should hold up at least for six months and, if the patients' natural living environments support the skills, be in evidence a year later. It is crucial to understand the conditions under which any skill is maintained over time, whether demonstrated by a normal person or a person with a learning disability caused by schizophrenia. None of us can reliably persist in demonstrating a skill unless our real world environments give us opportunities, encouragement and reinforcement for using the skill. A good example is cardiopulmonary resuscitation (CPR), which physicians are expected to be able to use in medical emergencies. Since very few physicians actually employ CPR from one year to the next, the American Red Cross and hospitals across the USA must re-train and re-certify physicians in CPR on an annual basis.

Durability of skills learned in the *Medication and Symptom Management Modules*, as evidenced by the schizophrenic subjects in the VA outpatient clinic study described above, was evaluated by comparing the post-treatment means with the six-month follow-up means and then comparing the six-month follow-up means with the means at the 12-month follow-up. For patients who were exposed to the modules, there was little erosion of skill levels through the one year of follow-up assessment. Gradual and modest accretion of knowledge and skills by the patients receiving supportive group therapy was probably a result of their repeated medication clinic visits and discussions with their nurse, practitioner, psychiatrist and case manager; however, the differences between treatment conditions were highly statistically significant at the post-treatment, six months and 12 months follow-up assessments.

One-year follow-up assessments also were made of the knowledge and performance of patients participating in the three modules offered in the residential and day treatment programs described above (Wallace et al., 1992). The data analysis from each module test indicated that subjects in each of the three modules significantly increased their skills as a function of participating in the modules, with no differences between post-testing and follow-up testing. It should be carefully noted, however, that durability of skills depends upon at least a modicum of opportunities, encouragement and reinforcement for using the skills in real life settings.

DO SKILLS GENERALIZE TO OTHER SETTING AND IMPROVE SOCIAL AND QUALITY OF LIFE?

In the study of outpatients with schizophrenia at the VA clinic (Eckman et al., 1992), subjects were systematically interviewed for evidence of their utilization of their *Medication and Symptom Management* skills in interactions with family members, residential care operators, physicians, and other health care providers. Patients who were exposed to the skills training modules reported significantly greater utilization than their counterparts who received supportive group therapy. In this same study, self-reported functioning over a two-year period, on the Social Adjustment Scale, revealed statistically significant generalization of social skills training to interpersonal closeness, personal well-being, and at a borderline level of significance, social activities in general.

In another study of 80 schizophrenic patients randomly assigned to six months of intensive outpatient social skills training versus traditional psychosocial occupational therapy (Vaccaro et al., 1992), utilization of skills in everyday life was measured by the Independent Living Skills Survey (Wallace, 1986). The patients receiving training in four of the modules in the UCLA Social and Independent Living Skills program showed statistically significant improvements in their total, cumulative score as well as in subscales measuring food preparation, money management, and job finding. The skills trained subjects also showed statistically significant improvements in their subjectively reported quality of life, using the Lehman Quality of Life Scale (Lehman, 1983).

Thus, the evidence accumulated from four independent studies which have employed the modules from the UCLA Social and Independent Living Skills program clearly indicates that a wide array of schizophrenic patients can learn and retain skills relevant to community life and self-management of their illness. Moreover, the learning of skills appears to lead to utilization of these skills in everyday life with consequent improvements in social adjustment and quality of life.

HOW MUCH TRAINING OF TRAINERS IS REQUIRED FOR PRACTITIONERS TO USE THE MODULES WITH FIDELITY?

To evaluate the need for training and supervision of clinicians who wished to implement one or more of the modules, 28 field sites from throughout the USA and Canada were assigned to "Training + Consultation" versus "Consultation Alone" conditions (Eckman et al., 1990). The sites in both conditions, selected on the basis of their response to a circular describing the opportunity to participate in a field test of the Medication Management Module, represented a wide geographic distribution and a broad range of inpatient and partial hospitalization programs located in public and private psychiatric hospitals, community mental health programs, and residential care facilities. Clinicians who participated as trainers came from a variety of disciplines, including psychiatry, psychology, social work, nursing, occupational therapy and paraprofessionals.

In the implementation phase of the field test, a total of 160 patients participated in the module - all patients were candidates for maintenance antipsychotic medication, had a history of at least two previous hospitalizations, and had a primary diagnosis of schizophrenia. Clinicians in the "Training + Consultation" condition received a two-day course of instruction, including observation of the module and its learning activities in action with expert trainers and guided practice in the learning activities. The other half of the clinician - trainers simply received the module in the mail and were encouraged to discuss and roleplay the learning activities with co-workers before implementing the procedures with real patients. Clinician trainers in both conditions received telephone consultation on a weekly or biweekly basis throughout the three month implementation phase.

Measures of clinician trainer competency, based on direct observation of the module in process at the 28 field sites, indicated that the module leaders learned the procedures specified in the Trainer's Manual and delivered them with a high degree of fidelity. While clinicians who had the benefit of the two-day experiential workshop were somewhat superior in the precision and confidence with which they led their patient groups, patients in *both* conditions showed statistically significant gains in knowledge, skill, skill utilization, and medication compliance.

The importance of faithful and systematic application of the full set of learning activities prescribed in the Trainer's Manual was highlighted by one module leader in a community-based residential care facility who skipped the roleplay and problem-solving activities with the result that her patients did not demonstrate any significant gain in knowledge or skills. At an additional field site in California - a mental health unit within a state prison - those patients who completed 18 or more module sessions showed 77% greater learning than those who participated in five or fewer sessions.

DISSEMINATION AND ADOPTION OF THE MODULES

Since the first module was produced in 1985, over 5000 modules have been distributed to mental health and rehabilitation facilities throughout the USA. To gauge the long-term use of the modules by agencies, programs and hospitals, and practitioners which initially showed interest in them, 126 facilities were polled for their experiences with and adoption of the *Medication Management Module*, one to two years after they first received a module. Sixty-one per cent of the facilities reported continued use of the module and another 35 per cent reported using the module at least once with intention to use it again. Only 4 percent of the respondents reported that they did not intend to use the module again. Ninety-six percent of the respondents reported that patients participating in the module had gained as much or more from their learning experiences than had been expected. Spin-off benefits yielded by the modules were reported to include (1) enlivened participation by patients in groups; (2) teacher - student, rather than therapist - patient, relationships established with improved treatment alliances and collaboration; (3) patients' gains in assertiveness and responsibility as they became better informed consumers of their medication.

The Medication and Symptom Management Modules have been translated into French, German, Swedish, Norwegian, Polish and Japanese, and other translations are underway into Bulgarian, Dutch, Spanish, Italian, Chinese, and Korean. Controlled field tests in Quebec, France, Switzerland, and Germany suggest that these modules are effective in those countries as well as in the USA (Liberman, 1993). Anecdotal comments made by both trainers and patients indicated that the modules were experienced as "user friendly", valuable and enjoyable. Furthermore, many trainers were able to adapt the modular learning activities into other facets of their clinical work-especially roleplaying and problem-solving exercises.

FUTURE DIRECTIONS FOR SKILLS TESTING

We are hopeful that the favorable results achieved to date with the modules will stimulate other clinicians to design and produce additional, user-friendly, treatment and rehabilitation methods with video-assisted training, roleplaying and problem-solving.   Treatment modules that provide clinicians with completely specified teaching tools promote the use of efficacious learning principles-such as cues for modeling and social reinforcement-without requiring a wholesale retraining of staff or reorganization of a treatment facility's structure, personnel and program. Moreover, the modules are sufficiently prescriptive so that even paraprofessionals, volunteers, and consumers themselves can effectively train the seriously mentally ill. One such program, established in a small city in Oregon and led by advocate Marv Higgins and National Alliance for the Mentally Ill volunteers appears to be securing its rehabilitative goals. Paraprofessionals and volunteers can be effective trainers if they have social skills, enthusiasm, and experience and comfort interacting with patients so the latter are seen and treated as individuals doing their very best with the limitations and disability their illness produces.

The demonstrated replicability of the skills training modules also overshadows concerns that psychosocial rehabilitation is applicable only to a small proportion of highly functioning individuals with chronic mental disorders. The modules equally improved patients' knowledge and skills from their baseline performance, regardless of initial levels of functioning, although lower functioning and more symptomatic patients required much more prompting, modeling, and repetition to learn the skills (Eckman et al., 1992).

The advent of the Americans with Disabilities Act heralds new and improved potentialities for skills training to overcome handicaps of the mentally ill in the coming decades. With the weight of the law influencing employers to provide accommodations to individuals with disabilities so they can take jobs and achieve the dignity and self-respect of the role of "worker", mental health and rehabilitation workers will be able to improve the "person - environment fit" of their clientele.   There will be new options for professionals to work collaboratively with employers and the public to create opportunities, encouragement and reinforcement for individuals with mental disorders to use the skills they have learned naturally or through training programs, thereby tailoring the environment to the person. In turn, these new avenues for rehabilitation will stimulate strategies and techniques for treatment and rehabilitation teams to modify the natural residential, work, and recreational environments of persons with mental disabilities so that their tentative use of newly learned skills will be strengthened and supported.

Future improvement in the delivery of modular skills to the seriously mentally ill will require an integration of skills training with assertive, outreach forms of case management and continuous clinical treatment. While skills can be suitably learned in a classroom-like setting, their ultimate application in patients' real life situations is "where the rubber hits the road". Case managers, if trained in behavioral learning principles, can amplify the generalization and utilization of skills by (1) using active-directive training techniques (e.g., in vivo modeling, prompting and reinforcement) in community settings where patients actually face problems and stressors; (2) liaising and consulting with the natural caregivers, relatives, and employers, thereby serving as "brokers" or "change agents" to open up opportunities, encouragement and reinforcement for patients' use of their skills; and (3) bridging the gap between training and application of the skills through supportive and practical therapeutic alliances with the patients (Vaccaro et al., 1992; Baker and Intagliata, 1992).

By the year 2000, we expect that life adjustment teams and personal services aides will employ structured skills-training techniques while interacting with patients in naturalistic settings in the community. Indeed, this approach has already been implemented in one demonstration study, conducted in a small suburban county between Oxford and London, England, which showed how early and therapeutically aggressive intervention using the full range of assessment, diagnosis, pharmacological, and cognitive-behavioral therapies, appeared to stymie the full development of chronic schizophrenia in most young adults who had shown prodromal or early psychotic signs and symptoms (Falloon et al., 1990).

REFERENCES

Anthony, W.A. (1979) "Principles of Psychiatric Rehabilitation", University Park Press, Baltimore.

Baker, F. abd Intagliata, J. (1992). "Case management". In Handbook of Psychiatric Rehabilitation (ed R.P. Liberman), Macmillan, New York, pp. 213 - 243.

Eckman, T.A., Liberman, R.P., Blair, K., and Phipps, C.C. (1990). "Teaching medication management skills to schizophrenic patients", J. Clin. Psychopharmacol, 10, 33 -38.

Eckman, T.A., Wirshing, W.C., Marder, S.R., Liberman, R.P., Johnston-Cronk, K., Zimmerman, K. Mintz, J. (1992). "Technique for training schizophrenic patients in illness self-management: a controlled trial ", Am. J. Psychiatry, 149, 1549-1555.

Falloon, I.R.H., Boyd, J.L., McGill, C.W., et al. (1985). "Family management in the prevention of morbidity of schizophrenia: clinical outcome of a two year longitudinal study", Arch. Gen. Psychiatry, 42, 887 - 896.

Falloon, I.R.H., Shanahan, W., LaPorta, M. and Krekorian, H.A.R. (1990). "Integrated family, general practice and mental health care in the management of schizophrenia", J. R. Soc. Med., 83, 225 - 228.

Gordon, R.E., Patterson, R.L., Eberly, D.A. and Penner L (1980). "Modular treatment of psychiatric patients". In Current Psychiatric Therapies (ed. J. Masserman), V. 19., Grune & Stratton, New York, 129 - 141.

Hogarty, G.E., Anderson, C.M., Reiss D.J., et al. (1986). "Family psychoeducation, social skills training, and maintenance chemotherapy in the aftercare treatment of schizophrenia", Arch. Gen. Psychiatry, 43, 633 - 642.

Leff, J.P., Kuipers, L., Berkowitz, R., Sturgeon, D. (1985). "A controlled trial of social intervention in the families of schizophrenic patients: two year follow-up", Br.J. Psychiatry, 146, 594 - 600.

Lehman, A. (1983). "The well-being of chronic mental patients", Arch. Gen. Psychiatry,, 40, 369 - 373.

Liberman, R.P. (1988) Psychiatric Rehabilitation of Chronic Mental Patients, American Psychiatric Press, Washington, DC.

Liberman, R.P. (1993). "International studies of the modules in the UCLA Program for Social and Independent Living Skills", Symposium presented to the annual meeting of the American Psychiatric Association, San Francisco, May 25, 1993.

Liberman, R.P., DeRisi, W.J., Mueser, K.T. (1989). Social Skills Training for Psychiatric Patients, Pergamon Press, New York.

Tarrier, N., Barrowclough, C., Vaughn, C.E., et al. (1988). "The community management of schizophrenia: a controlled clinical trial of a behavioral intervention with families to reduce relapse", Br. J. Psychiatry, 153, 532 - 542.

Test, M.A. (1992). "Training in community living". In Handbook of Psychiatric Rehabilitation (ed. R.P. Liberman), Macmillan, New York, pp 153 - 170.

Vaccaro, J.V., Liberman, R.P., Blackwell, G. and Wallace, C.J. (1992) "Combining social skills training and assertive case management". In New Directions for Mental Health Services: Effective Psychiatric Rehabilitation (ed. R.P. Liberman), Jossey-Bass, San Francisco, pp. 33 - 42.

Wallace, C.J. (1986). "Functional assessment in rehabilitation", Schizophr. Bull., 12, 604 - 630.

Wallace, C.J., Boone, S.E., Donahoe, C.P. and Foy D.W. (1985) "The chronically mentally ill: independent living skills training". In Clinical Handbook of Psychological Disorders (ed. D. Barlow), Guilford Press, New York, 462 - 501

Wallace, C.J., Liberman, R.P., MacKain, S.J., Blackwell, G. and Eckman, T.A. (1992). "Effectiveness and replicability of modules for teaching social and instrumental skills to the severely mentally ill", Am. J. Psychiatry, 149, 654 - 658.

Wallace C.J. and Liberman R.P. (1985). "Social skills training for patients with schizophrenia: a controlled clinical trial", Psychiatr. Res, 15, 239 - 247.

4

APPLYING PSYCHIATRIC REHABILITATION PRINCIPLES TO EMPLOYMENT: RECENT FINDINGS

Gary R. Bond

This chapter reviews recent research applying five psychiatric principles to helping persons with serious mental illness (SMI) attain competitive employment. Research on vocational programs has lagged behind other rehabilitation domains for several reasons. Historically, vocational services for the psychiatric population in the United States have been embraced by neither the mental health system nor the vocational rehabilitation (VR) system. As a consequence, relatively few persons with SMI have had access to comprehensive vocational programs (Tashjian et al., 1989). Moreover, the employment outcomes for the psychiatric population have been discouraging, even for individuals participating in model programs (Bond, 1992a). As the research below indicates, however, there may be reason for renewed optimism in light of the emergence of supported employment (SE) and related employment strategies.

Psychiatric rehabilitation has a diverse history, with a number of influential conceptualizations (e.g., Anthony, 1980; Dincin, 1975; Flexer and Solomon, 1993; Spaniol, in press). The purpose of the current chapter is not to offer an alternate conceptual framework, nor to provide an exhaustive inventory of critical ingredients. The purpose is rather to begin to consolidate areas of substantial empirical evidence. This need to collate and interpret the empirical bases for our intervention and program models has become even more urgent in

Schizophrenia: Exploring the Spectrum of Psychosis. Edited by R. Ancill © 1994
John Wiley & Sons Ltd.

the em of increased managed care and emphasis on accountability (Jacobs and Moxley, 1993).

HISTORICAL CONTEXT

Bond (in press) has suggested four historical phases in psychiatric rehabilitation, each associated with a vocational strategy: institutionalization, transitionalism, community support, and consumer empowerment.   Although all are still in common use, each strategy was most popular during one decade since the onset of deinstitutionalization.

Institutional models predominated in the 1950s. According to this philosophy, clients are trained in institutional settings segregated from society, in hopes that they will develop the skills necessary to function in community jobs (Black, 1988).   Skills training (as offered in psychiatric hospitals and in partial hospitalization programs), prevocational work crews, and sheltered workshops are examples of institutional approaches.

First popularized in the 1960s, transitional approaches are based on the concept of a continuum of vocational options, some more demanding than others (Dincin, 1975). Under this philosophy, clients improve their work habits and job performance by meeting expectations in successively more demanding work environments, beginning with relatively low-demand environments. As clients move through a rehabilitation continuum, their behaviors are shaped to satisfy community employment standards. Exemplifying the transitional philosophy are agencies offering a graded continuum of vocational options, such as prevocational work crews and transitional employment (TE) (i.e., temporary jobs in the community, through arrangements with the rehabilitation program).

The community support approach was articulated in a set of principles developed in the United States in the 1970s in response to the perceived failure of community mental health centers (CMHCs) to address the needs of persons with SMI (Tumer AND TenHoor, 1978). Features of a community support program (CSP) include the identification of a core service agency responsible for the comprehensive needs of clients and the use of "natural supports" to assist clients achieve community adjustment. Many CSP concepts developed in the 1970s foreshadowed the principles of supported employment, developed in the 1980s, with its emphasis on direct entry into community employment settings combined with ongoing and individualized support.

Consumer empowerment became a major theme with the emergence of the mental health consumer self-help movement in the 1980s (Chamberlin et al., 1989). The consumer movement has emphasized the importance of consumer preferences in the employment process, an element noticeably lacking in those vocational programs that stress the importance of gaining employment experience, regardless of the type of job obtained. Illustrating the consumer empowerment trend is a consumer run vocational program assisting individuals with SMI who have professional training to find employment in their area of expertise (Minnesota Mainstream, 1993). Instead of offering placement in unskilled jobs, this program links mental health consumers trained in engineering, accounting, social work, and other professions to community mentors (professionals in the field in which a client is seeking work), as one of the steps toward returning to work.

FIVE PRINCIPLES

Current psychiatric rehabilitation programs draw on a wide range of principles from these historical roots. Five ingredients found in many psychiatric rehabilitation models are examined here. They are: assertive outreach, time-unlimited support, team approach, assessment and training in natural settings, and attention to client preferences.

1. Assertive Outreach

The rationale for assertive outreach can be put very simply: for clients to benefit from treatment or rehabilitation, they must participate. Merely referring clients to services is not enough to ensure their participation. Moreover, clients who drop out of programs prematurely benefit little (Bond, 1984). For people with SMI, "assertive availability of services" is often necessary to combat high vulnerability to stress, poor interpersonal skills, low motivation, extreme dependency, and passivity, and other factors that interfere with participation (Test, 1994).

Treatment noncompliance is a major problem in mental health systems. Axelrod and Wetzler (1989) found that only 40% of a sample of clients were attending aftercare six months following discharge from an emergency admission in a municipal hospital. Dropout rates from community programs are even higher for frequent users of psychiatric hospitals. Surles and McGuffin (1987) found that 70% of a sample of 1499 "heavy users" of psychiatric hospitals refused outpatient care, compared to only 5% of a sample of 35,250 patients using other services.

Many mental health programs throughout the United States and Canada have adopted assertive outreach approaches to engage clients who are reluctant to use day treatment programs. There is little doubt that such programs can increase retention rates in mental health services. In their meta-analysis of nine studies of an assertive outreach model for frequent users of psychiatric hospitals, Bond et al., (in press) found that 83% of 451 assertive outreach clients were still receiving mental health services after one year, compared to 52% of 167 controls.

The principle of assertive outreach has yet to be applied on a broad scale to vocational programs, even though high attrition rates are common (Bond, 1992a). Individuals with SMI have particular difficulty negotiating the VR eligibility process. For example, Marshak et al. (1990) found that the successful closure rates among rehabilitation clients with psychiatric disabilities was only half that for persons with physical disabilities. A closer analysis of their data revealed that a large proportion (31%) of clients with psychiatric disabilities never finished the VR eligibility process, because they had trouble completing their "individual written rehabilitation plans" (IWRPs). Even in programs with the stated goal of accelerating the eligibility process, it is not uncommon for clients to wait months before their paperwork allows them to begin a vocational program (Bond, 1992a). During this time, some clients lose their resolve to pursue employment.

To improve the engagement process for clients who express the desire to seek employment, both micro-level and macro-level strategies need to be considered. Marrone's (1991) study of "speedy IWRP" is an example of an intervention at the micro level. He instructed six VR counselors to write IWRPs for clients based on their initial client interviews. A comparison group of six VR counselors followed standard procedures of waiting to write IWRPs until all reports from collaterals were received. Marrone found that 83% of the IWRPs written according to the experimental procedures did not require changes with additional information. Moreover, the time required to complete the VR eligibility process averaged 4.1 months for VR counselors using the experimental method, compared to 5.2 months for the counselors following standard procedures. Once used to the new procedures, VR counselors liked it as well as their habitual method. Further, they noticed that they were paying closer attention to the expressed needs of clients.

An Ohio project gives an example of a state-level intervention (Saveanu and Roth, 1986). Through a deliberate effort to recruit and retain clients with psychiatric disabilities, Ohio showed a small, but demonstrable, impact on both engagement and retention. Over a four-year period, 7,164 clients with SMI were referred for VR services, of whom 71% completed the eligibility process, compared to the national rate of 65% for this population (Andrews et al., 1992). Of those accepted for services, 60% were classified as rehabilitated at closure; the comparison rate from the national survey was 50%.

Perhaps changes at the federal level will ultimately prove to be the most effective. Consistent with Marrone's study, the 1992 Amendments to the Rehabilitation Act mandate that VR eligibility determination be done in a timely fashion. The 1992 guidelines stipulate that applicants for rehabilitation services should be certified within 60 days, barring extenuating circumstances.

Assertive outreach extends beyond facilitating the engagement process for VR applicants. It also involves "talking up work" with clients who are fearful or hesitant about working (Russert and Frey, 1991). Assertive outreach may make a difference for persons not only considered good candidates for employment programs. In an outreach program designed specifically to increase employment among homeless adults with SMI, Kirzner et al. (1991), reported that not only were 86 such individuals successfully engaged in treatment, but also that 70% were employed at some time over an 18-month period, and that 39% remained employed for at least 13 weeks.

2. Time-Unlimited Support

The importance of time-unlimited support in providing mental health and rehabilitation services. For example, when model programs are closed down, clients terminated from these programs tend to regress (Bond, 1990; Test, 1984). Perhaps the largest-scale study to examine the impact of a time-limited rehabilitation program is the recently completed study of the United States VR system (GAO, 1993). In the United States, clients historically have received few VR services once they reached "closure" status, as is the case if they successfully complete two months of competitive employment. The GAO report examined the short-term and long-term employment outcomes for 865,000 VR applicants whose cases were closed in 1980. Among clients with emotional disabilities (i.e., mental illness or substance abuse), the percentage with earnings from wages increased from 70% for the two years prior to referral to over 80% during the year of closure, suggesting a positive short-term impact of VR services. Unfortunately, the percentage dropped below baseline within the following year. The absence of any mechanism for continued support for VR clients after they attained closure status probably contributed to the dismal long-term employment rates.

Although the VR system has undergone nominal changes in recognizing the need for long-term support since this 1980 database was compiled, the findings are still relevant. The large majority of VR clients still receive traditional rehabilitation services, with time-limited support (Revell et al., 1994).

Another recent study offers further evidence for the importance of time-unlimited support for job retention. In a descriptive study of 448 clients followed up six months after terminating from a psychiatric rehabilitation agency, Cook and Rosenberg (in press) found that clients who received continuous follow-along support after termination were significantly more likely to be working than those who received either intermittent support or stopped receiving support altogether.

3. Team Approach

The concept of a team approach was popularized by Stein and Test (1980) in the development of the assertive community treatment (ACT) model. Their approach uses a multi-disciplinary team (e.g., psychiatrist, nurse, social workers, vocational counselor, and professionals), who together pool their expertise and knowledge of clients to develop effective treatment plans and to ensure continuity of treatment (Test, 1979). The Thresholds Bridge program, in their adaptation of the ACT model, did not retain the multi-disciplinary element, but did maintain the team concept, with its emphasis on shared caseloads, daily team meetings, and joint problem-solving (Bond, 1991).

Test (1979) hypothesized that one advantage of a team approach was preventing burnout. By working together, mental health staff feel less isolated and more supported, despite their challenging work. A case manager survey has offered support for Test's hypothesis (Boyer, 1991; Boyer and Bond, 1992). Boyer compared attitudes about work between 118 ACT case managers and 97 traditional case managers with individual caseloads. Although ACT case managers had the advantage of smaller caseloads (an average of 12 clients per case manager, compared to 29 for the individual case managers), the ACT teams served clients with more serious psychiatric problems (e.g., more clients with schizophrenia and clients who averaged more prior hospitalizations, both potential factors in burnout).

Boyer found that ACT workers generally experienced less job burnout than individual case managers. ACT workers also reported feeling more involved, less pressure, greater role clarity, and greater control over their environment. Also revealing were the variables correlating with burnout within each subsample. Consistent with the burnout literature, individual case managers were more likely to report burnout the longer they were in their current job. They were also more likely to report burnout if they had a higher proportion of clients with schizophrenia. Neither of these variables predicted burnout for ACT workers, however, providing further support for Test's hypothesis.

A team approach also helps ensure continuity of services (Test, 1979). A study by Bond et al. (1991), illustrates this point. They compared two case management programs designed for heavy users of psychiatric emergency rooms and hospitals. One program used a team approach, whereas the other consisted of a single case manager assigned an individual caseload of 15 clients. The individual case manager, although effective in reducing hospital admissions, resigned his position after one year, and was replaced by a second case manager, who also resigned after a year. The periods of staff turnover coincided with a substantial increase in hospital admissions. By contrast, the team approach showed a linear trend of reduced hospital use during each successive time period. The post hoc interpretation of the study findings was that the continuity of case manager-client relationships in the team approach provided the stability necessary to avoid the types of upheavals apparently experienced by clients with an individual case manager when the person filling that position changed.

Test (1979) also has noted the advantages of a multi-disciplinary team that integrates mental health and rehabilitation services. This philosophy has not been widely adopted, despite its intuitive appeal. Bond et al. (1993), examined employment outcomes for clients enrolled in two types of supported employment (SE) programs. At one site, the employment specialists were employed by the CMIRC. The mental health case managers and employment specialists had the same supervisor, and all worked closely together on mental health and rehabilitation goals. Thus, this site used a "service-integrated' approach. The second agency providing SE services was a rehabilitation agency that historically had provided a range of optional rehabilitation services, organized around a sheltered workshop. It previously had completed a successful SE pilot project with a local CMHC. The SE program developed by this second agency involved separate agreements with each of four CMHCS; hence, this site used an "interagency collaboration" approach.

The employment outcomes by the second year of the study significantly favored the service-integrated approach. The agency using interagency collaboration provided a microcosm of the well-documented problems with fragmentation of services and intermittent breakdowns in communication found throughout mental health systems in which brokering of services is a norm. Referrals were slower in the interagency collaboration approach, and the employment specialists had far less contact with mental health case managers and psychiatrists. In addition, case manager and employment specialists more frequently gave mixed messages to clients about their work readiness.

4. Assessment and Training in Natural Settings

The concept of transitionalism described above is deeply embedded in rehabilitation practice, not only for clients with SMI, but for other severe disabilities as well. Traditional VR services begin with an assessment and training phase preceding job placement. The SE movement, which owed its origins to demonstration projects for persons with mental retardation, has challenged the "Train-Place" paradigm by suggesting that training and assessment might best be accomplished after a client has begun a competitive employment position (Wehman, 1986). Independent of the SE movement, some researchers examining the impact of psychiatric rehabilitation programs during the 1980s were drawing similar conclusions.

Several studies suggest that clients are more motivated to work and are more likely to receive more favorable ratings of work performance if they are placed in paid community jobs rather than in unpaid prevocational settings. Bond and Friedmeyer (1987) examined staff ratings of work performance for clients who had been assigned either to TE or unpaid prevocational work crews. Clients assigned to TE had more favorable work evaluations than their prevocational counterparts. The authors speculated that clients placed in an unpaid work setting may have been less energetic than their paid counterparts, because they lacked both monetary incentives and challenging work. Schultheis and Bond (1993) found a similar pattern when the same clients were observed in both paid community jobs and unpaid prevocational settings. They concluded that work performance may actually decline if clients return to a prevocational setting after having worked in the community. Bell et al. (1993), compared attendance patterns over a six-month period for 100 clients with SMI randomly assigned to paid and unpaid work crews. Attendance differed dramatically and significantly throughout the six-month period. In the first week, 97% of the paid clients participated, compared to 37% of the unpaid clients. By the last week, 35% of the paid clients and 5% clients were still participating.

A number of recent studies suggest the feasibility of placing clients in community jobs without extensive prevocational preparation. Bond and Dincin (1986) compared examined employment outcomes for 107 clients randomly assigned to either a "gradual" or "accelerated" vocational approach. The gradual condition represented the standard approach for the agency: clients were required to stay a minimum of four months in the prevocational work crews before they were eligible for TE positions. In the accelerated condition, clients were placed in group TE positions one month after program admission. At the end of the nine-month follow-up period, significantly more accelerated participants were in paid employment positions (either competitive employment or TE), compared to gradual participants. By the 15-month follow-up, accelerated participants were significantly more likely to be employed full time. They also had accumulated significantly more weeks of paid employment.

Using a similar design, Bond et al. (1993) examined 74 clients with SMI who were randomly assigned either to an accelerated approach to SE which bypassed traditional prevocational preparation, or to a gradual approach which consisted of a minimum of four months in prevocational preparation before they were eligible for SE services. Results after one year suggested significantly better employment outcomes for accelerated participants. Over three years later, follow-up at one site indicated that 59% of the accelerated participants were competitively employed, compared to only 6% of gradual participants.

Gervey and Bedell (1993) compared employment outcomes for 34 young adults with SMI who were randomly assigned either to an SE program or to paid work crews within a CMHC. Whereas 73% of the SE clients obtained community jobs within the first year, only 17% of the sheltered work crew clients obtained competitive employment. Job tenure in competitive employment was much higher for SE clients ($\underline{M}$ = 117 days) than sheltered clients ($\underline{M}$ = 15 days).

Drake et al. (in press) compared 183 clients enrolled in two rehabilitation day treatment programs, one of which converted its services over to SE, and the other which continued to offer day treatment and to use traditional brokered VR services to assist clients seeking employment. In the program converting to SE, the rate of competitive employment increased from 25% to 39% over a year's time. Results were especially favorable for regular attendees, whose rate of employment increased from 33% to 56%. By contrast, in the day treatment program not converting to SE, employment rates did not change for either the total group (13% in the baseline year and 13% during the study year) or its regular attendees (14% during the baseline year and 8% during the study year). No negative outcomes (e.g., increased hospitalization, incarceration, homelessness, dropouts) were detected for the program converting to SE. This report is the only published study describing specific outcomes of converting from day treatment to SE. The study further suggests the capacity for the costs of SE programs to be offset by savings in reduced costs of day treatment (Clark and Bond, in press).

Meisel et al. (1993) examined 21 month outcomes for a California demonstration site known as the Village. The vocational program offered clients an extensive array of agency-run transitional work sites and individual placements. The emphasis on employment was demonstrated by the fact that 40% of all direct service staff time was devoted to client vocational goals. A total of 203 clients were randomly assigned to the Village or to a control group receiving usual mental health services. By the end of the follow-up period, 52% of Village clients and 7% of controls were employed. Moreover, 20 of the 52 Village clients working were employed competitively, and 44% of the total wages earned by the experimental group were from employers in the community.

Two interesting facets of this study should be noted. First, it was one of three demonstration projects begun at the same time. The three sites shared similar values about the importance of work, but only the Village had a major impact on employment outcomes. What appeared to differentiate the Village was a total commitment to employment goals, rather than making employment an "add-on". Second, the vocational focus at the successful site was obtained without any apparent negative impact on mental health outcomes (e.g., hospital rates, self-esteem, symptomatology, independent living, etc.), as compared to the control group or to the other two demonstration programs.

The aforementioned studies have emphasized the individual placement model of SE, which helps clients find jobs in the community. Providence Farm on Vancouver Island, British Columbia, offers a remarkable example of reversing the usual formula for helping mental health consumers to become fully contributing members of society (Hutton, 1994). Instead of finding jobs for consumers in usual places of work, Providence Farm has created new jobs on site with the community's involvement. Over the past 14 years, this 400-acre farm has been transformed into a caring community providing mental health consumers a wide array of employment options. Its enterprises include a greenhouse, a therapeutic horseback-riding facility, sponsorship and concessions for several outdoor concerts each year, and carpentry projects. Diametrically opposed to an isolated asylum, Providence Farm has attracted extensive involvement of townspeople in its commerce and activities.

The use of natural settings for assessment and training provides many advantages. Unlike institutional and transitional approaches, which have dismal competitive employment rates (Bond, 1992a), the SE approaches described in this section have reported solid employment findings. With regard to assessment, client behavior is more realistic and more predictive of future work behavior when observed under actual conditions. Moreover, if clients are observed in actual work settings, environmental factors can be observed at the same time. By eliminating extensive prevocational training, vocational programs can avoid the "institutional dependency" that some programs appear to foster (Bond, 1987). Finally, focusing training efforts on actual work settings reduces the difficulties in transfer of training and skill generalization found in artificial settings (Dilk, 1994).

5. Attention to Client Preferences

Historically, the role of mental health consumer preferences has been most extensively researched in the area of housing (Carling, 1993). It has been found, for example, that individuals who are satisfied with their living situation are more likely to remain stabley housed (Livingston et al., 1991). It also appears that clients who participate in choosing where they live are more likely to be satisfied with decisions about housing. An illustration comes from an evaluation of quality and costs of housing and resident satisfaction among formerly homeless persons with SMI served by outreach teams in two cities (Levstek and Bond, 1993). Client choice emerged as the single best predictor of satisfaction with housing, more powerful at predicting satisfaction than objective measures of housing quality.

Client surveys have been quite consistent in showing the types of living circumstances clients prefer. In most surveys, the most popular choice is living in one's own apartment, with support from professionals (Tanzman, 1993). In contrast, professionals are inclined to view many of their clients as needing structured group homes (Blanch et al., 1988). Unfortunately, many residential programs have been designed without any consideration of the client perspective.

Many of these observations can be readily transposed to the vocational domain, where prevocational programs predominate without regard to client preferences. In one study, Bond et al. (1993) surveyed client preferences among those who were about to be randomly assigned to prevocational training or to an SE program. Altogether, 73% expressed a preference for immediate entry into the SE program, 5% said they preferred to begin with prevocational preparation, and 22% said they had no preference. The slogan, "Prevoc is no voc", summarizes the attitude of many clients (Bell et al., 1993). However, unlike the housing domain, few large-scale surveys of client preferences for different vocational approaches have been reported.

In practice, most rehabilitation and mental health programs probably devote more attention to correcting skill deficits than to identifying factors influencing client satisfaction on the job. Yet both factors are undoubtedly important. According to a well-validated theory, job tenure is influenced by both job performance and job satisfaction (Dawis, 1976; Lofquist and Dawis, 1980). In one recent study examining job retention for 32 clients with SMI in SE positions, job satisfaction was more highly correlated with job retention ($r = .57$) than either employer ratings of job performance ($r = .41$) or staff ratings of the quality of the employment site ($r = .32$) (Bond, 1992b).

Attention to consumer preferences also suggests the creation of programs with career ladders. For example, there are programs are being developed to train and hire mental health consumers as direct service staff within mental health and other human service programs (Sherman and Porter, 1991). Warner and Polak (1993) have reported 70 graduates of a Denver consumer case manager aide training program, of whom 62% had completed a year or more of successful employment.

CONCLUSION

The five principles described in this chapter have been extensively discussed in the psychiatric rehabilitation literature. Research is needed to determine the best ways to operationalize these principles, the conditions under which these principles operate, and the identification of rehabilitation domains for which each principle applies. The studies reviewed here suggest ways in which these principles might be and have been applied to the vocational domain. Much work remains to be done to determine whether vocational programs based on these principles can be disseminated and sustained, and whether early promising results of program effectiveness can be replicated.

REFERENCES

Andrews H., Barker, J., Pittman, J., Mars, L., Struening, E. and LaRocca, N. (1992). "National trends in vocational rehabilitation: a comparison of individuals with physical disabilities and individuals with psychiatric disabilities" J. Rehabil., 51(1), 7 - 16.

Anthony, W.A. (1980). The Principles of Psychiatric Rehabilitation. University Park Press, Baltimore.

Axelrod, S. and Wetzler, S. (1989). "Factors associated with better compliance with psychiatric aftercare", Hosp. Comm. Psychiatry, 40, 397 - 401.

Bell, M.D., Milstein, R.M. and Lysaker, P.H. (1993). "Pay as an incentive in work participation by patients with severe mental illness", Hosp. Comm. Psychiatry, 44, 684 - 686.

Black, B.J. (1988). Work and Mental Illness: Transitions to Employment. Johns Hopkins Press, Baltimore.

Blanch, A.K., Carling, P.J. and Ridgway, P. (1988). "Normal housing with specialized supports: a psychiatric rehabilitation approach to living in the community", Rehabil. Psychol., 31, 47 - 55.

Bond, G.R. (1984). "An economic analysis of psychosocial rehabilitation", Hosp. Comm. Psychiatry, 35, 356 - 362.

Bond, G.P. (1987). "Supported work as a modification of the transitional employment model for clients with psychiatric disabilities", Psychosoc. Rehabil. J., 11(2), 55 - 73.

Bond, G.R. (1990). "Intensive case management", Hosp. Comm. Psychiatry, 41, 927.

Bond, G.R. (1991). "Variations in an assertive outreach model", New Dir. Ment. Health Serv., 51, 65 - 80.

Bond, G.R. (1992a). "Vocational rehabilitation". In Handbook of Psychiatric Rehabilitation, (ed R.P. Liberman.), pp. 244 - 275, Macmillan, New York.

Bond, G.R. (1992b). Job satisfaction and related measures for use with persons with serious mental illness. Unpublished manuscript (in press). Psychiatric rehabilitation. In Encyclopedia of disability and rehabilitation (eds A.E. Dell Orto and R.P.), Macmillan, New York.

Bond, G.R., Dietzen, L.L., McGrew, J.H. and Miller, L.D. (1993). Accelerating entry into supported employment for persons with severe psychiatric disabilities", (under review).

Bond, G.R. and Dincin, J. (1986). "Accelerating entry into transitional employment in a psychosocial rehabilitation agency", Rehabil.Psychol., 31, 143 - 155.

Bond, G.R. and Friedmeyer, M.H. (1987). "Predictive validity of situational assessment at a psychiatric rehabilitation center", Rehabil. Psychol., 22, 99 - 112.

Bond, G.R., McGrew, J.H. and Fekete, D. (in press). "Assertive outreach for frequent users of psychiatric hospitals: a meta-analysis", J. Ment. Health Admin.

Bond, G.R., Pensec, M., Dietzen, L., McCafferty, D., Giemza, R. and Sipple, H.W. (1991). "Intensive case management for frequent users of psychiatric hospitals in a large city: a comparison of team and individual caseloads", Psychosoc. Rehabil. J., 15(1), 90 - 98.

Boyer, S.L. (1991). A comparisonson of assertive community treatment case management and traditional case management on burnout and job satisfaction. Unpublished dissertation, Department of Psychology, Indiana University-Purdue University at Indianapolis.

Boyer, S.L. and Bond, G.R. (1992). "A comparison of assertive community treatment and traditional case management on burnout and job satisfaction", Outlook, 2(2), 13 - 15.

Carling, P.J. (1993). "Housing and supports for persons with mental illness: emerging approaches to research and practice", Comm. Psychiatry, 44, 439 - 449.

Chamberlin, I., Rogers, J.A. and Sneed, C.S. (1989). "Consumers, families, and community support systems", Psychosoc. Rehabil. J., 12(3), 93 - 106.

Clark, R.E. and Bond, G.R. (in press). "Costs and benefits of vocational programs for people with serious mental illness". In The Economics of Schizophrenia. (ed M. Moscarelli.), Wiley, Chichester.

Cook, J.A. and Rosenberg, H. (in press). "Predicting community employment among persons with psychiatric disability: a logistic regression analysis", J. Rehabil. Admin.

Dawis, R.V. (1976). "The Minnesota theory of work adjustment". In Handbook of Measurement and Evaluation (ed B. Bolton) pp. 227 - 248, University Park Press, Baltimore.

Dilk, M.N. (1994). Meta-analytic evaluation of skills training research for persons with severe mental illness. Unpublished dissertation, Department of Psychology, Indiana University-Purdue University at Indianapolis.

Dincin, J. (1975). "Psychiatric rehabilitation." Schizophr. Bull., 1, 131 - 148.

Drake, R.E., Becker D.R., Biesanz J.C., Torrey, W.C., McHugo, G.J. and Wyzik, P.F. (in press). "Partial hospitalization vs. supported employment: 1. vocational outcomes. Comm. Ment. Health J.

Flexer, R.W. and Solomon, P.L. (1993). Psychiatric Rehabilitation in Practice. Andover Medical Publishers, Boston.

General Accounting Office (GAO) (1993). Vocational Rehabilitation: Evidence for Federal Program's Effectiveness is Mixed. PEMD-93-19. US General Accounting Office, Washington, DC.

Gervey, R. and Bedell, J.R. (1993). Supported employment. In <u>Psychological Assessments and Treatment of Persons with Severe Mental Disorders,</u> (ed J.R. Bedell), pp. 139 - 163, Taylor & Francis, Washington, DC.

Hutton, J. (1994). <u>Providence Farm: From Dream to Reality</u>. Presentation at the annual meeting of the British Columbia Chapter of the International Association of Psychosocial Rehabilitation Services, Victoria, BC.

Jacobs, D.R. and Moxley, D.P. (1993). Anticipating managed mental health care: implications for psychosocial rehabilitation agencies. <u>Psychosoc. Rehabil. J.</u>, 17(2), 15 - 3 1.

Kirszner, M.L., McKay, C.D. and Tippett, M.L. (1991). "Homeless and mental health replication of the PACT model in Delaware", <u>Proceedings from the Second Annual Conference on State Mental Health Agency Services Research</u>, pp. 68 - 82, NASMHPD Research Institute, Alexandria, VA.

Levstek, D.A. and Bond, G.R. (1993). "Housing cost, quality, and satisfaction among formerly homeless persons with serious mental illness in two cities", <u>Innovations Res.</u>, 2(3), 1 - 8.

Livingston, J.A., Gordon, L., King, D.A. and Srebnik, D. (1991). <u>Implementing the Supported Housing Approach: A National Evaluation of NIMH Supported Housing Demonstration Projects</u>, Center for Comniunity Change Through Housing and Support, Burlington, VT.

Lofquist, L.H. and Dawis, R.V. (1980). "Vocational needs, work reinforcers, and job satisfaction". In <u>Rehabilitation: Client Assessment</u> (eds B. Bolton & D. W. Cook), pp. 234 - 243, University Park Press, Baltimore, MD.

Marrone, J. (1991). "Project on consumer responsiveness and speedy IWRP", unpublished manuscript.

Marshak, L.E., Bostick, D. and Turton, L.J. (1990). "Closure outcomes for clients with psychiatric disabilities served by the vocational rehabilitation system", <u>Rehabil. Counselling Bull.</u>, 31, 247 - 250.

Meisel, J., McGowen, M., Patotzka, D., Madison, K. and Chandler, D. (1993). <u>Evaluation of AB 3777 client and cost outcomes: July 1990 through March 1992</u>. Report prepared by Lewin-VHI, Inc. Available from California Dept. of Mental Health. 1600 9th St., Sacramento, CA 95814. Minnesota Mainstream (1993). Program brochure, Spring Lake Park, MN.

Revell, W.G., West, M. and Kregel, J. (1994). "Programmatic and administrative trends affecting the future of supported employment: a fifty state analysis", In <u>Supported</u>

Employment: Challenges for the 1990s, (eds P. Wehman and J. Kregel), Virginia Commonwealth University Rehabilitation Research and Training Center. Richmond, VA.

Russert, M.G. and Frey, J.L. (1991). "The PACT vocational model: a step into the future", Psychosoc. Rehabil. J., 14(4), 7 - 18.

Saveanu, T.I. and Roth, D. (1986). "Evaluation of the impact of a state-level interdepartmental agreement for the provision of rehabilitation services to severely mentally disabled persons in Ohio", unpublished report, Ohio Department of Mental Health, Columbus, OH.

Schultheis, A.M. and Bond, G.R. (1993). Situational assessment ratings of work behaviors: changes across time and between settings. Psychosoc. Rehabil. J., 13(2), 107 - 119.

Sherman, P.S. and Porter, R. (1991). "Mental health consumers as case management aides. Hosp. Comm. Psychiatry, 42, 494 - 498.

Spaniol, L. et al. (eds) (in press). An Introduction to Psychiatric Rehbabilitation. Center for Psychiatric Rehabilitation, Boston.

Stein, L.I. and Test, M.A. (1980). "An alternative to mental health treatment. 1: Conceptual model, treatment program, and clinical evaluation", Arch. Gen. Psychiatry, 37, 392 - 397.

Surles, R.C. and McGurrin, M.C. (1987). "Increased use of psychiatric emergency services by young chronic mentally ill patients", Hosp. Comm. Psychiatry, 38, 401 - 405.

Tanzman, B. (1993). "An overview of surveys of mental health consumers' preferences for housing and support services", Hosp. Comm. Psychiatry. 44, 450 - 455.

Tashjian, M.D., Hayward, B.J., Stoddard, S. and Kraus, L. (1989). Best Practice Study of Vocational Rehabilitation Services to Severely Mentally Ill Persons. Policy Study Associates, Washington, DC.

Test M.A. (1979). "Continuity of care in community treatment", New Dir. Ment. Health Serv., 2, 15 - 23.

Test, M.A. (1984). "Effective community treatment of the chronically mentally ill: what is necessary? J. Soc. Issues, 31(3), 7186.

Tumer, J.C. and TenHoor, W.J. (1978). "The NIMH community support program: pilot approach to a needed social reform". Schizophr. Bull., 4, 319 - 348.

Warner, R. and Polak, P. (1993). An Economic Development Approach to the Mentally Ill in the Community. Available from the Community Support Program, Center for Mental Health Services, SAMHSA, Rockville, MD.

Wehman, P. (1986). "Supported competitive employment for persons with severe disabilities", J. Appl. Rehabil. Counseling, 17, 24 - 29.

5

A NEURODEVELOPMENTAL PERSPECTIVE ON NORMAL BRAIN FUNCTIONING, PLASTICITY AND SCHIZOPHRENIA

Kathryn J. Kotrla and Daniel R. Weinberger

INTRODUCTION

Clinical neuroscience has utilized modern structural and functional neuroimaging technology to make tremendous inroads into our conceptualization of schizophrenia. There are now viable hypotheses about dysfunction in specific neuroanatomicalal networks in the disorder; this aids in the understanding of the neuroanatomicalal basis of clinical symptoms (Weinberger, 1993). Controversy remains, however, about whether schizophrenia is a single disorder or a final common expression of different neuroanatomicalal and molecular dysfunctions which result in a chronic psychotic state. Likewise, although there is an emerging consensus that at least some cases of schizophrenia are most likely due to a neurodevelopmental event (Weinberger, 1987; Weinberger, in press; Mednick et al., 1991; Bloom, 1993), hypotheses about the nature of the event remain unsatisfactory. Since clinical neuroscience has had difficulty with these issues, perhaps taking a basic neuroscience approach will suggest testable hypotheses.

Basic neuroscience has recently undergone an explosion of information. Tremendous advances have been made both in elucidating the neuroanatomicalal circuits that underlie human cognition and behavior, and the cellular properties that regulate the neurons within those circuits. Understanding

Schizophrenia: Exploring the Spectrum of Psychosis. Edited by R. Ancill. © 1994
John Wiley & Sons Ltd.

the principles that guide *normal* neurodevelopment and functioning should enable us to better understand schizophrenia. First, what are the normal neuroanatomical circuits that subserve attention, executive function, memory, language, and social interaction? Do these circuits correspond to the functional deficits seen in schizophrenia? Secondly, how are the circuits normally formed; how does a neuron know its proper cellular fate and find its proper synaptic connections? Do the principles of neuronal determination and differentiation suggest potential etiologic factors in schizophrenia? Third, what are the cellular and molecular mechanisms regulating neuronal functioning, and how do they impact the functioning and interaction between circuits? Are molecular mechanisms likely to be involved in the expression and treatment of schizophrenia?

What this chapter will highlight is that within the vast complexity of the brain, neurons are governed by guiding principles. One of these is that distributed neuronal networks subserve virtually all behavioral functions. Another is that the brain, although being constrained by genetics, is wonderfully plastic and dynamic, responding to the environment both in development and throughout postnatal life. Lastly, this environmental responsiveness is due to intracellular processes that integrate input, translate it into dynamic genomic changes, and result in structural synaptic modification. While this analysis may suggest possible areas that go awry to produce the symptoms of schizophrenia, the reality is that it will raise more questions than it will answer.

NORMAL CEREBRAL FUNCTIONING

Distributed Neural Networks

Initially, the idea of neuroanatomical circuits controlling behavior came from studies of abnormal states. The readily observed deficits in motor activity seen in Parkinson's disease and Huntington's disease spurred the elucidation of the neuronal pathways that control motor actions. Specific cortical areas project to segregated portions of the basal ganglia and thalamus, and project back on the frontal cortex, especially those areas providing input to the circuit. This creates a partially closed loop responsible for a particular aspect of behavior (Alexander et al., 1986). Alexander proposed five parallel but segregated, operationally analogous circuits which each act to carry out separate, distinct functions. These include the "motor" circuit involved in initiating, programming, and terminating complex motor behavior, the "oculomotor" circuit involved in the control of eye movements, and the dorsolateral prefrontal, cingulate, and orbito-frontal circuits involved presumably in more complex behavioral actions. Although the description of these circuits was based on "simple" motor behavior, the connections to the dorsolateral prefrontal, orbital frontal, and cingulate cortex suggest that these circuits are also involved in complex cognitive and emotional experience.

Indeed, it has been proposed (Mesulam,1990) that distributed neuronal networks exist for more complex functions such as language, attention, and memory, and almost every aspect of advanced cognition. The neuroanatomicalal basis for these circuits been suggested by patients, where a lesion in one or more nodes of the network leads to a specific dysfunction like aphasia, neglect, or amnesia. Direct support for distributed functional networks subserving a specific function in humans comes from functional neuroimaging studies of normal subjects. Positron emission tomography (PET) studies show specific network activations during language processing (Petersen et al., 1988; Demonet et al., 1992), musical processing (Sergent et al., 1992), attention (Corbetta et al., 1991; Pardo et al., 1990), memory (Raichle, 1993), and such "subjective" processes as will (Frith et al., 1991) and mood (George et al., 1993). Moreover, the neuroanatomical basis for these networks can be established in nonhuman primate studies. Tracer molecules for anterograde or retrograde transport can be injected intracortically. The efferent and afferent connections of the cortical network can then be mapped. Such work corroborates the neuroanatomicalal connections predicted from PET studies (Weinberger, 1993).

Memory provides a prime example of a distributed neuronal network subserving a seemingly ephemeral cognitive process, and raises several important principles about cerebral functioning. First, memory is not a single entity, but neuroanatomicalally appears to be of several distinct types and subtypes. For example, explicit, or declarative memory is the memory of which we are conscious, the memory of facts, events, and episodes. Loss of this type of memory leads to amnesia. Even some amnestic patients retain the ability to keep information in mind for several minutes, using "working" memory, a type of conscious but short-lived information rehearsal (Raichle, 1993). Moreover, while amnestic patients are unable to recognize a previously presented object (a type of declarative memory), they retain information about the abstract category to which the object belongs (Knowlton and Squire, 1993). Explicit memory can be contrasted to the unconscious process of implicit or nondeclarative memory which includes diverse abilities such as priming, operant or classical conditioning, motor learning, skill learning and habit formation (Squire and Zola-Morgan, 1991).

The neuroanatomicalal system underlying declarative memory involves specific areas of the mesial temporal lobe limbic system, diencephalon and the interconnected heteromodal association cortices in the frontal, parietal, and temporal lobes (Squire, 1986; Zola-Morgan and Squire, 1990; Mesulam, 1990). Data from PET studies suggest that working memory requires task-specific activation of the prefrontal cortex, in addition to interconnected cortical areas (Jonides et al., 1993; Petrides et al., 1993). Indeed, primate prefrontal cortex can be probed electrophysiologically during working memory tasks, demonstrating distinct cortical areas that process object identity as distinct from object location (Wilson et al 1993). Implicit memory is independent of mesial temporal lobe structures, but is thought to depend on cortico-striatal circuits involving sensory cortical areas, the caudate and putamen, and their indirect connections to the premotor cortical areas (Bachevalier, 1990).

That memory types can be neuroanatomicalally dissociated is graphically illustrated in patients. For example, after an ischemic episode, patient R.B. developed marked anterograde amnesia, but had little if any retrograde amnesia, and no other signs of cognitive impairment. The only lesion on neuropathological exam which could be associated with the memory defect was a circumscibed bilateral lesion of the CA1 hippocampal field (Squire, 1986). Thus although he lost the ability to form new explicit or declarative memories, he had normal working memory and implicit memory, and retained his long-term memories. Can an understanding of distributed neuronal networks help account for this apparent discrepancy?

Patients like R.B. and primate lesion studies provide strong evidence that the hippocampus and related perirhinal, entorhinal, and parahippocampal cortices play essential roles in the formation of long-term declarative memory (Squire and Zola-Morgan, 1991). It is thought that modality-specific neocortical areas underlie perception and short-term memory, accounting for amnestic patients retaining this ability. The role of the hippocampus and related cortices is to "bind" together the neocortically distributed pieces of information in a multi-modal memory into a pattern of neural activity that is recognized as the memory of an event. Without the hippocampus and related cortex, though, the activity patterns fade, and the isolated memory trace of one aspect of experience is lost. Once a memory is consolidated in the neocortex, it becomes independent of the mesial temporal lobe (Squire and Zola-Morgan, 1991), allowing R.B. to retain long-term established memories.

It has been hypothesized that consolidation involves synaptic remodeling whereby synapses that are active at the same time, as occurs in the memory of an event, become strengthened. As such, the memory eventually becomes independent of mesial temporal lobe structures as synaptic connections are remodeled in the neocortex (Squire and Zola-Morgan, 1991). Thus one principle of nervous system functioning that is exemplified by the process of learning new information is the plasticity the system has to respond to change. Coordinated patterns of activity in distributed groups of neurons may cause strengthened synaptic connectivity.

Another principle that memory illustrates is that different neural systems may come "on-line" at different developmental times. For example, it has been suggested that in monkeys or human infants, the explicit, or declarative memory system does not mature until after the neuroanatomicalally distinct corticostriatal or implicit system (Overman et al., 1992). Additionally, with the onset of adolescence, another network maturation occurs which impacts on memory function.

This latter occurrence was first noted in primates with frontal lobe lesions asked to perform a delayed response task, a task which requires "working" memory, to keep information on-line and available for short-term use. Monkeys who have their dorsolateral prefrontal cortex ablated in infancy perform normally as juveniles, but their performance deteriorates with the onset of puberty (Goldman, 1971). This suggests that the delayed response task is performed by a circuit unaffected by the prefrontal lesion during juvenile life. With the maturation that occurs around adolescence, the task becomes subserved by a neuronal network that is dependent on the normal functioning of the prefrontal cortex.

Memory, however, is simply an example. The idea is that all human cognition and experience can be reduced to the functions of discrete areas of cortex, brought on line as a "network" to perform specific tasks. With multiple distributed neuronal networks, how is one "choosen" to activate in response to an environmental challenge? What cerebral area monitors the results of network activation, and "decides" to shift to a different network? Where might such "executive" functioning reside? Interestingly, one cerebral area that many networks appear to have in common is the frontal lobe. Indeed, the frontal lobe is uniquely connected to the heteromodal association cortical areas, basal ganglia, limbic system, hypothalamus, and midbrain nuclei (Weinberger, 1993). As such its "executive" role may be one of selectively activating or inhibiting functional neuronal networks in a given situation. However, even the frontal lobe seems to be subject to a developmental time course, in which its role as "executive" may not fully emerge until after puberty. Also, it is expected that it will be subject to the same synaptic modifications by experience as the rest of the cortex.

Normal Developmental Plasticity

Thus, an organizing principle of neural functioning appears to be that discrete, functionally separate but probably overlapping neuroanatomicalal circuits are involved in the initiation and regulation of discrete aspects of experience and behavior, and that they may come into play at specific times in development. This begs the question, however, of how the connections between these networks are formed in the first place, and how the connections between them are remodeled in response to experience. This section provides a very brief review of normal prenatal development. For a more comprehensive review, see Weinberger, (1994).

The formation of the CNS depends on a number of complex processes loosely categorized as neurogenesis, neuronal migration, and neuronal differentiation. The decisions a neuron makes about cell identity and target selection depend on both genetic and epigenetic effects; neurons use cell surface molecules, extracellular matrix molecules, and trophic factors to guide the decision-making process. In short, an amazingly intricate minuet must take place between a neuron and its environment for it to assume its correct fate, find its proper synaptic targets, make its proper neurotransmitter, and express its proper complement of receptors. With such complexity, a misstep could have ramifications throughout the nervous system, and theoretically have tremendous impact on the formation and functioning of multiple neuronal networks.

The decision to become neural tissue appears to involve local inductive interactions, whereby ectoderm becomes committed to become "neural"; and position within the sheet of ectoderm is determined (Jessell and Kandel, 1993). From the neural ectoderm arise neuroblasts which "iive" in the ventricular germinal zone, and divide to produce a lineage of daughter cells. Neuroblasts are the precursor cells whose daughter cells migrate into the cortex to form cortical neurons. Aberrations in the formation of neural ectoderm or in the formation of neuroblasts are likely to result in gross abnormalities such as anencephaly or a lissencephalic brain (Weinberger, 1994).

Normally, the six cortical layers are generated in an orderly sequence, with first-born neurons residing in the deeper cortical layers, and later-born neurons residing in more superficial layers (Rakic, 1988). However, even the decision of the laminar identity of a daughter cell is not determined solely on a genetic basis. It is specified just before the time of final cell division in the ventricular germinal zone, and is based on environmental cues that must change over developmental time (McConnell and Kaznowski, 1991).

Once a neuron is born, having already received its proper laminar address, it must migrate to its proper cortical layer. Neurons do this by attaching to a transient radial glial fiber (Rakic, 1990). This process appears to depend on neuronal cell surface interactions for the neuronal decision to differentiate and migrate (Gao et al., 1992), on cell surface adhesion molecules between the neuron and glial fibers, and on NMDA receptors (Komuro and Rakic, 1993). Multiple environmental insults could interfere with the assignment of laminar address or migration, and thus with the final laminar position a neuron assumes (Weinberger, 1994).

From there comes the intricate problem of establishing connectivity. Neurons within a cortical area must become properly wired. For example, in the visual cortex, axons of layer 3 neurons bypass layer 4 to make specific connections with layer 5. The laminar address that cells obtain at their birth appears to convey the information needed for this type of connectivity. Even if layer 5 neurons are transplanted to foreign locations, they still send their axons to appropriate targets (Goodman and Shatz, 1993).

Another remarkable achievement is the wiring between different areas of cortex. How does a neuron extend its axon through the embryonic environment to find its correct target? The leading edge of the axon, the growth cone, has an array of molecules on its surface. It interacts with molecules on other cells, axons, and the extracellular matrix in the embryonic environment. The molecules are differentially adhesive or repellent, causing the growth cone to grow where it is "stickiest" and to avoid "repulsive" sites. As such, to choose among the number of possible pathways in the embryonic environment, the growth cone samples among the choices by means of its filopodia, and grows where it sticks. In addition to adhesion molecules, there appear to be diffusible gradients towards which some growth cones grow (Goodman and Shatz, 1993). The molecules involved in pathway selection are dynamic, changing on the surface of the axon, or even on specific parts of the axon over developmental time.

What happens when the developmental plan goes awry, and neurons lack some of these cell adhesive molecules? In the fruitfly, when one cell surface adhesion molecule is deleted by genetic methods, the fly develops a particular set of behavioral abnormalities; it can walk, jump, but not fly. It also has abnormalities of visual orientation and drinking behavior. This suggests that the molecule is involved in controlling the development of specific neural circuits. While fruitflies seemed impossibly removed from humans, the gene for this cell adhesion molecule does have a human homologue (Kolodkin et al., 1993). It has been suggested that the genetic defect in Kallman's syndrome, characterized by hypogonadism and anosmia, is the lack of a substrate adhesion molecule (Rugarli and Ballabio, 1993). This implies that a specific molecule, absent or aberrant even during a brief but critical time in development, could result in the dysfunction of a particular neuronal network and the behavior it subserves.

On a more dramatic scale, a whole area of cortex can have its fate altered by changing its afferent input. This is clearly seen in monkey experiments when geniculocalcarine afferents are abolished; not only does the size of area 17 diminish, but the cytoarchitecture of area 18 is altered as well (Rakic et al., 1991). In fact, in isolated kitten visual cortex deprived of its normal input, the laminar pattern of neurotransmitter receptor fails to undergo its normal pattern of redistribution (Shaw et al., 1988). Indeed, when auditory cortex in ferrets is deprived of its normal input, and is given aberrant visual input, it behaves like visual cortex (Pallas, 1990)!

A neuron's efferent connections also influence neuronal phenotype. Neuronal postsynaptic targets produce "differentiation" factors, which alter gene expression in the presynaptic neuron and influence the choice of neurotransmitter and neuropeptides synthesized. Even in postembryonic, functional neurons, normal fluctuations in neuronal activity or hormone levels, or an insult to the system can alter transmitter/neuropeptide expression (Patterson and Nawa, 1993).

It appears that the cortex, during and after the formation of connections, retains tremendous plasticity to respond to its environment. This may work to an evolutionary advantage. For example, when insults occur during critical windows early in development, the brain can often compensate, presumably because of its innate plasticity. Or, if a novel area of frontal lobe appears because of changes in neuroblast numbers, other brain areas may have little difficulty branching out and producing interesting and hopefully advantageous new connections. However, the price that is paid may be abnormalities in the functioning of neuronal circuits if the developmental plan goes awry.

Molecular Mechanisms of Plasticity

Even when neurons have the proper fate, reach the proper target, and make the appropriate connections, the nervous system retains tremendous plasticity. Synaptic plasticity appears to be a property of adult as well as developing cortex. If an adult monkey attends to a tactile stimulus to its finger, and is rewarded for learning frequency discrimination of the stimulus, the cortical spatiotemporal representations from that digit increase. There is no cortical change if the monkey experiences the same stimulus without attending to it (Merzenich and

Sameshima, 1993). In short, the cortex "learns" from experience. And, in fact, it is in learning and memory that the molecular mechanisms for synaptic plasticity and remodeling have been best explored.

Experientially, it is clear that we learn. We form new conscious memories and make new unconscious associations all the time. Just as behavior can be thought of in terms of neuronal networks which subserve specific functions, learning and memory can be reduced to the strengthening of existing synapses or the formation of new synapses within and between networks. Short-term memory appears to involve the strengthening of existing synapses through the covalent modification of existing proteins by the activation of second messenger systems. Long-term memory seems to involve neuronal gene expression and new protein synthesis, which results in the growth of new synaptic connections (Jessell and Kandel, 1993).

The most elegant work elucidating the molecular mechanisms of synaptic plasticity associated with learning has been in the sea slug, Aplysia. Because the slug has a relatively simple nervous system, the neurons involved in a behavior can be identified and analyzed at a molecular level. Aplysias exhibit classical conditioning, a type of implicit memory, and their learning can be observed behaviorally. One behavior is retracting their gill. There is a monosynaptic connection between a sensory neuron which responds when the siphon is touched, and a motor neuron which retracts the gill. Normally, repeated siphon touches lead to no response; in other words, it is a neutral stimulus and can be used as a conditioned stimulus (CS). It can be paired to a noxious, unconditioned stimulus (US) like a tail shock, which invariably leads to gill retraction (the unconditioned response). Learning involves strengthening the synapse between the siphon sensory neuron and the gill motor neuron so that a siphon touch causes the gill to retract. A single pairing of CS followed within one second by the US leads to short-term sensitization that lasts from minutes to hours; repeated trials can lead to long-term memory that lasts several weeks (Kandel, 1989).

How does the tail shock modulate the monosynaptic sensory neuron - motor neuron connection to make short and long-term memory at this synapse? A single tail shock results in short-term sensitization at the synapse. The tail shock causes facilitory neurons to release serotonin (5-HT) onto the sensory neuron, the presynaptic component of the "learning" synapse. Serotonin acts through a G protein to activate adenylate cyclase, resulting in increased cyclic adenosine monophosphate (cAMP) in the sensory neuron. cAMP activates a cAMP-dependent protein kinase, which adds a phosphate group onto a number of preexisting proteins. One of the targets of the kinase is a K^+ channel;

phosphorylation of the channel reduces the K^+ current which normally repolarizes the neuron. Since the sensory neuron stays depolarized longer, more C^{2+} flows into the synaptic terminal, resulting in enhanced transmitter release from the sensory neuron onto the motor neuron. Serotonin also activates another receptor-linked enzyme in the presynaptic sensory neuron, protein kinase C, which acts to enhance mobilization of transmitter, and maintain a higher level of transmitter release (Kandel, 1989). With more excitatory transmitter released onto the postsynaptic motor neuron, it consistently fires an action potential, retracting the gill. Thus without transcription or protein synthesis, a single application of serotonin results in short-term synaptic strengthening, observable as a change in behavior.

With repeated close temporal pairings of the CS and US, or repeated applications of 5-HT, long-term facilitation of the synapse occurs. This is associated with a growth of new synaptic connections between the sensory and motor neuron, and requires mRNA and protein synthesis (Bailey et al., 1992). Repeated applications of 5-HT activate the same cAMP-dependent protein kinase as in short-term facilitation. However, with repeated applications, the protein kinase is translocated to the nucleus of the presynaptic sensory neuron where it phosphorylates transcriptional activators to modulate the expression of specific genes (Kaang et al., 1993). Specifically, 5-HT produces an increase in ten proteins, and a decrease in five. Interestingly, one of the proteins which decreases is a cell surface adhesion molecule; a decrease in its presynaptic concentration may allow the growth of new synaptic contacts needed for long term learning (Mayford et al., 1992).

Learning can be seen not only in the beautifully simplistic sea slug. As discussed above, declarative long-term memory is dependent on the hippocampal formation and related cortices. One would predict that a similar mechanism for synaptic strengthening and remodeling exists in the hippocampus and neocortical areas for learning to occur. And indeed, related mechanisms can be invoked in the vertebrate central nervous system in the hippocampus and neocortex (Bear and Kirkwood, 1993).

In the hippocampus, a prolonged excitatory afferent stimulus results in long-term potentiation (LTP), where coincident activity in the pre- and postsynaptic neuron causes their synapses to strengthen. While the precise molecular mechanisms are being actively explored, some general principles have emerged. Coincident activity allows the influx of Ca^{2+} and the activation of several protein kinases. A retrograde messenger (possibly nitric oxide) from the postsynaptic cell results in enhanced neurotransmission from the presynaptic cell. For "long-term" LTP, however, protein synthesis is required (Jessell and Kandel, 1993), suggesting that a similar cascade leading to synaptic growth and remodeling is involved. Just as 5-HT triggered long term synaptic changes in Aplysia, dopamine appears to be a good candidate for neurotransmitter/neuromodulator in the hippocampus, because late LTP can be blocked by D_1 antagonists (Frey et al., 1993).

Protein kinases are essential for synaptic remodeling in Aplysia. What role do kinases play in LTP? Transgenic mice deficient in alpha-calcium-calmodulin (CaM) kinase II are impaired in their ability to produce LTP. Remarkably, these mice appear to function normally in a restricted lab environment, and evidence no gross abnormality of the hippocampus or neocortex (Silva et al., 1992a). However, they have a fascinating subset of deficits on testing, and appear much like rodents with hippocampal lesions. CaM kinase II deficient mice have impaired spatial learning even though they retain the ability to learn environmental associations. They have increased exploratory behavior and activity when placed in an open field. And they seem to have an abnormally enhanced acoustic startle response (Silva et al., 1992b). So the lack of a particular enzyme results in a specific behavioral deficit, linked to the neuroanatomical localization of the enzyme.

What genes may be involved in the cellular cascade that underlies learning? One day old chicks "learn" in a single trial to avoid a bitter tasting bead. In the areas of the brain shown to "learn", immediate early genes, c-fos and c-jun are induced with training. Immediate early genes encode transcription factors which can alter the expression of other gene products. With chick training, and c-fos and *c-jun* induction, there is enhanced synthesis of a variety of proteins, and increased fucosylation of membrane glycoproteins, molecules thought to act as cell adhesion signals; blocking fucosylation produces amnesia for the task (Rose, 1991). Structurally, 24 hours after training there is a 60% increase in the density of dendritic spines, increases in synaptic number, and a 60% increase in the numbers of synaptic vesicles per synapse (Rose, 1991). The net result is synaptic remodeling, with active synapses showing increased numbers of boutons.

So, the molecular basis of plasticity appears to follow set principles. Coincident activity releases neurotransmitters which trigger a cellular cascade involving second messenger systems, protein phosphorylation, gene induction, and ultimately synaptic growth and remodeling. The evidence again emphasizes the remarkable plasticity of the nervous system. Even when networks are formed, the precise connections within them remain responsive to environmental input. As such, perhaps it is time to think of neurotransmitters (5-HT and dopamine) not as simple monosynaptic signals, but rather as neuromodulators capable of inducing a cascade of cellular events resulting in changes in neuronal responsivity and in network remodeling. The guiding principle, both in final synaptic selections in development and in adult cortical plasticity is succinctly stated in the adage "neurons that fire together wire together" (Goodman and Shatz, 1993).

SCHIZOPHRENIA

The question that lurks beneath the surface of the preceding discussion is whether a cascade of neurodevelopmental events results in the final outcome we see as schizophrenia. How might we account for this illness in neurodevelopmental terms? How could we understand the difference in presentation between a "paranoid" and a "catatonic" schizophrenic? How do we account for medication-responsive delusions and hallucinations coexisting with the unresponsive cognitive decline that accompanies the onset of the disorder? How do we explain the difference in patients who were well until adolescence and in patients who always had evidence of subtle abnormalities of cerebral functioning? Clinically, lumping everyone into the category "schizophrenia", may not be particularly helpful in understanding the etiology of the disorder, or in devising particularly effective treatments.

This part of the chapter attempts to build upon the principles outlined in normal cerebral development and functioning. We will explore the relevance of neuronal networks to schizophrenia. We will briefly review work that suggests loci for developmental abnormalities and discuss this in the framework of developmental neurobiology. Lastly, we will discuss what little is known about the molecular underpinnings of the disease we seek to understand. So little is known at the basic level about schizophrenia that much of the discussion will be highly speculative.

Syndrome or Discrete Network Dysfunction?

Schizophrenia can be thought of as a tragic alteration in normal cerebral functioning. If normal functioning can be reduced to specific, intersecting behavioral components such as language, memory, executive function, attention, attachment, motivation, each with a neuroanatomical substrate, will this impact on our understanding of schizophrenia, and can it provide information about the neuroanatomicalal substrate of the disease?

While many investigators have begun to conceptualize specific neuronal networks involved in schizophrenia, interesting work is being done in attributing specific neural dysfunctions to specific symptom clusters. For example, in chronic patients, individual symptoms tend to cluster along three dimensions. These have been termed "psychomotor poverty" (alogia, decreased movement, affective flattening), "disorganization" (distractibility, inappropriate affect, disorders of thought form), and "reality distortion" (hallucinations and delusions) (Liddle and Barnes, 1990). There is some evidence that each syndrome is associated with impairment in specific neuropsychological tests (Liddle and Morris, 1991), and with distinct patterns of cerebral blood flow during resting state PET scans (Liddle et al., 1992). This suggests that clinical aspects of the disorder have specific neuroanatomicalal references. Interestingly, psychomotor poverty and disorganization were correlated with deficits in cerebral blood flow to different areas of the frontal lobes (Liddle et al., 1992).

Neuropsychological tests are helpful in delineating core cognitive deficits of the syndrome, and provide a tool to generate hypotheses about dysfunctional neuronal circuits. Although patients with schizophrenia demonstrate a generalized deficit in cognitive testing, they appear to have specific cognitive weaknesses in attention, memory, and executive functions (Gold and Harvey, 1993). In addition, the cognitive deficits seem to be dissociable from the symptoms of psychosis per se, and indeed appear to be essential features of the disorder. For example, although patients treated with clozapine show significant improvement in psychotic symptoms, their cognitive function for the most part remains unchanged (Goldberg et al., 1993). Can neuropsychological findings suggest neuroanatomicalal dysfunctions?

Memory again provides a solid reference point. As discussed earlier, memory resides in a distributed neuronal network, with relatively well delineated neuroanatomical loci. Explicit memory depends on a network linking mesial temporal lobe structures to heteromodal association cortices in the frontal and parietal lobes. Implicit memory is independent of the mesial temporal lobe and is likely to reside in cortico-striatal circuits. If patients with schizophrenia differ in their performance on explicit and implicit memory tasks, then greater dysfunction in a specific neuronal network is suggested. In fact, patients with schizophrenia, while performing exceptionally poorly on explicit memory tasks, appear to perform near normal on implicit memory tasks (Goldberg et al., 1993; Schwartz et al., 1993). Thus dysfunction in mesial temporal lobe and related prefrontal cortex is preferentially implicated.

However, the pattern of deficits in not analogous to that found in adult clinical samples with localized lesions of these cortical regions (Weinberger and Lipska, submitted). In an elegant neuropsychological study comparing patients with schizophrenia to patients with temporal lobe epilepsy (TLE), the relative roles of temporal and frontal dysfunction were dissected (Gold et al., in press). The TLE patients had documented temporal lobe lesions with childhood-onset epilepsy; as such, they allow one to ask the cognitive consequences of a presumably single locus lesion. While patients with schizophrenia had certain deficits in common with the patients with TLE, they also demonstrated a greater degree of attentional dyscontrol, suggesting frontal lobe in addition to temporal lobe dysfunction. The neuropsychological deficits suggest a pattern that involves dysfunction in both frontal and temporal regions (Randolph et al., in press).

As discussed earlier, the neuroanatomical pathways connecting the prefrontal cortex with the mesial temporal are well delineated (Weinberger, 1993). Neuropsychological tests suggest that schizophrenic patients have deficits in the tasks that involve these cortices. And indeed, in neuroimaging studies, there is evidence that the network that connects these cortices becomes dysfunctional during a task with working memory components.

The task in question is the Wisconsin Card Sorting Task (WCST). In this, subjects are asked to match a card to one of four other cards. On each card is one to four symbols: circles, triangles, crosses, or stars. The symbols can be in one of four different colors. Thus to match the card, the subject must decide whether to match on color, number, or shape of symbol. After ten correct responses, the matching "rule" changes. This task requires subjects to generate internally driven responses, as the external environment does not contain sufficient information to guide a response. Additionally, subjects must keep information "on-line", and keep continually updating information. When normals perform the task during PET imaging, a distributed pattern of activation is seen in areas of the prefrontal, parietal, and temporal cortices (Berman et al., 1991; Berman et al., submitted).

In rCBF studies of monozygotic twins discordant for schizophrenia, patients with schizophrenia can be compared to an ideal control for each affected individual. Monozygotic twins share the same genes and the same environment; differences in cerebral functioning can be attributed to the disease, per se. The twin with schizophrenia invariably shows decreased frontal blood flow, even if the performance scores for the WCST do not differ. This hypofrontality is not seen during simple tasks that do not require frontal - temporal connectivity (Berman et al., 1992). Moreover, in almost every twin pair, while the frontal cortex is hypoperfused, the mesial temporal lobe is invariably hyperfunctional (Weinberger et al., 1993). Thus the network that underlies the performance of the WCST appears to be fundamentally abnormal in schizophrenia.

If a fundamental neuronal network has abnormal functioning, how can children who are destined to become schizophrenic appear normal during childhood? The normal developmental time course of neuronal circuits at least provides a speculative explanation for this phenomenon (Weinberger, 1987). As seen in primate studies, the frontal component of a working memory network does not seem to be critical until adolescence. After adolescence, though, the absence of this area results in impaired performance on working memory tasks (Goldman, 1971). Thus the normal developmental time course of this network may be coincident with the onset of schizophrenia in late adolescence (Weinberger, 1987). Neuropsychological evidence is consistent with this hypothesis. Schizophrenics show relative strength in performing tasks which depend on premorbid abilities; their performance after illness onset suggests a deterioration in cognitive functioning (Gold et al., in press).

Thus dysfunction in at least one crucial neuronal network has been linked to schizophrenia. Clinically, schizophrenia is a complex disorder with a spectrum of presentations. Both the frontal and temporal lobes have extensive cerebral connections and likely function in multiple networks. Therefore, dysfunction in these areas may lead to dysfunction in multiple aspects of human behavior. For example, primate work is probing the relationship between mesial temporal lobe dysfunctions and social relatedness (Bachevalier, submitted), and "will" and "motivation" have been linked to fronto-striato-thalamic networks (Laplane et al., 1989). Perhaps further exploration of other neuronal networks will offer insights into the heterogeneity of clinical symptoms in schizophrenia and suggest more effective treatments.

Development Gone Awry?

Both neuropsychological and neuroimaging results suggest combined dysfunction of the frontal and mesial temporal lobe. What does this suggest about the etiology of the disorder? Does it arise from multiple areas of cortical abnormalities? Or can dysfunction in one cortical or subcortical structure lead to abnormalities in a network of interconnected cortical areas? The principles of developmental neurobiology do not provide answers but they do suggest possibilities which can be explored experimentally. This allows questions to be asked at two levels. First, is there evidence for abnormalities in the processes of brain development in schizophrenia? How does our understanding of developmental neurobiology suggest possibilities for the formation and ramifications of these abnormalities? Secondly, can we manipulate the system experimentally to further understand possibilities for the etiologic process?

In patients with schizophrenia, in vivo imaging studies have found focal morphometric changes in the mesial temporal and prefrontal cortex, and indeed may implicate even more widespread cortical abnormalities (Weinberger and Lipska, submitted). Postmortem morphometric studies have, for the most part, confirmed the in vivo results. Moreover, postmortem studies allow one to address specific developmental questions of laminar and migratory abnormalities. Jakob and Beckman (1986) described cytoArch.itectural disorganization of the entorhinal region, with too few neurons in the superficial layers and too many neurons in deeper layers. Such findings have been replicated (Arnold et al., 1991), and extended to cingulate (Benes et al., 1991), prefrontal, lateral temporal, and limbic cortices (Akbarian et al., 1993a, 1993b). It should be stressed that gliosis is not found in most postmortem studies, further supporting the hypothesis that schizophrenia arises from a neurodevelopmental event. These postmortem results add to the view that the areas of cortex implicated as dysfunctional by neuropsychologic and PET studies reflect specific morphologic anomalies.

What possible mechanisms could result in these abnormalities, and what are the potential consequences? As discussed previously, laminar identity depends on environmental input shortly before the neuron is born (McConnell and Kaznowski, 1991). For a correctly determined neuron to achieve its destined position appears to depend on cell surface differentiation factors to initiate migration (Gao et al., 1992), and glialneuronal cell surface interactions to migrate to the proper laminar position (Rakic, 1990). Abnormalities at any one of these steps, even for discrete times in development, could result in anomalous laminar patterns.

Abnormalities in laminar location could result in interesting "downstream" effects, as well. It appears from transplantation studies and culture experiments that once a neuron "knows" its laminar identity, it will connect with the correct cortical layer or subcortical structure (Goodman and Shatz, 1993). However, it is not clear that the modality of information will be correct. For example, even when isolated in culture, cortex and thalamus will connect to the proper layers. But it is possible in this extremely artificial situation that the information is not properly segregated by modality (Yamamoto et al., 1992). As studies have shown, different afferent input can change the nature of the cortex, from its information processing capacities (Pallas, 1990) to its receptor expression (Shaw et al., 1988). Given that the networks implicated as dysfunctional in schizophrenia are those that receive processed information from multiple modalities, this raises the possibility of very subtle abnormalities of connection resulting from anomalous cortical lamination.

Thus an abnormality of even one area of cortex could lead to resulting abnormalities of connections and hence functioning in interconnected cortices. This can be visualized even in human adults where a discrete structural lesion will result in dysfunction in its distributed network of connected cortex (Laplane et al., 1989). How might a discretely localized lesion early in development be manifest later in life?

Rats provide an intriguing model because their first postnatal week of cortical development corresponds roughly to the second trimester of gestation for a primate (Weinberger and Lipska, submitted). Lesions made neonatally in the rat are in effect lesions made during a critical period of cortical development, and their effects on connected cortical areas can be explored. Lesions can be produced in the ventral hippocampal region of neonatal rats with ibotenic acid, a glutamate receptor agonist which acts as an excitotoxin. Stereotactic injection of ibotenic acid destroys intrinsic and projection neurons but spares most presynaptic afferents, synapses, and fibers passing through the region (Lipska et al., 1993; Lipska and Weinberger, 1993), thus producing limited, discrete damage. Because of this, one can ask what effect a discrete lesion has on other areas of cortex.

Prior to puberty, lesioned rats, when compared to sham operated controls, show few if any behavioral abnormalities on testing. The tests include monitoring exploratory behavior in a novel environment, and monitoring activity and stereotypies to dopaminergic pharmacologic challenges. After puberty (three weeks later), if left undisturbed, the rats do not show obvious behavioral or neurochemical abnormalities (Weinberger and Lipska, submitted). However, during testing the hippocampal lesioned rats show exaggerated exploratory behavior in response to stress and to amphetamine, presumably because of hyperresponsiveness of their limbic dopamine systems (Lipska et al., 1993). Likewise, stereotypic motor behaviors are induced after administration of apomorphine (Lipska and Weinberger, 1993), and the rats show a deficit in prepulse inhibition of startle analogous to that seen in patients with schizophrenia (Lipska et al., in press). Not surprisingly, the exaggerated dopamine-related behaviors of these lesioned rats are ameliorated by antipsychotic drugs, and are uniquely responsive to the action of clozapine (Lipska and Weinberger, in press,a). Castration prior to puberty does not prevent the emergence of these behaviors (Lipska and Weinberger, in press,b), suggesting that it is not hormones per se that induce the behavior, but the normal postnatal development of cerebral function.

One striking aspect of this work is that the deficits are not immediately apparent; they present themselves only after puberty. This again suggests that the behaviors are subserved by a limbic - frontal network which comes "on-line" after puberty.

Another important and surprising result is the nature of the behavioral abnormalities. The behavioral changes are different in several ways from those following an identical hippocampal lesion produced in adult animals, and appear more like a combination of adult lesions of limbic and prefrontal cortices (Weinberger and Lipska, submitted). This implies that a discrete lesion during critical periods of cortical development can influence other cortical areas; in this case, a discrete ventral hippocampal lesion is sufficient to induce behaviors consistent with adult frontal lesions. While this does not directly address the etiology of schizophrenia, it underscores the principle that even a localized developmental event can have widespread cerebral consequences postnatally.

Molecular Mechanisms in Schizophrenia?

Molecular biology has yet to provide great insights into schizophrenia. The seArch. for the schizophrenia gene has to date been disappointing. However, the molecular basis of neuronal plasticity and responsiveness are principles that apply to all neuronal functioning, be it normal or abnormal. In the rat work discussed above, ventral hippocampal lesions induced perinatally have been shown to induce abnormalities of behavior during puberty that combine aspects of frontal and limbic dysfunction. The resulting behavioral abnormalities appear to be linked pharmacologically to hyperfunctioning of the dopamine system, as they are ameliorated by antipsychotics. Could the molecular analysis of learning, for example, add to our understanding of the workings of the rat limbic- frontal system?

As seen clearly in development and in learning and memory, neurotransmitters are not only a single discrete signal; they act on several transducing proteins (e.g., G proteins) to initiate a cellular cascade impacting on gene expression and on long-term cellular functioning. As noted above, dopamine has been implicated as the initiator in late LTP, which involves protein synthesis and synaptic remodeling (Frey et al., 1993).

This raises the speculative possibility that the "dopaminergic" dysfunction of schizophrenia may be due to an as yet unknown abnormality of cellular functioning. This could arise in dopamine receptors, G proteins, any of the multiple second messenger systems, or in the genes induced by this cascade. Is there evidence to support this possibility?

With advances in molecular technology, it is possible to map changes in cerebral gene expression in response to environmental manipulations. For example, the immediate early genes which have been implicated in learning, c-fos and c-jun, appear to be responsive to neuronal activation; their induction and the expression of their proteins, Fos and Jun, can be routinely mapped. Are these genes and their products affected by dopaminergic manipulations?

In rats, the acute administration of clinical doses of typical (haloperidol) or atypical antipsychotic agents (clozapine, raclopride, remoxipride) induce Fos in the nucleus accumbens. Moreover, an effect that is common to all such drugs is seen only within a specific region of the nucleus accumbens, the shell region. No other brain region has yet been shown to be a site of Fos induction common to all these drugs at clinical doses. This strongly suggests that despite the variable pharmacological and clinical effects of these agents, their shared antipsychotic action relates to a change in gene expression in the nucleus accumbens (Weinberger and Lipska, submitted).

Additionally, antagonists of dopamine type 2 receptors (haloperidol, remoxipride, raclopride, and YM-09151), all of which can produce extrapyramidal side effects, induce Fos in the dorsal striatum. So does metoclopramide, known clinically to produce extrapyramidal effects but lacking antipsychotic efficacy. Clozapine, which at clinical doses does not cause extrapyramidal side effects, does not induce Fos in this region. This suggests that extrapyramidal and antipsychotic effects can be dissociated at the regional molecular level (Weinberger and Lipska, submitted). It also provides tantalizing information about the neuroanatomical circuits involved in psychosis versus movement disorders. Indeed, clozapine also appears to be unique in inducing Fos in medial portions of the prefrontal cortex; at clinically equivalent doses, it is the only antipsychotic drug to date found to have this effect (Weinberger and Lipska, submitted).

Such molecular analyses suggest that it may be fruitful to look for antipsychotic effects (and the mechanism of psychosis) not at the level of receptors or receptor subtypes, but at the level of regulation of second messenger systems and gene expression. The expression of immediate early genes is likely to provide more information about the sum of a neuron's experience representing the integration of multiple second messenger processes corresponding to multiple extracellular stimuli. It would follow then that antipsychotic agents which have novel clinical impact would evidence novel patterns of gene expression in the brain. It would also follow that the location of this expression would provide information about the network(s) involved in psychosis.

Indeed, the prefrontal clozapine-induced Fos data again implicates the limbic-frontal network emphasized throughout this chapter. But how to integrate into our speculation the Fos expression in the nucleus accumbens? Interestingly, the nucleus accumbens is a convergence site for inputs from both prefrontal and limbic cortices. The frontal and hippocampal formation both project preferentially to the shell region of the nucleus accumbens, the region that shows Fos induction in response to antipsychotic agents. This raises the possibility that antidopaminergic drugs act as antipsychotics because their site of action in the nucleus accumbens allows them to initiate a series of intracellular molecular events that modulate the dysfunctional prefrontal- limbic network (Weinberger and Lipska, submitted).

We have seen that a gross lesion in the ventral hippocampus results in rats which appear normal in the lab, but show hippocampal and frontal deficits when tested after puberty. These rats were created to test the hypothesis that a discrete developmental limbic lesion can result in widespread behavioral abnormalities within a developmentally regulated network. As discussed previously, transgenic mice manipulated for very different reasons show strikingly similar behavioral deficits. Silva et al. (1992b) created transgenic mice deficient in alpha-CaM kinase II to test the role of this protein kinase in LTP. As noted previously, these mice behave as if they received hippocampal lesions. This strongly suggests that an abnormality in a particular enzyme, active in the intracellular cascade whereby a neuron responds to its environment, can lead to a defined set of behavioral anomalies that result from dysfunction in discrete neuronal networks. As such, these studies open the door to a myriad of possible abnormalities that could potentially be linked to the dysfunction of schizophrenia.

CONCLUSIONS

This chapter suggests that appreciating the complexities of normal neural development and functioning will further our understanding of the complexities of schizophrenia. We selectively discussed several principles of neuronal functioning. First, behavioral and cognitive functions can be understood neuroanatomicalally in terms of distributed neuronal networks that subserve specific functions. Next, the formation of these networks depends on the normal processes that underlie cerebral development. While constrained by their genome, neurons look to their environment for pathway and target selection, and once in place, to their afferent and efferent connections to make the final decisions of differentiation. The plasticity so evident in development persists to a certain extent into adulthood, as is best exemplified by the synaptic strengthening and remodeling that underlies learning and memory. Neurons with coincident activity develop stronger synaptic connections through the activation of intracellular cascades that involve signal transduction, second messenger systems, protein kinases, genomic regulation, and ultimately structural synaptic remodeling.

Basic neurosciences have not solved the riddle of schizophrenia, but have offered a solid base for further exploration. This chapter has argued that better understanding of schizophrenia will come from understanding the neuronal networks that subserve specific symptoms. Specificially, we have discussed evidence suggesting that a mesial temporal lobe - prefrontal cortical network is dysfunctional in the disorder. Postmortem studies in schizophrenia suggest that a neurodevelopmental event results in abnormalities in frontal and temporal cortices; developmental neurobiology offers multiple mechanisms to account for such an event. Rat studies indicate that even a discrete perinatal hippocampal lesion produces delayed behavioral deficits consistent with both hippocampal and frontal cortical dysfunction. Lastly, we have discussed the insights that molecular biology may bring to our understanding of neurotransmitter function and pharmacologic actions. The evidence suggests that neurotransmitters and the pharmacologic agents which mimic them are dynamic influences on neuronal gene expression and functioning, and may modulate the workings of a network. As such, deficits that arise in any area of cell biology, from the signal, to the signal transduction, to the genome, may be implicated in the complex behavioral, cognitive, and affective presentation that is labelled schizophrenia.

REFERENCES

Akbarian, S., Bunney Jr, W.E., Potkin, S.G., Wigal, S.B., Hagman, J.O., Sandman, C.A., and Jones, E.G. (1993a). "Altered distribution of nicotinamide-adenine dinucleotide phosphate-diaphorase cells in frontal lobe of schizophrenics implies disturbances of cortical development", Arch. Gen. Psychiatry, 50, 169 - 177.

Akbarian, S., Vinuela, A., Kim, J.J., Potkin, S.G., Bunney, W.E., and Jones, E.G. (1993). "Distorted distribution of nicotinamide-adenine dinucleotide phosphate-diaphorase neurons in temporal lobe of schizophrenics implies anomalous cortical development", Arch.. Gen. Psychiatry, 50, 178 - 187.

Alexander, G.E., DeLong, M.R. and Strick, P.L. (1986). "Parallel organization of functionally segregated circuits linking basal ganglia and cortex", Annu. Rev. Neurosci., 9, 357 - 381.

Arnold, S.E., Hyman, B.T., van Hoesen, G.W., and Damasio, A.R. (1991) "Some cytoArch.itectural abnormalities of the entorhinal cortex in schizophrenia", Arch. Gen Psychiatry, 48, 625 - 632.

Bachevalier, J. (1990). "Ontogenetic development of habit and memory formation in primates", Ann. NY Acad. Sci., 608, 457 - 484.

Bachevalier, J. (Submitted). "Medial temporal lobe structures and autism: a review of clinical and experimental findings", Neuropsychologia.

Bailey, C.H., Chen, M., Keller, F. and Kandel, E.R. (1992). "Serotonin-mediated endocytosis of apCAM: an early step of learning related synaptic growth in Aplysia", Science, 256, 645 - 649.

Bear, M.F., and Kirkwood, A. (1993). "Neocortical long-term potentiation", Curr. Opin. Neurobiol., 3, 197 - 202.

Benes, F.M., McSparren, J., Bird, E.D., SanGiovanni, J.P., and Vincent, S.L. (1991) "Deficits in small interneurons in prefrontal and cingulate cortices of schizophrenic and schizoaffective patients", Arch. Gen Psychiatry, 48, 996 - 1001.

Berman, K.F., Zec, R.F., and Weinberger, D.R. (1986). "Physiological dysfunction of dorsolateral prefrontal cortex in schizophrenia, II: role of medication, attention, and mental effort", Arch. Gen Psychiatry, 43, 126 - 135.

Berman, K.F., Randolph, C., Gold, J., Holt, D., Jones, D.W., Goldberg, T.E., Carson, R., R.E., Herscovitch, P., and Weinberger, D.R. (1991). "Physiological activation of frontal lobe studied with positron emission tomography and O^{15} water during working memory tasks", J. Cereb. Blood Flow Metab., 11 (Suppl. 2), 851.

Berman, K.F., Torrey, E.F., Daniel, D.G., and Weinberger, D.R. (1992) "Regional cerebral blood flow in monozygotic twins discordant and concordant for schizophrenia", Arch. Gen. Psychiatry, 49, 927 - 934.

Berman, K.F., Ostrem, J.L., Randolph, C., Gold, J., Goldberg, T.E., Coppola, R., Carson, R.E., Herscovitch, P. and Weinberger, D.R. (submitted). "Activation of a cortical network during performance of the Wisconsin Card Sorting Test: a PET study".

Bloom, F.E. (1993). "Advancing a neurodevelopmental origin for schizophrenia", Arch. Gen. Psychiatry, 50, 224 - 227.

Corbetta, M., Miezin, F.M., Dobmeyer, S., Shulman, G.L., and Petersen, S.E. (1991). "Selective and divided attention during visual discriminations of shape, color, and speed: functional anatomy by positron emission tomography", J. Neurosci., 11, 2383 -2402.

Demonet, J.F., Chollet, F., Ramsay, S., Cardebat, D., Nespoulous, J.L., Wise, R., Rascol, A., and Frackowiak, F. (1992). "The anatomy of phonological and semantic processing in normal subjects", Brain, 115, 1753 - 1768.

Frey, U., Huang, Y.Y. and Kandel, E.R. (1993). "Effects of CAMP simulate a late stage of LTP in hippocampal CA1 neurons", Science, 260, 1661 - 1664.

Frith, C.D., Friston, K., Liddle, P.F., and Frackowiak, R.S.J. (1991). "Willed action and the prefrontal cortex in man: a study with PET", Proc. R. Soc. Lond. Biol., 244, 241-246.

Gao, W.Q., Liu, X.L. and Hatten, M.E. (1992). "The weaver gene encodes a nonautonomous signal for CNS neuronal differentiation", Cell, 68, 841 - 854.

George, M.S., Ketter, T.A., and Post, R.M. (1993) "SPECT and PET Imaging in Mood Disorders", J Clin Psychiatry, 54(Suppl.), 6-13.

Gold, J.M., and Harvey, P.D. (1993). "Cognitive deficits in schizophrenia", Psychiatr. Clin. North Am., 16, 295 - 312.

Gold, J.M., Hermann, B.P., Randolph, C., Wyler, A.R., Goldberg, T.E. and Weinberger, D.R. (in press). "Schizophrenia and temporal lobe epilepsy: a neuropsychological analysis", Arch. Gen. Psychiatry.

Goldberg, T.E., Greenberg, R.D., Griffin, S.J., Gold, J.M., Kleinman, J.E., Pickar, D., Schulz, S.C. and Weinberger, D.R. (1993). "The effect of clozapine on cognition and psychiatric symptoms in patients with schizophrenia", Br. J. Psychiatry 162, 43 - 48.

Goldberg, T.E., Torrey, E.F., Gold, J.M., Ragland, J.D., Bigelow, L.B., and Weinberger, D.R. (1993). "Learning and memory in monozygotic twins discordant for schizophrenia", Psychol. Med., 23, 71 - 85.

Goldman, P.S. (1971). "Functional development of the prefrontal cortex in early life and the problem of neuronal plasticity", Exp Neurol., 32, 366 - 387.

Goodman, C.S. and Shatz, C.J. (1993). "Developmental mechanisms that generate precise patterns of neuronal connectivity", Cell, 72(Suppl), 77 - 98.

Jakob, H. and Beckman, H. (1986). "Prenatal developmental disturbances in the limbic allocortex in schizophrenics", J. Neural Transm, 65, 303 - 326.

Jessell, T.M., and Kandel, E.R. (1993). "Synaptic transmission: a bidirectional and self-modifiable form of cell - cell communication", Cell, 72(Suppl), 1 - 30.

Jonides, J., Smith, E.A., Koeppe, R.A., Awh, E., Minoshima, S. and Mintun, M.A. (1993). "Spatial working memory in humans as revealed by PET", Nature, 363, 623 -625.

Kaang, B.K., Kandel, E.R., and Grant, S.G.N. (1993). "Activation of cAMP-responsive genes by stimuli that produce long-term facilitation in Aplysia sensory neurons",Neuron, 10, 427 - 435.

Kandel, E.R. (1989). "Genes, nerve cells, and the remembrance of things past", J. Neuropsychiatry Clin. Neurosci., 1, 103 - 125.

Knowlton, B.J., and Squire, L.R. (1993). "The learning of categories: parallel brain systems for item memory and category knowledge", Science, 262, 1747 - 1749.

Kolodkin, A.L., Matthes, D.J., and Goodman, C.S. (1993). "The semaphorin genes encode a family of transmembrane and secreted growth cone guidance molecules",Cell, 75, 1389 - 1399.

Komuro, H. and Rakic, P. (1993). "Modulation of neuronal migration by NMDA receptors", Science, 260, 95-97.

Laplane, D., Levasseur, M., Pillon, B., Dubois, B., Baulac, M., Mazoyer, B., Tran Dinh, S., Sette, G., Danze, F. and Baron, J.C. (1989). "Obsessive-compulsive and other behavioral changes with bilateral basal ganglia lesions", Brain, 32, 699 - 725.

Liddle, P.F. and Barnes, T.R.E. (1990). "Syndromes of chronic schizophrenia",Br. J. Psychiatry, 157, 558 - 561.

Liddle, P.F. and Morris, D.L. (1991). "Schizophrenic syndromes and frontal lobe performance", Br. J. Psychiatry, 158, 340 - 345.

Liddle, P.F., Friston, K.J., Frith, C.D., Hirsch, S.R., Jones, T. and Frackowiak, R.S.J. (1992). "Patterns of cerebral blood flow in schizophrenia",Br. J. Psychiatry, 160, 179 - 186.

Lipska, B.K. and Weinberger, D.R. (1993). "Delayed effects of neonatal hippocampal damage on haloperidol-induced catalepsy and apomorphine-induced stereotypic behaviors in the rat", Dev. Brain Res., 75, 213 - 222.

Lipska, B.K. and Weinberger, D.R. (In pressa). "Behavioral effects of subchronic treatment with haloperidol or clozapine in rats with neonatal excitotoxic hippocampal damage", Neuropsychopharmacology.

Lipska, B.K. and Weinberger, D.R. (in pressb) "Gonadectomy does not prevent novelty or drug-induced motor hyperresponsiveness in rats with neonatal hippocampal damage", Dev. Brain Res.

Lipska, B.K., Jaskiw, G.E. and Weinberger, D.R. (1993). "Postpubertal emergence of hyperresponsiveness to stress and to amphetamine after neonatal excitotoxic hippocampal damage: a potential animal model of schizophrenia", Neuropsychopharmacology, 9, 67 - 75.

Lipska, B.K., Jaskiw, G.E. and Weinberger, D.R. (in press). "The effects of combined prefrontal cortical and hippocampal damage on dopamine-related behaviors in rats", Pharmacol. Biochem. Behav..

Mayford, M., Barzilai, A., Keller, F., Schacher, S. and Kandel, E.R. (1992). "Modulation of an NCAM-related adhesion molecule with long-term synaptic plasticity in Aplysia", Science, 256, 638 - 644.

McConnell, S.K. and Kaznowski, C.E. (1991). "Cell cycle dependence of laminar determination in developing neocortex", Science 254, 282 - 285.

Mednick, S.A., Cannon, T.D., Barr, C.E., and Lyon, M., eds. (1991). Fetal Neural Development and Adult Schizophrenia, Cambridge University Press, Cambridge.

Merzenich, M.M. and Samesha, K. (1993). "Cortical plasticity and memory", Curr. Opin. Neurobiology, 3, 187 - 196.

Mesulam, M.M. (1990). "Large-scale neurocognitive networks and distributed processing for attention, language, and memory", Ann. Neurol., 28, 597 - 613.

Overman, W.M., Bachevalier, J., Turner, M. and Peuster, A. (1992). "Object recognition versus object discrimination: comparison between human infants and infant monkeys", Behav. Neurosci. 1, 15 - 29.

Pallas, S.L. (1990). "Cross-modal plasticity in sensory cortex". In The Neocortex (eds B.L. Finlay et al.), pp 205 - 218, Plenum Press, New York.

Pardo, J.V., Pardo, P.J., Janer, K.W. and Raichle, M.E. (1990). "The anterior cingulate cortex mediates processing selection in the Stroop attentional conflict paradigm", Proc. Natl. Acad. Sci. USA, 87, 256 - 259.

Patterson, P.H., and Nawa, H. (1993). "Neuronal differentiation factors/cytokines and synaptic plasticity", Cell, 72 (Suppl), 123 - 137.

Petersen, S.E., Fox, P.T., Posner, M.I., Mintun, M. and Raichle, M.E. (1988). "Positron emission tomographic studies of the cortical anatomy of single-word processing", Nature, 331, 585 - 589.

Petrides, M., Alivisatos, B., Evans, A.C. and Meyer, E. (1993). "Dissociation of human mid-dorsolateral from posterior dorsolateral frontal cortex in memory processing", Proc. Natl Acad. Sci. USA, 90, 873 - 877.

Raichle, M.E. (1993). "The scratchpad of the mind", Nature, 363, 583 - 584.

Randolph, C., Goldberg, T.E. and Weinberger, D.R. (in press). "The neuropsychology of schizophrenia". In Clinical Neuropsychology Third Edition (eds K.M. Heilman and E. Valenstein), Oxford, New York.

Rakic, P. (1988). "Specification of cerebral cortical areas", Science, 241, 170 - 176.

Rakic, P. (1990). "Principles of neural cell migration", Experientia, 46, 882 - 891.

Rakic, P., Suner, I. and Williams, R.W. (1991). "A novel cytoarchitectonic area induced experimentally within the primate visual cortex", Proc. Natl Acad. Sci. USA, 88, 2083 - 2087.

Rose, S.P.R. (1991) "How chicks make memories: the cellular cascade from c-fos to dendritic remodeling", TINS, 14, 390 - 396.

Rugarli, E.I. and Ballabio, A. (1993). "Kallmann syndrome: from genetics to neurobiology", JAMA, 270, 2713 - 2716.

Schwartz, B.L., Rosse, RB. and Deutsch, S.I. (1993). "Limits of the processing view in accounting for dissociations among memory measures in a clinical population", Memory Cognition, 21, 63 - 72.

Sergent, J., Zuck, E., Terriah, S. and MacDonald, B. (1992). "Distributed neural network underlying musical sight-reading and keyboard performance", Science 257, 106 - 109.

Shaw, C., Prusky, G. and Cynader, M. (1988). "Surgical undercutting prevents receptor redistribution in developing kitten visual cortex", Visual Neurosci., 1, 205 -210.

Silva, A.J., Stevens, C.F., Tonegawa, S. and Wang, Y. (1992a). "Deficient hippocampal long-term potentiation in alpha-calcium-calmodulin kinase II mutant mice", Science, 257, 201 - 206.

Silva, A.J., Paylor, R., Wehner, J.M. and Tonegawa, S. (1992b). "Impaired spatial learning in alpha-calcium-calmodulin kinase II mutant mice", Science 257, 206 - 211.

Squire, L.R. (1986). "Mechanisms of memory", Science, 232, 1610 - 1619.

Squire, L.R. and Zola-Morgan, S. (1991). "The medial temporal lobe memory system", Science, 253, 1380 - 1386.

Weinberger, D.R. (1987). "Implications of normal brain development for the pathogenesis of schizophrenia", Arch. Gen. Psychiatry, 44, 660 - 669.

Weinberger, D.R. (1993). "A connectionist approach to the prefrontal cortex", J. Neuropsychiatry Clin. Neurosci., 5, 241 - 253.

Weinberger, D.R. (1994, in press). "Schizophrenia as a neurodevelopmental disorder: a review of the concept". In Schizophrenia (eds D.R. Hirsch and D.R. Weinberger), Blackwood Press, London.

Weinberger, D.R. and Lipska, B.K. (submitted). "Cortical maldevelopment, antipsychotic drugs, and schizophrenia: a neuroanatomicalal reductionism", Arch. Gen. Psychiatry.

Weinberger, D.R., Berman, K.F., Ostrem, J.L., Abi-Dargham, A., and Torrey, E.F. (1993). "Disorganization of prefrontal-hippocampal connectivity in schizophrenia: a PET studies of discordant MZ twins", Soc. Neurosci. Abstracts, 19, 7.

Wilson, F.A.W., O'Scalaidhe, S.P. and Goldman-Rakic, P.S. (1993) "Dissociation of object and spatial processing domains in primate prefrontal cortex", Science, 260, 1955 - 1958.

Yamamoto, N., Yamada, K., Kurotani, T. and Toyama, K. (1992). "Laminar specificity of extrinsic cortical connections studied in coculture preparations", Neuron, 9, 217 - 228.

Zola-Morgan, S. and Squire, L.R. (1990). "The neuropsychology of memory: parallel findings in humans and nonhuman primates", Ann. N.Y. Acad. Sci, 608, 434 - 456.

6

THE AETIOLOGY OF BRAIN ABNORMALITIES IN SCHIZOPHRENIA

P.W.R. Woodruff, R.M. Murray

INTRODUCTION

The distinction between schizophrenia and other "functional" psychoses has been based traditionally on the presence or absence of clinical features thought to be characteristic of the former, e.g. first rank symptoms. These clinical features have been operationalized to produce internationally agreed criteria such as DSM-III or ICD-10 which can be used by researchers to diagnose the schizophrenia syndrome in a highly reliable fashion. Unfortunately, the comparative validity of the different criteria remains quite uncertain, and they classify widely different numbers of patients as schizophrenic (Castle et al., 1991).

As our understanding of psychosis has developed, researchers have begun to turn to theories of aetiology in an attempt to devise more biologically meaningful ways of classifying psychotic patients (Murray et al., 1985). For instance, Crow (1990) argues that schizophrenia and manic depression lie on a continuum of genetic risk, while Murray et al. (1992) contend that the psychoses can best be distinguished on the basis of characteristics acquired either congenitally or in adult life.

These divergent theories have in common the belief that there exist

Schizophrenia: Exploring the Spectrum of Psychosis. Edited by R. Ancill. © 1994 John Wiley & Sons Ltd

developmental abnormalities in the brains of many schizophrenic patients. However, before we uncritically accept the developmental model of schizophrenia, it is necessary to understand not only the cerebral abnormalities found in schizophrenia but also the processes underlying normal brain development, how these processes are determined, and the way they interact with factors potentially damaging to healthy brain development.

NEUROIMAGING AND NEUROPATHOLOGICAL STUDIES OF SCHIZOPHRENIA

There is now reasonable consensus between computed tomography (CT) and magnetic resonance imaging (MRI) studies that lateral ventricles, and to a lesser extent third and fourth ventricles, are enlarged in schizophrenia. Ventricular enlargement is present at the onset of symptoms (Turner et al., 1986; DeLisi et al., 1992), and there is little evidence of progression on follow-up for up to eight years (Illowsky et al.,1988; Vita et al.,1988), although DeLisi et al. (1994) has recently questioned this.

These in vivo findings have been confirmed by modern neuropathological techniques. In addition, reduced cortical volume and reduced neuronal density in frontal regions of brains of schizophrenics have been described by Pakkenberg (1987) and Benes (1991), though not confirmed by Heckers et al., (1991). Likewise, the findings that brains of schizophrenics were lighter by 5 -8% and shorter by 4% (Brown et al., 1986; Bruton et al., 1990) was not demonstrated by Heckers et al. (1991).

There is more consensus among studies that have looked at the temporo-limbic regions. The finding that the temporal horn of the left lateral ventricle is especially enlarged in schizophrenics supports the idea that there may be tissue loss in surrounding medial temporal structures (Brown et al., 1986). More direct evidence of temporo-limbic pathology in schizophrenia includes observations of: (1) reduced grey and white matter volume of hippocampus, amygdala and parahippocampal gyrus; (2) reduced neuronal number, size or abnormal arrangements in hippocampus, parahippocampal, gyrus and entorhinal cortex (see Bogerts, 1993).

What can neuropathology tell us about the origins of these abnormalities? Since reactive gliosis is thought only to occur after the second trimester of pregnancy, brain abnormalities in the absence of gliosis probably indicate abnormalities of brain development as opposed to degeneration. Of the 10 studies reviewed by Bogerts (1993) that looked for gliosis, none found any in the medial temporal lobe, cingulate or thalamus, despite evidence of other abnormalities in the temporal region such as cell loss, reduced volume and disrupted cell orientation,

Abnormalities of brain asymmetry may also provide insight into the timing of the cerebral lesions in schizophrenia. In the normal brain, the left Sylvian fissure is longer than that on the right; the right frontal lobe, right temporal lobe and left planum temporale are larger than those on the opposite side. Recent post-mortem studies report that asymmetry is lost or reduced in schizophrenic brains (Falkai et al., 1992; Crow et al., 1992), observations supported by some MRI studies (e.g. of the planum temporale, Rossi et al., 1992), but not others (Falkai et al., 1994).

Further support for a developmental aetiology for schizophrenia comes from studies that demonstrate frank developmental anomalies in the brains of patients. Using CT and MRI, an association between psychosis and dysgenesis of the corpus callosum, first noted by Lewis et al. (1988), has been confirmed by others (Swayze et al., 1990). An anomaly related developmentally to the corpus callosum is cavum septum pellucidum and an association between the presence of cavum septum pellucidum and schizophrenia has also been described (Lewis and Mezey, 1985; Degreef et al., 1992a). Lewis et al. (1988) inferred from these associations that neurodevelopmental damage to the corpus callosum may predispose to the later onset of psychosis. There is, of course, evidence of callosal dysfunction in schizophrenia (David, 1987, Coger and Serafinitides, 1989). Failed neuronal development or myelination might account for this and for the altered corpus callosum size reported in schizophrenia (Woodruff et al., 1993; David, 1993). In addition, patterns of asymmetry of temporal lobe structures may be related to morphology of the corpus callosum. For example, Woodruff et al. (1993) found that the isthmus of the corpus callosum, which transmits fibres between both superior temporal gyri, was particularly reduced in size in schizophrenics.

Brain asymmetry is thought to develop late in pregnancy. As the left temporal lobe normally develops later than the right, it might be more susceptible to injury during fetal brain development. Therefore environmental factors that affect the normal control of cerebral asymmetry may operate during this critical time during development. On the other hand, cerebral asymmetry, like handedness, may be largely genetically determined. Thus, impairment of asymmetrical brain development may result from the interaction of genetic and environmental processes. Some support for this idea comes from the work of Bilder et al. (1994), who found schizophrenics showed less cerebral asymmetry in the volumes of five cortical regions than controls, but that these volumes did not correlate with sulcal prominence. They speculate that processes underlying cerebral asymmetry and other brain abnormalities such as sulcal prominence in schizophrenia are independent.

THE RELEVANCE OF NORMAL BRAIN DEVELOPMENT TO THE AETIOLOGY OF SCHIZOPHRENIA

The development of the CNS involves the production of the neural tube (neurulation), neuronal proliferation, migration and differentiation. These events occur in concert such that development of each neurone influences the subsequent development of others, and the connections they later form. Brain development consists of numerous processes occurring simultaneously and in succession. Table 1 shows the peak times for stages of brain development and the main disorders associated with disrupted development at these periods (Volpe, 1991). The timing of brain developmental processes gives us vital clues as to the potential insults that can adversely affect them.

During early development, the neural tube develops from primitive ectoderm. The lumen of the neural tube becomes the ventricular system and the wall becomes the brain substance. Factors determining this process (genetic) or operating at this time of development (environmental) might also influence development of other tissues derived from ectoderm such as skin. Minor physical anomalies (MPAs) such as malformed ears or palate occur in patients with developmental disorders (Smith, 1976). MPAs occur more frequently in schizophrenics than controls (Gualtieri et al., 1982; Guy et al., 1983; Green et al., 1987). An environmental insult operating at this early stage of brain development might be expected to result in more obvious gross brain abnormalities than are generally observed in schizophrenia. However, some reports suggest that MPAs predict a younger age of onset of schizophrenia and occur in those with cognitive impairment indicating more severe consequences of subtle but early brain impairment (Green et al, 1987; Waddington et al., 1990). The development of dermatoglyphics of the hand occurs simultaneously with neural cell migration to the cortex (Rakic, 1988). Minor dermatoglyphic abnormalities have been observed more commonly in schizophrenics than controls (Mellor, 1992) and in schizophrenic monozygotic twins compared with their well cotwins (Bracha et al., 1991). Since both twins are genetically identical and share their intrauterine environment the latter observation does not help to separate genetic from early environmental influences. However, the finding of dermatoglyphic abnormalities in schizophrenics without a family history support environmental aetiological influences (Fananas et al., 1994). Neurones are produced by proliferation during the developmental period until

Table 1. Stages of Brain Development and Associated Clinical Disorders

Stage	Peak time period	Events	Disorders
Primary neurulation	3 - 4 weeks	Production neural crest	Anencephaly Meningo-myelocoel Cortical malformations
Prosencephalic development	2 - 3 months	Face and forebrain development Cerebral hemispheres thalamus, hypothalamus, midline, e.g. corpus callosum, septum pellucidum	Holoprosencephaly, facial abnormalities
Neuronal proliferation	3 - 4 months	All neurones and glia derived from Ventricular and sub-ventricular zones	Microcephaly Macroencephaly
Neuronal migration	3 - 5 months	Cells move to permanent sites	Schizencephaly, tissencephaly, pachygyria, polymicrogyria, heterotopias, focal cerebrocortical dysgenesis Agenesis of corpus callosum
Neuronal organization	5 months - years	Realignment of neurones, growth axons and dendrites. Synaptogenesis, selective elimination processes and synapses. Glial proliferation / differentiation	Mental retardation ± seizures, infantile autism, Down's syndrome, Duchenne muscular dystrophy, familial disorder of axonal development, necrotizing myopathy, cardiomyopathy and cataracts. Congenital absence of cortico-spinal fibres. Ventilator-dependent premature infants, perinatal and post-natal insults
Myelination	6 months - adult	Myelin sheaths develop	Cerebral white matter hypoplasia, amino acidopathies, post-natal undernutrition, congenital hypothyroidism, periventricular leukomalacia. Other post-natal insults

Three to six months after birth. Cell proliferation occurs in two zones: a ventricular zone lining the ventricles and a subventricular zone. Cells move from their site of proliferation to their final position as a result of migration. Cells of the cerebral cortex undergo active migration along a scaffolding of radially aligned glial fibres away from the proliferative zones. Younger cells occupy the superficial layers by overtaking older ones that remain closer to the ventricular surface. The neurone migrates along the glial fibres until detaching itself and making connections from its final position.

Disruption of neuronal migration results in abnormal cell positions. Of particular clinical importance in schizophrenia are abnormally arranged neurones in cortical regions as these probably indicate early disturbance of brain development which can result in a range of syndromes from mild behavioural disorders to severe mental retardation. The finding of similar neuropathological abnormalities in hippocampi, frontal cortex and cingulate gyrus in schizophrenic brains further supports the idea of disturbed early brain development (Roberts, 1991). Evidence of ectopic neurones in area CA1/CA2 of the hippocampus in schizophrenia (Kovelman and Scheibel, 1984) and suggests abnormal cell migration in this condition. Recently, Akbarian et al. (1993a, 1993b) found abnormally positioned dinucleotide phosphate-diaphorase (NADPH-d) containing neurones in frontal and temporal cortex in schizophrenics. Reduced numbers in the outer cortical layers and excess in underlying white matter provide strong evidence for defective migration of neurones during development.

In the final stage of cell differentiation axons grow out, become myelinated and form their respective synaptic links and neurotransmitters. As the axon grows it extends to a post-synaptic cell. There then follows a process of axon elimination that results in the final pattern. Axonal collaterals are either retracted from target cells or neurones themselves die. A complex series of processes are likely to influence these events which may continue into adulthood. Misplaced neurones would therefore result in aberrant connections and patterns of axonal elimination. Abnormal patterns of axonal elimination would result in further aberrant connections.

In schizophrenia, there may be little evidence of gross neurological disorder, and symptoms often develop in adult life. Since disruption to early brain development would lead to severe brain abnormalities, it is likely that the subtle brain abnormalities responsible for schizophrenia occur later, e.g. at the stages of neuronal organization or myelination in the 2nd and 3rd trimester of pregnancy, perinatally or later.

As fetal brain tissue expands, the proportion of ventricle to brain volume decreases. Therefore increased ventricular size in relation to brain size in schizophrenia may represent incomplete maturation of surrounding brain regions. The ventricular region is surrounded by areas such as the amygdala, hippocampus and parahippocampal gyrus. These structures contain neuronal networks concerned with activities including selection, association and integration of sensory information, memory and control of basic drives and emotions. The particularly increased volume of left temporo-frontal horns of the lateral ventricles found in some studies of schizophrenics are consistent with most MRI studies that demonstrate left-sided temporal lobe abnormalities (Degreef et al., 1992b). For instance, of 13 recent MRI studies that have compared temporal lobe volume between schizophrenics and controls, 12 demonstrated volume reduction on the left (statistically significant in seven studies) and 9 on the right (statistically significant in three studies) (see Woodruff, 1994).

If processes like neuronal proliferation and migration that originate in the ventricular wall were impaired, then lack of development of hippocampus and other temporal structures might be associated with enlarged "immature" ventricles. That hippocampal volume was inversely related to ventricular size supports such a notion (Nasrallah et al., 1990).

THE ANATOMY AND PHYSIOLOGY OF SCHIZOPHRENIC SYMPTOMS

Are immature patterns of brain structure and function linked with the clinical symptoms and neuropsychological deficits manifest in schizophrenia? The clinical parameter most strongly associated with structural abnormality in schizophrenia is poor outcome. For example, in a prospective follow-up of 140 psychotic patients, Van Os et al, (1994a) found that structural abnormality, especially increased Sylvian fissure and third ventricle volume, predicted negative symptoms and unemployment over the next four years. Two recent studies suggest that loss of cortical grey matter may be diffuse (Harvey et al., 1993; Zipursky et al., 1992). Reduced brain or cortical volume is sometimes accompanied by increased cerebrospinal fluid in schizophrenics. Harvey et al.

(1993) found this to be related to poor pre-morbid function, a further indication of impaired development, and also again to unemployment.

Some studies have also found reduced frontal lobe volumes in schizophrenia (Breier et al., 1992). Patients with frontal lobe damage, in common with schizophrenics with negative symptoms, may exhibit deficits of attention, abstract thinking, judgment, motivation, affect and emotion, impulse control, as well as decreased spontaneous speech, verbal fluency and voluntary motor behaviour. This similarity was first pointed out by Kleist in 1930 when he stated "Patients with brain disease and war wounds in the left temporal lobe also demonstrated the same gross speech disorders - the paraphasias and word amnesias - and even the same fine deficits - the characteristic word errors, formation of new words and the strange formation of sentences-that one sees in schizophrenics".

Furthermore, schizophrenics may show impaired performance on neuropsychological tasks that require adequate frontal lobe function (Goldberg et al., 1993, Park et al., 1992). The question is whether this frontal lobe underactivity is reflected in abnormalities of underlying brain structure. It has been shown that those patients with decreased prefrontal volume do show particular impairment in tests of frontal lobe function (Raine et al., 1992, Woodruff et al., 1994b).

Differences in patterns of grey and white matter loss may be focused in particular brain areas. Three studies examined white and grey matter separately in the temporal lobes; all reported grey matter reduction, one white matter reduction bilaterally, and one white matter reduction on the left and increase on the right (Woodruff, 1994).

Reduced volume of the superior temporal gyrus has been associated with auditory hallucinations (Barta et al., 1991) and with thought disorder (Shenton et al., 1992). Within the dominant temporal lobe lie many auditory and language functions that may underlie abnormalities of thought, speech, and auditory perception in schizophrenia. Temporal lobe lesions may, therefore, provide an important link between abnormalities of brain development and the positive symptoms of schizophrenia.

Structural abnormalities have been complemented by studies of regional cerebral blood flow (rCBF) or glucose metabolism using positron emission tomography or single photon emission tomography. These have demonstrated dysfunction of frontal, parietal and temporal lobes when activated by various tasks (see Liddle, 1994). Of particular relevance to aetiology has been the validation of the three syndromes of psychomotor poverty, disorganization and delusional disorder in terms of patterns of abnormal rCBF, first described by Liddle et al., (1992) and recently largely replicated by Ebmeier et al. (1993). Van Os et al. (1994b) have examined the relationship between childhood deficits and psychopathological syndromes resembling those of Liddle. Psychomotor poverty was associated with early onset of psychosis, negative symptoms, male sex and low premorbid IQ. Disorganization showed similar but less striking association with premorbid dysfunction and illness course. A third syndrome characteristic more affective symptoms was associated with female sex and more benign course.

These findings therefore provide some circumstantial evidence in favour of links between possible structural and functional "immaturity" of the brain, and propensity to develop symptoms of schizophrenia. Explanations are that a developmental abnormality might interact with either normal maturation (Weinberger, 1987) or an additional progressive process, to produce symptoms at a later date (usually early adulthood).

The conclusion from such diversity of structural abnormalities may be that a process or processes are operating over some time during brain development, i.e. during neuronal organization and/or myelination. There is some circumstantial evidence that social deprivation during gestation and early life predisposes to later schizophrenia (Castle et al., 1993). Social deprivation may be linked to a number of variables, including overcrowding and poorer nutrition which are known to influence brain development. These considerations are relevant to the finding of Lewis et al. (1992), who showed the incidence of schizophrenia was 1.65 times higher in men brought up in cities than those from rural regions. However, genetic factors are also important.

GENETICS

There is, of course, long-standing evidence of a genetic contribution to schizophrenia (Murray et al., 1986) but as yet linkage and association studies have failed to locate or identify the gene of genes that transmit this liability (Gill et al., 1993). Are the structural brain abnormalities which are found in schizophrenia genetically or environmentally determined? Considerable argument has occurred over whether non-familial schizophrenics show, on average, greater ventricular volume than their familial counterparts (McGrath and Murray, 1994). Vita et al. (1994) carried out a recent meta-analysis which reported a significant trend in this direction but also carried out a valuable clarifying analysis in a large series of their own. There were no differences in ventricular volume between female familial and sporadic cases but male sporadic cases had significantly larger lateral ventricles. This finding has been exactly replicated by Jones et al. (1994a) in a CT study of 162 schizophrenics.

Canon et al. (1993) suggest that increased ventricular volume in schizophrenics may reflect environmentally determined damage while cortical abnormality may reflect genetic predisposition. Families multiply affected with schizophrenia have, therefore, begun to be studied. Basset, (1989) reported temporal lobe abnormalities in an uncle and nephew with schizophrenia in association with a partial trisomy of chromosome 5, and in the young man's mother (an obligate carrier) who nevertheless was clinically well. In a most interesting preliminary report, Honer et al. (1992) carried out CT examinations of 42 individuals from six multiply-affected families. Sulcal enlargement in the lateral temporal cortex, and ventricular and cisternal enlargement in the medial temporal region, were significantly more prominent in the psychotic than non-psychotic family members.

It seems that both genetic and environmental factors contribute to the cerebral abnormalities found in schizophrenia but that the different pathologies are differently caused. Jones and Murray (1991) pointed out that the genetic effect may be through mutations in the genes that control the process of early brain development that we have outlined above, a view subsequently endorsed by Bloom (1993). A more recent refinement of this view points out that maturational brain changes continue through adolescence and early adult life, and that such processes are also largely genetically determined. Thus, a genetic defect in the control of cortical pruning during adolescence would be one possible explanation for the tendency for schizophrenia to have its onset at this time (Keshavanet al., 1994).

SEX DIFFERENCES IN SCHIZOPHRENIA AND THEIR BEARING ON AETIOLOGY

Generally, ventricular enlargement, in common with other brain regions, is more pronounced in male as opposed to female schizophrenics and control groups (see Woodruff, 1994). It may be therefore that male schizophrenics are more likely to exhibit "developmental" brain abnormalities. Such a view is consistent with other observations of sex differences between schizophrenics (Castle and Murray, 1991). Males compared with females show an earlier age 14 of onset of schizophrenia (Lewine, 1988). Male schizophrenics exhibited more abnormalities of premorbid personality and poorer premorbid social adjustment than female schizophrenics or patients with affective disorder (Foerster et al., 1991). Low IQ, poor school performance and increased "soft" neurological signs were noted more frequently in males than females who later developed schizophrenia (Jones et al., 1994b).

The generalized cognitive deficits noted particularly in male pre-schizophrenic children may suggest generalized brain disturbance. This is supported by MRI. Studies have demonstrated particularly reduced brain size in schizophrenic males. However, in addition to generalized changes, abnormalities in specific brain regions like the temporal lobe and corpus callosum tend to be more pronounced in males (Bogerts et al., 1990; Woodruff et al., 1993).

There is some evidence that schizophrenia in females is more highly heritable. For example, concordance for schizophrenia is higher in female than male Mz twins, and some studies suggest that the relatives of female schizophrenics have a higher risk of schizophrenia than the relatives of male schizophrenics (Sham et al., 1994). In contrast, schizophrenic males are more likely to have a history of obstetric complications (Foerster et al., 1991).

OBSTETRIC COMPLICATIONS

There is now a consensus that schizophrenia is more often preceded by a history of obstetric complications than in controls (Lewis and Murray, 1987). These are associated with earlier onset of schizophrenia and with of a more chronic form of the illness (Foerster et al., 1991). Several studies have reported that the increased frequency of obstetric complications in the histories of male than female schizophrenics may contribute to the earlier onset of schizophrenia in males. Indeed, Kirov et al. (1994) have shown, in a large series, that when one removes those cases of schizophrenia who have suffered obstetric complications (predominantly male), the gender difference in age of onset disappears. This finding is consistent with evidence that schizophrenics from families multiply affected with schizophrenia (i.e. in whom the aetiology is presumed to be genetic) do not show the usual gender difference in age of onset (Walsh et al., 1994).

The observation that obstetric complications occur more frequently in those patients without a family history has been used to support the theory that they predispose individuals who are not genetically loaded to develop schizophrenia (Lewis and Murray, 1987). The mechanism by which they would do this could be through disrupting neuronal organization or myelination. Some studies suggest a possible link between obstetric complications and ventricular enlargement but others do not (Done et al., 1993; McGrath and Murray, 1994). Perinatal complications can result in periventricular hemorrhage with or without subsequent hydrocephalus, such as occurs in very-low-birth-weight infants (Silverton et al., 1985). In support of this, it has been suggested that "bowing" of the corpus callosum in schizophrenia is related to ventricular enlargement due to low-grade chronic hydrocephalus (Casanova et al., 1990). Alternatively, detectable obstetric complications (which are mainly perinatal) could be secondary to some earlier but hitherto unrecognized factor, e.g.maternal under-nutrition (Susser and Lin, 1992) or viral infection during pregnancy.

PRE-NATAL EXPOSURE TO INFLUENZA

A current controversial issue is whether pre-natal exposure to influenza predisposes individuals to schizophrenia. Some studies indicate that the incidence of schizophrenia reaches a peak in those born during or just after major influenza pandemics such as occurred in 1957 (Mednick et al., 1988; O'Callaghan et al., 1991; Sham et al., 1992). However, other studies report no such relationship (e.g. Crow and Done, 1992). Circumstantial evidence has linked influenza exposure to enlarged cerebral ventricles (Degreef et al., 1988; Zipursky and Schulz, 1987). If a true association this would link such exposure to possible structural developmental brain abnormalities. Peak risk of exposure appears to be about the 5th month of gestation. If so, a range of developmental stages could be affected including neuronal proliferation, migration, organization and myelination (Table 1)

CONCLUSIONS

Evidence from epidemiological, neuropathological and neuroimaging research supports the existence of developmental brain abnormalities in schizophrenia. Neuroimaging studies have demonstrated both generalized and regional grey and white matter abnormalities in cerebral cortex, frontal and temporal lobes, hippocampi and corpus callosum. These changes appear to be non-progressive and occur more commonly in males with a poor outcome. They support the idea that sex differences in schizophrenia have a neurodevelopmental basis. Both structural and functional imaging of the brain have helped define schizophrenic symptoms which may be determined by developmental abnormalities. Neuropathological studies showing aberrant arrangements of nerve cells suggest that these abnormalities occur around the time of neuronal migration in the latter stages of gestation. Associations between brain developmental abnormalities and schizophrenia help to define the timing of possible deviations in the development of the brain.

There is further need to relate specific brain abnormalities in schizophrenia with putative aetiological factors. Thus, we need to link molecular genetic and neuroimaging studies in families multiply affected with schizophrenia in order to establish the role of mutations in developmental genes in producing the pathological phenotype. Similarly, we need to utilize the modern techniques of imaging the neonatal and foetal brain in order to establish whether specific gestational events produce damage to neuronal systems so specific as to induce schizophrenic symptoms two or three decades later in the absence of susceptibility genes.

REFERENCES

Akbafian, S., Bunney, NY.E., Potkin, S.O., Wigal, S.B., Hagman, LO., Sandman, CA and Jones, E.G. (1993a). "Altered distribution of nicotinamide-adenosine dinucleotide phosphatediaphorase cells in frontal lobe of schizophrenics implies disturbances of cortical developtnent", Arch. Gen. Psychiatry, 50, 169 - 177.

Akbarian, S., Vinuela, A., Kim, J.J., Potkin, S.G., Bunney, W.E., Jones and E.G. (1993b). "Altered distribution of nicotinamide-adenosine dinucleotide phosphate diaphorase cells in frontal lobe of schizophrenics implies disturbances of cortical development". Arch. Gen. Psychiatry, 50, 178 - 187.

Barta, P.E., Pearlson, G.D., Powers, R.E,, Richards, S.S. and Tune, L.E. (1990). "Auditory hallucinations and smaller superior temporal gyral volume in schizophrenia, Am. J. Psychiatry , 147, 1457 - 1462.

Bassett, A.S. (1989). "Chromosome 5 and schizophrenia: implications for genetic linkage studies", Schizophr. Bull., 15, 393 - 402.

Benes, F.M., McSparren, J. Bird, E.D., San Giovanni, J.P. and Vincent, S.L. (1991). "Defcits in small interneurons in prefrontal and cingulate cortices of schizophrenic and schizoaffective patients". Arch. Gen. Psychiatry, 48, 996 - 1001.

Bilder, R.M., Wu, H., Bogerts, B., Snyder, P., Lantos, G., Ashtari, M. and Lieberman, LA. (1994) "Abnormal cortical asymmetry and sulcal prominence are independent predictors of schizophrenia". Schizophr. Res, 11, 131.

Bloom, F.E. (1993). "Advancing a neurodevelopmental origin for schizophrenia",Arch. Gen. Psychiatry, 50, 224 - 227.

Bogerts, B. (1993). "Recent advances in the neuropathology of schizophrenia", Schizophr Bull. 19, 431 - 445.

Bogerts, B., Ashtari, M., Degreef, G., Alvir, J.M.J., Bilder, R.M. and Lieberman, LA. (1990). "Reduced temporal limbic structure volumes on magnetic resonance images in first episode schizophrenia", Psychiatry Res. Neuroimag, 35, 1 - 13.

Bracha, H.S., Torrey, E.F., Bigelow, L.B., Lohr, J.B. and Linington, B.B. (1991) "Subtle signs of prenatal rnaldevelopment of the hand ectoderm in schizophrenia - a preliminary monozygotic twin study, Biol Psychiatry", 30, 719 - 725.

Breier, A., Buchanan, R.W., Elkashef, A., Munson, R.C., Kirkpatrick, B. and Gellad, F. (1992) "A magnetic resonance imaging study of limbic, prefrontal cortex, and caudate structures" Arch. Gen. Psychiatry, 49, 921 - 925.

Brown, R. Colter, N., Corsellis, J.A.N., Crow, T.J., Frith, C.D., Jagoes, R., Johnstone, E.C. and Marsh, L. (1986). "Postmortem evidence of structural brain changes in schizophrenia; Differences in brain weight, temporal horn area, and parahippocampal gyrus compared with affective disorder", Arch. Gen. Psychiatry, 43, 36 - 42.

Bruton, C.J., Crow, T.J., Frith, C.D., Johnstone, E.C., Owens, D.O.C. and Roberts G.W. "Schizophrenia and the brain: a prospective clinico-neuropathological study", Psychol. Med., 20, 285 - 304.

Canon, T.D., Mednick, S.A., Parnas, I., Schulsinger, F., Praestholm, I. and Vestergaard, A. (1993). "Developmental brain abnormalities in the offspring of schizophrenicmothers", Arch. Gen. Psych., 50, 551 - 564.

Casanova, M.F., Sanders, R.D., Goldberg, T.E., et al. (1990). "Morphometry of the corpus callosum in monozygotic twins discordant for schizophrenia: a magnetic resonance imaging study", J. Neurol. Neurosurg. Psychiatry, 53, 416 - 421.

Castle, D.J. and Murray, R.M. (1991). "The neurodevelopmental basis of sex differences in schizophrenia", Psychol. Med, 21, 565 - 575.

Castle, D.J.,Scott, K., Wessely, S., Murray, R.M, (1993). "Does social deprivation during gestation and early life predispose to later schizophrenia?", Soc. Psychiatry Psychiatr. Epidemiol., 28, 1 - 4.

Coger, R.W. and Serafetinides, E.A. (1990) "Schizophrenia, corpus callosum, and interhemispheric communication: a review", Psychiatry Res, 34, 163 - 84.

Crow, T.J. (1990). "The continuum of psychosis and its genetic origins: the sixty-fifth Maudsley lecture", Br. J. Psychiatry, 156, 788 - 797.

Crow, T.J. and Done, D.J. (1992). "Prenatal exposure to influenza does not cause schizophrenia" Br. J. Psychiatry, 161, 390 - 393.

Crow, T.I., Brown, R., Bruton, CJ., Fritb, C.D. and Gray, V. (1992). "Loss of Sylvian fissure asymmetry in schizophrenia: findings in the Runwell 2 series of brains", Schizophr. Res. 6, 152 - 153.

David, A.S. (1987). "Tachistoscopic tests of colour naniing and matching in schizophrenia: evidence for posterior callosal dysfunction?", Psychol. Med, 17, 621 -30.

David, A.S. (1993). "Callosal transfer in schizophrenia: too much or too little?" J. Abnorm. Psychol., 102, 573 - 579.

Degreef, G., Mukherjee, S., Bilder, R., et al., (1988). "Season of birth and CT findings in schizophrenic patients", Biol. Psychiatry, 24, 461 - 464.

Degreef, G., Bogerts, B., Falkai P., Greve, B., Lantos, G., Ashtari, M. and Liebermann, J. (1992a). "'Increased prevalence of cavum septum pellucidum in magnetic resonance scans and postmortem brains of schizophrenic patients", Psychiatry Res, 45, 1 - 13.

Degreef G., Ashtari M., Bogerts B., et al. (1992b). "Volumes of ventricular system subdivisions measured from magnetic resonance images in first-episode schizophrenic patients", Arch. Gen. Psychiatry, 49, 531 - 7.

De Lisi, L.E, Stritzke, P., Riordan, H., et al. (1992). "The timing of brain morphological changes in schizophrenia and their relationship to clinical outcome", Biol. Psychiatry, 31, 241 - 54.

De Lisi, L.E,, Grimson, R., Kushner, M., Lee, G., Sakuma, M., Gao, T. and Kantawal, K. (1994). "Is there progressive brain change following a first hospitalization for schizophrenia? A 4 year follow-up", Schizophr. Res, 11, 135 - 136.

Done, D.J., Sacker, A. and Crow, T.J. (1993). "Obstetric complications and schizophrenia". Br. Med. J.., 306, 269.

Ebmeier, K.P., Blackwood, D.H.R., Murray, C., Souza V., Walker, M., Dougall, N., Moffoot, A.P.R. O'Carroll, R.E. and Goodwin, G.M. (1993). "Single photon emission tomography with 99mTc-exametazime in unmedicated schizophrenic patients", Biol. Psychiatry, 33, 487 - 495.

Falkai, P. Bogerts, B. Greve, B. Pfeiffer, U. Machus, B. Folsch-Reeta, B. Majtenyi, C. and Ovary, I. (1992). "Loss of Sylvian fissure asymmetry in schizophrenia. A quantitative post mortem study", Schizophr. Res.,7, 23 - 32.

Falkai, P., Bogerts, B., Kleinschmidt, A., Steinmetz, H., Schneider, Th., Greve, B., Pilz, K., Gonsiorcyzk, C. and Pfeiffer, U. (1994) "The planum temporale in schizophrenia: a comparison of postmortem and MRI data", Schizophr. Res 11, 131.

Fananas, L., Van Os, J., and Murray, R.M. (1994). "Dermatoglyphic ridge count as a possible marker for developmental insult in schizophrenia" (submitted).

Foerster, A., Lewis, S., Owen, M. and Murray, R.M. (1991). "Premorbid personality on psychosis: effects of sex and diagnosis", Br. J. Psychiatry, 158, 171 - 176.

Gill, M., McGuffin, P., Parfitt, E., et.al., (1993) "A linkage study of schizophrenia with DNA markers from the long arm of chromosome 11",. Psychol. Med, 23, 27 - 44.

Goldberg, T.E., Fuller Torrey, E., Gold, J.M., Ragland, J.D., Bigelow, L.B. and Weinberger, D.R. (1993) "Learning and memory in monozygotic twins discordant for schizophrenia", Psychol. Med., 23, 71 - 85.

Green, M.F., Satz, P., Soper, H.V. and Kharabi, F. (1987). "Relationship between physical anomalies and age of onset of schizophrenia, Am. J. Psychiatry 144, 666 - 667.

Gualtieri, C.T., Adams, A., Shen, C.D. and Loiselle, D. (1982). "Minor physical anomalies in alcoholic and schizophrenic adults and hyperactive and and autistic children", Am. J. Psychiatry, 139, 640 - 643,

Guy, J.D., Majorski, L.V., Wallace, C,J., and Guy, M.P. (1983). "'The incidence of minor physical anomalies in adult male schizophrenics", Schizophr. Bull, 9, 571 - 582.

Harvey, I., Ron, M..A., DuBoulay, G., Wicks, D., Lewis, S.W. and Murray, R.M. (1993). "Reduction of cortical volume in schizophrenia on magnetic resonance imaging", Psychol. Med., 23, 591 - 604.

Heckers, S., Heinsen, H., Heinsen, Y.C. and Beckman, H. (1991). "Cortex, white matter and basal ganglia in schizophrenia: a volumetric postmortem study". Biol Psychiatry., 29, 556 - 566,

Honer, W.G., Bassett, S.A., MacEwan,   et al., (1992). "Structural brain imaging abnormalities associated with schizophrenia and partial trisomy of chromosome 5", Psychol. Med., 22, 519 - 524.

Illowsky, B., Juliano, D.M., Bigelow, L.B. and Weinberger, D.R. (1988). "Stability of CT scan findings in schizophrenia", J. Neurol. Neurosurg. Psychiatry 51, 209 - 213.

Jones, P. and Murray, R.M. (1991) "The genetics of schizophrenia is the genetics of neurodevelopment" Br. J. Psychiatry, 158, 615 - 623.

Jones, P. and Murray, R.M. (1991) "The genetics of schizophrenia is the genetics of neurodevelopment" Br. J. Psychiatry , 158, 615 - 623.

Jones, P.R., Harvey, I., Lewis, S.W., Toone, B.K., Van Os., J., Williams, M., and Murray, R.M. (1994a). "Cerebral ventricle dimensions as risk factors for schizophrenia and affective psychosis, an epidemiological approach to analysis" (submitted).

Jones, P.B., Guth, C., Lewis, S.M. and Murray, R.M. (1994) "Low intelligence and poor educational achievement precede early onset schizophrenic psychosis". In The Neuropsychology of Schizophrenia, (eds. A.S. David, J. Cutting), Lawrence Erlbaum.

Keshaven, M.S., Reynolds, C.F., Montrose, D., Haas, G.L., Swezney, J. and Miewald, L (1994). "Sleep abnormalities in psychosis: gender and age effects", Schizophr. Res., 11, 192.

Kirov, G., Jones, P., Harvey, I., Lewis, S.W., Toone, B., Sham, P. and Murray, R.M. (1994). "Do obstetric complications cause gender differences in schizophrenia?" (submitted)

Kovelman, J.A. and Scheibel, A.B. (1984). "A neurohistological correlate of schizophrenia", Biol. Psychiatry, 19, 1601 - 1621.

Lewine, R.J. (1988). "Gender and schizophrenia" In Handbook of Schizophrenia, Vol. 3 (ed. H.A. Nasrallah), Elsevier, Amsterdam, pp. 379 - 397.

Lewis, G., David, A., Andreasson, S. and Allebeck, P. (1992). "Schizophrenia and city life", Lancet, 34, 137 - 140.

Lewis, S.W. and Mezey, C. (1985). "Clinical correlates of septum pellucidum cavities: an unusual association with psychosis", Psychol. Med., 15, 1 - 12.

Lewis, S.W. and Murray, R.M. (1987). "Obstetric complications, neurodevelopmental deviance and risk of schizophrenia", J. Psychiatr. Res., 21, 413 - 421.

Lewis, S.W., Reveley, M..A., David A.S., Ron, M.A. (1988). "Agenesis of the corpus callosum and schizophrenia: a case report", Psychobiol.. Med., 18, 341-347.

Liddle, P.F. (1994). "Neurobiology of schizophrenia", Curr. Opin. Psychiatry,. 7, 43 - 46.

Liddle, P.F., Friston, K.J., Frith, C.D., Hirsch, S.R., Jones, T., Frackowiak, R.S.I. (1992). "Patterns of cerebral blood flow in schizophrenia", Br. J. Psychiatry, 160, 179 - 186.

McGrath, J., Murray, R.M. (1994). "Risk factors for schizophrenia, from conception to birth" (submitted).

Mellor, C.S. (1992). "Dermatoglyphic evidence of fluctuating asymmetry in schizophrenia", Br. J. Psychiatry, 160, 467 - 472.

Murray, R.M., Lewis, S.W. and Reveley, A.M., (1985) 'Towards an aetiological classification of schizophrenia", Lancet, i, 1023 - 1026.

Murray, R.M., Reveley, A.M. and Clifford, C.A. (1986). "Genetic vulnerability to schizophrenia", Psychiatr. Clin. North Am, 9, 3 - 16.

Murray, R.M., O'Callaghan, E., Castle, D.J. and Lewis, S.W. (1992). "A neurodevelopmental approach to the classification of schizophrenia", Schizophr. Bull., 18 (2), 319 - 332.

Nasrallah, H.A., Bogerts, B., Olson, S., Schwartzkopf, S.B. and Coffman, J.A. (1990) "Correlates of hippocampus hypoplasia in schizophrenia", Proc. Am. Psychiatr. Assoc., Annual meeting, New York, 304.

Nowakowski, R.S., Rakic, P. (1981). "The site of origin and route and rate of migration of neurones to the hippocampal region of the rhesus monkey",J. Comp. Neurol., 196, 129 - 159.

O'Callaghan, E., Sham, P., Takei, N., Glover, G. and Murray, R.M. (1991) "Schizophrenia after prenatal exposure to 1957 A2 influenza epidemic", Lancet, I, 1248 - 1250.

O'Callaghan, E., Buckley, P., Redmond, O., Stack, J., Ennis, J.T., Larkin, C., Waddington, J.L. (1992). "Abnormalities of cerebral structure in schizophrenia on magnetic resonance imaging: interpretation in relation to the neurodevelopmental hypothesis", J. R. Soc. Med, 85, 227 - 231.

Pakkenberg, B. (1987). "Post mortem study of chronic schizophrenic brains", Br. J. Psychiatry, 151, 744 - 752.

Park, S. and Holzman, P.S. (1992). "Schizophrenics show spatial working memory deficits", Arch. Gen. Psychiatry, 49, 975 - 982.

Raine, A., Lencz, T., Reynolds, G.P., Harrison, G., Sheard, C., Medley, I., Reynolds, L.M. and Cooper, J.E. (1992). "An evaluation of structural and functional prefrontal deficits in schizophrenia.: MRI and neuropsychological measures", Psychiatry Res., 45, 123 - 137.

Rakic, P. (1988). "Specification of cerebral cortical areas", Science, 241, 170.

Roberts, G.W. (1991). "Schizophrenia: a neuropathological perspective", Br. J. Psychiatry, 158, 8 - 17.

Rossi, A., Stratta, P., Mattei, P., Cupillari, M., Bozzao, Gallucci, M. and Casacchia, M. (1992). "Planum temporale in schizophrenia: a magnetic resonance study". (1992) Schizophr Res., 7, 19 - 22.

Sham, P., O'Callaghan, E., Takei, N., Murray, G., Hare, E. and Murray, R. (1992). "Schizophrenic births following influenza epidemics: 1939 - 1960",Br. J. Psychiatry, 160, 461-466.

Sham, P.C., Jones, P.B., Russell, A.J., Gilvarry, K., Bebbington, P., Lewis, S.W., Toone, D.K. and Murray, R..M. (1994). "Age at onset, sex, and familial psychiatric morbidity in schizophrenia: report from the Camberwell Collaborative Psychosis Study", Br. J. Psychiatry, (in press).

Shenton, M.E., Kikinis, R., Jolesz, F.A., et al. (1992). "Left-lateralized temporal lobe abnormalities in schizophrenia and their relationship to thought disorder: a conmputerized quantitive MRI study", N. Engl. J. Med, 327, 604 - 612.

Silverton, L., Finello, K.M., Mednick, S.A., Schulsingrr, F. Pamas, J. (1985). "Birthweight, schizophrenia and ventricular enlargement in a high risk sample",J. Abnorm. Psychol., 94, 405 - 409.

Smith, D.W. (1976). Recognizable Patterns of Human Malformation: Genetic, Embryologic and Clinical Aspects, W.B. Saunders, Philadelphia.

Susser, E.S., Lin, S.P. (1992). "Schizophrenia after prenatal exposure to the Dutch hunger winter of 1944 - 1945", Arch. Gen. Psychiatry 49, 983 - 988.

Swayze W., Andreasen, N.C., Erhardt, J.C., Yuh W.T.C., Allinger R.J. and Cohen G.A. (1990). "Development abnormalities of the corpus callosum in schizophrenia: an MRI study", Arch. Neurol., 47, 805 - 808.

Turner, S.W., Toone, B.K., Brett-Jones and J.R. (1986). "Computerised tomographic scan changes in early schizophrenia", Psychol. Med, 16, 219 - 225.

Van Os, L., Fahy, T., Jones, P., Harvey, I., Lewis, S., Toone, B. and Murray, R..M. (1994a). "Intracerebral CSF spaces predict unemployment and negative symptoms in psychotic illness: a prospective study" (submitted).

Van Os, J., Faby, T., Jones, P., Harvey, I., Lewis, S., Toone, B. and Murray, R.M. (1994b). "Psychopathological syndromes in the functional psychoses: associations with premorbid functioning and outcome" (submitted).

Vita, A. (1994) (pers. comm.).

Vita, A., Sacchetti, R., Valvassori, G. and Cazzullo, C.L. (1988). "Brain morphology in schizophrenia: a 2 - 5 year CT scan follow-up study", Acta Psychiatr. Scand., 78, 618 - 621.

Volpe, L.J. (1991). "Brain development-normal and abnormal", J. Perinat. Med., 19, 29 - 34.

Waddington, J.L., O'Callaghan, E. and Larkin, E. (1990). "Physical anomalies and neurodevelopmental abnormality in schizophrenia: new clinical correlates", Schizophr. Res., 3, 90.

Walsh, C., Asherson, P., Sham, P., Castle, D., Williams, J., Taylor, C., Clements, A., Watt, D., Sargeant, M., Owen, M., Gill, M., McGuffin, P. and Murray, R.M. (1994). "Age of onset of schizophrenia in multiply affected families is early and shows no sex difference" (submitted).

Weinberger, D.R. (1987). "Implications of normal brain development for the pathogenesis of schizophrenia", Arch. Gen. Psychiatry, 44, 660 - 669.

Woodruff, P.W.R. (1994) "Structural magnetic resonance imaging in psychiatry". in Cambridge Medical Reviews: Neurobiology and Psychiatry 3 (eds R. Kerwin, D. Dawbarn, J. McCulloch and C. Tarnminga), Cambridge University Press, (in press).

Woodruff, P.W.R., Pearlson, O.D., Geer, M.J., Barta, P.E. and Chilcoat, H.D. (1993). "A computerized magnetic resonance imaging study of corpus callosum morphology in schizophrenia", Psychol. Med., 23, 45 - 56.

Woodruff, P.W.R., Howard, R., Rushe, T., Graves, M. and Murray., R.M. (1994). "Frontal lobe volume and cognitive estimation in schizophrenia", Schizophr. Res., 11, 133 - 134.

Zipursky, R.B. and Schulz, S.C., (1987). "Seasonality of birth and CT findings in schizophrenia" Biol. Psychiatry, 22, 1289 - 1292.

Zipursky, R.B., Lim, K.O. and Sullivan, E.V. (1992). "Widespread cerebral grey matter volume in schizophrenia", Arch. Gen. Psychiatry, 49, 195 - 205.

7

MAGNETIC RESONANCE IMAGING IN SCHIZOPHRENIA: A REVIEW OF CLINICAL AND METHODOLOGICAL ISSUES

L.D. Hall, J.J. Herrod, T.A. Carpenter and P.J. McKenna

INTRODUCTION

According to current nosology, schizophrenia is considered to be a distinct clinical entity with identifiable symptoms, outcome and response to treatment. As such, it should also have an identifiable aetiology. Considerable circumstantial evidence suggests that the disorder has its root cause in some biological disturbance of brain function, but the precise nature of this remains elusive. As a consequence, one of the major goals in psychiatry has been to find a biological marker for schizophrenia, be it a gene or gene product, a biochemical abnormality, or direct evidence of a brain disorder. One of the main elements of this endeavour has been the search for a structural brain lesion in the disorder.

Investigation of structural brain abnormality in schizophrenia began at the start of the era of (X-ray computed tomography) (CT) scanning. The first study (Johnstone et al., 1976) revealed lateral ventricular enlargement, and after nearly 50 further studies this remains the only widely reproduced finding (Andreasen et al, 1990a; Lewis, 1990). Enlargement of the third ventricle, sulcal widening and a miscellany of other findings have been reported, but have not been reliably

Schizophrenia: Exploring the Spectrum of Psychosis. Edited by R. Ancill. © 1994
John Wiley & Sons Ltd

replicated. Even lateral ventricular enlargement itself has not been universally found, and it is clear that it is at most modest.

In the wake of CT studies, and having been a neglected area of research for most of this century, post-mortem studies of schizophrenic brain began to be undertaken. A notable feature of these studies has been a succession of claims for size reductions in limbic structures, in particular the hippocampus, amygdala and parahippocampal gyrus (see Bogerts, 1993a for a review). However, the differences between patients and controls have been small and the findings have not been consistently replicated. In addition, quantitative post-mortem studies themselves face formidable methodological difficulties.

Magnetic Resonance Imaging (MRI) is not only technically superior to CT in terms of resolution of brain substance versus cerebrospinal fluid (CSF), but its ability to distinguish grey and white matter permits comparisons of the size of particular cortical and subcortical regions during life. This imaging technique thus offers distinct advantages over both CT and post-mortem studies, and has the potential to delineate any structural brain pathology in schizophrenia clearly and unequivocally. This review examines the MRI studies of schizophrenia to date, from both clinical and methodological standpoints and with particular reference to the questions of lateral ventricular enlargement and regional size reductions.

CLINICAL ISSUES

Ventricular system

One of the major difficulties which emerged from CT scan studies of schizophrenia was the problem involving selection of controls (Buckley et al., 1992) (See Table 1). Early studies tended to rely on scans drawn from radiology files which had been reported as normal by radiologists; for example those carried out on patients investigated for headache with negative results or on the asymptomatic relatives of patients with Huntington's disease. Unfortunately, using such a method is liable to result in the exclusion of scans from normal individuals who have ventricles which are merely at the extreme upper end of the size distribution-some such individuals will inevitably be reported as being borderline or questionably abnormal. Systematic bias can thus creep in, and Smith and Iacono (1986) were able to make a strong case that at least some of the findings of lateral ventricular enlargement in schizophrenia were actually due to smallness of the ventricles in the control groups.

A recent large and rigorous CT scan study (Andreasen et al., 1990a), which employed as controls prospectively ascertained normal volunteers who were screened for head injury, neurological disease, alcohol and drug abuse, has recently confirmed the presence of lateral ventricular enlargement in schizophrenia. However, that study also indicated that the degree of enlargement is slight, and that there was a wide overlap between patients and controls. In fact significant differences could only be demonstrated for male, and not for female schizophrenic patients.

Studies using MRI have been carried out on schizophrenic patients since 1983. Almost all of these have employed prospectively ascertained normal volunteers as controls. In addition, many (but not all) of the studies have matched their groups for age and sex - an important consideration when small size differences are being sought. The findings of studies on the size of the ventricular system are shown in Table 1; only those studies which used normal volunteers as controls are shown, but those which did not match for age and sex are included. A number of these studies (Kelsoe et al, 1988; Suddath et al, 1989; Andreasen et al., 1990a; Gur et al, 1991; Bornstein et al, 1992; Zipursky et al, 1992) have confirmed the CT scan finding of lateral ventricular enlargement in schizophrenia, although there have been almost as many exceptions (Johnstone et al, 1989; Rossi et al, 1990; Young et al, 1991; Shenton et al, 1992; Harvey et al, 1993). A similar approximately equal division of positive and negative findings is also evident for third ventricular enlargement.

One possible explanation of the inconsistencies in these findings is that lateral ventricular enlargement may be restricted to subgroups of patients. As found by Andreasen et al. (1990) using CT, one important determinant of lateral ventricular enlargement may be male sex: this was apparent in the MRI studies of Andreasen et al. (1990b), Bogerts et al. (1990), Gur et al (1991) and Harvey et al (1993). Other possible reasons for the lack of consensus in MRI studies of this finding have not as yet been addressed.

Table 1. MRI Studies of the Ventricular System in Schizophrenia

Study	Sample	Lateral ventricles	Third ventricle	Comment
Smith et al (1987)	29 patients 21 controls	Normal	-	Groups age-matched
Kelsoe et al (1988)	24 patients 14 controls	Larger	Larger	Groups age and sex-matched Trend only to lateral-ventricular enlargement on right
Johnstone et al (1989)	21 patients 20 MDP* patients 21 controls	Normal	-	Groups age and sex-matched
Suddath et al (1990)	17 patients 17 controls	Larger	-	Groups age and sex-matched
Suddath et al (1990)	15 patients 15 controls	Larger	Larger	Control group consisted of unaffected MZ co-twins Affected co-twin could be identified visually by size of lateral ventricles in 12 of 15 cases
Andreasen et al (1990b)	54 patients 47 controls	Larger	-	Groups age and sex-matched Increase in lateral ventricular size restricted to males
Rossi et al (1990)	17 patients 13 controls	Normal	-	Sample not closely matched for age and sex
Dauphinias et al (1990)	28 patients 28 controls (2 overlapping groups of 21)	Normal / Larger	Larger	Groups age and sex-matched Compared with 2nd control group lateral ventricles larger on left and VBR larger bilaterally

Study	Sample			Comments
Jernigan et al (1991)	42 patients 24 controls	Normal	Normal	Groups age and sex-matched Trend towards larger total ventricular volume in patients 23 of patient group also had alcohol or other substance abuse
Gur et al (1991)	42 patients 43 controls	?Larger	?Larger	Groups age and sex-matched Patients had higher whole-brain CSF volume and higher ratio of ventricular/sulcal CSF to volume
Young et al (1991)	31 patients 33 controls	Normal	Normal	Groups age and sex-matched
Shenton et al (1992)	15 patients 15 controls	Normal	Normal	Groups age and sex-matched
Zipursky et al (1992)	22 patients 20 controls	Larger	Normal	Groups age and sex-matched
Bornstein et al (1992)	72 patients 31 controls	Larger	Larger	Groups not age or sex-matched Differences in lateral ventricular size due to significant increases in female patients only
Kawasaki et al (1992)	20 patients 10 controls	?	Normal	Groups age and sex-matched
Harvey et al (1993)	48 patients 34 controls	Normal	-	Groups age but not-sex matched

* MDP - manic depressive psychosis

Brain Substance

Whole Brain

The relevant studies are summarized in Table 2. Once again, only studies which used normal volunteers as controls are included. The results are far from consistent: only three out of 11 studies found an overall reduction in brain size. One of these studies (Zipursky et al., 1992) employed small numbers of patients (22), and in another (Andreasen et al., 1986) the patient and control groups were not matched for sex (however, the size reduction remained significant when the sex differences were controlled for). It is also interesting to note that this finding of Andreasen et al (1986) was not replicated in a subsequent study by the same group (Andreasen et al, 1990b). Possible reasons for that failure to replicate were explored in detail by Andreasen et al (1990b); no obvious explanation was forthcoming, but it was felt that matching for educational level between patients and controls might be important for future studies.

Frontal Lobes

As shown in Table 2, four of 13 studies found reductions in the size of the frontal lobes, with one further study (Raine et al, 1992) yielding equivocal evidence of this. In the study of Harvey et al (1993), a reduction in the volume of the frontal and anterior parietal lobes was reported, but that finding seems only to have emerged after regression analysis was used to control for overall brain size and other variables such as sex, age and height. As above, an initial positive finding by Andreasen et al (1986) was not replicated subsequently (Andreasen et al, 1990b).

Temporal Lobes and Limbic Structures

The results for overall temporal lobe size are also shown in Table 2. The results are approximately equally divided: five of 13 studies found an overall reduction in the size of the temporal lobe. One further study (Johnstone et al, 1989) found a trend towards smaller size, and one (Suddath et al, 1990) found a significant size reduction on the left only.

A natural extension of these findings has been to consider whether the temporal lobe changes found reflect grey or white matter reductions, and whether, in particular, temporal lobe subcortical nuclei, i.e. the hippocampus and amygdala, are affected. It is clear from Table 2 that, once again, positive and negative findings are equally divided: five of 11 studies found evidence for a reduction in

Table 2. MRI Studies of Whole Brain and Various Regions in Schizophrenia

Study	Sample	Whole brain	Frontal lobe	Temporal lobe	Subcortical structures	Comment
Andreasen et al (1986)	38 patients 49 controls	Smaller	Smaller	-	-	Groups not sex-matched Whole brain and frontal reductions persisted after controlling for sex, height and weight
DeMyer et al (1988)	24 patients 24 controls	Smaller right hemisphere	Smaller	-	-	Groups age and sex-matched Only left frontal area smaller with additional educational matching
Kelsoe et al (1988)	24 patients 14 controls	Normal	Normal (prefrontal)	Normal	Normal amygdala/ hippocampus	Groups not sex-matched Non-blind ratings
Johnstone et al (1989)	21 patients 21 controls	Normal	-	Normal	-	Groups age and sex-matched Trend towards smaller temporal lobe size in patients
Suddath et al (1989)	17 patients 17 controls	-	Normal (prefrontal)	Smaller	Smaller amygdala/ hippocampus	Groups age and sex-matched Temporal lobe size reductions due to smaller amygdala and anterior hippocampal grey matter
Andreasen et al (1990b)	54 patients 47 controls	Normal	Normal	Normal	-	Groups age and sex-matched

(Table Continues)

Table 2. MRI Studies of Whole Brain and Various Regions in Schizophrenia (continued)

Study	Sample	Whole brain	Frontal lobe	Temporal lobe	Subcortical structures	Comment
Suddath et al (1990)	15 patients 15 controls	-	Normal (grey matter)	Smaller on left	Smaller hippocampus	Control group were non-schizophrenic monozygotic co-twins of patients
Bogerts et al (1990)	34 patients 25 Normals	-	-	-	Normal hippocampus	Groups age and sex-matched 7 controls were drawn from radiology files Left hippocampus smaller in males
Dauphinias et al (1990)	28 patients 28 controls	Normal (excluding temporal lobes)	Normal	Smaller	Normal amygdala/ hippocampus	Groups age and sex-matched Right amygdala/hippocampus smaller in one of two analyses
Gur et al (1991)	42 patients 43 controls	Normal	-	-	-	Groups age and sex-matched
Jernigan et al (1991)	42 patients 24 controls	-	Smaller (inferior)	Smaller (medial)	-	Groups age and sex-matched
Young et al (1991)	31 patients 33 controls	-	Normal	Normal	Normal amygdala/ hippocampus	Groups age and sex-matched Hippocampal gyrus normal
Breier et al (1992)	44 patients 29 controls	-	Smaller (white matter)	-	Smaller amygdala Smaller left hippocampus	Groups age and sex-matched Trend towards smaller hippocampus on right
Di Michele et al (1992)	25 patients 25 controls	-	-	Smaller	-	Groups age and sex-matched Reductions more marked on left

Study	Sample					Comments
Raine et al (1992)	17 patients 19 controls	-	?Smaller	-	-	Groups age and sex-matched Significant differences between patients and controls in 2 of 3 prefrontal cuts and 1 of 3 right prefrontal cuts
Shenton et al (1992)	15 patients 15 controls	Normal	-	?	Smaller amygdala/ hippocampus on left	Groups age and sex-matched Smaller superior temporal gyrus on left Smaller parahippocampal gyrus bilaterally
Zipursky et al (1992)	22 patients 20 controls	Smaller (grey matter)	-	-	-	Groups age and sex-matched
Bogerts et al (1993b)	19 patients 18 controls	-	-	-	Smaller amygdala/ hippocampus	Groups age and sex-matched Amygdala/hippocampal size reductions accounted for by reductions in posterior portion of complex, i.e. hippocampus
Colombo et al (1993)	18 patients 18 controls	-	-	Normal	Normal hippocampus	Groups age and sex-matched
Harvey et al (1993)	48 patients 34 controls	Normal	?Smaller	Smaller	-	Groups not closely matched for sex Decrease in anterior cerebral volume
Kawasaki et al (1993)	20 patients 10 controls	Normal	Normal	Normal	Normal amygdala/ hippocampus	Groups age and sex-matched

size of the hippocampus/amygdala complex, or one or other component of this. One of these studies (Shenton et al., 1992) also found reductions in the size of the parahippocampal gyrus, and another found this cortical region to be smaller on the left (Kawasaki et al., 1992); however a third study (Young et al., 1991) which examined this structure found it to be normal.

An interesting study of this type is that of Suddath et al. (1990), who compared a series of 15 monozygotic twins discordant for schizophrenia. Quantitative analysis of sections through the hippocampus revealed this structure to be smaller on the left in the affected member of 14 of 15 pairs, and smaller on the right in 13 of the 15.

METHODOLOGICAL CONSIDERATIONS

Ventricular System

The technical aspects of the studies reviewed above are shown in Table 3. The earlier MRI studies (Andreasen et al, 1986, 1990b; Kelsoe et al, 1988; Dauphinias et al, 1990) used inversion recovery spin echo sequences (usually with an inversion time of 600 ms) to achieve excellent tissue contrast in combination with relatively thick slices - typically 10 mm. Ventricular area was then estimated by manual methods from films of each slice, summed over slices to yield a figure for ventricular volume.

This approach is associated with a number of problems. First, with thick slices volume measurement is compromised to some extent - the so-called partial volume effect. Secondly, determination of where the ventricle edge lies from radiographic film is subject to vagaries of photographic processing and development. Thirdly, defining regions of interest by manually tracing ventricular area inevitably produces some loss of fidelity. A graphic example of the number of steps that such methods interpose between the original data and its measurement is provided by the study of Andreasen et al (1986). In this study, the MR images were first recorded on film; the film was then placed on an overhead projector; then the ventricles were traced; and finally the area of the tracing was measured using a planimeter.

Table 3. MRI Methodology

Study	Field (T)	Protocol	SLTH (mm)	ISDI (mm)	FOV (mm)	Orien	NSI	Quantitation	Inter-rater reliability	System/ Phantom
Smith et al (1987)	0.3	SE30	8	?	?	T	?	planimetry from film	0.85	
DeMyer et al (1988)	0.15	IR400/ 1250/30	1			T		planimetry from film	0.8 - 0.95	
Kelsoe et al (1988)	0.5	IR600/?/3 583	10	?	?	C	12	manual ROI on imager	~0.97	
Johnstone et al (1989)	0.15	SE44/544	8	10	?	C	10	"Film, then image analyser" using fixed threshold		
Suddath et al (1989)	1.5	SE20/800	5	5	?	TC	30	manual ROI offline	0.99	?
Suddath et al (1990)										
Andreasen (1990)	0.5	IR600/ 1600	10	10	?	C/TC?	8	Film projected/traced by hand	>0.9	
Rossi et al (1990)	0.5	SE30/450	8	?	?	(T)C	7	Areas by planimeter "VBR, redigitized film"	0.96	
Dauphinais et al (1990)	0.5	IR600/30 /3583	10	10	?	C	12	Film/image analyser or manual ROI off line	0.93 - 0.98	?

(Table Continues)

Table 3. MRI Methodology (Continued)

Study	Field (T)	Protocol	SLTH (mm)	ISDI (mm)	FOV (mm)	Orien	NSI	Quantitation	Inter-rater reliability	System/Phantom
Jernigan et al (1991)	1.5	TE25/70/2000	5	7.25	240	T	?	Classification/manual ROI	?	107 controls
Gur et al (1991)	1.5	TE30/80/3000	5	5	?	T	?	Classification/semi-automatic segmentation operator provides seed for boundary	0.96 to 0.99	0.998 for phantom
Young et al (1991)	0.08	FE?/800/60	8	?	?	C	10	Quantimet from films	"10%"	
Shenton et al (1992)	1.5	TE30/80/3000	3	3	240	T	54	Classification/automatic segmentation		6% on phantom
		FE5/35/45 (3D)	1.5	1.5	240	3D	124	Manual ROI with reference to atlas	0.86	
Zipursky et al (1992)	1.5	TE20/80/2000*	5	7.5	240	T(C)	10	Semi-automatic/using both echoes Histogram on sum of echoes	0.98	
Harvey et al (1993)	0.5	IR150/40/4420	5	5	300	C(T)		semi-automatic/threshold fill	0.99	
		SE70/2400	5	5	300	T		Brain structures		

Study						Orien		Method	Reliability	Validity
Andreasen et al (1986)	0.5	IR600/?/1 600	?	?	?	S	1	"Films ohp, hand trace/planimeter"	0.81 to 0.97	
Bogerts et al (1990)	1	FE15/40/ 40	3.1	?	3	3D	63	Semi-automatic? (manual ROI)	0.85 to 0.93 interrater and repeats	2.5% compared to PM brains
Bogerts et al (1993)	1	FE15/40/ 50	3.1	?	3	3D	63	"Semi-automatic (manual ROI)"	0.85 to 0.94 interrater and repeats	2.5% compared to PM brains
Breier et al (1992)	1.5	SE600/17	3	?	3	C	?	"Thresholding, then manual ROI?"	0.91	

* = cardiac gated

Key:
SLTH = slice thickness
FE = field echo
C = coronal
3D = three-dimensional
ohp = overhead projector

ISDI = inter-slice distance
SE = spin echo
S = sagittal
ROI = region of interest

FOV = field of view
IR = inversion recovery
T = transverse
VBR = ventricle to brain ratio

Orien = orientation
CT = coronal/transverse oblique

In more recent studies such cumbersome measurement techniques have been largely replaced by direct analysis of digital images by means of regions of interest manually selected on a computer screen. Another innovation has been the use of double spin echo sequences in the axial plane (e.g. Jernigan et al, 1991; Gur, 1991; Shenton et al, 1992; Zipursky et al, 1992). Consequently subtraction of the first from the second-echo image yields an image which highlights CSF. This means that a simple threshold can be used to classify pixels corresponding to ventricle, and subsequently the ventricular area can be measured automatically by the computer. This technique has been shown to give good results when applied to phantoms (Shenton et al., 1992).

Initial MRI studies of ventricular size followed the previously established CT methodology and used a single slice to compute ventricle to brain ratio (VBR). The shortcomings of that approach have been demonstrated by Woods et al. (1990): using a coronal slice in which the area of the lateral ventricle appeared maximal, they found that a 1 mm variation in slice position resulted in an 8 -10% change in VBR, and that a 2 - 3 degree changes in rotational head tilt also resulted in sizeable effect. Since VBR differences between schizophrenic patients and controls are often of the order of 10%, it is possible for uncertainties of measurement to exceed the differences between patients and controls. Those problems can be avoided by calculation of ventricular volume either from multiple slices or by using 3D data acquisition.

Brain Structure

The technical aspects of those studies are also shown in Table 3. As in the studies of the ventricular system, some studies, particularly the earlier ones, used a manually defined region of interest derived by drawing round the appropriate areas on film. However, replacing this approach with an automated, computerized method has proven difficult because of the poor contrast between grey and white matter; as yet no technique has been developed to overcome this difficulty. Some of the more recent studies have continued to use a manually defined region of interest, but applied directly to digitised data (or digitised film). Others have also identified the regions of interest in conjunction with an anatomical atlas. One group (Bogerts et al, 1990, 1993) also standardized MR images against post-mortem brains and have shown a good correlation between MRI and histologically defined structures. The most recent studies have used 3D imaging in conjunction with semi-automatic, user-initiated region-of-interest estimations. 3D imaging has the advantage over conventional 2D images of being based on thinner slices, and hence causing smaller partial volume effects; grey/white matter contrast in such images is, however, poorer.

Combined Clinical and Methodological Issues

Considered on methodological grounds, seven of the studies reviewed above stand out as being particularly rigorous and sophisticated and consequently are best suited to demonstrate small differences between schizophrenic patients and controls at the required level of significance. That differentiation is based on a combination of most or all of the following features: thin multi-slice or three-dimensional image acquisition; computerized analysis of images; use of standard anatomical atlases for localization of structures (or referencing against post-mortem brain); and careful use of MRI controls, such as reproductibility and reliability of images and instrument parameters.

Six of those seven studies are summarized in Table 4 (one study, Bornstein et al, 1992, is not included as it fails to meet the clinical requirement of age and sex matching). As regards lateral ventricular size, one study (22 patients) found significant enlargement, another (42 patients) significant enlargement of the total ventricular system, one (42 patients) demonstrated a trend towards enlargement, and one (15 patients) no significant difference. These findings do not permit any definite conclusions to be drawn. However, they might be consistent with the previous CT studies of lateral ventricular enlargement, bearing in mind that it is known from CT studies that the differences are small.

As regards overall brain size and the size of subregions, interpretation of the MR studies must be even more guarded. There seems to be little compelling support for the claim of reductions in overall brain size in schizophrenia, with, in particular, one large study (Gur et al., 1991) failing to find positive evidence for this. Only one study (Jernigan et al., 1991) addressed frontal and temporal lobe size and so it is impossible to draw any conclusions. More interestingly, two (Shenton et al, 1992., Bogerts et al., 1993) of three studies reported positive findings with respect to the hippocampus/amygdala complex; these two studies are very recent, and used refined techniques.

Table 4. MRI Findings in Schizophrenia from Six Best Studies Methodologically

Study	Sample	Lateral ventricles	Third ventricle	Whole brain	Frontal lobe	Temporal lobe	Subcortical structures
Bogerts et al. (1990)	34 patients 25 normals	-	-	-	-	-	Normal hippocampus
Gur et al (1991)	42 patients 43 controls	?Larger	?Larger	Normal	-	-	-
Jernigan et al (1991)	42 patients 24 controls	Normal	Normal	-	Smaller (inferior)	Smaller (medial)	-
Zipursky et al (1992)	22 patients 20 controls	Larger	Normal	Smaller (grey matter)	-	-	-
Shenton et al (1992)	15 patients 15 controls	Normal	Normal	Normal	-	Smaller superior temporal and para-hippocampal gyri	Smaller amygdala/ hippocampus on left
Bogerts et al (1993)	19 patients 18 controls	-	-	-	-	-	Smaller amygdala/ hippocampus

CONCLUSION

Nearly 20 years of CT and post-mortem brain research in schizophrenia has made it abundantly clear that there is no gross structural pathology associated with the disorder. Consequently, the search for a measurable brain lesion has had to focus on differences between patients and the normal population which are too small to be apparent on visual inspection but which can be demonstrated statistically. Even so, those searches have not been an unqualified success, and MRI studies in particular have not as yet yielded a consensus on the presence of any abnormality in schizophrenia.

The major clinical difficulty that can be identified from this review concerns the sample sizes employed, of patients and especially of controls. Given that the differences being sought are small and that overall brain size varies considerably — from individual to individual, between males and females, and with age— it is perhaps surprising that the studies have been content to rely on patient numbers of less than 50, and control numbers which have invariably been smaller than the patient numbers. As well as providing an obvious explanation for the lack of any convergence of evidence in the studies to date, it is apparent that the currently used sample sizes are barely able to support an adequate statistical analysis or forestall objections that any differences found are an artefact of multiple comparisons. A useful strategy for future studies might be the development of normative data for MRI scans of the brain— of, say, 150 normal individuals of both sexes and with a wide age distribution. Such a database might also eliminate the necessity for large sample sizes of patients: for example, relatively small groups of schizophrenic patients could be examined to see what proportion fall below the 10th, 5th and 1st percentiles for a particular structure, and it could be determined to what extent age and sex were important considerations.

At a technical level, two main conclusions emerge from this appraisal of the literature. The first is the necessity of developing an objective, statistically sound, automated method of measuring particular brain structures, notably subcortical nuclei such as the hippocampus and amygdala. This is particularly pertinent now that whole-brain 3D images consisting of 128 or more "slices" are routinely obtainable. Such technology will of course need to be coupled with computerized analysis, as the volume of data to be analysed is otherwise prohibitively large. Secondly, even with such improved technology, it remains at present difficult to establish differences between patients and controls which are anticipated to be of the order of less than 10%; even with sophisticated technology this tests the limits of accuracy of the MRI method. A feasible strategy might be to concentrate initially on ventricular volume, perhaps using larger sample sizes or a normative data set as described above.

It may legitimately be asked if there are any convincing abnormalities of brain structure in schizophrenia. Notwithstanding the present uncertainties in the MRI literature, the answer is likely to be yes. First, lateral ventricular enlargement is a relatively well-substantiated abnormality in CT studies, if not in MRI studies. Secondly, while the MRI studies of overall brain size and size of various subregions have been internally inconsistent, when differences have been found they have always indicated a reduction in brain size for schizophrenic patients. If there were truly no differences between schizophrenic patients and normals it might be expected that approximately as many studies should find the relevant structures to be larger in schizophrenia as smaller. Other underlying consistencies can also be discerned in the literature, for example the concentration of abnormalities in male schizophrenic patients and perhaps also the preponderance of left-sided pathology.

ACKNOWLEDGEMENTS

It is a pleasure to thank Dr. Herchel Smith for an Endowment (LDH and TAC).

REFERENCES

Andreasen, N.C., Nasrallah, H.A., Dunn, V., Olsen, S.C., Grove, W.M., Ehrhardt, J.C., Coffman, J.A. and Crossett, J.H.W. (1986) "Structural abnormalities in the frontal system in schizophrenia", Arch. Gen. Psychiatry, 43, 136 - 144.

Andreasen, N.C., Swayze, V.W. 2, Flaum, M., Yates, W.R., Arndt, S. and McChesney, C. (1990a) "Ventricular enlargement in schizophrenia evaluated with computed tomographic scanning", Arch. Gen. Psychiatry, 47, 1008 - 1015.

Andreasen, N.C., Ehrhardt, J.C., Swayze, V.W. 2, Alliger, R.J., Yuh, W.T.C., Cohen, G. and Zebell, S. (1990b). "Magnetic resonance imaging of the brain in schizophrenia", Arch. Gen. Psychiatry, 47, 35 - 44.

Bogerts, B., Ashtari, M., Degreef, G., Alvir, J.M.J., Bilder, R.M. and Lieberman J.A. (1990). "Reduced temporal limbic structure volumes on magnetic resonance images in first episode schizophrenia", Psychiatry Res. Neuroimaging, 35, 1 - 13.

Bogerts, B. (1993). "Recent advances in the neuropathology of schizophrenia", Schizophr. Bull., 19, 431 - 445.

Bogerts, B., Lieberman, J.A., Ashtari, M., Bilder, R.M., Degreef, G., Lerner, G., Johns, C. and Masiar, S. (1993b). "Hippocampus - amygdala volumes and psychopathology in chronic schizophrenia", Biol. Psychiatry, 33, 236 - 246.

Bornstein, R.A., Schwarzkopf, S.B., Olson, S.C. and Nasrallah, H.A. (1992). "Third-ventricle enlargement and neuropsychological deficit in schizophrenia", Biol. Psychiatry, 31, 954 - 961.

Breier, A., Buchanan, R.W., Elkashef, A., Munson, R.C., Kirkpatrick, B. and Gellaad, F. (1992). "Brain morphology and schizophrenia", Arch. Gen. Psychiatry, 49, 921 - 926.

Buckley, P., O'Callaghan, E., Larkin, C. and Waddington, J.L. (1992). "Schizohrenia research: the problem of controls", Biol. Psychiatry, 32, 215 - 217.

Colombo, C., Abbruzzese, M., Livian, S., Scotti, G., Locatelli, M., Bonfanti, A. and Scarone, S. (1993). "Memory functions and temporal - limbic morphology in schizophrenia", Psychiatry Res. Neuroimaging, 50, 45 - 56.

Dauphinias, I.D., DeLisi, L.E., Crow, T.J., Alexandropoulos, K., Colter, N., Tuma, I. and Gershon, E.S. (1990). "Reduction in temporal lobe size in siblings with schizophrenia", Psych. Res. Neuroimaging, 35, 137 - 147.

DeMyer, M.K., Gilmor, R.L., Hendrie, H.C., DeMyer, W.E., Augustyn, G.T. and Jackson, R.K. (1988). "Magnetic resonance brain images in schizophrenia and normal subjects: influence of diagnosis and education", Schizophr. Bull, 14, 21 - 32

Di Michele, V., Rossi, A., Stratta, P., Schiazza, G., Bolino, F., Giordano, L. and Casacchia, M. (1992). "Neuropsychological and clinical correlates of temporal lobe anatomy in schizophrenia", Acta Psychiatr. Scand, 85, 484 - 488.

Gur, R.E., Mozley, P.D., Resnick, S.M., Shtasel, D., Kohn, M., Zimmerman, R., Herman, G., Atlas, S., Grossman, R., Erwin, R. and Gur, R.C. (1991). "Magnetic resonance imaging in schizophrenia", Arch. Gen. Psychiatry, 48, 407 - 412.

Harvey, I., Ron, M.A., Du Boulay, G., Wicks, D., Lewis, S.W. and Murray, R.M. (1993). "Reduction of cortical volume in schizophrenia on magnetic resonance imaging", Psychol. Med., 23, 591 - 604.

Jernigan, T.L., Zisook, S., Heaton, R.K., Moranville, J.T., Hesselink, J.R. and Braff, D.L. (1991). "Magnetic resonance imaging abnormalities in lenticular nuclei and cerebral cortex in schizophrenia", Arch. Gen. Psychiatry, 48, 881 - 890.

Johnstone, E.C., Crow, T.J., Frith, C.D., Husband, J. and Kreel, L. (1976). "Cerebral ventricular size and cognitive impairment in chronic schizophrenia", Lancet, ii , 924 - 926.

Johnstone, E.C., Owens, D.G.C., Crow, T.J., Frith, C.D., Alexandroplis, K., Bydder, G. and Colter, N. (1989). "Temporal lobe structure as determined by nuclear magnetic resonance in schizophrenia and bipolar affective disorder", J. Neurol. Neurosurg. Psychiatry, 52, 736 - 741.

Kawasaki, Y., Maeda, Y., Urata, K., Higashima, M., Yamaguchi, N., Suzuki, M., Takashima, T. and Ide, Y. (1993). "A quantitative magnetic resonance imaging study of patients with schizophrenia", Eur. Arch. Psychiatry Clin. Neurosci, 242, 268 - 272.

Kelsoe, J., Cadet, J.L., Pickar, D. and Weinberger, D.R. (1988). "Quantitative neuroanatomy in schizophrenia", Arch. Gen. Psychiatry, 45, 533 - 541.

Lewis, S.W. (1990). "Computerized tomography in schizophrenia 15 years on",Br. J. Psychiatry, Supplement 9, 16 - 24.

Raine, A., Lencz, T., Reynolds, G.P., Harrison, G., Sheard, C., Medley, I., Reynolds, L.M. and Cooper, J.E. (1992). "Evaluation of structural and functional prefrontal deficits in schizophrenia", Psychiatry Res. Neuroimaging, 45, 123 - 137.

Rossi, A., Stratta, P., D'Albenzio, L., Tartaro, A., Schiazza, G., Di Michele, V., Bolino, F. and Casacchia, M. (1990) "Reduced temporal lobe areas in schizopohrenia",Biol. Psychiatry, 27, 61 - 68.

Shenton, M.E., Kikinis, R., Jolesz, F.A., Pollak, S.D., LeMay, M., Wible, C.G., Hokama, H., Martin, J., Metcalf, D., Coleman, M. and McCarley, R.W. (1992). "Abnormalities of the left temporal lobe and thought disorder in schizophrenia", N. Engl. J. Med., 327, 604 - 612.

Smith, G.N. and Iacano, W.G. (1986). "Lateral ventricular size in schizophrenia and choice of control group", Lancet, I, 1450.

Smith, R.C., Baumgartner, R. and Calderon, M. (1987). "Magnetic resonance imaging studies of the brains of schizophrenic patients", Pyschiatry Res, 20, 33 - 46

Suddath, R.L., Casanova, M.F., Goldberg, T.E., Daniel, D.G., Kelsoe, J.R. and Weinberger, D.R. (1989). "Temporal lobe pathology in schizophrenia: a quantitative magnetic resonance imaging study", Am. J. of Psychiatry, 146, 464 - 472.

Suddath, R.L., Christison, G.W., Torrey, E.F., Casanova, M.F. and Weinberger, D.R. (1990). "Anatomical abnormalities in the brains of monozygotic twins discordant for schizophrenia", N. Engl. J. Med., 322, 789 - 794.

Woods, T.B., Douglass, A. and Gescuk, B. (1990). "Is the VBR still a useful measure of changes in the cerebral ventricles?", Psychiatry Res. Neuroimaging, 40, 1 - 10.

Young, A.H., Blackwood, D.H.R., Roxborough, H., McQueen, J.K., Martin, M.J. and Kean, D. (1991). "A magnetic resonance imaging study of schizophrenia", Br. J. Psychiatry, 158, 158 - 164.

Zipursky, R.B., Lim, K.O., Sullivan, E.V., Byron, B.W. and Pfefferbaum, A. (1992). "Widespread cerebral grey matter volume deficits in schizophrenia", Arch. Gen. Psychiatry, 49, 195 - 205.

8

NEW THERAPEUTIC ADVANCES IN SCHIZOPHRENIA

Stephen M. Stahl

INTRODUCTION

Treatments for schizophrenia are advancing from research using two synergistic approaches: (1) fortuitous clinical observations, as well as (2) improvements in our understanding of the neurobiological basis of schizophrenia. These approaches are currently accelerating the pace at which new therapeutic agents for schizophrenia are being developed. Here we will review a wide range of research efforts to find new drug therapies. We will trace the entire therapeutic pipeline, starting with those new medications already spilling into clinical practice, and proceeding back through the drug development maze to new drugs in late clinical trials in schizophrenia, to those in early human trials, to those in preclinical research and finally to those only conceptualized but not yet discovered. Those remaining to be discovered will undoubtedly be based upon recent advances in our understanding of the neurobiological basis of schizophrenia. Some of these key ideas will therefore also be discussed.

These various approaches to drug development in schizophrenia are outlined in Figure 1. Much of the information available for drugs not yet marketed comes from unpublished trials, unpublished abstracts, and the results of multicenter trials still in progress or still in the process of data and statistical analysis. Often, negative results from studies of clinical efficacy are never published, and positive results not published until multicenter trials are completed, and

Schizophrenia: Exploring the Spectrum of Psychosis. Edited by R. Ancill. © 1994
John Wiley & Sons Ltd

marketing approval granted many years after initiation of clinical trials in schizophrenic patients. Literature will be quoted when available, and information from studies in progress or not yet published will be included whenever available, although the nature of the latter information is necessarily less complete and less well documented. It may nevertheless be useful to include information from studies in progress to update the reader on the current state of the art rather than relying only on published clinical trials which often follow many years after the ideas upon which they are based were conceptualized. Here we emphasize current concepts now generating both the discovery of new agents and the contemporary testing of them in schizophrenic patients.

Figure 1. Current Approaches to Drug Discovery in Schizophrenia

---

Targeting dopamine and serotonin receptor subtypes selectively (see Figure 2)

Targeting other novel receptor sites:
Peptide receptors
G proteins

Neuroprotection, exitotoxicity and the glutamate system:
NMDA sites
Glycine sites
Sigma sites
Ion channel sites
Glutamate receptor subtypes
Free radical scavengers (lazaroids)

Molecular appproaches to drug discovery

Neurodevelopmental approaches to drug dicovery

VARIATIONS ON THE THEME OF SELECTIVELY TARGETING DOPAMINE AND SEROTONIN RECEPTOR SUBTYPES

Atypical Neuroleptics

The traditional (i.e., typical) antipsychotic/neuroleptic drugs were first observed (serendipitously) to have clinical efficacy in schizophrenic patients, and then their action of blocking dopamine receptors was discovered (Meltzer and Stahl, 1976). Research into the pharmacology of dopamine receptors has discovered that dopamine receptors in the nigrostriatal dopamine pathway mediate the extrapyramidal side effects of neuroleptics, but that the dopamine receptors in the mesolimbic dopamine pathway are more likely to mediate the antipsychotic therapeutic actions of neuroleptics (Stahl and Wets, 1987). Drug discovery efforts have sought to produce agents which were more selective for mesolimbic dopamine receptors than for nigrostriatal dopamine receptors, in order theoretically to generate an improved side effect profile. Hints that this might be a useful approach are already available from clinical observations of certain neuroleptics already used in clinical practice. Notably, thioridazine and sulpiride, for example, seem to have less propensity to produce extrapyramidal side effects, while still showing good antipsychotic properties when compared to "typical" neuroleptic agents such as thorazine or haloperidol. Thus, the term "atypical" was coined and first applied to the concept of typical efficacy with atypical side effects (see Figure 2).

A series of benzamide compounds structurally related to sulpiride have been synthesized and have been found to exhibit the desired "atypical profile" of preference for mesolimbic over nigrostriatal dopamine receptors in animal models. Several of these have been tested in schizophrenia patients, and the first of these to come into clinical practice is remoxipride (Roxiam), which was introduced in Europe and Canada in the past few years and has been awaiting FDA approval following extensive clinical testing in the United States (Chouinard, 1990). Unfortunately, reports of aplastic anemia have thrown a cloud of doubt over the safety of this compound (Ayd, 1994). It therefore may never reach the US market, and there is the threat of its being withdrawn from worldwide markets. A related compound, raclopride, is more potent than remoxipride, has been a useful tool in PET scan studies (Farde et al., 1992), and may eventually enter the market as an atypical neuroleptic upon completion of clinical testing now in progress.

Other atypical neuroleptics, with promising profiles in animal models, are melperone, amperozide and zotepine. Clinical testing of these particular compounds is either incomplete or suspended, in some cases because of inconclusive data from clinical trials, and in other cases because of the greater perceived promise of other approaches listed below. These latter drugs are thus unlikely to be marketed, at least in the US, according to current projections.

Clozapine was recognized for its atypical properties soon after its introduction into clinical practice in Europe. Clozapine is thus an atypical neuroleptic in the sense that it has few if any extrapyramidal side effects, while being an effective antipsychotic. However, it is also unusual in another key manner, namely that it can be more effective than typical neuroleptics, especially in patients who have failed to respond adequately to other neuroleptics (Kane et al., 1988). Some investigators have expanded the concept of "atypical" to being that of enhanced efficacy as well as diminished side effects compared to typical neuroleptics, and as exemplified uniquely by clozapine. This has spawned a race for a clozapine - like compound, but which would not have clozapine's dangerous bone marrow toxicity (agranulocytosis). In order to do this, pharmacologists have been attempting to define what it is about clozapine's biochemical mechanism of action which makes it "clozapine-like" and different from other neuroleptics. Apparently, site-selective action on mesolimbic versus nigrostriatal dopamine receptors is not sufficient to explain this since "atypical" neuroleptics such as the benzamides discussed above may have an improved side effect profile, but there is no evidence to suggest that they have the special efficacy properties of clozapine (Meltzer, 1993).

Serotonin-Dopamine Antagonists

Following the classical pattern of therapeutic discoveries in schizophrenia, the special efficacy of clozapine was first observed clinically, and now scientists are trying to work out the neurobiological basis for clozapine's unique therapeutic actions. The leading hypotheses for this involve a variety of unique aspects of dopamine and serotonin pharmacology which have been attributed to clozapine and which are therefore candidates for mediating clozapine's unique clinical actions (Meltzer, 1993; Lindenmayer, 1993). The most prominent among these, is the theory that simultaneous blockade of dopamine 2 receptors and serotonin 2 receptors accounts for the unique properties of clozapine. This possibility has already led to a plethora of related drugs now known as SDAs (serotonin dopamine antagonists). These are outlined in Table 2 and include risperidone (Risperdone), olanzepine, sertindole, CP88-059, seroquel, RWJ 37796, HP398, among others.

Figure 2. Variation on the Theme of Selectively Targeting Dopamine and Serotonin Receptor Subtypes

Atypical neuroleptics	Serotonin-dopamine antagonists (SDAs)
Clozapine (Clozaril)	Clozapine (Clozaril)
Remoxipride (Roxiam)	Risperidone (Risperdone)
Raclopride	Olanzepine
Sulpiride (Dogmatil)	Sertindole
Amisulpride	Seroquel
Thioridazine (Mellaril)	CP89059
Amonapride	HP398
Melperone	RWJ37796
Zotepine	Org 5222
	Amperozide
	Savoxepine
	SM9018
	Fluperlapine
Dopamine 4 antagonists	Dopamine 1 antagonists
Clozapine (Clozaril)	Clozapine (Clozaril)
Some SDAs	SCH23390
	SCH39166
Dopamine partial agonists	Dopamine autoreceptor selective
Terguride	agonists
Roxindole	3-PPP
BHT920	UH301
SDZ HDC 912	
Serotonin 3 antagonists	Silent serotonin 1a antagonists
Clozapine (Clozaril)	WAY 100135
Ondansetron	
GR68755C	
MDL 73147EF	
MDL 72222	
Tropisetron	
Granisetron	
Combined serotonin 1A partial agonists/dopamine 2 antagonists	Serotonin 1c antagonists clozapine (Clozaril)

The individual members within the SDA series differ from one another in the relative amounts of dopamine 2 versus serotonin 2 receptors they block at a given dose. The drugs in this class also differ from one another in the amount to which they block additional receptors such as alpha adrenergic, muscarinic and histaminic receptors. Generally, these latter receptors are considered to be responsible for various side effects rather than for therapeutic effects. Clozapine is a powerful blocker of all these receptors as well, but the SDA hypothesis considers these actions of clozapine to be irrelevant to its desired properties. The SDAs hope to deliver the special efficacy of clozapine without the undesired bone marrow toxicity.

One of the possibilities of how SDAs may mediate the special properties of clozapine is that there may be less blockade of dopamine 2 receptors required for therapeutic action in schizophrenia when serotonin 2 receptors are blocked simultaneously. PET scanning techniques (using labeled raclopride to bind dopamine 2 sites or N-methyl-spiperone to label dopamine 2 sites in the caudate and serotonin 2 sites in the cortex) are beginning to clarify how much blockade of dopamine 2 and serotonin 2 receptors is optimal (Farde et al, 1992).

That is, approximately 70 - 90 % of dopamine 2 receptors are blocked at therapeutic doses of typical neuroleptics, but only 30 - 60 % of dopamine 2 receptors are blocked at therapeutic doses of clozapine. PET scanning studies are in progress now for some of the new SDAs in clinical trials, also attempting to explore how much serotonin 2 receptor blockade is occurring simultaneously with dopamine 2 receptor blockade. Thus, 85 - 90% of serotonin 2 receptors are blocked by a dose of clozapine which simultaneously blocks only 20% of dopamine 2 receptors. On the other hand, essentially no serotonin receptors are blocked by an antipsychotic dose of haloperidol which blocks more than 80% of dopamine 2 receptors. Evidently, the atypical neuroleptic thioridazine also blocks a high percentage of serotonin 2 receptors as it simultaneously blocks a high percentage of dopamine 2 receptors.

Early studies with the novel recently marketed SDA risperidone suggest that an antipsychotic dose blocks approximately 50% of serotonin 2 receptors and, simultaneously, 50% of dopamine 2 receptors. The ability to study blockade of dopamine 2 receptors and serotonin 2 receptors in vivo with PET scanning techniques in schizophrenic patients is helping to clarify what is the optimal profile for an SDA in terms of relative receptor blockade which is desired. One thing that appears evident from clinical trials so far is that some degree of dopamine 2 antagonism is desired since the pure serotonin 2 antagonist ritanserin, which does not block dopamine 2 receptors at all, appears to have little efficacy in positive symptoms of schizophrenia, although it may reduce negative symptoms, and not induce extrapyramidal side effects.

Many clinical trials are now in progress for the SDAs, but it is too early to tell how advantageous the SDAs will be compared to clozapine. Currently, it is proven that the first drug in this class, risperidone, has clinical efficacy comparable to haloperidol in schizophrenia (Chouinard et al, 1993). There are indications of an improved side effect profile, but this is not as well established as its efficacy. Also, risperidone has not yet been demonstrated to be superior to typical neuroleptics in efficacy, nor comparable to clozapine in refractory cases. Such studies are in progress as this compound now enters marketing in various countries including the United States. Several other SDAs are now demonstrating clinical efficacy superior to placebo and comparable to typical neuroleptics such as haloperidol, but are not yet marketed.

It is generally only after marketing that the truly unique properties of new therapeutic agents for schizophrenia are identified. The possibility that SDAs are clozapine-like is beginning to be investigated, as are other aspects of the SDAs which hope to differentiate themselves more clearly from the typical neuroleptics and perhaps in ways not yet recognized from clozapine.

Dopamine 4 Antagonists

Receptor subtyping for dopamine receptors is proceeding at a fast pace as molecular biology is identifying unique genes for multiple subtypes. At least four pharmacological and molecular subtypes (each with multiple possible additional molecular isoforms) have now been classified (Van Tol et al., 1991; Seeman, 1992). Mapping the properties of clozapine across these receptor subtypes, it appears to be a more powerful antagonist of D4 receptors than the typical neuroleptics (Meltzer, 1993). Interestingly, many of the SDAs also have powerful antagonist properties at D4 receptors. The hunt is now on for drugs which are selective antagonists for D4 receptors and no other receptor, to see if such agents would have special advantages in schizophrenia. No published data yet exist on selective D4 antagonists, including no clinical research studies.

Dopamine 1 Antagonists

Clozapine also blocks D1 receptors, and queries have been posed whether a selective D1 antagonist, which has no actions at any other receptor, would be a useful treatment in schizophrenia. The prototype agent is SCH23390, but it has poor bioavailability, and has not progressed in clinical development. It has been used as a preclinical pharmacological tool, and a prototype for other agents in earlier development. No widespread clinical testing of selective D1 antagonists in schizophrenia has been published.

Dopamine Partial Agonists

An interesting new concept in pharmacology is that of dopamine partial agonists. These compounds mimic the naturally occurring neurotransmitter dopamine, which is a full agonist; however, the partial agonists generate only a portion of the response that the full agonist dopamine generates (thus the designation *partial* agonist). Partial agonists can exist for any neurotransmitter, and have the interesting property of being either an agonist, or an antagonist, depending upon the amount of naturally occurring full agonist which is present. Thus, a dopamine partial agonist would be a net agonist in the absence of dopamine (such as may exist in dorsolateral prefrontal cortex and relate to the negative symptoms of schizophrenia) and simultaneously would be a net antagonist when dopamine is in excess (such as postulated for the mesolimbic dopamine pathway and relating to the positive symptoms of schizophrenia). Also, where normal dopamine activity may exist (such as in nigrostriatal neurons), a partial agonist may not generate extrapyramidal side effects as easily as would the full antagonist typical neuroleptics. Although several dopamine partial agonists are in preclinical research, relatively little is yet known about their potential clinical activity in schizophrenia.

Dopamine Autoreceptor Selective Agonists

The presynaptic autoreceptor of the dopamine neuron is responsible for detecting the amount of synaptic dopamine, and turning off release of further dopamine from the presynaptic neuron when activity becomes excessive. Dopamine itself and most known dopamine agonists are not able to distinguish between the presynaptic autoreceptor and the postsynaptic receptor. Therefore, when dopamine or dopamine agonists turn off the presynaptic neuron, this is ultimately self-defeating since they simultaneously directly stimulate the post-synaptic receptors.

One possible therapeutic intervention for reducing theoretically excessive dopamine activity is to synthesize an agonist which detects the presynaptic autoreceptor but not postsynaptic dopamine receptors, having the net pharmacological effect of turning off dopamine release and reducing net dopamine activity. One such compound is 3-PPP, which seems to act as an autoreceptor agonist in animal models. Little is yet known about the promise of this approach from published results in clinical trials.

Serotonin 3 Antagonists

Blockade of serotonin 3 receptors can counter the activity of excessive dopamine in some preclinical models. This has led to the proposal that a novel way of diminishing theoretically increased dopamine activity in schizophrenia would be to block serotonin 3 receptors. Preliminary results, largely unpublished, from clinical trials, however, have been disappointing so far.

Silent Serotonin 1A Antagonists

Most serotonin 1A antagonists are really weak partial agonists, and this complicates the interpretation of their pharmacological action at pre- and postsynaptic serotonin 1A receptors. WAY 100135 is a prototype of a true (sometimes called silent) serotonin 1A antagonist which has no degree of partial agonist property whatsoever. Serotonin 1A receptors are increased in autopsy studies of cortex from postmortem schizophrenic patients' brains. Perhaps reducing the serotonin 1A receptor activity by true silent antagonists would be therapeutic. No direct testing of this hypothesis has yet been completed in schizophrenic patients.

Combined Serotonin 1A Partial Agonists/Dopamine 2 Antagonists

Preclinical data have shown that serotonin 1A partial agonists can reduce some of the extrapyramidal side effects of typical dopamine 2 receptor blocking neuroleptic agents. This has led to the proposal that combination of these two properties in the same molecule would give an enhanced side effect profile. Although preclinical studies of two agents given simultaneously have been published, no known clinical studies have been published on any such combinations of compounds administered to patients.

Serotonin 1C Antagonists

Clozapine is, among its many other unique pharmacological properties mentioned above, also a serotonin 1C antagonist (Meltzer, 1993). Also, administration of the serotonin 1C agonist mCPP can cause worsening of schizophrenic symptoms in schizophrenic patients (Kahn et al, 1993). Thus, blocking this receptor may not only reduce symptoms in schizophrenia, but possibly also replicate the special properties of clozapine. No serotonin 1C antagonists have been tested yet in schizophrenic patients.

TARGETING OTHER NOVEL RECEPTOR SITES

Peptide Receptors

Certain peptide neuromodulators are known to be co-transmitters in the same neurons which utilize dopamine. Thus, it is possible that dopamine neuronal activity might be modified by actions on receptors for companion neurotransmitters. The most prominent of these are cholecystokinin (CCK) and neurotensin. Although experimental antagonists for CCK A and CCK B receptors have been identified, little is yet known about any potential therapeutic actions of these compounds in schizophrenia. Neurotensin receptor agonists and antagonists have not yet been identified for clinical trials.

G Proteins

Many receptors, including dopamine receptors, are linked to the production of second messengers through a protein called a G protein. G proteins link many neurotransmitter and hormone receptors to the stimulation and inhibition of second messenger synthesis, including both cyclic AMP and phosphatidyl inositol (PI). It is not yet well explored whether G proteins differ from neurotransmitter system to neurotransmitter system, or whether drugs could be specifically targeted to the G proteins in the dopamine system. However, this possibility is being aggressively pursued with the synthesis of various agents capable of blocking G proteins in different systems. No such agents are yet available for testing in schizophrenia as of this date.

NEUROPROTECTION, EXCITOTOXICITY AND THE GLUTAMATE SYSTEM

Another approach to novel therapeutics in schizophrenia is to target the glutamate system, which might mediate progressive neurodegeneration in schizophrenia by an excitotoxic mechanism. Antagonists of this putative neurodegenerative process can act at a number of receptor sites around the

NMDA (n-methyl-D-aspartate) type of glutamate receptor, including modulatory glycine sites. Such antagonists are being developed and will soon begin testing in schizophrenia. This therapeutic approach follows clinical observations that schizophrenia is not a static disorder, but in many cases a progressive disorder, suggesting an active and ongoing neurobiological process underlying the disorder in such patients.

Excitotoxicity is a major current hypothesis for a neuropathological process capable of mediating such a neurodegenerative course of disease. The idea is that the normal process of excitatory neurotransmission runs amok, and instead of normal excitatory neurotransmission, things get out of hand, and the neuron is literally excited to death. This may actually be a normal function of the cell at those times when it needs to revise its synapses, and prune out connections which become no longer necessary. If this excitotoxic mechanism is turned on inappropriately, or runs out of control, then it is possible that important and necessary synapses or even entire neurons could be wiped out by this process, killing neurons by a neurodegenerative process.

The therapeutic idea is to stop any such activity which is inappropriate or excessive and thereby halt the progressive neurodegenerative course of some patients with schizophrenia. The excitotoxic mechanism is thought to begin with a pathological process which triggers excessive glutamate activity, then causes excessive opening of the calcium channel, with poisoning of the cell by this excessive calcium, resulting in the production of free radicals which overwhelm the cell with toxic actions on its membrane and organelles, ultimately killing it.

The subtype of glutamate receptor which is thought to mediate neurodegenerative excitotoxic actions is the NMDA subtype. There exist various theoretical mechanisms to block this receptor, and numerous drugs which act on these multiple mechanisms have been discovered, tested in preclinical models, and are beginning to advance into clinical trials. For example, the NMDA site can itself be blocked by competitive antagonists. It can also be blocked by noncompetitive antagonists which act at various allosteric sites around the NMDA receptor and its associated calcium channel. Notably, this includes ion channel antagonist sites, which is where phencyclidine is thought to exert its psychotomimetic actions and where dissociative anesthetics are also thought to work. Another site is the glycine modulatory site: glycine enhances glutamate activity and blocking the ability of glycine to do this would have a net antagonist action on the NMDA site, and possibly on the neurodegenerative process hypothesized to be occurring in schizophrenia.

Free radicals are generated in this neurodegenerative process, and some drugs exist which are free radical scavengers and soak up these toxic free radicals like a chemical sponge. A weak scavenger which has been tested in Parkinson's disease and tardive dyskinesia is vitamin E. A more powerful set of agents, currently available for clinical testing only in intravenous dosage formulations, are the lazaroids (so named because of their putative Lazarus-like actions of raising degenerating neurons from the dead). Other modulatory sites are also being identified at this site, and numerous pharmacological agents are being synthesized which target such sites. There is intense research interest in this approach, since neurodegenerative excitotoxicity is thought possibly to underlie many diseases in addition to schizophrenia, including stroke, Alzheimer's dementia, Huntington's disease, Parkinson's disease, amyotrophic lateral sclerosis, and others. This approach holds promise for schizophrenia and other neurodegenerative disorders, but no data yet exist with testing of such compounds in schizophrenia.

It is possible that the effect of psychosis itself is damaging to the brain and that such damage of neurons during the psychotic process could be mediated by excitotoxicity. Psychosis seems to beget psychosis and a course of uncontrolled psychosis leads to a poorer prognosis than does a course of illness where the number and duration of active psychotic episodes and symptoms are reduced. These conclusions are based upon data from studies showing that patients who are ill for less time before treatment with standard neuroleptics are begun are more likely to respond more rapidly than those with longer duration of symptoms before treatment. These results suggest that the active phase of psychosis reflects a morbid process that, if allowed to persist, can impair the patient's ability to respond to treatment when finally instituted. In a similar manner, data suggest that over subsequent episodes of illness the time it takes patients to reach the same level of remission increases.

A receptor related to the NMDA receptor is the sigma receptor, originally classified as one of the opiate receptors, which may mediate pychotomimetic actions of opiates and other drugs such as phencyclidine. Antagonists of sigma sites have some theoretical appeal for schizophrenia, and preliminary results have included testing of tiospirone and BMY14802. It is too early to tell whether this approach will yield an effective therapeutic approach to schizophrenia.

MOLECULAR APPROACHES TO DRUG DISCOVERY

Another approach to therapeutics is predicated upon the genetics of schizophrenia. Scientists are trying to identify abnormal genes in schizophrenia, and the consequences which such abnormal genes have on molecular regulation in neurons of schizophrenic patients. If a degenerative process is "turned on" genetically at the beginning of the course of the illness, perhaps it could be "turned off" pharmacologically to prevent further progression. It will not be possible to make a specific therapeutic agent until this abnormal process is discovered and clarified, so there are no specific therapeutic agents which have yet been identified. However, various therapeutic approaches, such as the antisense knockout strategies, are being developed in order to block the expression of the gene or genes once they are discovered.

A related molecular approach is to identify the genes activated by known antipsychotics, rather than those genes associated with the disease itself. It might be possible to mimic the action of clozapine or other antipsychotic drugs on the genome with drugs acting by new mechanisms compared to the usual neuroleptic agents. Progress is being made on the genetic mechanisms activated by antipsychotic agents, but no novel drugs have yet been identified utilizing this approach.

Another genetic approach is based upon the hypothesis that there is not only an abnormal gene (or set of genes) in schizophrenia, but also some additional mechanism for "turning them on". That is, in subjects with identical copies of the exact complement of genes (i.e. monozygotic twins) only about half of them get the disease schizophrenia, and the other half is apparently without the disease despite having the same postulated defective gene(s). A question which has long puzzled schizophrenia genetic researchers is what makes one twin get schizophrenia and the other not? A related issue is that in the general population, perhaps twice as many people have the genetic risk for schizophrenia as the number who actually develop the disease.

This has led to theories to explain why some individuals with the abnormal genes get the disease and others do not. One possibility is that developmental influences or stressful life events somehow activate the schizophrenia gene, and thus initiate the disease. Theoretically, those without such activating influences would not get the disease despite harboring the abnormal gene. A related idea is that some additional biochemical event must occur in order for the schizophrenia disease to be activated, be that a virus, an intrauterine problem, an environmental toxin or something else.

Gaining an understanding of the manner in which the onset of the schizophrenic disease process might be prevented in those at risk for it due to having an abnormal gene will require identification not only of an abnormal gene or genes; it will also require identification of the various behavioral and biochemical processes which regulate such genes, and cause them to be expressed, causing disease, or lie dormant, causing no disease. Perhaps once the regulation of this process is understood, it would be possible not only to prevent the activation of the genetically mediated disease, but also to turn it back off in the subject who is currently manifesting the symptoms of schizophrenia. Developing therapies using this approach are only in the conceptualization stage, and no specific treatments are yet available for testing in patients.

NEURODEVELOPMENTAL APPROACHES TO DRUG DISCOVERY

Studies of neuronal functioning, from neuroimaging studies and tests of cognitive functioning of schizophrenic patients, suggest that schizophrenia may not actually start when the psychotic symptoms arise. The disease process may actually be the result of abnormal development of the brain from the beginning of life, when neurons fail to migrate to the correct parts of the brain, fail to form appropriate connections, and then are subject to breakdown when used by the individual in late adolescence and early adulthood. If the abnormal disease process is essentially a developmental problem, which is completed very early in brain development, and then the die is cast, with no further disease process in action, then it may be very difficult indeed to modify such a situation. On the other hand, it is difficult to conceive that a process which would be completed early in life would be entirely asymptomatic until the disease process begins, and that the downhill course and waxing and waning symptomatology of schizophrenia would be due to an entirely static pathophysiological mechanism in the brain. It may well prove that any neurodevelopmental difficulties caused in early development may be difficult to reverse directly in an adult. However, there may be rational means to compensate for these difficulties by other mechanisms, and to interrupt any ongoing mechanism still present in the symptomatic patient. Therefore, it is critical to learn what possible neurodevelopmental abnormalities exist in schizophrenia and which are present long before the disease symptoms announce themselves in order to learn how to reduce the impact of these in the ultimately symptomatic patient. It may eventually be possible to reawaken neuronal plasticity selectively for therapeutic applications even in the symptomatic adult by using appropriate genetic therapies capable of instructing the genes of the neuron. Such interventions may also stop any ongoing process, and if reversed, may actually have the theoretical capability of repairing the brain and the developmental damage. These are bold and unsubstantiated theoretical extrapolations based upon the most optimistic therapeutic possibilities which current molecular and neurodevelopmental approaches suggest. Although therapeutic applications may take many years to discover and test, the vision of such therapies is an encouraging possibility to render hope to our patients with schizophrenia today.

REFERENCES

Ayd, F.J. (1994). "Aplastic anemia associated with remoxipride", Int. Drug Ther. Newsletter, 29, 3.

Chouinard, G., Jones, B., Remington, G., et al. (1993). "A Canadian multicenter placebo - controlled study of fixed doses of risperidone and haloperidol in the treatment of chronic schizophrenic patients", J. Clin. Pharmacol., 13, 25 - 40.

Chouinard, G. (1990). "A placebo-controlled clinical trial of remoxipride and chlorpromazine in newly admitted schizophrenic patients with acute exacerbation", Acta Psychiatr. Scand., 82 (suppl). 111 - 119.

Farde, L., Nordstrom, A.L., Wiesel, F-A., et al. (1992). "Positron emission tomagraphic analysis of central dopamine receptor occupancy in patients treated with classical neuroleptics and clozapine: relationship to extrapyramidal side effects", Arch. Gen. Psychiatry, 49, 538 - 544.

Kahn, R.S., Siever, L., Davidson, M., et al. (1993). "Haloperidol and clozapine treatment and their effect on M-chlorophenyl-piperazine mediated responses in schizophrenia: implications for the mechanism of action of clozapine", Psychopharmacology, 112, S90 - S94.

Kane, J., Honigfeld, G., Singer, J., et al. (1988). "Clozapine for the treatment-resistant schizophrenic: a double-blind comparison with chlorpromazine", Arch. Gen. Psychiatry, 45, 789 - 796.

Lindenmayer, J.P. (1993). "Recent advances in pharmacotherapy of schizophrenia", Psychiatr. Ann., 23, 201 - 208.

Meltzer, H.Y. (1993). "Serotonin dopamine interactions and atypical antipsychotic drugs", Psychiatr. Ann., 23, 193 - 200.

Meltzer, H.Y. and Stahl, S.M. (1976). "The dopamine hypothesis of schizophrenia: a review", Schizophr. Bull, 2(1), 19 - 76.

Seeman, P. (1992). "Dopamine receptor sequences: therapeutic levels of neuroleptics occupy D_2 receptors, clozapine occupies D_4", Neuropsychopharmacology,. 7, 261 - 284.

Stahl, S.M. and Wets, K. (1987). "Indoleamines and schizophrenia". In: Handbook of Schizophrenia Vol. # 2: Neurochemistry and Neuropharmacology of Schizophrenia, (eds F.A. Henn and L.E. DeLisi), Elsevier Science Publishers, Amsterdam, pp. 257-296.

Van Tol, H.H.M., Bunzow, J.R., Guan, H.C., et al. (1991). "Cloning of the gene for a human dopamine D_4 receptor with affinity for the antipsychotic clozapine", Nature, 350, 610 - 614.

9

AN EXAMINATION OF THE COMPLEXITIES IN THE MEASUREMENT OF RECOVERY IN SEVERE PSYCHIATRIC DISORDERS

Courtenay M. Harding

Results from five recent investigations studying the very long-term"outcome" of schizophrenia (in Switzerland, Germany, and the United States) indicate that no matter how chronic the cohorts were, approximately 25% of the subjects achieved recovery at follow-up, with an additional 25 - 40% improved, with achievement of wide heterogeneity as the rule rather than the exception (Bleuler, 1972; Ciompi and Moller, 1976; Harding et al., 1987b, Huber et al., 1979; Tsuang et al., 1979). In fact, these studies and other shorter ones (Bland and Orn, 1980; Gardos et al., 1982; Hawk et al., 1975, Strauss and Carpenter, 1974; Strauss et al., 1978; WHO, 1979) have shown that the course of severe psychiatric disorder is a complex, dynamic, and heterogeneous process, which is non-linear in its patterns moving toward significant improvement over time and helped along by an active, developing person in interaction with his or her environment (Harding and Strauss, 1985).

Our new appreciation about this process evokes many questions. For instance, just what is meant by the use of the word "recovery"? Is the subject simply no longer symptomatic? Is she or he considered to be "recovered" or just "in remission"? Has the person re-found (or recovered) all his or her initial levels of functioning which were lost during a psychotic episode or do we mean that he or she is functioning more soundly and stronger than ever before? Against which

Schizophrenia: Exploring the Spectrum of Psychosis. Edited by R. Ancill. © 1994
John Wiley & Sons Ltd

baseline do we make such judgments? Is a new episode after "recovery" considered to be a new illness? What do we mean when we discuss "outcome"?

After the completion of two three-decade studies of the long-distance course of schizophrenia, the author examines some of these questions which arise in the measurement of recovery from severe psychiatric disorder. She suggests that constructs such as "outcome" and "end state" often lead to inaccurate conclusions about disorders. In contrast to cross-sectional measures, longitudinal assessments are portrayed as essential to an accurate understanding of prolonged illness.

To cope with these challenges, puzzled investigators have employed four primary strategies to determine the amount of recovery and improvement. The strategies comprise the following: (1) measurement against each subject's own baseline, (2) employment of grouped means, (3) comparison across studies, and (4) assessment against a construct of "normal" behavior. This chapter will discuss these strategies and present additional suggestions proposed by the Vermont and Maine Longitudinal Research Project teams as we attempted to undertake this prodigious task ourselves. We have organized our thinking along five major themes and propose that: (1) the concept of outcome is a research artifact, (2) "two cross-sectionals do not a longitudinal make", (3) global measures of psychopathology and recovery are not sufficient, (4) double standards are often employed in assessments, and (5) a rater's epistemological framework about illness, recovery, and human beings plays an important role in measurement in that "what you are trained to ask about and observe, strongly determines what you ask about and observe". The author concludes with the suggestion that these factors do indeed color the judgment of which patients are considered to be recovered and which are not.

AN OVERVIEW OF THE VERMONT AND MAINE LONGITUDINAL STUDIES OF SEVERE PSYCHIATRIC DISORDER

In the Vermont Project, 269 Vermont State Hospital patients with severe and persistent psychiatric disorders (especially with schizophrenia) were originally selected for very chronic disability, rehabilitated in a model demonstration program, and released to the community in the mid-1950s (Chittick et al., 1961). At the time of entry into this project in the 1950's, these subjects had an average of six years of continuous psychiatric hospitalization and sixteen years of disability. A five to ten-year follow-up study in the 1960s revealed that two thirds of the subjects were in the community maintained by considerable investment of time, money, and effort (Deane and Brooks, 1967).

Twenty to twenty-five years after their entry into this program, 97% of this group were located and assessed. The catamnestic period averaged 32 years. Two field interviews were conducted by raters blind to record information. The first interview provided a multivariate cross-sectional assessment of outcome. The second interview included a Meyerian/Leighton Life Chart (Leighton and Leighton, 1949; Meyer, 1919) and contributed a longitudinal documentation of patterns, shifts, and trends in the course of life for members of the cohort. These patterns were derived from a multidimensional year-by-year documentation of the 20 to 25-year period. Close relatives and others, who knew the subjects well, were interviewed to verify current status and historical data for both the live and deceased subjects. New and traditional scales were used to provide structured measures of outcome. Hospital and Vocational Rehabilitation records were independently reviewed with the Hospital Record Review Form battery (HRRF), compiled from a modification of WHO's Psychiatric and Personal History form (WHO, 1979) and Strauss's Case Record Rating Scale (Strauss and Harder, 1981). The record raters were blind to outcome and field data. All batteries were subjected to inter-rater trials and inter-item concordance testing (Harding et al., 1987a; 1987b).

In order to make our subjects comparable to today's patients we then, applied the DSM-III criteria (APA, 1980) to their index status with records that were stripped of all previous diagnostic assignments (Harding et al., 1987b). John Strauss at Yale and Alan Breier at NIMH completed the rediagnostic work after two sets of inter-rater trials. Analysis of the long-term outcome for those subjects, who once qualified for DSM-III schizophrenia, revealed wide heterogeneity. For one-half to two-thirds of the group, course was neither downward nor marginal. This finding was remarkable because these patients represented those in the "bottom third" of the schizophrenia spectrum and the back wards in the hospital. Most people resided in the community, were able to care for themselves, had become actively involved with family and friends, and made productive contributions to their families and communities with little or no residual display of symptomatology (Harding et al., 1987b). These findings mirrored those derived for the full cohort, which included patients with a wide variety of other DSM-III diagnoses (Harding et al., 1987a). Thus, the more stringent criteria of DSM-III were not associated with uniformly poor outcome as expected (APA, 1980). The definition of recovery included the following factors measured at follow-up: no signs or symptoms of psychiatric disorder, no psychotropic medications, working or retired appropriately after a work history (especially important because the average age at follow-up was 61 ranging up to 79 years of age), maintaining mutually satisfying interdependent relationships, the absence of behavioral or contextual indicators that they were former mental patients, and integration into the community as full-fledged citizens. We agreed with Vaillant's conclusion after his ten-year study, that "diagnosis and prognosis should be treated as two different dimensions of psychosis" (Vaillant, 1975).

The Vermonters received a ten-year pioneering and comprehensive psychosocial and vocational rehabilitation program. We were unable to determine if the program had made an impact upon the outcome findings because all the patients, who were in the back wards of the state's only state hospital, were selected with the exception of those on legal mandates, developmental disabilities, or over 62 years of age. However, Augusta State Hospital in Maine was another New England hospital with a similar catchment area and hospital which did not give a rehabilitation program to its patients. We achieved a comparison sample, person by person computer-matched to the Vermont cohort members on age, sex, diagnosis, and length of hospitalization during the window of 1956-61. The Maine cohort was then followed with the same protocol, the same diagnostic criteria, and instrument batteries with both intra- and inter-project reliabilities established as well as blindness in the data collection. Ninety-four per cent of the Mainers were assessed at an average of 36 catamnestic years. This event was the first time in longitudinal research that two such long-term studies had matched samples, protocols, diagnostic criteria, and historical periods (DeSisto et al., submitted, a).

The Mainers did significantly less well than did the Vermonters both in the quantity and quality of recovery, especially in areas of work, symptoms, global outcome (even covarying out other significant modifiers (e.g. acute onset, education, urban/rural settings). Longitudinal year by year patterns also showed more positive and independent trajectories for Vermonters. We concluded that rehabilitation and the opportunity to be out of the hospital joined with biological correction mechanisms to potentiate a return to the highest level of function possible for each person (DeSisto et al., submitted, b).

THE MEASUREMENT OF RECOVERY

Outcome is a Research Artifact

The Vermont and Maine Projects are considered to be studies about the long-term outcome of schizophrenia. They represent some of the longest studies in the world literature, with catamneses of 22 to 62 years after first admission as well as projects with the most stringent methodology. Other studies have looked at 5, 10, 20, and 25 years post admission and each of those projects is also called an outcome study. I propose that each one of those studies is a research artifact;

that one investigator's "outcome" level is another investigator's "course". For example, those projects which have completed a 10-year follow-up consider a 5-year marker as part of the course; a 20-year follow-up considers both the 10-year and the 5-year points in time as part of the course of the 20 years (Harding and Strauss, 1985). The Vermont marker at 62 years has been superseded by Luc Ciompi's study at 64 years (Ciompi, 1980), ad infinitum, to its own logical conclusion. Therefore, we suggest that instead of assessing outcome we are actually studying markers in the course of life (Harding and Strauss, 1985) in which illness is only a part.

The largest misnomer to date is the so-called "end state", used by Manfred Bleuler (1978) and other Europeans to describe plateau states of five years in which subjects have achieved a certain level of recovery and a stabilized period. Use of the words "end state" gives the incorrect impression that a person will stay at that state and that it is the final state. In fact, Bleuler (1978) did not intend to imply such a finality (pp. 190 - 192). Bleuler, himself, said that there were sometimes late improvements after as many as 30 to 40 years of illness (Bleuler, 1978, pp. 228 - 233). In reality, the words usually denote an end state for the research project itself. Although an investigator's device, the phenomenon might be re-labeled and described from a different vantage point. The knowledge of plateaus and late improvements might be valuable contributions to the biopsychosocial understanding of the course of schizophrenia and should have a new name.

"Two Cross-Sectionals Do Not a Longitudinal Make"

Many investigations start by achieving a baseline measurement on all subjects, and then a number of years later secure another cross-sectional measurement at that point in time - or vice versa. These studies have been labeled longitudinal, and we have suggested that "two cross-sectionals do not a longitudinal make" (Harding and Strauss, 1985, p. 3421). By way of analogy, a cross-sectional could be likened to a black-and-white portrait. The observer can tell gender, approximate age, something about the surrounding background, but is unable to determine whether the wrinkles around the forehead and the eyes come from a lot of laughter or many frowns. Raters are unable to tell whether that background is a usual one or not; nor are they able to tell how the subject got to that spot where he or she is today. In the cross-sectional part of the interviews with both the Vermont and Maine cohorts, we were aware of the fact that the month we happened to interview people was purely arbitrary. We knew that we had found some people who were having a good month when they ordinarily did not, but we realized that the opposite was also true, and hoped they balanced out.

However, a longitudinal can be a follow-along or a follow-back through a block of time year after year with many measures across many domains. Because human life is very difficult to capture in all its dynamic ebbs and flows, and since it is a longitudinal process, a year-by-year accounting comes much closer to reality. Continuing the earlier analogy, this strategy would be more akin to watching a theater-in-the-round in which one can gain perspective from looking at the same person from different angles over time with characters interacting and changing. Given this distinct bias, I would venture an opinion that few judgments can be made about degrees of recovery or lack of it unless there is a longitudinal documentation of course.

Ways to Assess a Heterogeneous Process

Early investigators, such as E. Bleuler (1950), Holt and Holt (1952), Stephens (1970) and others, used global and often undefined terms of "recovered or "not recovered". Other researchers divided recovery into symptom recovery and social recovery, quite often loosely defined but at least a step in the right direction (e.g., Harris et al., 1956; Holmbe and Astrup, 1957; Lo and Lo, 1977; Rennie, 1939). The question remains, "How do we define and measure recovery?"

The Vermont and Maine Projects chose to triangulate data by using measures of functioning, such as the Global Assessment Scale (GAS) by Endicott et al. (1976); Levels of Function Scale (LOF), by Strauss and Carpenter (LOF) by Hawk, Carpenter and Strauss, (1975); the Brief Psychiatric Rating Scale (BPRS) by Overall and Gorham (1962), as well as 12 other classic scales rating twenty-one domains (Harding et al., 1987a). From the cumulative data acquired over three hours of field interviews with the probands themselves, we subsequently also rated them for adjustment - another guise for "recovery". The Community Adjustment Scale (CAS) was designed by Consalvo et al. (l981) to measure adjustment based on scores for productivity, intimacy, and behavior (see Figure 1 below).

The findings from this scale were significantly related to those generated by the GAS and Level of Function Scale in a chi-square analysis (p= <.001 [CAS vs. GAS] and p= <.004 [CAS vs LOF]). A little over one quarter (29%) of the Vermont cohort were rated as functioning well across all domains. Recovery is not difficult to determine or defend with that group. A group of about 36% of the Vermonters, whose functioning across all domains was very poor, also was not difficult to define as "not recovered".

However, there were 35% in Vermont who were in between those two extremes. They presented serious problems for the rater. There were people who still had positive signs of schizophrenia (e.g., hallucinations, and/or delusions) but who were quite functional people. They retained mild impairment, but no disability. They worked, had families, friends, were generally satisfied with life, and had

Figure 1. Community Adjustment Scale (CAS)* (Consalvo et al., 1981)

1. Criteria

1. Degree of productivity based on work (housework, volunteer, avocation), or retired and functioning at a level appropriate to age and health. Rate on a one to five scale.

2. Degree of intimacy achieved, based on the nature of interpersonal relationships (e.g., marriage, friendship, kinship), and the possession of interpersonal skills. Rate on a one to five scale.

3. The relative absence of behavioral (e.g., bizarre speech, actions, appearance), or contextual (e.g., living in a boarding home), indications that they are former mental patients. Rate on a one to five scale.

2. Ratings for overall adjustment: Use total points from above three criteria.

1. Well adjusted. Individuals in this group exhibit a moderate to high level of adjustment in all three areas and would be described as without any indications of being a former mental patient. Total range 12 - 15 points.

2. Well adjusted but... Individuals in this group ordinarily have a moderate to high level of adjustment in all areas but one, or a marginally moderate level of adjustment in at least two of the three criteria categories. Such individuals would give no clear indication that they were ever former mental patients but their overall level of adjustment would not rule out that possibility. Total range 8 - 11 points.

3. Maladjusted. These individuals display poor adjustment in at least two criteria areas and could at least be viewed as probable former mental patients. Total point range 3- 7 points.

---

* It should be noted that this scale was completed after a comprehensive structured interview across 21 areas of functioning and psychological status.

learned to control their symptoms. Would they be labeled recovered? We said they are significantly improved and rated them 'Well, but..." There was another group which was quite sociable, maintained supportive interpersonal relationships, had hobbies, and was quite happy, but did not work. They told us of the disincentives in the entitlement systems and its environmental impact on their lives. Another group worked well, but was composed of self-described "loners" with no family and no friends with whom to interact. Is this group improved? Many raters would hastily say "No, not even improved." Let us suppose that some of those so-called loners have always been loners and preferred their own company to others? Was their behavior prodromal and now considered to be residual? Or, are there not substantial numbers of people, both outside of or working for the mental health system who live alone. They are quite happily functioning at work and caring for themselves and who do not maintain relationships? Are we not asserting our own conceptions about "normal" behavior?

STRATEGIES TO DETERMINE CURRENT STATUS

Strategy #1: Assessment of Abnormality Against Societal Norms

What then is the range of normal human functioning? Hogarty and Katz (1971) produced some work in the early 1970s assessing 450 non-patients in one Maryland county to acquire norms for their instruments. They discovered that patterns of behavior for age, marital status, social class, and gender must be taken into consideration when making judgments (e.g., normal adolescents were reported to show negativism, general psychopathology, and less stability). They asked: "Is it valid to point in absoluteness to the belligerence, negativism, and poor performance of juvenile offenders and otherwise 'disturbed adolescents' when corresponding norms of age-related behavior are so characterized?" (Hogarty and Katz, 1971, p.479). It is a very important question.

As another example, the difference in gender functioning has only recently become appreciated. Holstein and Harding (1992) have assessed the data for women only from the Yale Longitudinal Study in which we were following people intensively for the first two years after episode (Strauss et al., 1985). We found that those women who were rated as more symptomatic were often those who carried dual work roles and were quite functional in caring for home and family, as well as working. These dual roles, their stressors, and the level of function required, were complexities not accounted for in the primary analysis. We found that, while women's experience is now perceived as different from men's, this phenomenon is rarely investigated systematically or written into research protocols (Holstein and Harding, 1992). Some exceptions to the rule are the investigations by M. Bleuler (1978), Gilligan (1982), Seeman (1985), and Test and Berlin (1983).

Strategy #2: Comparison Across Similar Studies

The five studies cited earlier in the chapter possess the same goals but use different diagnostic systems for determining schizophrenia, varying lengths of follow-up and methodology, among other factors, which make comparison between them difficult. They give a strong indication of the trend toward recovery only when all five are clumped together because, despite their differences, the similarity of their findings is remarkable (see Table 1). One-half to two-thirds of nearly 1200 patients followed over two to three decades significantly improved or recovered. The reason that the Vermont/Maine comparison is so important is the fact that these are the only two studies in the very long-term literature of schizophrenia and other serious mental illness which were matched in sample, catchment area, treatment eras, diagnostic criteria, design, and methodology (DeSisto et al., submitted, a, submitted, b).

Table 1. Five Recent Long-Term Studies of Schizophrenia

Investigators	Sample size	Average length In years	% Subjects recovered and/or improved significantly
M. Bleuler (1972), Burghölzli - Zurich	208	23	(53 - 66)
Huber et al. (1979), Bonn Studies	502	22	57
Ciompi and Müller (1976), Lausanne investigations	289	37	53
Tsuang et al. (1979), Iowa 500	189	35	46
Harding et al. (1987), Vermont	118	32	62 - 68

Strategy #3: Subgroup Analysis Within the Same Study

A third technique has been to clump life course markers as grouped means within certain subgroup categories (e.g., type of onset, severity, degree of chronicity, diagnosis, age of onset, demographics, etc.). We discovered that with a seemingly simple sub-grouping such as dividing the cohort into age brackets and correlating these groups with outcome measures, we found no significant relationships. The between-subject heterogeneity in other time-related variables (such as age at admission and duration of time since first admission) washed out the effects of presumed homogeneous subgroupings (Harding et al., 1987c). As an experiment, we then chose every subject with a 42-year course. Wide heterogeneity appeared. The age range for those subjects went from 57 to 84. When we subtracted the 42 years course from each person's age, we ranged from age 15 to age 42 as their ages at first admission. These differences should reflect diverse prognostic indicators. This problem of heterogeneity underlying key measures points to the need for an analysis in which the association of age with outcome is assessed by partialing out the effects of age at first admission and thus length of course (Harding, et al., 1987c). In pursuing this strategy, we discovered that the oldest subjects who had the shortest course (20 - 29 years) achieved the best Global Assessment Scale (Endicott, et al, 1986) scores at outcome. In addition to the importance of these methodologic questions for interpreting results, it should be pointed out that the relevant developmental issues confronting people at various ages of onset have not begun even to be characterized (Harding et al. 1987c). We have wondered if we finally achieve some sense of true homogeneous subgroups, whether our cell sizes will become too small to provide meaningful analyses at all?

Strategy #4: The Individual as His or her Own Control

Should a person be measured against his own baseline? Such a strategy might be a good idea, but engenders the following problems. First, the investigators should know the subjects across the period under scrutiny. In the Vermont Project, we were fortunate that the five clinicians of the original project team were able to maintain contact across 32 years with many members of the cohort and are in a good position to say, for example, that: "Barbara has come a long way. She was once withdrawn and apathetic and now, after several years of improvements and regressions, she consistently goes out once a week in the company of friends through her own initiative." M. Bleuler (1978) is also in a position to make such judgments.

In addition, we came to appreciate that a person's baseline keeps changing as he or she proceeds through developmental tasks. Looking for a return to premorbid status may not be as valid an indicator of recovery as we think it is. Who wants to be judged by their 18-year-old status when they are emerging from an illness at age 35? Further, adult development appears to proceed across domains of function in a fashion close to Piaget's notion of "horizontal decalage" (see Ginsberg and Opper, 1979). (We have re-interpreted his term to describe such natural adult behaviors as the use of *dialectical thinking* in a discussion on ethics; *formal operations* when dealing with the bank; *concreteness* when cooking lunch; and being *pre-operational* when dealing with statistics [all in the same hour]. Are not the varying degrees of functioning within the same person further evidence for Strauss and Carpenter's idea of open-linked systems (Strauss and Carpenter, 1974)? Therefore, given all the underlying complexities, if we measure people against their own baselines, we would probably have 269 single case studies and lose our funding.

THE EFFECT OF THE RATER'S EPISTEMOLOGY

Underlying all efforts is the pervasive problem of recovery measured against the theoretical constructs evolved by the current state of the art and individually interpreted by the investigator. The epistemological framework would define whether recovery meant cured, in remission, or a retreat to underlying vulnerability (such as suggested by Zubin and Spring, 1977). To be cured would mean that a new episode would be considered a new illness. Some cultures believe in this idea very strongly, even about schizophrenia. For example, Waxler (1979) described the Sri Lankan viewpoint as a contributor to a better recovery rate due to the resulting higher expectation of functioning and the lightening of the psychological burden of on-going illness from the patient and his family.

We note that being "in remission" carries with it a heavy impending time bomb effect. Robert Cancro (1982) once commented that women are not considered to be latently pregnant. Further, he suggested that theoretical frameworks made you decide whether a Kansan who moved to Missouri could now be considered a Missourian, or if the person was *born* in Kansas, was he or she a Kansan no matter where he or she went or how long he or she lived elsewhere? Although Cancro was referring to the genetics of schizophrenia, we might refocus the discussion and pose the question, "How long is remission before recovery can be claimed?

We suggest replacing the outlook, which views a person as having a lifetime of illness with intervals of remission included, with the view of a person with a life course of work and relationships, developmental lags and spurts with episodes of illness included. When considering a subject as having a "life", we then must focus on the person behind the disorder (Bleuler, 1978) and not on the illness itself. Paul Lieberman (1984) at Dartmouth has suggested. The same patient is never the same person at each admission". There seems to be a person x illness x environment interaction which continues to reshape the on-going process (Harding and Strauss, 1985; Strauss, et al. 1985).

DOUBLE STANDARDS IN JUDGING RECOVERY

Participation in case conferences and review of instrument batteries has led us to wonder if we, as clinicians and investigators, tend to have a double set of standards in judging how well someone is functioning? We all seem to have a certain but nebulous sense of what is "normal". I wonder if our standard for patients is not "super normal" (e.g., as in Maslow's (1954) self-actualized persons, few and famous? For example, the top rating for the Global Assessment Scale (91-100) uses the following criteria: "No symptoms, superior functioning in a wide range of activities, life's problems never seem to get out of hand, and is sought out by others because of his warmth and integrity" (Endicott et al., 1976).

Quite possibly we secretly harbor the idea that maybe everyone else we know is happier, handles things better, does not worry about the mortgage coming due, spreading waistlines, gray hair, or falling on one's face during an important presentation. When we do discover that other people worry too, get depressed, stumble and fall, only to laugh again, it is a celebration and quite often the glue that binds a friendship. For ourselves and our friends we may tend to accept the sets of idiosyncrasies and horizontal decalage because we know where we have come from and the direction in which we are going with a thorough-going appreciation of underlying continuities. Do these understandings permeate clinicians' judgments and investigators' ratings often, or do patients have to perform twice as well to be considered half as good?

SUMMARY

In summary, this chapter examined some of the complexities surrounding the measurement of recovery from severe psychiatric disorder. Investigators must be careful in employing the words "outcome" or "end state" because they end up being interpreted by clinicians and clients alike as a real phenomenon. It has been suggested that we substitute outcome with the phrase "markers of course" or simply "at this point in the life course." Longitudinal documentation comes closer to recapturing course of life than do two cross-sectional assessments.

Questions about the measurement and meaning of recovery can best be answered by assessment of multiple domains across long periods of time. The problems in declaring recovery begin with the realization that human beings develop differentially across domains of functioning and across time. Four strategies for assessment have been discussed: 1) a person might be measured against his or her own baseline; 2) the employment of grouped means within sub-samples; 3) the possibility of comparison of groups across studies; and 4) measurement against some construct of normal behavior or outcome. The advantages and disadvantages of each approach were presented.

A philosophical look at the impact of epistemology upon one's view of recovery as cure, remission, or underlying vulnerability was discussed as well as a postulated double standard employed by clinicians for rating recovery in patients versus rating functioning in friends. We joke about the fact that no one we know as colleagues, including ourselves, could meet the GAS score of 91 to 100, yet we persisted in using this scale and others as earnest assessments of subjects. It should be noted that the Global Assessment of Functioning (GAF) which recently replaced the GAS has dropped the 91-100 rating (APA, 1987, pp 12 and 20).

In conclusion, I would venture to say that to designate someone as recovered from severe psychiatric disorder is a judgment call as challenging as the decision made about when to call behavior an illness. It is trying to pin down a constantly moving target. In addition, the process encompasses cultural expectations, the state of the art, and the personality of the investigator, all of which influence the theoretical framework in which he or she constructs and selects the questions for the assessment, the manner in which they are asked, and how the data are analyzed.

ACKNOWLEDGEMENTS

This chapter is a revision of an article which appeared in the Psychiatric Journal of the University of Ottawa, 11 (4),1986 and is reproduced by permission of Yvon La Pierre, M.D., Chairman, and the Journal Management Committee, Department of Psychiatry at the University of Ottawa. The article was first a banquet presentation for G.W.A.N. (The International Psychiatric Research Society), given on November 23, 1985, in Toronto, Ontario. This effort was also supported in part by NIMH Grants R 01 MH29575 and R 01 MH40607. The ideas contained in this chapter have been sifted from hundreds of conversations across the last 15 years within the Vermont and Maine Project Teams as well as with friends and colleagues ... anyone who would sit still long enough to discuss the issues.

REFERENCES

American Psychiatric Assn. (1980). Diagnostic and Statistical Manual, 111, APA Press, Washington, DC.

American Psychiatric Assn. (1987). Diagnostic and Statistical Manual, III-R, APA Press, Washington, DC.

Bland, R.C. and Orn, H. (1980). "Schizophrenia: Schneider's first-rank symptoms and outcome", Br. J. Psychiatry, 137, 63 - 68.

Bleuler, E. (1950). Dementia Praecox or the Group of Schizophrenias (translated by J. Zinkin), International Universities Press, New York.

Bleuler, M. (1978). Die schizophrenen Geistesst6rungen im Lichte Kranken - und Familiengeschiten. George Thieme Verlag, Stuttgart (1972) (Translated by S.M. Clemens, The Schizophrenic Disorders, Long-term Patient and Family Studies, Yale University Press, New Haven.

Cancro, R. (1982). "The role of genetic factors in the etiology of schizophrenic disorders", The Schizophrenic Disorders. Part 11 of the Annual Review, 135th annual meeting, American Psychiatric Association.

Chiftick, R.A., Brooks, G.W., Irons, F.S. and Deane, W.N. (1961). The Vermont Story, Queen City Printers, Burlington, VT.

Ciompi, L. (1980). "Catamnestic long-term study on the course of life and aging in schizophrenia", Schizophr. Bull., 6(4), 592 - 605.

Ciompi, L. and Moller, C. (1976). Lebensweg und Alter Schizophrenen. Eine katamnestic Lonzeitstudies bis ins senum, Springer - Veriag, Berlin.

Consalvo, C.M., Harding, C.M., Landerl, P.D. and Mikkelsen, J., (1981). The Community Assessment Scale (CAS), Waterbury, VT.

Deane, W.N., Brooks, G.W. (1967). Five-year follow-up of chronic hospitalized patients, Report from Vermont State Hospital, Waterbury, VT.

DeSisto, M., Harding, C.M., Ashikaga, T., McCormick, R. and Brooks, G.W. (submitted, a). "The Maine - Vermont Project: a matched cohort comparison of long-term outcome 1. Methodology, study samples, design, overall 36-year outcome for the Maine cohort."

DeSisto, M., Harding, C.M., Ashikaga, T., McCormick, R. and Brooks, G.W.(submitted, b) "The Maine - Vermont Project: a matched cohort comparison of long-term outcome II. Cross-sectional outcome for both cohorts".

Endicott, J., Spitzer, R.L., Fleiss, J.L. and Cohen, R. (1976). "The Global Assessment Scale: a procedure for measuring overall severity of psychiatric disturbance", Arch. Gen. Psychiatry, 33, 766 - 771.

Gardos, G., Cole, J.O. and LaBrie, R.A. (1982). "A 12-year follow-up study of chronic schizophrenics", Hosp. Community Psychiatry, 33(12), 983 - 984.

Gilligan, C. (1982). In a Different Voice: Psychological Theory and Women's Development, Harvard University Press, Cambridge, MA.

Ginsberg, H. and Opper, S. (1979). Piaget's Theory of Intellectual Development,2nd edn, Prentice - Hall, EnglewoodCliffs, pp. 152,109,159.

Harding, C.M. and Strauss, J.S. (1985). "The course of schizophrenia: an evolving concept". In Controversies in Schizophrenia: Changes and Constancies (ed. M. Alpert), Guilford Press, New York, pp. 339 - 353.

Harding, C.M., Brooks, G.W., Ashikaga, T., Strauss, J.S. and Breier, A. (1987a). "The Vermont longitudinal study of persons with severe mental illness: 1. Methodology, study sample, and overall status 32 years later", Am. J. Psychiatry, 144(6), 718 - 726.

Harding, C.M., Brooks, G.W., Ashikaga, T., Strauss, J.S., Breier, A. (1987b). "The Vermont longitudinal study: II. Long-term outcome of subjects who retrospectively met the criteria for DSM-111 schizophrenia", Am. J. Psychiatry, 144(6), 727 - 735.

Harding, C.M., Brooks, G.W., Ashikaga, T., Strauss, J.S. and Landerl. P.D. "Aging and social functioning in once-chronic schizophrenic patients 22 - 62 years after first admission: The Vermont Story". In Schizophrenia, Paranoia and Schizophreniform Disorders in Later Life (eds N. Miller and G.D. Cohen), Guilford Press, New York, pp. 160 - 166.

Harris, A., Linker, I., Norris, V. and Shepherd, M. (1956). "Schizophrenia: a prognostic and social study", Br. J. Prev.Soc. Med., 10, 107.

Hawk, A.B., Carpenter, W.T. and Strauss, J.S. (1975). "Diagnostic criteria and 5-year outcome in schizophrenia: a report from the International Pilot Study of Schizophrenia", Arch. Gen. Psychiatrv, 32, 343 - 347.

Hogarty, G.E. and Katz, M.M. (1971). "Norms of adjustment and social behavior", Arch. Gen. Psychiatry, 25(11), 470 - 480.

Holmbe, R. and Astrup, A. (1957). "A follow-up study of 255 patients with acute schizophrenia and schizophreniform psychosis", Acta Psychiatr. Scand, Suppl. 115.

Holstein, A.R. and Harding, C.M. (1992). "Omissions in assessment of work roles: implications for evaluating social functioning and mental health", J. Orthopsychiatry, 62(3), 469 - 474.

Holt, W.L., Jr and Holt, W.M. (1952). "Long-term prognosis in mental illness: a thirty-year follow-up of 141 mental patients", Am. J. Psychiatry, 108, 735 - 739.

Huber, G., Gross, G. and SchOttler, R. (1979). Schizophrenie: Verlaufs und sozialpsychiatrische Lanqzeitundersuchungen an den 1945 bis 1959 in Bonn Hospitalisierten schizophrenen Kranken. Monographien aus dem Gesamtgebiete der Psychiatrie. Bd. 21., Springer - Verlag, Berlin.

Leighton, A.H. and Leighton, D.P. (1949). "Gregorio, the handtrembler: a psychobiological personality study of a Navaho Indian", Peabody Museum Papers, Harvard University Press, Cambridge, MA.

Lieberman, P. (1984). Personal Communication.

Lo, W.H. and Lo, T. (1977). "A ten-year follow-up study of Chinese schizophrenics in Hong Kong", Br. J. Psychiatry, 131, 63 - 66.

Maslow, A. (1954). Motivation and Personality. Harper & Row, New York.

Meyer, A. (1919). "The life chart", In Contributions to Medical and Biological Research. Paul B. Hoeber, New York.

Overall, J.E. and Gorham, D.R. (1962). Brief Psychiatric Rating Scale (BPRS). Psychol. Rep., 10, 799 - 812.

Rennie, T.A.C. (1939). "Follow-up study of five hundred patients with schizophrenia admitted to the hospital", Arch. Neurol. Psychiatry, 42(5), 877 - 891.

Seeman, M.V. (1985). "Sex and schizophrenia", Can. J. Psychiatry, 30(8), 313 - 315.

Stephens, J.H. (1970). "Long-term course and prognosis in schizophrenia", Semin. Psychiatry, 2(4), 464 - 485.

Strauss, J.S. and Carpenter, W.T. (1974). "Prediction of outcome in schizophrenia. II. Relationships between predictor and outcome variables", Arch. Gen. Psychiatry, 31, 37 - 42.

Strauss, J.S. and Harder, D.W. (1981). "The case record rating scale: a method for rating symptom and social function data from case records", Psychiatry Res, 4, 333 - 345.

Strauss, J.S., Kokes, R.F., Ritzler, B., Harder, D.W. and VanOrd, A. (1978). "Patterns of disorder in first admission psychiatric patients", J. Nerv. Ment. Dis., 166(9), 611 - 625.

Strauss, J.S., Hafez, H., Lieberman, P. and Harding, C.M. (1985). "The course of psychiatric disorder: longitudinal principles", Am. J. Psychiatry, 142(3), 289 - 296.

Test, M.A. and Berlin, S.B. (1981). "Issues of special concern to chronically mentally ill women", Professional Psychol., 12(1), 136 - 145.

Tsuang, M.T., Woolson, R.F. and Fleming, J.A. (1979). "Long-term outcome of major psychoses. 1. Schizophrenia and affective disorders compared with psychiatrically symptom-free surgical conditions", Arch. Gen. Psychiatry, 36, 1295 - 131.

Vaillant, G.E. (1975). Paper presented at the 128th annual meeting of the American Psychiatric Association, Anaheim, CA.

Waxler, N. (1979). "Is outcome for schizophrenia better in non-industrial societies? The case of Sri Lanka", J. Nerv. Ment. Dis., 67, 144 - 158.

World Health Organization (1973). The International Pilot Study of Schizophrenia, WHO Press, Geneva.

World Health Organization (1979). Schizophrenia: An International Follow-up Study, Wiley, Chichester.

Zubin, J. and Spring, B. (1977). "Vulnerability: a new view of schizophrenia", J. Abnorm. Psychology, 86, 103 - 126.

10

DEPOT NEUROLEPTICS

Gary J. Remington and Martha E. Adams

The clinical introduction of chlorpromazine in the early 1950s represented a turning point in the treatment of schizophrenia, and in 1955 the term "neuroleptic" was coined to identify this new class of medications characterized by their antipsychotic efficacy. Efforts to develop new agents have been continuous since, to the point where there are now approximately 50 neuroleptics representing 12 different chemical families (Deniker, 1990). From the earliest trials it was apparent that ongoing neuroleptic treatment was required in order to maintain symptom control, and depot neuroleptics were first introduced in the 1960s as a practical alternative to oral neuroleptics for the long-term management of schizophrenia. The present chapter reviews depot neuroleptics and the role they now play in the pharmacotherapy of schizophrenia.

RATIONALE FOR USE

Advantages

Compliance

Neuroleptic therapy represents the cornerstone of treatment programs for schizophrenia. For example, reported relapse rates at one year in first-episode schizophrenic patients treated with placebo versus neuroleptic were 41% and 0%, respectively (Kane et al., 1982). Similarly, Rabiner and coworkers (1986) noted that 95.7% of patients with a first-episode psychosis who relapsed at one year were not on medications. Unfortunately, compliance is a major problem in this population and estimates of noncompliance range from 15 - 35% in inpatients to 20 - 65% in outpatients (Curry, 1985). Noncompliance itself is a complex process involving a number of factors such as symptomatology, stage and duration of illness, and side effects (Coorigan et al., 1990; Van Putten, 1974). It is held that depot neuroleptic therapy improves compliance, and in doing so decreases relapse rates; however, acceptance of depot neuroleptic therapy does not guarantee compliance. It has been reported that approximately one-third of patients fail to become established on depot neuroleptics following discharge (Falloon et al., 1978; Quitkin et al., 1978), and in a seven-year follow-up study of schizophrenics originally designated as good compliers with depot treatment 40% had compliance problems (Curson et al., 1985). Two surveys have reported noncompliance or refusal over a twoyear period to be 10-15% (Johnson and Freeman, 1973; Johnson and Wright, 1990).

A review comparing depot and oral neuroleptic therapy (Davis and Andriukaitis, 1986) documented six controlled studies (Crawford and Forrest, 1974; del Giudice et al., 1975; Falloon et al., 1978; Hogarty et al., 1979; Rifkin et al., 1977; Schooler et al., 1979), with the percentage of patients relapsing on oral versus depot ranging from minus 16% to 48% and three of the six studies reporting a difference of at least 20% (Crawford and Forrest 1974; del Giudice et al., 1975; Hogarty et al., 1979). Taken together, it would appear that relapse rates decrease approximately 15% on depot versus oral therapy (Glazer and Kane, 1992). The advantages of depot versus oral neuroleptic treatment, particularly in unstable and poorly remitted patients, are readily apparent within the first year (Conley and Johnson, 1991; Johnson, 1991).

Noncompliance versus Treatment Resistance

Relapse may be related to noncompliance, which is a well-recognized problem in the management of schizophrenia, rather than treatment resistance. Having the opportunity to accurately document noncompliance can, therefore, prove useful in making such a distinction.

Clinical Administration

Depending on the specific agent, depot neuroleptics are routinely administered from once weekly to once monthly. For the patient this offers a convenience when compared to the requirement of daily administration with oral agents, as well as a less frequent reminder of his or her illness. Administration of depots in the context of medication clinics can provide regular patient contact and a focus around which social programs can be implemented, while at the same time streamlining services with the potential of cost savings. Finally, depot neuroleptics avoid the risk of abuse or overdose that can occur with oral medications.

Bioavailability

Oral neuroleptics can be converted to inactive metabolites by nonspecific enzymes in the gut wall, and they are rapidly metabolized through the liver's first-pass effect (Bames, 1991). Conversely, depot neuroleptics bypass oral absorption variability, gut wall metabolism, and first-pass extraction (Jann et al., 1985). First-pass metabolism, in particular, may be an important source of the interindividual variability which has been noted with oral neuroleptics (Marder et al., 1989). In patients who prove refractory to oral agents because of bioavailability difficulties, depot agents represent a useful alternative. It has been postulated, however, that such problems are rare (Van Putten et al., 1991), and that the improved efficacy of depots is more likely attributable to greater compliance (Bames, 1991).

With patients where hepatic function may be compromised, as in the case of individuals with a history of alcohol abuse, depot neuroleptics may prove a useful alternative to their oral counterparts.

Pharmacokinetics

By avoiding first-pass metabolism, depot neuroleptics minimize the impact of metabolites (Marder et al., 1989), and altering parent-to-metabolite relationship through use of depot agents could have implications in terms of both clinical efficacy and side effect profile (Ereshefsky et al., 1984a; Marder et al., 1989). For example, the active metabolite of haloperidol, reduced haloperidol, is significantly less potent and high ratios of reduced haloperidol/haloperidol have been associated with poorer antipsychotic response (Altamura et al., 1988; Ereshefsky et al., 1984b; Shostak et al., 1987).

It has been reported that depot neuroleptics are associated with lower plasma levels when compared to their oral counterparts (Ereshefsky et al., 1984a; Marder et al., 1989; Nair et al., 1986), and this would be in keeping with the recommendation that the lowest possible dose be utilized for maintenance therapy. Because depot neuroleptics produce a more gradual rise and decline in plasma levels, there is less fluctuation between minimum and maximum levels (Jann et al., 1985; Marder et al., 1989). The clinical impact of this remains to be further investigated; however, there are data, for example, noting a correlation between side effects and higher plasma levels (Casper et al., 1979; Ereshefsky et al., 1984a; Hansen et al., 1981; Marder et al., 1991; see review by Van Putten et al., 1991).

Disadvantages

Dose Titration and Steady-State Levels

As with oral neuroleptics, it is customary to start depot therapy with lower doses and to titrate upwards. Dosing schedules with these agents, e.g. once monthly, prevent the flexibility possible with oral agents, and it is therefore often necessary to augment the depot during conversion with oral supplementation. Generally, doses of the oral neuroleptic are decreased while the depot is initiated and increased, but precise guidelines for dose equivalents regarding oral to depot conversion are lacking (Marder et al., 1989; Yadalam and Simpson, 1988). The problem is complicated further when switching from one neuroleptic to another, as once again precise dose equivalents are not available. Moreover, it has been reported that patients stabilized on one neuroleptic and then switched to another are placed at a significant risk of relapse (Gardos, 1974), and many oral neuroleptics do not have a depot counterpart.

Approximately 4-5 half-lives are required to attain steady-state levels (Rowland and Tozer, 1989), during which time oral supplementation may be required. There may be considerable variability though, and it has been reported in one study involving haloperidol decanoate that in 3 of 11 patients (27%), steady-state levels were only achieved after 11 monthly injections (Wiles et al., 1990).

Because of the slow absorption rate of depot neuroleptics, as well as the slow distribution from deep compartments, i.e. injection sites, accumulation may occur and require dose reductions after several months of therapy (Jann et al., 1985).

Table 1. Comparison of Depot Neuroleptics

Neuroleptic	Fatty acid chain	Vehicle	Usual dose range (mg)*	Chemical class	Duration of action (weeks)*	Time to peak (days)	Half-life (days)
Flupenthixol	Decanaote	Viscoleo	20 - 100	Thioxanthene	3	3 - 17 Jorgensen, 1978a,b,1980; Jorgensen and Gottfries,1972; Jorgensen and Overo, 1980	8 - 17 Jorgensen and Overo, 1980
Fluphenazine	Decanaote	Sesame oil	12.5 - 100	Piperazine phenothiazine	4	1 - 2 Chang et al, 1985; Curry et al, 1979; Ereshefsky et al., 1984; Jann et al., 1985; Midha et al., 1985; Wiles and Gelder, 1979	6 - 9 Curry et al, 1979; Ereshefsky et al, 1984
Fluphenazine	Enanthate	Sesame oil	25 - 100	Piperazine phenothiazine	2	2 - 3 Ereshefsky et al., 1984; Jann et al., 1985	Ereshefsky et al, 1984
Fluspirilene	No	Aqueous solution	2 - 10	Diphenylbutyl-piperidine	1.5	Not available	Not available
Haloperidol	Decanaote	Sesame oil	5 - 300	Butyrophenone	4	3 - 10 Bersford and Ward, 1987; Deberdt et al., 1980; De Buck et al., 1981; De Cuyper et al., 1986; Gelders, 1986; Meco et al., 1990	21 Bersford and Ward, 1987; Ereshefsky et al.,1984; Reyntjens et al. 1982
Pipotiazine	Palmitate	Sesame oil	50 - 250	Piperidine phenothiazine	4	Not available	Not available

*Bezchlibnyk-Butler et al. (1994).

CHARACTERISTICS OF DEPOT NEUROLEPTICS

Formulations

In Canada there are six depot agents currently available (see Table 1). This is in keeping with Europe where approximately eight different depots are available but in sharp contrast to the United States which has only three available (Marder et al., 1986). These differences appear reflected in depot use between regions, as will be discussed later.

Other agents in depot form include clopenthixol decanoate (Carney, 1984; Carney and Rutherford, 1981), perphenazine enanthate and decanoate (Baruch et al., 1989; Knudsen et al., 1985b, 1985c, 1985d, 1985e; Rapp et al., 1986), pipotiazine undecylenate (Ahlfors, 1973; Brown-Thomsen, 1973; Simpson, 1984), oxyprothepine decanoate (Balon, 1994; Ceskova et al., 1993), and bromperidol decanoate (Levi Minzi and Laviani, 1992).

Pharmacokinetics

As a rule, depot neuroleptics are synthesized by esterification of their hydroxyl group to form a long-chain fatty acid (Ereshefsky et al., 1984a; Jann et al., 1985)(see Figure 1). An exception to this is fluspirilene, which is formulated as an aqueous microcorystalline suspension and is immediately active upon injection without having to be hydrolyzed (Simpson, 1984).

The ester is dissolved in a vehicle, routinely sesame seed oil or vegetable oil (Viscoleo), and is injected into the muscle, and over a period of days the esterified compounds are taken up into various fat stores where slow release occurs (Ereshefsky et al., 1984a; Groves, 1979). In the bloodstream, hydrolysis by plasma esterases occurs rapidly to produce free fatty acid and unbound neuroleptic (Dreyfuss et al., 1976; Jorgensen et al., 1977; Knudsen et al., 1985a) (see Figure 1). Compared to Viscoleo, sesame oil vehicle may retard this process of hydrolysis (Dreyfuss et al., 1976; Jann et al., 1985; Jorgensen and Gottfries, 1972; Knudsen et al., 1985a).

Because of their slow release following injection, depot neuroleptics have a very slow "absorption phase": that period following administration when plasma concentrations rise to a maximum. Accordingly, the pharmacokinetic rate-limiting step for depots is the absorption rather than "elimination" phase, and this also appears to be the most significant factor in establishing steady state levels

(Ereshefsky et al., 1984a). Because rate of absorption is slower than rate of elimination, pharmacokinetics of depot neuroleptics reflect a "flip-flop" model (Ereshefsky et al., 1984a;; Jann et al., 1985; Marder et al., 1989).

A single-compartment pharmacokinetic model is not applicable to depot neuroleptics or, in fact, to other lipophilic drugs. Unbound neuroleptic can be actively or passively transported from plasma, or the "central" compartment, to "deeper" compartments such as fat or skeletal muscle, and steady state concentrations cannot be attained until equilibrium is reached between these deeper compartments and the central compartment (Ereshefsky et al., 1984a). Approximately 4-5 half-lives may be required (Rowland and Tozer, 1989), although considerable variability exists (Wiles et al., 1990).

Time to reach peak plasma concentrations is also quite variable between depot agents (Balant-Gorgia and Balant, 1987), and for fluphenazine decanoate a rapid peak within the first several days after injection has been reported (Chang et al., 1985; Curry et al., 1978, 1979; Wiles and Gelder, 1979; Wiles, 1990). It is possible that increased side effects and need for antiparkinsonian medications will occur during this period of "dumping" (Ayd, 1973; Marder et al., 1989).

The multicompartment model for depot neuroleptics makes conclusions regarding elimination difficult, as the curve is contaminated by leaching of drug from old injection sites, as well as deeper compartments, e.g., fatty tissues (Marder et al., 1989). As a result, plasma levels can often be detected for months following the cessation of treatment (Gitlin et al., 1988; Wistedt et al., 1981, 1982), and this may influence both risk of relapse and side effect profile.

The pharmacokinetic profile of individual depot agents does not seem to be significantly modified by the different concentrations available (Reyntjens et al., 1982; Stauning et al., 1979; Suy et al., 1982).

Plasma Levels

As with oral neuroleptics, plasma levels for depot agents have demonstrated considerable inter-individual, as well as intra-individual, variability (Furet et al., 1991; Nasrallah et al., 1979; Wiles and Gelder, (1979). Wiles and Gelder (1979), for example, reported a four-fold variation in plasma levels between patients receiving the same dose of fluphenazine decanoate. At the same time, depot neuroleptics circumvent the variability associated with intestinal absorption and the hepatic "first-pass" effect, and plasma levels of depot neuroleptics might therefore better correlate with clinical response (Ereshefsky et al., 1984a).

Positive correlations between dose and plasma level have been reported for a number of depot agents, including haloperidol decanoate (De Buck et al., 1981; Reyntjens et al., 1982; De Cuyper et al., 1986; Altamura et al., 1990), fluphenazine decanoate (Wiles and Gelder, 1979), perphenazine decanoate and cis (z)-flupenthixol decanoate. The relationship between plasma level and dose may also be related to the specific neuroleptic. For example, less variation has been reported for haloperidol decanoate versus fluphenazine decanoate, and it has been postulated that this may be due to the fact that metabolism of phenothiazines such as fluphenazine is more complex and involves more metabolites than with a butyrophenone such as haloperidol (McCreadie et al., 1986; Marder et al., 1989).

Correlating plasma levels with clinical response and side effect profile has proven more difficult. Both oral and depot neuroleptic studies share the same difficulties here, related to such problems as clinical measures, time of assessment, concomitant treatments, and so on. Reviewing this topic, Marder et al. (1993) have suggested that a therapeutic range or "window" exists for fluphenazine decanoate between 0.8 and 1.2 ng/ml. They argue that data are lacking for other depot neuroleptics, and while a therapeutic range has been suggested for oral haloperidol this may not apply to the depot form. More specifically, data from plasma levels for oral neuroleptics cannot be extrapolated to their depot counterparts because of differences in kinetics (Marder et al., 1993). Indeed, various reports have suggested that therapeutic efficacy can be maintained at lower plasma levels when depot neuroleptics are employed (Ereshefsky et al., 1984a; Marder et al., 1989; Nair et al., 1986). It is unclear, however, whether this finding is related to pharmacokinetic (Nair et al., 1986) or pharmacodynamic (Ereshefsky et al., 1984a) differences between the two formulations.

Figure 1. Pharmacokinetics of Depot Neuroleptics

a) Flusprillene is not esterified, but rather is formulated as an aqueous microcrystalline solution.

b) Hydrolysis of the esterified drug can also occur with esterases found in the muscle tissue.

c) Interconversion can occur between metabolites and the parent compound, e.g. reduced haloperidol and haloperidol (Korpl and Wyatt, 1984).

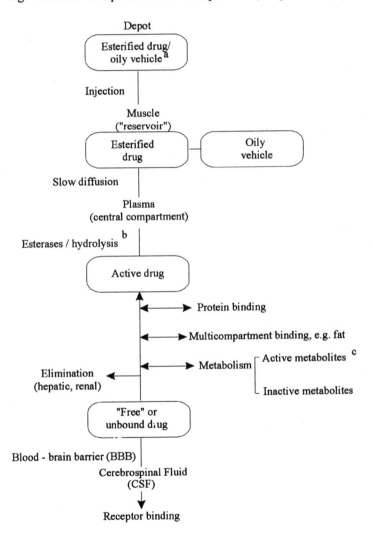

CLINICAL USE OF DEPOT NEUROLEPTICS

Depot versus Oral Treatment

As a rule neuroleptic treatment is initiated with oral agents, but may be switched to depot therapy for various reasons (see Table 2). Patients doing well on oral neuroleptics are often not given the alternative of depot medications, although they may find the latter more convenient and less stigmatizing from the standpoint of having to take medications daily (Diamond, 1983). Depots are routinely considered in patients who are noncompliant but, as noted earlier, they do not ensure compliance. However, they do permit a more accurate recording of medication use which can be useful in distinguishing between noncompliance and treatment resistance. Medicolegal cases may, in particular, benefit from such documentation. The use of depot agents has been recommended in patients who have frequent relapses, and Johnson et al., (1984) have argued that they should be routine treatment for anyone with two or more relapses. In cases where bioavailability is an issue depot neuroleptics are worthwhile considering, although once again this is not thought to be very common (Van Putten et al., 1991). Finally, in this time of decreasing dollars for health care costs, more serious consideration may need to be given to treatments which diminish relapse rates. Although well-controlled studies are lacking, the possibility also exists that organized depot clinics may provide a more economic means of long-term patient management.

Clinical Demographics

The use of depot neuroleptics has been shown to be influenced by both geographic and demographic variables. It has been estimated, for example, that in Britain and other parts of Europe approximately 40% of patients with chronic schizophrenia receive depot neuroleptics, in contrast to only 5% in the United States (Bourin et al., 1990; Simpson, 1984). Here in Canada, a review of a chronic population followed in a major teaching hospital indicated that over 50% of patients were receiving two depot neuroleptics (Remington et al., 1993). Differences in philosophies of treatment, i.e. focusing on chronic versus acute care, health care systems, and number of depot agents available may account for the discrepancy between United Sates and other countries such as Great Britain and Canada (Conley and Johnson, 1991; Remington, 1992). A substantial number of patients on depots may be followed by general practitioners, with or without psychiatric supervision (Wesby et al., 1993).

Differences exist in the type of patient receiving depot neuroteptics. In a borough of London, England, depot use has been reported to be more frequent in patients who were West Indian born, compared to those who were born in the United Kingdom (Glover and Malcolm, 1988). In a review of 397 outpatients maintained on depot treatment through one health centre, patients tended to be young, male, and black (Price et al., 1985). Depot neuroleptics also have been reported to be used more frequently with involuntary medicated patients (Coumos et al., 1991).

As noted earlier, treatment with a depot agent does not guarantee compliance. In a seven-year follow-up study of patients on depot treatment, Curson et al. (1985) found that 40% had problems with compliance during this time. Two measures of poor compliance, that is poor attendance record and receiving the injection at home rather than the clinic, were associated with more frequent relapse. Irregular attendees at a depot clinic were not noted to have increased EPS or altered health beliefs compared to those who came regularly, but they were significantly more depressed (Pan and Tantam, 1989). Johnson and Freeman (1973) reported a noncompliance rate of 18% in patients on depot therapy, with the greatest risk during the first six months. Contributing factors included more than patient refusal, such as side effects, and moves which resulted in loss of contact with medical services.

Polypharmacy, that is the ongoing use of a depot and oral antipsychotic concomitantly, remains an ongoing problem that has been associated with high neuroleptic doses (Remington et al., 1993) and poor outcome (Babiker, 1987). Increased risk of relapse has been reported in converting individuals from combined depot/oral treatment to only depot medication, but this could reflect problems with current conversion formulae and/or pharmacokinetic factors, i.e., time to reach steady state with depots. While the use of depots has been on the increase, combined depot and oral neuroleptic treatment appears to be declining (Johnson and Wright, 1990).

Table 2. Double Blind Studies Comparing Depot Neuroleptics

Reference	Comparison	Sample Size	Dose (mg)	Injection Interval	Duration	Clinical Effect	Extrapyramidal Symptoms (EPS)
Chouinard et al., 1984, 1989	HD vs FD	72	HD15 - 900 (median 225) FD 2.5 - 300 (median 75)	2-4	32	HD = FD	HD = FD
Kissling et al., 1985	HD vs FD	31	HD 82 - 68 FD 22 - 10	4 2	32	HD = FD	HD < FD
McKane et al., 1984	HD vs FD	38	HD 127 - 120 FD 106 - 105	4	60	HD < FD	HD = FD
Meco et al., 1984	HD vs FD	20	HD 50 - 150 FD 25 - 75	4	24	HD = FD	HD ≤ FD
Wistedt et al., 1984	HD vs FD	51	HD 122 (mean) FD 84 (mean)	4	20	HD > FD	HD = FD
Eberhard and Hellborn, 1986	HD vs FPD	32	HD 131 - 151 FPD 56 - 66	4	24	HD >FPD	HD =FPD
Bechelli et al., 1985	HD vs PP	41	HD 50 - 150 (mean 100) PP 50 - 125 (mean 65)	4	28	HD = PP	HD = PP
Chouinard et al., 1982	FD vs FE	50	FD 2.5 - 250 (median 25) FE 2.5 - 325 (median 50)	4 2	48	FD = FE	FD = FE
Donion et al., 1976	FD vs FE	41	FD 50 FE 50	2-3/ week	8	FD = FE	FD = FE
MacCrimmon et al., 1976	FD vs FE	39	FD 25 * 6 months FE 37.5 * 6 months same	1-6 2-6	1 year	FD = FE	FD < FE
Van Praag and Dois, 1973	FD vs FE	30	FD 25 FE 25	4	4	FD = FE	FD < FE
Chowdhany et al., 1980	FD vs FPD	26	FD 25 FPD 40	1-4	32	FD = FPD	FD = FPD
Haslam et al., 1975	FD vs FPD	24	FD 25 - 50 FPD 20 - 40	4	18	FD = FPD	FD = FPD

Study	Comparison	N	Dose range		Duration	Outcome	Outcome
Johnson and Malik, 1975	FD vs FPD	40	FD 25 / FPD 40	4	8	FD = FPD	FD = FPD
Knights et al., 1979	FD vs FPD	57	FD 25 / FPD 40	3	24	FD = FPD	FD = FPD
Wistedt and Ranta, 1983	FD vs FPD	32	FD 27 / FPD 31	3	2 years	FD = FPD	FD = FPD
Frangos et al., 1978	FD vs FLUS	50	FD 25 - 150 (mean 76) / FLUS 2 - 20 (mean 12)	2 / 1	16	FD =FLUS	FD >FLUS
Russell et al., 1982	FD vs FLUS	28	FD 25.5 - 10 / FLUS 3 - 10	2-3 / 2	24	FD =FLUS	FD =FLUS
Winter et al., 1973	FD vs FLUS	23	FD 25 / FLUS 2 - 8	3 / 1	40	FD =FLUS	Not Reported
Dencker et al., 1973	FD vs PP	67	(crossover / 12 weeks each) FD 3.1 - 50 (mean 16.8 1 - 6 months, 16.2 6 - 12 months) PP 25 - 400 (mean 131.5 1 - 6 months, 145.7 6 - 12 months)	4	1year	FD = PP	FD > PP
Lapierre et al., 1979	FD vs PP	43	FD 12.5 - 59.6 (mean) / PP 12.5 - 77.5 (mean)	4	1year	FD = PP	FD = PP
Schlosberg and Shadmi (Weber), 1976	FD vs PP	75	FD 6.25 - 37.5 (mean - 27.5) PP Same	4	15 months	FD= PP	FD= PP
Chouinard et al., 1978	FE vs PP	32	FE 6.25 - 100 / PP 12.5 - 450	2 / 4	36	FE ≥ PP	FE ≥ PP
Singh and Saxena, 1979	FE vs PP	30	FE 25-75 (mean 44.2) / PP 100-200 (mean 125)	2 / 4	44	FE ≤ PP	FE > PP
Malm et al., 1974	FE vs FLUS	62	FE7.5-50 (mean 28.51) / FLUS 1-14 (mean 5.7)	2 / 1	12	FE = FLUS	FE . FLUS
Steinert et al., 1986	FPD vs PP	39	FPD 20-40 / PP 50-100	2 / 4	1 year	FPD ≤ PP	FPD = PP

(HD: haloperidol decanoate; FD: fluphenazine decanoate; FE: fluphenazine enanthate; FLUS: flusppirilene; FPD: flupenthixol decanoate; PP: pipotiazine palmitate)

Choice of Depot Neuroleptic

Prior to the advent of 'atypical' neuroleptics such as clozapine, it has generally been agreed that the various oral neuroleptics were equal in terms of clinical efficacy (Carpenter and Keith, 1986; Kane, 1987). As there are no commercially available depot neuroleptics to date that represent this new class of atypical agents, it is generally held that depots are also equivalent with respect to clinical response. A review of double-blind studies comparing those depots commercially available in North America confirms this (see Table 2).

Table 3. Choosing a depot neuroleptic

A. Depot vs oral neuroteptic
Patient's preference
Compliance
Frequent relapses
Refractory
Bioavailability
Medicolegal
B. Choice of Specific Depot
Current neuroleptic
Previous neuroleptic response
History of side effects
Desired injection interval
Familial response
Patient's preference

Factors influencing choice of depot neuroleptic include current neuroleptic, history of previous response or side effects, patient choice, familiarity with particular agent(s), desired dosing interval, accessibility, and cost.

Administration

Many patients, at least initially, are reluctant to consider neuroleptic therapy so it is essential that the procedure be made as easy and painless as possible. It is important to respond to patients' questions and concerns, and attention to such details as needle gauge and injection site can diminish problems with the injection itself (McConnell, 1982). Self-administration may be an option and can increase the individual's sense of autonomy and control (Mound et al., 1990). Leakage can occur, particularly after intramuscular injections (Glazer et al., 1987), and various procedures, including the Z-track technique of injection, can diminish this problem as well as injection site complications (Belanger and Chouinard, 1982; Middlemiss and Beeber, 1989).

Several recent reports have suggested the higher concentration of haloperidol decancate, that is 100 mg/ml versus 5 mg/ml, have an increased risk of injection site reactions (Hamann and Wells, 1992; Hamann et al., 1990; Reinke and Wiesert, 1992). Conversely, high doses that require greater volume injections i.e., over 3 ml, have also been associated with an increased risk of indurations (McGee et al., 1983).

Dosing

Well-defined dosing guidelines are not available for depot neuroleptics, although recommendations for each have been made based on our pharmacokinetic understanding of the individual agents. Because of the"irreversibility" of depots following administration and their duration of action, a very low "test dose" is sometimes administered before routine administration is commenced (Ayd, 1975; Groves, 1979). Even if a test dose is not used, it is generally recommended that treatment begin with doses at the lower range, employing oral supplementation as required during dose titration (Johnson et al., 1984). Only more recently has the concept of "loading doses" with depot neuroleptics been raised as an alternative approach (De Cuyper et al., 1986; Ereshefsky et al., 1990).

As with oral neuroleptic therapy, dosing guidelines with the depots are also being influenced by the trend towards lower doses which has taken place in recent years (Johnson et al., 1987; Kane, 1986; Kane et al., 1985, 1986; Yadalam and Simpson, 1988). Table 1 outlines general dosing ranges, as well as other parameters, relevant to the depot neuroleptics currently available in North America.

Specific conversion formulae are available for various depot agents, based on the oral neuroleptic dose at the time of switchover, Most of the focus has been on fluphenazine decanoate and haloperidol decanoate, perhaps not so surprising since aside from fluphenazine enanthate which has largely been replaced by the decanoate formulation, these are the only depot neuroleptics commercially available in the United States. Before reviewing these formulae, several issues are worth consideration.

Many formulae are not based on pharmacokinetic data, and were developed at a time when higher neuroleptic doses were being recommended (Yadalam and Simpson, 1988). As a result, a number of more recent investigations have employed a comparative approach using a predefined "low-dose" group. Looking at fluphenazine decanoate, for example, a number of studies have indicated that with low-dose strategies, e.g. 1.25 - 10 mg every two weeks, increased relapse rates may occur when compared to standard doses e.g., 12.5-50 mg. Differences are not always significant though, and the risk may be countered by decreased side effects, particularly with respect to those that can mimic negative symptomatology, and improved measures of psychosocial functioning (Hogarty, 1984; Kane, 1986; Kane et al., 1983, 1985, 1986).

Establishing standardized conversion formulae based on pharmacokinetic data may itself be questionable, given that plasma levels for depot agents, just as with the oral neuroleptics, can be quite variable (Beresford and Ward, 1987; Jann et al., 1985; Marder et al., 1986). Yadalam and Simpson (1988) note intraindividual variation may be such that high levels associated with an oral agent do not necessarily ensure the same with a depot, making assumptions concerning conversion formulae even more difficult. There is a school of thought which simply recommends conversion to a specific dose of the depot agent, usually at its lowest dose. For example, in switching from an oral neuroleptic to pipotiazine palmitate, Ayd (1983) has first recommended a one-week drug holiday to prevent superimposing the depot on the accumulated oral neuroleptic. At that point, the pipotiazine may be initiated at the lowest possible dose, usually 25 mg, and increased accordingly.

If further medication is required during the titration phase it can be done in the form of shortened intervals between injections, or oral supplementation. Oral supplementation as routine practice should be avoided, since it can further contribute to excessively high neuroleptic doses, and may simply not be required. More specifically, it appears to take from three to seven months after drug discontinuation for relapse to occur (Kane et al., 1986).

With these caveats in mind, a number of conversion formulae will now be reviewed.

Fluphenazine decanoate

Mason and Granacher (1976) recommended the index of fluphenazine decanoate 20 mg biweekly for up to 20 mg of oral fluphenazine daily. An increase in the depot of 12.5 mg per injection is then added for each 5 mg above 20 mg of oral fluphenazine per day.

Stimmel (1985) has advocated that the dose of fluphenazine decanoate be given weekly and be equal to the first increase in 12.5 mg increments beyond the daily oral dose, e.g., 20 mg oral fluphenazine daily = 25 mg fluphenazine decanoate weekly.

Ereshefsky and coworkers (1985) utilized pharmacokinetic data to recommend that the dose of fluphenazine decanoate/week = 1.6 times the daily oral dose of fluphenazine in mg/day. They argue against the need for overlap between oral and depot therapy, and suggest that following four to six weeks on an initial dose which appears clinically effective, consideration be given to decreasing the dose or increasing the injection interval.

Yadalam and Simpson (1988) have recommended a test dose of 6.25 mg to evaluate sensitivity to the sesame oil. If the oral fluphenazine dose was low, subsequent injections of 6.25 mg are administered on days 7, 21, 42, and every two weeks thereafter. In the case of moderate to high doses of oral fluphenazine, the depot dose would be 12.5 - 25.0 mg administered according to a similar schedule.

Haloperidol Decancoate

Early studies utilizing data on bioavailability of oral haloperidol and a monthly injection interval for haloperidol decanoate established a theoretical rationale for employing a conversion formulae of 20 times the daily oral dose of haloperidol (Deberdt et al., 1980; De Buck et al., 1981; Suy et al., 1982; Zuardi et al., 1983).

In an investigation evaluating doses of haloperidol decanoate monthly that were 10, 20, or 30 times the daily oral haloperidol dose, it was noted that the conversion factor of 20 provided optimal plasma concentrations (Deberdt et al., 1980).

Suarez Richards et al. (1982) reported a conversion formula of 13 times the daily oral haloperidol dose to be therapeutically effective, while Viukari and coworkers (1982) found a conversion factor of 15 times clinically adequate in geriatric patients.

Nair et al. (1986) found haloperidol decanoate, administered monthly in doses of 9.2 to 15 times the daily oral haloperidol dose, to be as efficacious, despite lower plasma haloperidol concentrations, and it was concluded that the optimal conversion formula is 10 - 15 times the daily oral dose of haloperidol.

Ereshefsky et al. (1990) have described the use of a "loading dose" technique which employs a conversion factor of 20 times the daily oral haloperidol dose, administered in divided doses of 100 - 150 mg every three to seven days until the full amount is given. Concomitant oral therapy is not used, and the dosing schedule for the second month is based on clinical response. Using this approach, lower plasma haloperidol concentrations with the decanoate were recorded during the first month compared to oral haloperidol, but therapeutically equivalent concentrations were achieved more quickly. This approach is only recommended in those individuals who have been on oral haloperidol for at least two weeks to establish the correct oral dose.

Flupenthixol Decanoate

Jorgensen and Gottfries (1972) suggested that flupenthixol decanoate 40 mg biweekly = oral flupenthixol 3 mg daily.

Finally, a standard approach to conversion from any oral neuroleptic to a depot agent has also been described (Bezchlibnyk-Butler et al., 1994). The dose of the oral agent is converted to chlorpromazine (CPZ) equivalents and this value is then converted to the desired depot dose per day. This daily depot dose is then multiplied by the number of days in the chosen injection interval. While this approach has the advantage of being applicable to all depot agents, it is based on the assumption that conversion formulae to CPZ equivalents for the various neuroleptics are well established and this is not the case, e.g., fluphenazine (Brotman and McCormick, 1989; Haffmans et al., 1990; Inderbitzin et al., 1989; Rittmansberger, 1990; Schiff, 1989).

Depot Neuroleptics in Acute Treatment

Several reports have now documented the use of depot agents in the treatment of acutely psychotic patients (Bechelli and Navas-Filho, 1986; Turns et al., 1987).

More recently, it has been reported that co-injecting zuclopenthixol acetate and decanoate can be done safely with chronic psychotic patients who are experiencing an acute exacerbation of their symptoms (Hebenstreit, 1990). The acetate formulation offers the advantage of a rapidly acting, shorter duration treatment i.e., two to three days, while the decanoate offers longer-term treatment of approximately two to four weeks (Kazi, 1986; Wistedt et al., 1991).

Side Effects

Side effect profiles for the depot agents generally parallel their oral counterparts, or that particular chemical class of neuroleptics. There is no evidence to indicate that depot neuroleptics are associated with an increased risk of extrapyramidal side effects (EPS) or tardive dyskinesia (Barnes, 1991; Glazer and Kane, 1992; Marder, 1986). In fact, it has been suggested that haloperidol decanoate may be at a decreased risk of EPS compared to oral haloperidol (Bames, 1991; Beresford and Ward, 1987). Double-blind studies comparing depot agents fail to demonstrate marked differences between the different formulations, with the exception of fluphenazine enanthate, which has a greater risk of EPS than fluphenazine decanoate (Groves and Mandel, 1975). Use of excessively high doses, or simply individual susceptibility, can result in adverse effects which may be prolonged in the case of depot therapy. Particularly worrisome is a side effect such as neuroleptic malignant syndrome (NMS), for although there is again no evidence to indicate depots are at a greater risk of causing such a side effect, their slow elimination theoretically could increase the risk of mortality were it to occur (Glazer and Kane, 1992).

CONCLUSIONS

The investigation of depot neuroleptics lags considerably behind oral agents, despite the fact that depots have been now been available for approximately three decades. The availability of fewer depot neuroleptics in the United States and the lower frequency of use there, compared to many other countries, likely contributes to this discrepancy. At the same time, our understanding of depot neuroleptics has progressed considerably over the years, and a number of conclusions can be drawn from the current body of evidence.

1. Depot neuroleptics represent an effective, but likely underutilized, alternative to oral agents, particularly in the United States.
2. Depot neuroleptics offer distinct advantages associated with bioavailability, duration of action, and so on, but they also have disadvantages e.g., dose titration.
3. Relapse rates are diminished with depot compared to oral neuroleptics, but not to the extent that might be anticipated.
4. Depot neuroleptics are not a panacea. They do not ensure compliance, although they do permit better documentation of noncompliance in a way that can help distinguish this from treatment resistance.
5. Depots appear equally effective in terms of clinical response, and they do not appear to have a greater risk of side effects.
6. The conversion from oral to depot neuroleptics is not well established for any of the depot neuroleptics and is influenced, at least in part, by the recent trend towards lower neuroleptic doses.
7. Plasma levels for depots correlate better with closed than with clinical response or side effects.

In the face of diminishing health care dollars, deinstitutionalization, and greater emphasis on outpatient programs, depot neuroleptics are likely to take on a more important role in the long-term treatment of schizophrenia. To this end, we need to expand our knowledge of depot neuroleptics further, particularly in terms of pharmacokinetics, dosing, and clinical demographics. In light of the development of newer oral neuroleptics with atypical features, it will also be important to pursue. The development of depots which can offer these same clinical advantages.

REFERENCES

Ahlfors, U.G. (1973). "Controlled clinical evaluation of depot neuroleptics: a double - blind trial with pipotiazine undecylenate and fluphenazine enanthate", Acta Psychiatr. Scand., Suppl. 241, 95 - 99.

Altamura, C., Mauri, M., Cavallaro, R., Colacurcio, F., Gorni, A. and Bareggi, S. (1988). "Reduced haloperidol/haloperidol ratio and clinical outcome in schizophrenia: preliminary evidence", Prog. Neuropsychopharmacol. Biol. Psychiatry 12, 689 - 694.

Altamura, C.A., Colacurcio, F., Maurt, M.C., Moro, A.R. and De Novellis, F. (1990). "Haloperidol decanoate in chronic schizophrenia: a study of 12 months with plasma levels", Prog. Neuropsychopharmacol. Biol. Psychiatry, 14, 25 - 35.

Ayd, F.J., Jr (1973). "Side effects of depot fluphenazines", Int. Drug Ther. Newsletter, 69 - 76.

Ayd, F.J., Jr (1975). "The depot fluphenazines: a reappraisal after 10 years' clinical experience", Am. J. Psychiatry, 132, 491 - 500.

Ayd, F.J., Jr (1983). "Depot pipotiazine palmitate: thirteen years later", Int. Drug. Ther. Newsletter, 18, 5 - 8.

Babiker, I.E. (1987). "Comparative efficacy of long-acting depot, and oral neuroleptic medications in preventing schizophrenic recidivism", J. Clin. Psychiatry 48, 9497.

Balant-Gorgia, A.E. and Balant, L. (1987). "Antipsychotic drugs: clinical pharmacokinetics of potential candidates for plasma concentration monitoring", Pharmacokinetics, 13, 65 - 90.

Balon, R. (1994). "The underutilization of depot neuroleptic therapy", J. Clin.Psychiatry, 55, 39.

Bames, T.R.E. (1991). "Depot antipsychotic drugs and prevention of psychotic relapse", Clin. Neuropharmacol., 14, S1 - S6.

Baruch, P., Brion, S., Broussolle, P., Gayral, L.F., Ropert, R., Volmat, R. and Porot, M. (1989). "Enanthate de perphenazine", Encéphale, 15, 449 - 455.

Bechelli, L.P.C. and Navas - Filho, F. (1986). "Short-term double-blind trial of pipotiazine palmitate and haloperidol in the acute phase of schizophrenia",Encéphale, 12, 121 - 125.

Bechelli, L.P.G., Lecco, M.C., Acioli, A. and Pontes, M.C. (1985). "A double-blind trial of haloperidol decanoate and pipothiazine palmitate in the maintenance treatment of schizophrenics in a public out-patient clinic", Curr. Ther. Res, 37, 662 - 671.

Belanger, M.C. and Chouinard, G. (1982). "Technique for injecting long-acting neuroleptics", Br. J. Psychiatry, 141, 316.

Beresford, R. and Ward, A. (1987). "Haloperidol decanoate: a preliminary review of its pharmacodynamic and pharmacokinetic properties and therapeutic use in psychosis", Drugs, 33, 31 - 49.

Bezchlibnyk-Butier, K.Z., Jeffries, J.J. and Martin, B. (1994)., Clinical Handbook of Psychotropic Drugs, Hans Huber, Toronto.

Bourin, M., Venisse, J.L. and Lecuyer, F. (1990). "Résultats d'une enquete sur l'utilisation en psychiatric des neuroleptiques à action prolongée", Encéphale 16, 363 - 369.

Brotman, A.W. and McCormick, S. (1989). "Converting doses of fluphenazine decanoate to oral equivalents", Am. J. Psychiatry, 146, 815 - 816.

Brown-Thomsen, J. (1973). "Review of clinical trials with pipotiazine, pipotiazine undecylenate and pipotiazine palmitate", Acta Psychiatr. Scand, Suppl. 241, 119 - 138.

Carney, M.W.P. (1984). "A 5-year follow-up study of chronic schizophrenics treated with clopenthixol decanoate", Pharmacotherapeutica 4, 57 - 63.

Carney, M.W.P. and Rutherford, P. (1981). "Clopenthixol decanoate in schizophrenia", Curr. Med. Res. Opin., 7, 205 - 211.

Carpenter, W.T. and Keith, S.J. (1986). "Integrating treatments in schizophrenia", Psychiatr. Clin. North Am., 9, 153 - 164.

Casper, R.C., Davis, J.M., Garver, D.L., Dekirmenjian, H. and Chang, S. (1979). "Phenothiazine plasma and red blood cell concentrations, their relationships to side effects and clinical efficacy", In Biological Psychiatry Today (eds J. Obiols, C. Ballus, E. Gonzalez Monclus and J. Pujol), pp. 939 - 942, Elsevier, Amsterdam.

Ceskova, E., Svestka, J. and Rysanek, R. (1993). "Intraindividual comparison of haloperidol decanoate and oxyprothepine in maintenance therapy in schizophrenic patients", Cesk. Psychiatr., 89, 11 - 14.

Chang, S.S., Javaid, J.I., Dysken, M.W., Casper, R.C., Janicak, P.G. and Davis, J.M. (1985). "Plasma levels of fluphenazine during fluphenazine decanoate treatment in schizophrenia", Psychopharmacology 87, 55 - 58.

Chouinard, G., Annable, L. and Kropsky, M. (1978). "A double-blind controlled study of pipothiazine palmitate in the maintenance treatment of schizophrenic patients", Clin. Pharmacol., 18, 148 - 154.

Chouinard, G., Annable, L. and Ross - Chouinard, A. (1982). 'Fluphenazine enanthate and fluphenazine decanoate in the treatment of schizophrenic outpatients: extrapyramidal symptoms and therapeutic effect", Am. J. Psychiatry, 139, 312 - 318.

Chouinard, G., Annable L. and Campbell, W. (1989). "A randomized clinical trial of haloperidol decanoate and fluphenazine decanoate in the outpatient treatment of schizophrenia", J. Clin. Psychopharmacol, 9, 247 - 253.

Chouinard, G., Annable, L., Campbell, W., Boisvert, D. and Bradwejn, J. (1984). "A double-blind, controlled clinical trial of haloperidol decanoate and fluphenazine decanoate in the maintenance treatment of schizophrenia", Psychopharmacol. Bull, 20, 108 - 109.

Chowdhury, M.E. and Chacon, C. (1980). "Depot fluphenazine and flupenthixol in the treatment of stabilized schizophrenics: a double-blind comparative trial", Compr. Psychiatry, 21, 135 - 139.

Conley, R.R. and Johnson, D.A.W. (1991). "British versus United States usage of depot neuroleptics", Relapse, 1, 1 - 2.

Coorigan, P.W., Liberman, R.P. and Engel, J.D. (1990). "From noncompliance to collaboration in the treatment of schizophrenia", Hosp. Community Psychiatry, 41, 1203 - 1211.

Coumos, F., McKinnon, K. and Stanley, B. (1991). "Outcome of involuntary medication in a state hospital system", Am. J. Psychiatry, 148, 489 - 494.

Crawford, R. and Forrest, A. (1974). "Controlled trial of depot fluphenazine in out-patient schizophrenics", Br. J. Psychiatry, 124, 385 - 391.

Curry, S.H. (1985). "Commentary: the strategy and value of neuroleptic drug monitoring", J. Clin. Psychopharmacol, 5, 263 - 267.

Curry, S.H., Whelpton, R., Deschepper, P.J., Vrancks, S. and Schiff, A.A. (1978). "Plasma fluphenazine concentrations after injections of long-acting esters", Lancet, i, 1217 - 1218.

Curry, S.H., Whelpton, R., Deschepper, P.J., Vrancks, S. and Schiff, A.A. (1979). "Kinetics of fluphenazine after fluphenazine dihydrochloride, enanthate and decanoate administration to man", Br. J. Clin. Pharmacol, 7, 325 - 331.

Curson, D.A., Bames, T.R.E., Bamber, R.W.K., Platt, S.D., Hirsch, S.R. and Duffy, J.C. (1985). "Long-term depot maintenance of chronic schizophrenic outpatients: the seven year follow-up of the MRC fluphenazine/placebo trial", Br. J. Psychiatry, 146, 464 - 480.

Davis, J.M. and Andriukaitis, S. (1986). "The natural course of schizophrenia and effective maintenance drug treatment", J. Clin. Psychopharmacol, 6, 2S - 10S.

Deberdt, R., Elens, P., Berghmans, W., Heykants, J., Woestenborghs, R., Drelsens, F., Reyntijens, A. and Wijngaarden, I. (1980). 'Intramuscular haloperidol decanoate for neuroleptic maintenance therapy, efficacy, dosage schedule and plasma levels", Acta Psychiatr. Scand., 62, 356 - 363.

De Buck, R.P., Zelaschi, N., Gilles, C., Durdu, J. and Brauman, H. (1981). "Theoretical and practical importance of plasma levels of haloperidol. Correlations with clinical and computerized EEG data", Prog. Neuropsychopharmacol. 5, 499 - 502.

De Cuyper, H., Solien, J., Van Praag, H.M., and Verstraeten, D. (1986). "Pharmacokinetics and therapeutic efficacy of haloperidol decanoate after loading dose administration", Br. J. Psychiatry, 148, 560 - 566.

del Giudice, J., Clark, W.G. and Gocka, S. (1975). "Prevention of recidivism of schizophrenic outpatients treated with fluphenazine enanthate", Psychosomatics, 16, 32 - 36.

Dencker, S.J., Frankenberg, K., Maim, U. and Zell, B. (1973). "A controlled one - year study of pipothiazine palmitate and fluphenazine decanoate in chronic schizophrenic syndromes", Acta Psychiatr. Scand., Suppl. 241, 101 - 118.

Deniker, P. (1990). "The neuroleptics: a historical survey", Acta Psychiatr. Scand. 82(Suppl. 358), 83 - 87.

Diamond, R.J. (1983). "Enhancing medication use in schizophrenic patients", J. Clin. Psychiatry, 44, 253 - 261.

Donlon, P.T., Axeirad, A.D., Tupin, J.P. and Chien, C. (1976). "Comparison of depot fluphenazines: duration of action and incidence of side effects", Compr. Psychiatry, 17, 369 - 376.

Dreyfuss J., Shaw, J.M., and Ross, R.R. (1976). "Fluphenazine enanthate and fluphenazine decanoate: intramuscular injections and esterification as requirements for slow-release characteristics in dogs", J. Pharm. Sci., 63, 1310 - 1315.

Eberhard, G. and Hellbom, E. (1986). "Haloperidol-decanoate and flupenthixol decanoate in schizophrenia", Acta Psychiatr. Scand, 74, 255 - 262.

Ereshefsky, L., Saklad, S.R., Jann, M.W., Davis, C.M., Richards, A. and Seidel D.R. (1984a). "Future of depot neuroleptic therapy: pharmacokinetic and pharmacodynamics approaches", J. Clin. Psychiatry, 45, 50 - 59.

Ereshefsky, L. Davis, C.M., Harrington, C.A., Jann, M.W., Browning, J.L., Sakfad, S.R. and Burch, N.R. (1984b). "Haloperidol and reduced haloperidol plasma levels in selected schizophrenic patients", J. Clin. Psychopharmacol, 4, 138 - 142.

Ereshefsky, L., Richards, A.L., Grothe, D.R., Saklad, S.R. and Jann, M.W. (1985). "Pharmacokinetic and clinical evaluation of the conversion from oral to depot fluphenazine", unpublished data.

Ereshefsky, L., Sakfad, S.R., Tran-Johnson, T., Toney, G., Lyman, R.C. and Davis, C.M., (1990). "Kinetics and clinical evaluation of haloperidol decanoate loading dose regimen", Psychopharm. Bull., 26, 108 - 114.

Falloon, I., Watt, D.C. and Shepherd, M.A. (1978). A comparative controlled trial of pimozide and fluphenazine decanoate in the continuation therapy of schizophrenia", Psychol. Med., 8, 59 - 70.

Frangos, H., Zissis, N.P., Leontopoulos, I., Diamantas, N., Tsitouridis, S., Gavriil, I. and Tsolis, K. (1978). "Double-blind therapeutic evaluation of fluspirilene compared with fluphenazine decanoate in chronic schizophrenics", Acta Psychiatr. Scand, 57, 436 - 446.

Furet, Y., Breteau, M., and Etienne T. (1991). "Study of residual levels of delayed-action neuroleptics", Therapies, 46, 119 - 123.

Gardos, G. (1974). "Are antipsychotics interchangeable?", J. Nerv. Ment. Dis., 159, 343 - 348.

Gelders, Y.G. (1986). "Pharmacology, pharmacokinetics and clinical development of haloperidol decanoate", Int. Clin. Psychopharmacol, 1(s), 1 - 11.

Gitlin, M.J., Midha, K.K., Fogelson, D. and Nuechterlein, K. (1988). "Persistence of fluphenazine in plasma after decanoate withdrawal", J. Clin. Psychopharmacol., 8, 53 - 56.

Glazer, W.M., and Kane, J.M. (1992). "Depot neuroleptic therapy: an underutilized treatment option", J. Clin. Psychiatry, 53, 426 - 433.

Glazer, W.M., Maynard, C. and Berkman, C.S. (1987). "Injection site leakage of depot neuroleptics: intramuscular versus subcutaneous injection", J. Clin. Psychiatry, 48, 237 - 239.

Glover, G. and Malcolm, G. (1988). "The prevalence of depot neuroleptic treatment among West Indians and Asians in the London borough of Newham", Soc. Psychiatry Psychiatr. Epidemiol., 23, 281 - 284.

Groves, J.E. (1979). "Prescribing long-acting neuroleptics", Drug Therapy, 9, 89 - 93.

Groves, J.E. and Mandel, M.R. (1975). "The long-acting phenothiazines", Arch. Gen. Psychiatry, 32, 893 - 900.

Haffmans, P.M.J., Hoencamp, E., Jansen, G.S., and Van Kempen, G.M.J. (1990). "Dosage of fluphenazine", Am. J. Psychiatry, 147, 259.

Hamann, G.L. and Wells, B.G. (1992) "Drs. Hamman and Wells reply", J. Clin. Psychiatry, 53, 415 - 416.

Hamann, G.L., Egan, T.M., Wells, B.G., and Grimmig, J.E. (1990). "Injection site reactions after intramuscular administration of haloperidol decanoate 100 mg/mL", J. Clin. Psychiatry, 51, 502 - 504.

Hansen, L.B., Larsen, N-E. and Vestergard, P. (1981). "Plasma levels of perphenazine (Trilafon) related to development of extrapyramidal side effects", Psychopharmacology, 74, 306 - 309.

Haslam, M.T., Bromham, B.M. and Schiff, A.A. (1975). "A comparative trial of fluphenazine decanoate and flupenthixol decanoate", Acta Psychiatr. Scand, 51, 92 - 100.

Hebenstreit, G.F. (1990). "Clinical experience with zuclopenthixol acetate and co-injection of zuclopenthixol acetate and zuclopenthixol decanoate", In Psychiatry: A World Perspective, Volume 3 (eds C. N. Stefanis et al.), pp. 196 - 201, Elsevier, Amsterdam.

Hogarty, G.E. (1984). "Depot neuroleptics: the relevance of psychosocial factors a United States perspective", J. Clin. Psychiatry, 45, 36 - 42.

Hogarty, G.E., Schooler, N.R., Ulrich, R., Mussare, F., Ferro, P. and Herron, E. (1979). "Fluphenazine and social therapy in the aftercare of schizophrenic patients. Relapse analyses of a two-year controlled study of fluphenazine decanoate and fluphenazine hydrchloride", Arch. Gen. Psychiatry, 36, 1283 - 1294.

Inderbitzin, L.B., Lewine, R.R.J., Gloersen, B.A., Rosen, P.B., McDonald, S.C. and Vidanagama, B.P. (1989). "Fluphenazine decanoate: a clinical problem?", Am. J. Psychiatry, 146, 88 - 91.

Jann, M.W., Ereshefsky, L. and Saklad, S.R. (1985). "Clinical pharmacokinetics of the depot antipsychotics", Clin. Pharmacokinet, 10, 315 - 333.

Johnson, D.A.W. (1991). "Depot therapy: advantages, disadvantages and issues of dose". In Depot Antipsychotics in Chronic Schizophrenia: Proceedings of a Symposium (eds D.A.W. Johnson, M.P.W. Carney, S.J. Dencker and P.M. Kristjansen), pp. 14 - 86, Excerpta Medica, Amsterdam.

Johnson, D.A.W. and Freeman, H.L. (1973). "Drug defaulting by patients on late-acting phenothiazines", Psychol. Med, 3, 115 - 119.

Johnson, D.A.W. and Malik, N.A. (1975). "A double-blind comparison of fluphenazine decanoate and flupenthixol decanoate in the treatment of acute schizophrenia", Acta Psychiatr. Scand., 51, 257 - 267.

Johnson, D.A.W. and Wright, N. (1990). Drug prescribing to schizophrenic outpatients on depot injections: repeat surveys over eighteen years", Br. J. Psychiatry,156, 827 - 834.

Johnson, D.A.W., Kane, J.M. and Simpson, G. (1984). "I. The use of depot neuroleptics: clinical experience in the United States and the United Kingdom", presented at the International Conferences on Depot and Oral Neuroleptics Conferences, May 6, Los Angeles, California.

Johnson, D.A.W., Ludlow, J.M., Street, K. and Taylor, R.D.W. (1987). "Double-blind comparison of half-dose and standard-dose flupenthixol decanoate in the maintenance treatment of stabilized out-patients with schizophrenia", Br. J. Psychiatry , 151, 634 - 638.

Jorgensen, A. (1978a). "Pharmacokinetic studies of flupenthixol decanoate: a depot neuroleptic of the thioxanthine group", Drug Metab. Rev., 8, 235 - 249.

Jorgensen, A. (1978b). "A sensitive and specific radioimmunoassay for cis(z)flupenthixol in human serum", Life Sci., 23, 1533 - 1542.

Jorgensen, A. (1980). "Pharmacokinetic studies in volunteers of intravenous and oral cis(z)-flupenthixol and intramuscular cis(z)-flupenthixol decanoate in Viscoleo", Eur. J. Pharmacol., 18, 355 - 360.

Jorgensen, A. and Gottfries, C.G. (1972). "Pharmacokinetic studies on flupenthixol and flupenthixol decanoate in man using tritium labeled Illustration 2. d compounds", Psychopharmacology, 27, 1 - 10.

Jorgensen, A. and Overo, K.F. (1980). "Clopenthixol and flupenthixol depot preparations in outpatient schizophrenics. III. Serum levels. Acta Psychiatr. Scand., 61 (Suppl. 279), 41 - 54.

Jorgensen, T., Overo, K.F., Bogeso, K.P. and Jorgensen, A. (1977). "Pharmacokinetic studies on clopenthixol decanoate: a comparison with clopenthixol in dogs and cats", Acta Pharmacol. Toxicol., 41, 103 - 120.

Kane, J.M. (1986). "Dosage strategies with long-acting injectable neuroleptics, including haloperidol decanoate", J. Clin, Psychopharmacol, 6, 20S - 23S.

Kane, J.M. (1987). "Treatment of schizophrenia",Schizophr. Bull., 13, 133 - 156.

Kane, J.M., Rifkin, A., Quitkin, F., Nayak, D. and Ramos-Lorenzi, J. (1982). "Fluphenazine vs placebo in patients with remitted, acute first-episode schizophrenia", Arch. Gen. Psychiatry , 39, 70 - 73.

Kane, J.M., Rifkin, A., Woerner, M., Reardon, G., Sarantakos, S., Schiebel, D. and Ramos-Lorenzi, J. (1983). "Low-dose neuroleptic treatment of outpatient schizophrenics I. Preliminary results for relapse rates", Arch. Gen. Psychiatry, 40, 893 - 896.

Kane, J.M., Rifkin, A., Woerner, M., Reardon, G., Kreisman, D., Blumenthal, R. and Borenstein, M. (1985). "High-dose versus low-dose strategies in the treatment of schizophrenia", Psychopharmacol. Bull, 21, 533 - 537.

Kane, J.M., Woemer, M. and Sarantakos, S. (1986). "Depot neuroleptics: a comparative review of standard, intermediate and low-dose regimens", J. Clin. Psychiatry, 47 (Suppl. 5), 30 - 33.

Kazi, H.A.G. (1986). "An open clinical trial with the long-acting neuroleptic zuclopenthixol decanoate in the maintenance treatment of schizophrenia", Pharmacotherapeutica, 4, 555 - 560.

Kissling, W., Moller, H.J., Walter, K., Wittmann, B., Krueger, R. and Trenk, D. (1985). "Double-blind comparison of haloperidol decanoate and fluphenazine decanoate: effectiveness, side-effects, dosage, and serum levels during a six months' treatment for relapse prevention", Pharmacopsychiatry, 18, 240 - 245.

Knights, A., Okashs, M.S., Salin, M.A., and Hirsch, S.R. (1979). "Depressive and extrapyramidal symptoms and clinical effects: a trial of fluphenazine versus flupenthixol in maintenance of schizophrenic out-patients", Br. J. Psychiatry, 135, 515 - 523.

Knudsen, P., Hansen, L.B. and Larsen, N-E. (1985a). "Pharmacokinetic implications of different oil vehicles used in depot neuroleptic treatment", Acta Psychiatr. Scand., 72 (suppl. 322), 2 - 10.

Knudsen, P., Hansen, L.B. and Larsen, N-E. (1985b). "Perphenazine decanoate in sesame oil vs. perphenazine enanthate in sesame oil: a comparative study of pharmacokinetic properties and some clinical implications", Acta Psychiatr. Scand., 72 (suppl. 322), 11 - 14.

Knudsen, P., Hansen, L.B., Auken, G., Waehrens, J., Hojholdt, K. and Larsen, N-E. (1985c). "Perphenazine decanoate vs. perphenazine enanthate: efficacy and side effects in a 6 week double-blind, comparative study of 50 drug monitored psychotic patients", Acta Psychiatr. Scand., 72 (suppl. 322), 15 - 28.

Knudsen, P., Hansen, L.B., Hojholdt, K. and Larsen, N-E. (1985d). "Long-term depot neuroleptic treatment with perphenazine decanoate I. Efficacy and side effects in a 12 month study of 42 drug monitored psychotic patients", Acta Psychiatr. Scand, 72 (suppl. 322), 29 - 40.

Knudsen, P., Hansen, L.B., Hojholdt, K. and Larsen, N-E. (1985e). "Long-term neuroleptic treatment with perphenazine decanoate II. Different depot intervals in the last 6 months of a 12 month study of 42 drug monitored psychotic patients", Acta Psychiatr. Scand., 72 (suppl. 322), 41 - 50.

Korpi, E.R. and Wyatt, R.J. (1984). "Reduced haloperidol: effects on striatal dopamine metabolism and conversion to haloperidol in the rat", Psychopharmacology, 83, 34 - 37.

Kristrup, K., Gerlach, J., Aaes-Jorgensen, T. and Larsen, N - E. (1991). "Perphenazine decanoate and cis (z)-flupentixol decanoate in maintenance treatment of schizophrenic outpatients", Psychopharmacology, 105, 42 - 48.

Lapierre, Y.D., Berliss, H., Monpremier P. and Elie, R. (1979). "Methodology and results of a long-term study of long-acting neuroleptics: pipothiazine palmitate and fluphenazine decanoate", In Biological Psychiatry Today (eds J. Obiols, C. Ballus, E. Gonzalez Monclus and J. Pujol), pp 1087 - 1094, Elsevier/North-Holland Biochemical Press, Amsterdam.

Levi Minzi, A. and Laviani, M. (1992). "Evaluation of effectiveness and tolerance of the long-term treatment with bromperidol decanoate in psychotic disorders", Minerva Psychiatrica, 33, 51 - 55.

MacCrimmon, D.J., Saxena, B., Foley, P. and Grof, P. (1978). "Fluphenazine decanoate and fluphenazine enanthate in the outpatient management of chronic schizophrenia", Neuropsychobiology, 4, 360 - 365.

Malm, U., Perris, C., Rapp, W. and Wedren, G. (1974). "A multicenter controlled trial of fluspirilene and fluphenazine enanthate in chronic schizophrenic syndromes", Acta Psychiatr. Scand., Suppl. 249, 94 - 116.

Marder, S.R. (1986). "Depot neuroleptics: side effects and safety", J. Clin. Psychopharmacol., 6, 24S - 29S.

Marder, S.R., Van Putten, T., Mintz, J., McKenzie, J., Lebell, M., Faitico, G. and May, P.R.A. (1984). "Costs and benefits of two doses of fluphenazine", Arch. Gen. Psychiatry, 41, 1025 - 1029.

Marder, S.R., Hawes, E.M., Van Putten, T., Hubbard, J.W., McKay, G., Mintz, J., May, P.R. and Midha, K.K. (1986) "Fluphenazine plasma levels in patients receiving low and conventional doses of fluphenazine decanoate", Psychopharmacology 88, 480 - 483.

Marder, S.R., Hubbard, J.W., Van Putten, T. and Kamal, K.M. (1989). "Pharmacokinetics of long-acting injectable neuroleptic drugs: clinical implications", Psychopharmacolgy, 98, 433 - 439.

Marder, S.R., Midha, K.K., Van Putten, T., Aravagari, M., Hawes, E.M., Hubbard, J.W., McKay, G., and Mintz, J. (1991). "Plasma levels of fluphenazine in patients receiving fluphenazine decanoate: relationship to clinical response", Br. J. Psychiatry, 158, 658 - 665.

Marder, S.R., Van Putten, T., Aravagiri, M., Wirshing, W.C. and Midha, K.K (1993). "Plasma level monitoring for long-acting injectable neuroleptics", In Clinical Use of Neuroleptic Plasma Levels (eds S.R. Marder, J.M. Davis and P.G. Janicak), pp. 101 - 112, American Psychiatric Press, Washington, DC.

Mason, A.S. and Granacher, R.P. (1976). "Basic principles of rapid neuroleptization", Dis. Nerv. Syst., 37, 547 - 551.

McConnell, E.A. (1982). "The subtle art of really good injections", RN, February, 25 - 34.

McCreadie, R.G., McKane, J.P., Robinson, A.D.T., Wiles, O.H. and Stirling, G.S. (1986). "Depot neuroleptics as maintenance therapy in chronic schizophrenic in-patients", Int. Clin. Psychopharmacol., 1(s), 13 - 14.

McGee, H.M., Seeman, M.V. and Deck, J.H.N. (1983). "Fluspirilene neuroleptic depot injections and indurations", Can. J. Psychiatry, 28, 379 - 381.

McKane, J.P., Robinson, A.D., Wiles, D.H., McCreadie, R.G. and Stirling, G.S. (1987). "Haloperidol decanoate v. fluphenazine decanoate as maintenance therapy in chronic schizophrenic in-patients", Br. J. Psychiatry, 151, 333 - 336.

McLaren S., Cookson, J.C. and Silverstone, T. (1992). "Positive and negative symptoms, depression and social disability in chronic schizophrenia: a comparative trial of bromperidol and fluphenazine decanoates", Int. Clin. Psychopharmacol, 7, 67 - 72.

Meco, G., Casacchia, M., Atteni, M., Latrate, A., Castellana, F. and Ecari, U. (1983). "Haloperidol decanoate in schizophreniform disorders", Acta Psychiatr. Belg., 83, 57 - 68.

Middlemiss, M.A. and Beeber, L.S. (1989). "Issues in the use of depot antipsychotics", J. Psychosoc. Nurs. Ment. Health Serv., 27, 36 - 37.

Midha, K.K., Hawes, E.M., Hubbard, J.W., McKay, G., Rauw, G., Sardessai, M.S., Aravagirir, M. and Moore, M.D. (1988). "Radioimmunoassay for fluphenazine sulfoxide in human plasma", J. Pharmacol. Meth., 19, 63 - 74.

Mound, B., Flanagan, E. and O'Keefe, G. (1990). "Self-injection of neuroleptics", Can. Nurse, June, 31 - 32.

Nair, N.P.V., Suranyi-Cadorte, B., Schwartz, G., Thavundayil, J.X., Achim, A., Lizondo, E. and Nayak, R. (1986). "A clinical trial comparing intramuscular haloperidol and oral haloperidol in chronic schizophrenic patients: efficacy, safety, and dosage equivalence", J. Clin. Psychopharmacol., 1986, 6, 30S - 37S.

Nasrallah, H., Rivera-Catimlim, L., Pogot, A.D., Gillin, J.E. and Wyatt R.J., (1979). "Fluphenazine decanoate and prolactin: plasma concentrations and clinical response". In Pharmacokinetics of Psychoactive Drugs, Blood Levels and Clinical Response (eds. S. Mertis and L. Gottschalk), pp. 115 - 123, Spectrum, New York.

Pan, P.C. and Tantam, D. (1989). "Clinical characteristics, health beliefs and compliance with maintenance treatment: a comparison between regular and irregular attendees at a depot clinic", Acta Psychiatr. Scand., 79, 564 - 570.

Price, N., Glazer, W. and Morgenstern, H. (1985). "Demographic predictors of the use of injectable versus oral antipsychotic medications in outpatients", Am. J. Psychiatry, 142, 1491 - 1492.

Quitkin, F., Rifkin, A., Jane, J.M., Ramos - Lorenzi, J. and Klein, D. (1978). "Long-acting oral drugs vs injectable antipsychotic drugs in schizophrenics: a one-year double-blind comparison in multiple episode schizophrenics", Arch. Gen. Psychiatry, 35, 889 - 892.

Rabiner C.J., Wegner, J.T. and Kane, J.M. (1986). "Outcome study of first-episode psychosis, I: relapse rates after 1 year", Am. J. Psychiatry, 143, 1155 - 1158.

Rapp, W., Hellbom, E., Norrman, O., Palm, U., Rodhe, K., Forsman, A. and Larsson, M. (1986). "A double-blind crossover study comparing haloperidol decanoate and perphenazine enantate", Curr. Ther. Res., 39, 665 - 670.

Reinke, M. and Wiesert, K.N. (1992). "High incidence of haloperidol decanoate injection site reactions", J. Clin. Psychiatry, 53, 415.

Remington G.J. (1992). "A Canadian perspective on the use of depot neuroleptics", Relapse, 2, 3 - 4.

Remington, G.J., Prendergast, P. and Bezchlibnyk - Butter, K.Z. (1993). "Dosaging patterns in schizophrenia with depot, oral and combined neuroleptic therapy", Can. J. Psychiatry, 38, 159 - 161.

Reyntjens, A.J.M., Heykants, J.J.P., Woestenborghs, R.J.H., Gelders, Y.G. and Aerts, T.J.L. (1982). "Pharmacokinetics of haloperidol decanoate: a 2 - year follow-up", Int. Pharmacopsychiatry 17, 238 - 246.

Rifkin, A., Quitkin, F., Rabiner, C.J. and Klein, D.F. (1977). Fluphenazine decanoate, fluphenazine hydrochloride given orally and placebo in remitted schizophrenics, I. Relapse rates after one year", Arch. Gen. Psychiatry, 34, 43 - 47.

Rittmannsberger, H. (1990). "Dosage of fluphenazine", Am. J. Psychiatry, 147, 258 - 259.

Rowland, M. and Tozer, T.N. (1989). Clinical Pharmacokinetics: Concepts and Applications, Lea & Febiger, Philadelphia.

Russell, N., Landmark, J., Merskey, H. and Turpin, T. (1982). "A double-blind comparison of fluspirilene and fluphenazine decanoate in schizophrenia", Can. J. Psychiatry, 27, 593 - 596.

Schiff, A.A. (1989). "Dosage of oral and depot fluphenazine", Am. J. Psychiatry, 146, 1233.

Schlosberg, A. and Shadmi (Weber), M. (1978). "A comparative controlled study of two long-acting phenothiazines: pipothiazine palmitate and fluphenazine decanoate", Curr. Ther. Res., 24, 689 - 707.

Schooler, N.R., Levine, J. and Severe, J.B. (1979). "NIMH-PRB Collaborative Fluphenazine Study Group. Depot fluphenazine in the prevention of relapse in schizophrenia: evaluation of a treatment regimen", Psychopharmacol., Bull, 15, 44 - 47.

Shostak, M., Perel, J.M., Stiffer, R.L., Wyman, W. and Curran, S. (1987). "Plasma haloperidol and clinical response: a role for reduced haloperidol in antipsychotic activity?", J. Clin. Psychopharmacol., 7, 394 - 400.

Simpson, G.M. (1984). "A brief history of depot neuroleptics", J. Clin. Psychiatry, 45, 3 - 4.

Singh, A.N. and Saxena, B. (1979). "A comparative study of prolonged action (depot) neuroleptics: pipothiazine palmitate versus fluphenazine enanthate in chronic schizophrenic patients, Curr. Ther. Res., 25, 121 - 132.

Stauning, J.A., Kirk, L. and Jorgensen, A. (1979). "Comparison of serum levels after intramuscular injections of 2% and 10% cis (z)-flupenthixol decanoate in viscoleo to schizophrenic patients", Psychopharmacology, 65, 69 - 72.

Steinert, J., Erba, E., Pugh, C.R., Robinson, C. and Priest, R.G. (1986). "A comparative trial of depot pipothiazine", J. Int. Med. Res., 14, 72 - 77.

Stimmel, G. (1985). "Schizophrenia". In Clinical Pharmacy and Therapeutics (eds J.T. Coyle and S.J. Enna), Williams & Wilkins, Baltimore.

Suarez Richards, M., Actis Dato, A.C., Zelaschi, N.M., Balbo, F.A. and Canero, E.C. (1982). "Monthly haloperidol decanoate substitutes for daily neuroleptics in psychotic inpatients", Curr. Ther. Res., 32, 586 - 589.

Suy, E., Woestenborghs, R. and Heykants, J. (1982). "Bioavailability and clinical effect of two different concentrations of haloperidol decanoate", Curr. Ther. Res, 31, 982 - 991.

Turns, D.M., Pary, R., Tobias, C.R. and James, W.A. (1987). "Depot neuroleptics for acutely psychotic patients", Am. J. Psychiatry, 144, 1099.

Van Praag, H.M. and Dols, L.C. (1973). "Fluphenazine enanthate and fluphenazine decanoate: a comparison of their duration of action and motor side effects", Am. J. Psychiatry, 130, 801 - 804.

Van Putten, T. (1974). "Why do schizophrenics refuse to take their drugs?", Arch. Gen. Psychiatry, 31, 67 - 72.

Van Putten, T., Marder, S.R., Wirshing, W.C., Aravagiri, M., and Chabert, N. (1991). "Neuroleptic plasma levels", Schizophr. Bull., 17, 197 - 216.

Viukari, M., Salo, H., Lamminsivu, U. and Gordin, A. (1982). "Tolerance and serum levels of haloperidol during parenteral and oral haloperidol treatment in geriatric patients", Acta. Psychiatr. Scand., 65, 301 - 308.

Wesby, R., Earle, J., Bullmore, E. and Heavey, A. (1993). "Community care of patients receiving antipsychotic medication by depot injection", Br. J. Gen. Pract, 43, 83 - 84.

Wiles, D.H. and Gelder, M.G. (1979). "Plasma fluphenazine levels by radioimmunoassay in schizophrenic patients treated with depot injections of fluphenazine decanoate", Br. J. Clin. Pharmacol., 8, 565 - 570.

Wiles, D.H., McCreadie, R.G. and Whitehead, A. (1990). "Pharmacokinetics of haloperidol and fluphenazine decanoates in chronic schizophrenia", Psychopharmacology, 101, 274 - 281.

Winter, K., Fullerton, A.G., Hussain, K. and Tario, L. (1973). "A comparative double-blind trial of fluspirilene and fluphenazine decanoate in the treatment of chronic schizophrenia", Br. J. Clin. Pract., 27, 377 - 380.

Wistedt, B. and Ranta, J. (1983). "Comparative double-blind study of flupenthixol decanoate and fluphenazine decanoate in the treatment of patients relapsing in schizophrenic symptomatology", Acta. Psychiatr. Scand, 67, 378 - 388.

Wistedt, B., Wiles, D. and Kolakowska, T. (1981). "Slow decline in plasma drug and prolactin levels after discontinuation of chronic treatment with depot neuroleptics", Lancet, i, 1163.

Wistedt, B., Jorgensen, A. and Wiles, D. (1982). "A depot neuroleptic withdrawal study: plasma concentrations of fluphenazine and flupenthixol and relapse frequency", Psychopharmacology, 78, 301 - 304.

Wistedt, B., Persson, T. and Hellbom, E. (1984). "A clinical double-blind comparison between haloperidol decanoate and fluphenazine decanoate", Curr. Ther. Res., 35, 804 - 814.

Wistedt, B., Koskinen, T., Thelander, S., Nerdrum, T., Pedersen, V. and Molbjerg, C. (1991). "Zuclopenthixol decanoate and haloperidol decanoate in chronic schizophrenia: a double-blind multicentre study", Acta. Psychiatr. Scand, 84, 14 - 16.

Yadalam, D.G. and Simpson, G.M. (1988). "Changing from oral to depot fluphenazine", J. Clin. Psychiatry, 49, 346 - 348.

Youssef, H.A. (1982). "A one-year study of haloperidol decanoate in schizophrenic patients", Curr. Ther. Res., 31, 976 - 981.

Youssef, H.A. (1983). "Haloperidol decanoate in place of multiple drug therapy in chronic schizophrenic patients", Acta Therpeutica, 9, 215 - 225.

Zuardi, A.W., Giampetro, A.C., Grassi, E.C., Matos Uma, A.A. and Buoncompagno, E.M. (1983). "Double-blind comparison between two forms of haloperidol: an oral preparation and a new decanoate in the maintenance of schizophrenic inpatients", Curr. Ther. Res., 34, 253 - 261.

11

AFFECTIVE MOOD DISTURBANCE IN SCHIZOPHRENIA

Graham D. Burrows and Trevor R. Norman

INTRODUCTION

High rates of depression are a consistent finding in studies of patients with schizophrenia, despite methodological differences (Martin et al., 1985). Early clinical accounts noted that depressive symptoms emerged following the abatement of florid psychotic symptomatology (Roth, 1970). Other studies have noted the presence of depression in a high proportion of patients during admission for a psychotic episode (McGlashan and Carpenter, 1976a; Siris et al., 1984). In a small proportion of patients, depressive symptoms have been noted to occur following recovery from a psychotic episode and in the absence of pre-existing depressive symptoms (Bowers and Astrachan, 1967; Steinberg et al., 1967). The term post-psychotic depression has been applied to each of these three apparently distinct clinical groups. It has been suggested that the clinical efficacy of antidepressant drugs in treating post-psychotic depression may be different for each of these subtypes (Leff et al., 1988a). The importance of co-existing depression in schizophrenia has been underlined by the recognition that it is often associated with poor outcome (Black et al., 1985; Herz and Melville, 1980; Johnson, 1981; Falloon et al., 1978). This chapter presents a brief overview of post-psychotic depression and its treatment.

Schizophrenia: Exploring the Spectrum of Psychosis. Edited by R. Ancill © 1994
John Wiley & Sons Ltd

PREVALENCE OF DEPRESSION IN SCHIZOPHRENIA

Various studies have estimated that between 25% and 50% of patients may manifest depressive features during an acute episode of schizophrenia (Donlon et al., 1976; McGlashan and Carpenter, 1976a, 1976b; Johnson, 1981; Mandel et al., 1982). In chronic stabilized inpatients the incidence appears to be less. Johnson, (1981) found that about a third of patients had depressive symptoms while Barnes et al. (1989) noted that depressed mood was present in 13% of chronic institutionalized patients. In contrast to point prevalence studies, long-term follow-ups in schizophrenia show that nearly 60% of patients had a history of at least one depressive episode during the course of their illness (Martin et al., 1985). Similarly Roy (1981) found that 39% of chronic patients, with an illness duration of at least three years, had been treated for depression since the onset of their disorder.

AETIOLOGY OF DEPRESSION IN SCHIZOPHRENIA

The aetiology of the depressive syndrome in schizophrenia remains uncertain and is a matter of some controversy. Several hypotheses have been advanced to explain the emergence of depressive symptoms. Knights and Hirsch, (1981) coined the term "revealed depression" to imply that the depressive symptoms are part of the schizophrenic process. On the other hand a substantial body of evidence suggests that depressive symptoms and dysphoric mood are caused by antipsychotic drugs used to treat the illness. A third school of thought maintains that depression is confused with a syndrome of pseudo-parkinsonism and the term akinetic depression has been coined.

Drug-induced or pharmacogenetic depression

This aetiology has been most forcefully stated by Galdi (1993) and remains a popular view. A direct depression-causing effect of antipsychotic medication has been hypothesized to occur due to the effects of the drugs on adrenergic and dopaminergic receptors. Several reports in the literature implicate antipsychotic medications (Floru et al., 1975; Singh, 1976) and fluphenazine decanoate in particular (DeAlarcon and Carney, 1969; Johnson and Malik, 1975; Falloon et al., 1978; Johnson, 1984) in the aetiology of depression in patients with schizophrenia. The notion that this depression was pharmacogenetically induced was based on the observation that patients with schizophrenia who had first-degree relatives with depression were themselves more depressed four to six weeks after commencing antipsychotic therapy than patients receiving placebo (Galdi et al., 1981). Patients who had first-degree relatives with schizophrenia failed to show differences between placebo and antipsychotic drugs with respect to depressive responses. This finding was supported by the study of Hogarty et al. (1979) who reported a distinct "affective quality" in relapsed hospitalized patients with a first-degree relative with depression, than in non-relapsed patients.

The notion of pharmacogenetic depression has been refuted by several studies which have failed to find any evidence for a relationship between severity of depression and the dose of antipsychotic used (Siris et al., 1988; Roy, 1984; Leff et al., 1988b). Furthermore, in many other studies, depressive symptoms actually decreased when patients were treated with antipsychotic drugs (Leff et al., 1988b; Donlon et al., 1976; Knights and Hirsch, 1981). This has led to the hypothesis that the depression observed may be an integral part of the illness. Also opposing the notion that antipsychotic drugs may cause depression is the review documenting the usefulness of these agents in some cases of major depressive disorder (Robertson and Trimble, 1982).

Akinetic depression

Akinetic depression is essentially a variant of pharmacogenetic depression since it arises in the context of and is caused by the use of antipsychotic drugs. Van Putten and May (1978) first noted that depression occurs in antipsychotic treated patients as a symptom of drug-induced parkinsonism. Furthermore, they noted that this depression responded to anticholinergic treatment. Patients were described as having mild akinesia with anergia, and emotional withdrawal associated with drowsiness. This phenomenon was described by Rifkin et al. (1975) but was not regarded as a variant of depression. Since the syndrome responded to anticholinergic drugs they suggested, probably correctly, that this was identical to drug-induced extrapyramidal side-effects. Clearly the differentiation of akinetic depression from the Parkinsonian syndrome would be difficult clinically. Nevertheless, Galdi (1983) maintains that "pseudo-Parkinsonian depression" is a distinct clinical entity. Furthermore, he contends that they both have a biological basis through an interaction of antipsychotics with a defective nigrostriatal dopaminergic system. This defect may apparently be inherited.

Post-psychotic depression

This concept refers to the notion that depression may occur as patients with schizophrenia recover insight into their illness and life situation. The salient features of the disorder have been reviewed by McGlashan and Carpenter (1976b). According to these authors, post-psychotic depression is a phasic disorder of thought and behaviour in patients during remission from the acute phase of schizophrenia. It occurs in about 25% of patients who have been hospitalized with an acute episode of schizophrenia but is less common in chronically ill patients.

Clinically post-psychotic depression is most like a "retarded" depression with complaints of emptiness, lack of feelings, decreased interpersonal relationships and prominent suicidal ideation and acts. The illness is usually stable with a duration lasting from weeks to years. Treatment is difficult and it is usually resistant. The syndrome is regarded as arising either due to a reaction to the psychosis, to mourning the loss of established maladaptive ways of coping, or due to the difficulties to be faced in confronting the necessity to change (McGlashan and Carpenter, 1976b). These psychodynamic views are not exclusive of a biological aetiology, but given the difficulty of the diagnostic issues implied in the concept of post-psychotic depression, it would seem unlikely that much progress could be made before the nosology is clarified.

Overview

It seems likely that depression in schizophrenia has no single aetiology. The unmasking of depression (revealed depression) as proposed by Hirsch, that is, depression is an integral part of the syndrome of schizophrenia is a plausible explanation for the aetiology. The co-occurrence of dysphoric mood and other depressive features in the acute phase of the illness, as well as during recovery, when the more florid symptoms of schizophrenia have abated, certainly supports this notion for at least some cases. On the other hand, the notion of post-psychotic depression occurring as a result of regaining insight and the realisation of loss, i.e., a "reactive depression", has appeal from a psychodynamic point of view. The concept of pharmacogenetic depression does not appear to be sustained. Irrespective of the aetiology, the association of depression with suicidal ideation and the high suicide rates in schizophrenia (Black et al., 1985) makes further research on its cause and treatment a high priority.

DRUG TREATMENT OF DEPRESSED SCHIZOPHRENIA PATIENTS

While the emergence of depressive symptoms during an episode of schizophrenia is undisputed, the manner of its treatment remains controversial. While some authors have concluded that a tricyclic antidepressant should be added to the continuing antipsychotic regimen, controlled clinical trials do not unequivocally support this idea (Rifkin and Siris, 1987). A summary of controlled trials of antidepressant adjunctive treatments in schizophrenia is presented in Table 1. The results of these prospective controlled studies provide a mixed picture of the efficacy of antidepressants in post-psychotic depression. Few of the studies are without methodological flaws, in particular, operationally defined criteria for the diagnosis of schizophrenia. Another major difference between studies has been the state of psychosis of patients treated. In three studies, where adjunctive antidepressant therapy was more effective than placebo, most patients were outpatients with mildly active psychosis (Prusoff et al., 1979; Siris et al., 1987; Singh et al., 1978). This is in contrast to the study of Kramer et al. (1989) who used acutely psychotic patients and found that neither amitriptyline nor desipramine was more effective than placebo in alleviating depressive symptomatology as measured by the Hamilton Depression Rating Scale. Similar findings were also noted in acutely ill inpatients when bupropion or placebo was added to thiothixene treatment (Dufresne et al., 1988).

Many anecdotal reports suggest that antidepressant drugs may exacerbate psychosis in patients with schizophrenia (Siris et al., 1978). This has not been the case in most controlled studies where rather adjuvant antidepressants retarded recovery (Kramer et al., 1989; Prusoff et al., 1979; Dufresne et al., 1988). Therapeutic disadvantages may persist as long as 24 weeks in some patients treated with combined treatment.

On the other hand, a recent study reported therapeutic benefits for combined imipramine-fluphenazine decanoate treatment for six months (Siris et al., 1992). In this study none of the 23 patients completing the study had a depressive or psychotic relapse. However, all patients with post-psychotic depressions were selected for continued, open treatment on the basis of a favourable initial response.

The issue of whether to use antidepressant medications in post-psychotic depression may well be related to when during the course of the psychosis the symptoms appear. Moller and von Zerssen (1986) have suggested that the use of antidepressants is not warranted for depression occurring in acute psychotic episodes. Rather they argue that these depressive symptoms abate, along with the psychotic symptoms during the course of antipsychotic drug therapy. According to these authors, since the distinction between antipsychotic induced, akinesia, post-psychotic and other depressions in schizophrenia is often impossible, it is preferable to attempt to alleviate the problem by using a pragmatic approach:

(i)   decrease the dose of the antipsychotic;

(ii)   use parenteral anticholingeric medication on the assumption of an akinesia or akinetic depression;

(iii) if neither of the above are successful, an antidepressant should be tried.

Table 1. Adjunctive Antidepressant Treatment in Post-Psychotic Depression*

Indication	Antipsychotic	Antidepressants	Findings	Comment	Authors
DSM-111 Schiz	Perphenazine	Amitriptyline	Amitriptyline > placebo	dose psychosis amitriptyline too low	Prusoff et al. 1979
Schiz	Various	Maprotiline	Maprotiline not different from placebo	No criteria for schiz depr no ratings depression.	Waehrens & Gerlach1980
Feighner Schiz	Various	Trazodone	Trazodone> placebo	No syndromal definitions of depression.	Singh et al. 1978
Feighner Schiz.	Fluphenazine HCl Flupenthixol decanoate	Nortriptyline	Nortript not.. different from placebo	Dose of nortriptyline may be too high.	Johnson 1981
Schiz	Haloperidol Chlorpromazine	Viloxazine	Viloxazine not different from placebo	Trial too short; stage of psychosis not specified	Kurland & Nagaraju1981
RDC Schiz or Schizoaff	Fluphenazine	Imipramine	Imipramine		Siris et al. 1987
DSM-111 Schiz	Thiothixene	Bupropion not superior to placebo	Bupropion	Severity of psychosis not clearly defined.	Dufresne et al. 1988
RDC Schiz or Schizoaff.	Haloperidol	Amitriptyline or Desipramine	Neither antidepressant superior to placebo		Kramer et al. 1989

* modified from Kramer et al., (1989)

Abbreviations:Schiz: schizophrenia; Schizoaff: schizoaffective disorder; RDC: Research Diagnostic Criteria.

CONCLUSION

Depression in patients with schizophrenia represents an important clinical entity. Whether it arises as part of the syndrome, as an antipsychotic induced phenomenon or as a comorbid condition, cannot be decided on the basis of available data. Diagnostic criteria and the responsiveness to medications are required to establish practical treatment guidelines. Controlled trials of the use of antidepressants in these "post-psychotic depressive syndromes" have not provided unequivocal evidence of efficacy in these states. Perhaps the introduction and wider use of new antipsychotic agents which have mixed dopaminergic serotonergic antagonism, e.g., clozapine, risperidone, remoxipride, may provide greater relief from the full range of psychotic symptoms and associated depression.

REFERENCES

Barnes, T.R.E., Curson, D.A., Liddle, P.F. and Patel, M. (1989). "The nature and prevalence of depression in chronic schizophrenic inpatients", Br. J.Psychiatry, 154, 486 - 491.

Black, D.W., Winokur, G. and Warrock, G. (1985). "Suicide in schizophrenia: the Iowa record linkage study", J.Clin.Psychiatry, 46, 14 - 17.

Bowers, M.B. and Astrachan, B.M. (1967). "Depression in acute schizophrenic psychosis", Am. J.Psychiatry, 123, 976 - 979.

DeAlarcon, R. and Carney, M.W.P. (1969). "Severe depressive mood changes following slow-release intramuscular fluphenazine injection", Br..Med.J., 3, 564 - 567.

Donlon, P.T., Rada, R.T., and Arora, K.K. (1976). "Depression and the reintegration phase of acute schizophrenia", Am. .J. Psychiatry, 133, 1265 - 1268.

Dufresne, R.L., Kass, D.J. and Becker, R.E. (1988). "Bupropion and thiothixene versus placebo and thiothixene in the treatment of depression in schizophrenia", Drug.Dev.Res., 12, 259 - 266.

Falloon, I., Watt, D.C. and Shepherd, M. (1978). "A comparative controlled trial of pimozide and fluphenazine decanoate in the continuation therapy of schizophrenia", Psychol.Med., 8, 59 - 70.

Floru, L., Heinrich, K. and Wittek, F. (1975). "The problem of post-psychotic schizophrenic depressions and their pharmacological induction", Int. Pharmacopsychiatry, 10, 230 - 239.

Galdi, J. (1983). "The causality of depression in schizophrenia", Br.J.Psychiatry, 142, 621 -625.

Galdi, J., Reider, R.O., Silber, D. and Bonato, R.R. (1981). "Genetic factors in the response to neuroleptic in schizophrenia: a psychopharmacogenetic study", Psychol. Med., 11, 713 -728.

Galdi, J. (1983). "The causality of depression in schizophrenia", Br. J. Psychiatry, 142, 621 - 625.

Herz, M.I. and Melville, C. (1980). "Relapse in schizophrenia", Am. J. Psychiatry, 137, 801 - 805.

Hogarty, G.E., Schooler, N.R., Ulrich, R., et al. (1979). "Fluphenazine and social therapy in the aftercare of schizophrenic patients", Arch.Gen.Psychiatry, 36, 1283 - 1294.

Johnson, D.A.W. (1981). "Studies of depressive symptoms in schizophrenia I. The prevalence of depression and its possible cause",Br. J.Psychiat., 149, 89 - 101.

Johnson, D.A.W. (1984). "Observations on the use of long-acting depot neuroleptic injections in the maintenance therapy of schizophrenia", J. Clin. Psychiatry, 5, 13 - 21.

Johnson, D.A.W. and Malik, N.A. (1975). "A double-blind comparison of fluphenazine decanoate and flupenthixol decanoate in the treatment of acute schizophrenia", Acta. Psychiatr. Scand., 51, 257 - 267.

Knights, A. and Hirsch, S.R. (1981). "Revealed depression and drug treatment for schizophrenia", Arch.Gen.Psychiatry, 38, 806 - 811.

Kramer, M.S., Vogel, W.H., Johnson, C.D., Dewey, D.A., Sheves, P., Cavicchia, S., Litle, P., Schmidt, R. and Kimes, I. (1989). "Antidepressants in `depressed' schizophrenic inpatients. A controlled trial", Arch.Gen.Psychiatry, 46, 922 - 928.

Kurland, A.A. and Nagaraju, A. (1981). "Viloxazine and the depressed schizophrenic methodological issues", J.Clin.Pharmacol., 21, 37 - 41.

Leff, J., Tress, K. and Edwards, B. (1988a). "Post-psychotic depression: an umbrella term", Schizophr.Res., 1, 363 - 364.

Leff, J., Tress, K. and Edwards, B. (1988b). "The clinical course of depressive symptoms in schizophrenia", Schizophr.Res., 1, 25 - 30.

Mandel, M.R., Severe, J.B. and Schooler, N.R. (1982). "Development and prediction of postpsychotic depression in neuroleptic-treated schizophrenics", Arch.Gen.Psychiatry, 39, 197 - 203.

Martin, R.L., Cloninger, C.R., Guze, S.B. and Clayton, P.B. (1985). "Frequency and differential diagnosis of depressive syndromes in schizophrenia", J.Clin.Psychiatry 46, 9 -13.

McGlashan, T.H. and Carpenter W.T (1976a). "An investigation of the post psychotic depressive syndrome", Am.J.Psychiatry, 133, 14 - 19.

McGlashan, T. and Carpenter, W.T. (1976b). "Postpsychotic depression in schizophrenia", Arch.Gen.Psychiatry, 33, 231 - 239.

Moller, H.J. and von Zerssen, D. (1986). "Depression in schizophrenia". In Handbook of Studies on Schizophrenia Part 1 (eds. G.D. Burrows, T.R. Norman and G. Rubinstein), pp 183-191, Elsevier Science Publishers, Amsterdam.

Prusoff, B.A., Williams, D.H. and Weissman, M.M. (1979). "Treatment of secondary depression in schizophrenia", Arch.Gen.Psychiatry, 36, 569 - 575.

Rifkin, A., Quitkin, F. and Klein, D.F. (1975). "Akinesia: a poorly recognised drug induced extrapyramidal disorder", Arch.Gen.Psychiatry, 32, 672 - 674.

Rifkin, A. and Siris, S. (1987). "Drug treatment of acute schizophrenia". In Psychopharmacology: The Third Generation of Progress (ed. H.Y. Meltzer) pp 1095 -1101, Raven Press, New York.

Robertson, M. and Trimble, J. (1982). "Major tranquillizers used as antidepressants - a review", J.Affect.Dis., 4, 173 - 193.

Roth, S. (1970). "The seemingly ubiquitous depression following acute schizophrenic episodes, a neglected area of clinical discussion", Am. .J. Psychiatry, 127, 51 - 58.

Roy, A. (1981). "Depression in the course of chronic undifferentiated schizophrenia", Arch.Gen.Psychiatry, 38, 296 - 297.

Roy, A. (1984). "Do neuroleptics cause depression?", Biol.Psychiatry, 19, 777 - 781.

Singh, A.N., Saxena, B. and Nelson, H.L. (1978). "A controlled study of trazodone in chronic schizophrenic patients with pronounced depressive symptomatology", Curr.Ther.Res., 23, 485 - 499.

Singh, M.M. (1976). "Dysphoric response to neuroleptic treatment of schizophrenia and its prognostic significance", Dis.Nerv.Syst., 37, 191 - 196.

Siris, S.G., van Kammen, D.P. and Docherty, J.P. (1978). "Use of antidepressant drugs in schizophrenia", Arch.Gen.Psychiatry, 35, 1368 - 1377.

Siris, S.G., Rifkin, A., Reardon, G.T., Endicott, J., Pereira, D.H., Hayes, R. and Casey, E. (1984). "Course-related depressive syndromes in schizophrenia", Am. .J. .Psychiatry, 141, 1254 - 1257.

Siris, S.G., Morgan, V., Fagerstrom, R., Rifkin, A. and Cooper, T.B. (1987). "Adjunctive imipramine in the treatment of post-psychotic depression: a controlled trial", Arch.Gen.Psychiatry, 44, 533 - 539.

Siris, S.G., Strahan, A., Mandeli, J., Cooper, T.B. and Casey, E. (1988). "Fluphenazine decanoate dose and severity of depression in patients with post-psychotic depression", Schizophr.Res., 1, 31 - 35.

Siris, S.G., Bermanzohn, P.C., Mason, S.E., Shuwall, M.A. and Aseniero, M.A.R. (1992). "Continuation treatment with adjunctive imipramine in schizophrenia", Psychopharmacol.Bull., 28, 303 - 307.

Steinberg, A.R., Green, R. and Durrell, J. (1967). "Depression occurring during the course of recovery from schizophrenic symptoms", Am. .J. Psychiatry, 124, 153 - 156.

Van Putten, T. and May, P.R.A. (1978). "'Akinetic depression' in schizophrenia", Arch.Gen.Psychiat., 35, 1101 - 1107.

Waehrens, J. and Gerlach, J. (1980). "Antidepressant drugs in anergic schizophrenia: a double-blind cross-over study with maprotiline and placebo", Acta.Psychiatr. Scand., 61, 438 - 444.

12

ANXIETY AND PSYCHOSIS

Malcolm Lader

INTRODUCTION

Both anxiety and psychosis are very large and diffuse topics in psychiatry. It would be unhelpful to cover many aspects of these subjects inevitably in the most superficial way. Instead, I shall focus on a circumscribed but nevertheless important and intriguing area, namely the role of anxiety in prodromal symptoms of schizophrenia, most especially with respect to relapse. I shall also discuss the use of anxiolytics in the treatment of acute episodes of schizophrenia as this can be regarded as the obverse of the anxiety/schizophrenia relationship. I shall make particular relevance to sub-topics in which I have made personal observations and, hopefully, contributions.

It is customary but not obligatory to define one's terms before discussing them. I shall deliberately refrain from defining or even describing anxiety and schizophrenic psychosis, giving as an excuse exigencies of space, but in reality avoiding definitions which I believe will over-restrict consideration of these subjects, probably prematurely. It may prove easier to assess the relevance of one diffuse concept to another, the relationship proving more definable than the conditions themselves.

Anxiety As An Early Symptom of Schizophrenia

Even now, the literature dealing with the early diagnosis of schizophrenia is sparse. Following the introduction of Bleuler's concept of schizophrenia, a

Schizophrenia: Exploring the Spectrum of Psychosis. Edited by R. Ancill. © 1994
John Wiley & Sons Ltd

series of clinicians have emphasized the difficulty in distinguishing the early stages of the disorder from other psychiatric disorders, particularly anxiety and depression. Bellak (1958) based the diagnosis of schizophrenia on the degree of disturbance of ego functions and also on the pathological nature of the defences which the patient mobilized to stave off the dissolution of ego function. The crumbling of the defences is typified by "deja vu experiences, feelings of unreality, impaired sleeping, impaired appetite and a rising anxiety level .....". Thus, anxiety is regarded as a secondary phenomenon in early schizophrenia, a formulation which has never been seriously challenged and is generally accepted. Nevertheless, a secondary feature of an illness, or even an attempted compensatory mechanism, can be important in the pathogenesis of a disorder, and may form a legitimate target for therapeutic intervention.

One of the most comprehensive explorations of early schizophrenic symtomatology is that by Chapman (1966). He studied 40 patients, all but 2 male, aged between 17 and 32, and with less than 3 years illness history. Between 2 and 12 semistructured interviews, each approximately one hour in duration formed the basis for evaluation of symptoms. Chapman (1966) described how visual perception was altered, usually transiently but often severely, and how thought blocking was common, as was blocking of attention, perception, memory, speech and mobility. All of these phenomena were accompanied by anxiety and tension, particularly manifest when they occurred during the interview. Although early perceptual and cognitive changes might appear quite pleasant initially, as they progressed the patient became increasingly alarmed and aroused and developed intense anxiety. It appeared that delusional explanations served to lessen that anxiety. Of the 40 patients, 5 presented first with general anxiety and a further 10 or so with specific concern such as hypochondriacal fears. Such somatic complaints are a well-known early feature of schizophrenia (Offenkrantz, 1962).

A prospective approach was adopted by Hustig and Hafner (1990). They developed a self-report questionnaire which was filled in over 3 weeks by 12 patients with persistent auditory hallucinations. Clear correlation's were found between thought disturbance and the intrusion and distress caused by the hallucinations on the one hand, and anxiety and depression on the other.

In a study in Vancouver of Beiser et al. (1993), pairs of clinicians independently rated initial phases in the evolution of psychotic illness, such as first appearance of symptoms, first appearance of prominent psychotic symptoms, and the first time treatment was sought. Although good reliability was attained in assigning age at first appearance of psychotic symptoms and treatment-seeking, the onset of prodromal symptoms proved difficult to assess.

Anxiety may be more prone to occur at certain times and episodes of postpsychotic depression are well-known to occur. In one series of 45 schizophrenic and schizoaffective patients suffering such an episode, about a quarter had severe anxiety to the point of panic attacks (Cutler and Siris, 1991).

Sophisticated technology has been used to further study anxiety in psychosis. Twenty patients with schizophrenia and 10 controls underwent PETscan studies of regional brain glucose metabolism (Wik and Wiesel, 1991). Intensity of anxiety was rated after the scan. In all subjects, positive correlation's were found between the level of anxiety and the regional glucose metabolism. the patterns differed between patients and controls: the latter showed positive correlation's between anxiety and frontal/parietal regions of the left hemisphere; in patients, negative relationships were found to the relative metabolic rates in right medial frontal cortex and the left thalamus. The authors suggest that altered functions in fronto-limbic neuronal circuits may partly explain emotional impairments in some schizophrenic patients.

Anxiety As An Early Symptom of Relapse

Schizophrenic relapse is a complex process. One scheme which has been suggested involves 4 stages (Donlon and Blacker, 1975). The first comprises a massive psychological conflict which presses on an emotionally sensitive individual. The conflict is not soluble by normal or even neurotic mental processes. There is malaise and dysphoria with fluctuating cognitive-perceptual disturbances and subjective fear. Next, the individual tries to avert psychological disintegration by repetitive actions, often accompanied by panic symptoms. Depression may ensue and deepen. In the third stage, loss of control of thought processes and conceptual mechanisms signifies the failure to contain the psychotic process. finally, the patient achieves relief from anxiety, depression and the inner chaos of psychosis through compensatory mechanisms such as idiosyncratic thinking and pre-occupations. Anxiety and terror are relieved but at the cost of distorting reality. The importance of anxiety in this schema is quite apparent.

Direct observation of schizophrenic patients during relapse has revealed somewhat varied results with respect to symptomatology. In one such study (Subotnik and Nuechterlein, 1988), six-week periods prior to 17 psychotic relapses and to 10 depressive relapses were evaluated in 23 recent-onset schizophrenics, using the BPRS. The symptom patterns were compared with those during periods not heralding relapse for the same patients and for 27 schizophrenic patients who did not relapse. Before psychotic relapses, overall symptomatology increased mostly for symptoms related to thought disturbance and anxiety-depression factors of the BPRS. However, the individual BPRS item for Anxiety was not elevated. The authors interpreted this as indicating that anxiety is more characteristic of a general exacerbation of illness rather than being a specific harbinger of a full relapse.

An earlier study had involved giving 145 chronic schizophrenic patients (99 in Atlanta; 46 in Buffalo) and 80 family members in Atlanta a structured interview regarding early signs of relapse as detected by them (Herz and Melville, 1980). As expected, the families were more aware of prodromal changes than the patients themselves; 93% as compared with 70%. In about two-thirds of instances involving a patient and a family member, they agreed that early signs of decompensation were recognizable. In most of the cases, relapse took more than a week, giving an opportunity to intervene. The commonest prodromal symptom was becoming tense and anxious. Other phenomena reported included dysphoria, loss of appetite, poor sleep and social withdrawal. The predominance of anxiety symptoms in both groups of patients and the families is shown clearly in Table 1. Only the 10 most frequent in each group is listed. High consistency is apparent.

Recognizing these prodromal symptoms of relapse, and the observation that several days or even weeks elapse before this process is complete, offers the potential of early intervention to prevent relapse and commonly rehospitalisation. In a retrospective survey of the case-notes of 38 patients, two-thirds (24) were judged to have maintained insight, of whom only 2 relapsed; of the 14 patients without insight, 7 required rehospitalisation (Heinrichs et al., 1985). Birchwood and his colleagues (1989) developed an early sign scale (ESS) which combined self-report with observer report. Four separate groups of changes were noted, namely anxiety/agitation, depression/withdrawal, disinhibition and incipient psychotic features. About two-thirds of relatives reported anxiety, tension and sleep problems as prodromata. The ESS was then used prospectively to validate it as an instrument predicting relapse. Of 19 patients, 8 relapsed and 11 remained well. No early signs were found in the non-relapsers but were present in 6 who relapsed. Case examples show anxiety and agitation to increase markedly according to the subjective ratings but less so by observer ratings.

Table 1. Prodromal Symptoms Before Hospital Admission (Herz and Melville, 1990)

Atlanta Patients n = 99		Atlanta Families n = 80		Buffalo Patients n = 46	
Symptom	%	Symptom	%	Symptom	%
Tense and nervous	70.7	Tense and nervous	83.3	Tense and nervous	80
Depression	63.6	Restlessness	78.8	Eating less	71
Trouble sleeping	61.6	Trouble concentrating	76.3	Trouble concentrating	69
Restlessness	58.6	Nonsensical talk	76.3	Trouble sleeping	67
Trouble concentrating	56.6	Depression	76.3	Enjoy things less	65
Loss of interest	56.6	Loss of interest	73.8	Restlessness	63
Seeing friends less	54 5	Sleeping less	68.8	Can' t remember things	63
Enjoy things less	52.5	Enjoy things less	67.5	Depression	60
Am being laughed at	51.5	Preoccupied	65.0	Preoccupied	59
Eating less	49.5	Can't remember things	60.0	Seeing friends less	59

Other studies have concentrated on dysphoria and depression as primary foci of research interest. using an Early Signs Questionnaire (ESQ), Hirsch and Jolley (1989) examined the relationship between various symptoms including dysphoria and relapse in 54 schizophrenic patients, of whom 10 relapsed (one twice) during a year. A total of 44 dysphoric episodes were identified of which 8 (18%) were followed by relapse. The dysphoric episodes were characterized by depression, hostility, anxiety and paranoid feelings. The most frequent early symptom was 'fear of going crazy". Thus, dysphoric episodes were not necessarily related to relapse, and intervention such as increasing the antipsychotic dosage would have been designed to lessen the symptomatic distress rather than to prevent relapse.

A Canadian study has looked generally at symptoms of dysphoria and anxiety in schizophrenia, not just in relation to relapse (Norman and Malla, 1991). Diagnostic interviews were conducted on 95 schizophrenic patients and a range of questionnaires was completed by each patient. Depression and anxiety dimensions correlated strongly and were combined into one measure of dysphoria. This measure correlated more strongly with the positive than the negative symptoms of schizophrenia. The authors favored the explanation that the anxiety and depression, the dysphoria, was an integral part of the psychosis but admitted that other explanations could fit their correlational data such as the possibility that patients become dysphoric as a reaction to the high level of positive symptoms.

Anxiety and Schizophrenic Relapse - Theoretical Considerations

Birchwood (1992) has provided us with a coruscating review of the theoretical background to relapse, and clinical strategies designed to obviate it (Figure 1). he describes two stages in the process of relapse. The first is dysphoria comprising anxiety, restlessness, blunting of drives, followed by early psychotic symptoms such as suspiciousness, ideas of reference and misrepresentations. The interpretation of the first stage is problematic. He postulates that a mixture of symptoms occurs, some intrinsic to the illness, together with a psychological response that focuses on a search for the meaning of bizarre experiences and ways of controlling them. In the earlier stages of schizophrenia when few relapses have occurred, the patient is perplexed by the perceptual and thought changes and finds them difficult to describe: diffuse anxiety results. Later, with more experience, the patient recognizes these changes as dangerous and has a sense of foreboding: a more focused anxiety results that something is about to happen over which little or no control can be exercised. The stress, fear, anxiety, anticipation and sense of futility can themselves accelerate the process of relapse, i.e., they may prove maladaptive rather than defensive.

Figure 1. Psychological Process in the Stages of Psychotic Relapse (Birchwood, 1992)

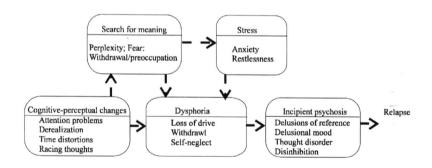

Mediating Mechanisms

For many years, my research team has been interested in the mediating mechanisms between environmental influences and fluctuations in the severity of mental disorders. About 15 years ago we collaborated with the Social Psychiatry Unit at the Institute of Psychiatry to investigate the area of schizophrenic relapse. This came soon after the well-known seminal work in that Unit which related relapse to an index of "Expressed Emotion" (EE) in the schizophrenic patient's environment, to the time spent with the key relative, and to the protective value of antipsychotic medication in a high EE milieu. Unexpected life events seemed to precipitate relapse despite the patient's taking phenothiazine medication. We hypothesized that high EE factors chronically increased arousal but this could be contained with medication, whereas life events elevated arousal acutely and to such an extent that medication proved ineffectual. By arousal, we meant generalized increase in neuronal activity, both centrally, manifest as anxiety and increased schizophrenic symtomatology, and peripherally, where it could be monitored by our psychophysiological measures.

Our first study involved 18 partly remitted schizophrenic patients living in the community and in age- and sex-matched normal control subjects; a third group comprised 10 chronic schizophrenic in-patients who had been withdrawn from medication for at least 4 weeks (Tarrier et al., 1978). Bilateral skin conductance was recorded in the laboratory during both a passive habituation procedure to tones and an active reaction time test. Heart-rate was also recorded and both groups of patients had faster heart-rates than the normal. However, no consistent electrodermal differences were found between patients and controls, between in-patients and community patients, or between patients living in high or low EE environments - an essentially negative study suggesting that laboratory conditions were inappropriate in investigating the type of environmental factors which interested us.

Next, we investigated 21 schizophrenic patients in the community who had taken part in a replication of the original EE study. Psychophysiological recordings were carried out on 3 occasions in the patient's home. Twenty-one normal control subjects were also recruited and tested in the same way, but only once. Electrodermal activity and heart-rate were recorded, first with only the experimenter present and then with the subject's key relative in the room. The investigator was unaware whether that relative had been rated previously high or low in EE (Tarrier et al., 1979). Information was also obtained about time spent in fact-to-fact contact with that key relative, medication taken, and then any life events in the three weeks prior to the testing.

Patients had significantly more electrodermal activity (spontaneous fluctuations) than controls. High EE and low EE patients had similar levels when only the experimenter was present but activity increased in high EE patients when the relative was present but dropped in the low EE patients (p<0.01). In other words, controls adapt throughout the recording, low EE patients when their relative is present, but high EE patients not at all (see figure 2). This difference only occurred on the first occasion. On the second occasion, both groups steadily declined in physiological activity and on the third, the patterns resembled those of the normal's tested once. Thus, the novel recording itself was a necessary stress factor to bring out the differences between the groups. Finally, recordings taken on occasions preceded by life events were more active than those not so preceded (p<0.02). The data suggested that the presence of the relative in high EE patients accentuated these life event differences. Our interpretation was that a series of factors can interact to increase physiological arousal and this is compatible with an increase in predisposition to relapse.

Figure 2. Effect of Key Relative on Spontaneous Fluctuations in Skin Conductance in Patients with High EE Relatives, Low EE Relatives, and Normal Controls.

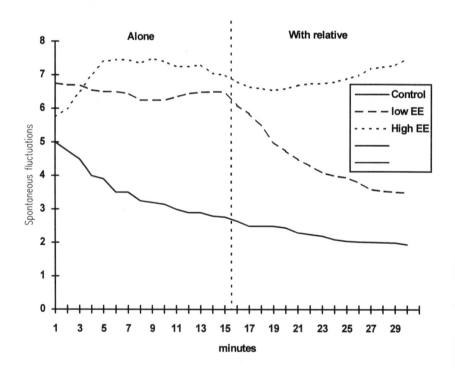

A partial replication of this study was achieved by Sturgeon et al. (1984) who recorded from high and low EE patients in a video studio, again with a relative absent/present design. Electrodermal activity was almost twice as high in high as low EE patients, but the presence of the relative made no difference. Tarrier and his group (1988) went on to carry out a much larger replication using 70 patients, newly admitted to hospitals. Electrodermal measurements were made with the patient talking to the experimenter for 15 minutes and then to the relative. Again there were no differences between high and low EE patients when the relative as absent but significantly more activity in the high than low EE patients when the relative was present. the arousal of the low EE patients lessened with the relative present, but increased in the high EE patients. Ratings of anxiety were made. The high EE group rated themselves more anxious and tense than the low EE group throughout. Patients with low EE relatives reported decreases in anxiety after the relative entered.

These studies provide insight into the possible associations between factors in the patient and possible mediating mechanisms, the latter being relatively non-specific. More recent studies (e.g. Stirling et al., 1993) have shown that EE is not a stable characteristic (nor is there any a priori reason why it should be), but the psychophysiological approach might enable this to be monitored. What it does emphasize, of course, is the possibility of family and social intervention strategies. It also has implications for my final topic, drug treatment.

Drug Prevention of Relapse

Relapse is a major event in the natural history of schizophrenia and the avoidance of these events is a major goal of therapy. The efficacy of antipsychotic medication in postponing relapses and perhaps even preventing them in some patients has been well-documented (David, 1975). However, long-term antipsychotic treatment carries with it a burden of unwanted effects which can distress the patient and compromise compliance (Marder et al., 1987). In particular, akinesia and akathisia can increase a patient's subjective experience of depression and anxiety. Alternative strategies have been attempted including low dose treatment and intermittent therapy.

Intermittent therapy involves withdrawing patients from maintenance treatment, closely monitoring the clinical state for prodromal signs of relapse and then instituting rapid but brief pharmacotherpay. One well-controlled study involved 54 asymptomatic, stable patients who were allocated randomly to receive active drug or placebo maintenance (Jolley et al., 1989; 1990). When a prodromal was identified, patients in both groups could receive "escape medication". patients were instructed how to detect an incipient relapse and told to contact the investigators. One-year outcome was fairly encouraging. Although more placebo maintenance patients experienced prodromal symptoms than did the drug maintenance group (76 vs 27%) and more relapsed (30 vs 7%), severe relapses were not common in either group, and the reduced drug side-effects in the placebo group were a definite advantage. However, at two years relapse was both more frequent (50 vs 12%) and more severe in the intermittent than in the continuous maintenance groups. In the second year most of the relapses were not preceded by identified prodromal symptoms. Another study had rather similar outcomes, and, in addition, the intermittent regimen was less popular with the patients (Carpenter et al., 1990).

Some of the difficulty lies with the need to identify prodromata, which as we saw earlier, vary greatly from patient to patient, although each patient tends to have his own pattern, anxiety often being important. In such patients, the possibility arises that the intervention could take the form of anxiolytic rather than antipsychotic medication. This has not been directly tested in a brief intervention paradigm, but benzodiazepine anxiolytics have been evaluated in schizophrenia in other contexts (Kellner et al., 1975; Wokowitz et al, 1988; Csernansky et al., 1988).

Lingjaerde (1991) has reviewed such studies, although he points out the difficulties in coming to definite conclusions because of the uncontrolled nature of so many of the studies. In conventional doses, benzodiazepines are anxiolytic in schizophrenic patients, but have "no convincing antipsychotic effect". Nevertheless, they may help stave off relapse (e.g. Gracia et al., 1990). In high dosage (up to 10 times usual), paranoid-hallucinatory patients may show a therapeutic response, anxiety, tension but also psychotic symptoms improving. Some patients may become disinhibited. In combination with antipsychotic c drugs, benzodiazepines have a useful potentiating effect, hallucinations in particular appearing to respond. The effect is prompt in onset. Differences among the benzodiazepines with regard to putative antipsychotic efficacy have been claimed but are not supported by adequate clinical trials.

CONCLUSIONS

We have ranged fairly widely over the topic of anxiety, schizophrenic relapse and drug treatment. Anxiety provides a unifying leitmotif through a whole series of areas of research. It is not fundamental to the schizophrenic process but can be viewed in three major ways. First, it is an index of the distress which the cardinal features of schizophrenia such as thought disturbance occasion. Secondly, it can provide a marker for incipient relapse as the anxiety spirals up out of control. Thirdly, it is a legitimate target for therapeutic intervention. In research terms, assessment of anxiety directly by mood reports or indirectly by psychophysiological variables can provide a useful research tool to examine both practical issues and theoretical constructs.

REFERENCES

Beiser M., Erickson D., Fleming J.A.E., and Iacono W.G. (1993). "Establishing the onset of psychotic illness", Am. J. Psychiatry, 150, 1349 - 1354.

Bellak L. (1958). "Schizophrenia: A review of the syndrome", Logos Press, New York.

Birchwood M. (1992). "Early intervention in schizohrenia: Theoretical background and clinical strategies", Br. J Clin. Psychol., 31, 257 - 278.

Birchwood M., Smith J., MacMillan F., Hogg B., Prasad R., Harvey C. and Bering S. (1989). "Predicting relapse in schizophrenia: the development and implementation of an early signs monitoring system using patients and families as observers: a preliminary investigation", Psychol. Med., 19, 649 - 656.

Carpenter W.I., Hanlon T.E., Heinrichs D.W., Summerfelt A.T., Kirkpatrick B., Levine J. and Buchanan R.W. (1990). "Early intervention in schizohrenia: Theoretical background and clinical strategies", Br. J Clin. Psychol., 31, 257 - 278.

Chapman J. (1966). "The early symptoms of schizophrenia", Br. J Psychiatry, 112, 225 - 251.

Csernansky J.G., Riney S.J., Lombrozo L., Overall J.E., Hollister L.E. (1988). "Double-blind comparison of alprazolam, diazepam, and placebo for the treatment of negative schizophrenic symptoms", Arch. Gen. Psychiatry, 45, 655 - 659.

Cutler J.L. and Siris S.G. (1991). " "Panic-like" symptomatology in schizohrenic and schizoaffective patients with postpsychotic depression: observations and implications", Comp. Psychiatry, 32, 465 - 473.

Davis J. (1975). "overview: maintenance therapy in psychiatry, I. Schizophrenia", Am. J. Psychiatry, 132, 1237 - 1245.

Donlon P.T. and Blacker K.H. (1975). "Clinical recognition of early schizophrenic decompensation", Dis. Nerv. System, 36, 323 - 330.

Gracia R.I., Gutierrez J.M., Faraone S.V., Tsuang M.T. (1990). "Use of lorazepam for increased anxiety after neuroleptic dose reduction", Hosp. Comm. Psychiatry, 41, 197 - 198.

Heinrichs D.W., Cohen B.P. and Carpenter W.T. (1985). "Early insight and the management of schizophrenic decompensation", J. Nerv. Ment. Dis., 173, 133 - 138.

Herz M.I. and Melville C. (1980). "Relapse in schizophrenia", Am. J. Psychiatry 137, 801 - 805.

Hirsch S.R. and Jolley A.G. (1989). "The dysphoric syndrome in schizophrenia and its implications for relapse", Br. J Psychiatry, 155 (Supp. 5), 46 - 50.

Hustig H.H. and Hafner R.J. (1990). "Persistent auditory hallucinations and their relationship to delusions and mood", J. Nerv. Ment. Dis., 178, 264 - 267

Jolley A.G., Hirsch S.R., Mcrink A. and Wilson L. (1989). "Trial of brief intermittent neuroleptic prophylaxis for selected schizophrenic outpatients: Clinical outcome at one year", Bri. Med. J., 301, 837 - 842.

Kellener R., Wilson R.M., Mudawer M.D., Pathak D. (1975). "Anxiety ins chizophrenia: the responses to chlordiazepoxide in an intensive design study", Arch. Gen. Psychiatry, 32, 1246 - 1254.

Lingjaerde O. (1991). "Benzodiazepines in the treatment of schizophrenia: an updated survey", Acta Psychiat. Scand., 84, 453 - 459.

Marder S.R., VanPutten T., Mintz J., McKenzie J., Labell M., Faltico G. and May R.P. (1987). "Low and conventional dose maintenance therapy with fluphenazine decanoate", Arch. Gen. Psychiatry, 44, 518 - 521.

Norman R.M.G. and Malla A.K. (1991). "dysphoric mood and symptomatology in schizophrenia", Psychol. Med., 21, 897 - 903.

Offrenkrantz W. (1962). "Multiple somatic complaints as a precursor of schizophrenia", Am. J. Psychiatry, 119, 258 - 9.

Stirling J., Tantam D., Thomas P., Newby D., Montague L., Ring N. and Rowe S. (1993). "Expressed emotion and schizophrenia: the ontogeny of EE during an 18-month follow up. Psychol. Med., 23, 771 - 778.

Sturgeon D., Turpin G., Berkowitz R., Kuipers L. and Leff J.P. (1984). "Psychophysiological responses of schizophrenic patients to high and low expressed emotion relatives: a follow-up study', Br. J Psychiatry, 146, 62 - 69.

Subotnik K.L. and Nuechterlein K.H. (1988). "Prodromal signs and symptoms of schizophrenic relapse", J. Abnorm. Psychol., 97, 405 - 412.

Tarrier N., Cooke E.C. and Lader M.H. (1978). "Electrodermal and heart-rate measurements in chronic and partially remitted schizophrenic patients", Acta Psychiatr. Scand., 57, 369 - 376.

Tarrier N., Lader M.H., Leff J.P. (1979). "bodily reactions to people and events in schizophrenics", Arch. Gen. Psychiatry, 36, 311 - 315.

Tarrier N., Barrowclough C., Porceddue K. and Watts S. (1988). "The assessment of psychophysiological reactivity ot the expressed emotion of the relatives of schizophrenic patients", Br. J Psychiatry, 152, 618 - 624.

Wik G. and Wiesel F-A (1991). "Regional brain glucose metabolism: correlations to biochemical measures and anxiety in patients with schizophrenia", Psychiatry Res.: Neuroimaging 40, 101 - 114.

Wolkowitz O.M., Brieier A., Doran A., Kelsoe J., Lucas P., Paul S.M.,Pickar D., (1988). "Alprazolam augmentation of the anti-psychotic effects of fluphenazine in schizophrenic patients: preliminary reports", Arch. Gen. Psychiatry, 45, 664 - 671.

13

DEPRESSION IN SCHIZOPHRENICS

Richard Williams

When Kraeplin (1917) introduced the concept of dementia praecox "for the purpose of preliminary enquiry", he believed in the unitary disease concept and saw "that in dementia praecox the emotions are silent, whilst the manic depressive patients complain in despairing accounts of the feelings of inward desolations and emptiness." Thus, Kraeplin acknowledges the sadness of schizophrenics, whilst yet separating dementia praecox from manic depressive illness. Bleuler (1950) suggested that the dysphoric mood found in many schizophrenics arose from the subjects, awareness of the disorder and its limiting influence on their lives. (See Figure 1.)

Figure 1. Possible Relationship of Depressive Symptoms to Schizophrenia

- Depression is an integral part of schizophrenia
- Neuroleptics treating schizophrenia cause depression
- Depression is a psychological reaction to accepting schizophrenia
- Depression and schizophrenia are two independent illnesses
- Depression and schizophrenia share aspects of common biology

THEORIES OF AETIOLOGY

Martin et al. (1985) reported that 60% of schizophrenics had experienced a depressive syndrome during the course of their illness. Knights and Hirsch

Schizophrenia: Exploring the Spectrum of Psychosis. Edited by R. Ancill. © 1994
John Wiley & Sons Ltd

(1981) prefer to talk of revealed depression with 25% of their schizophrenic subjects showing depressive symptomatology after resolution of psychosis. They, like Mandel et al. (1982), regard depressive symptoms as an integral part of the schizophrenic illness, (they believe these symptoms are frequently masked by the more florid signs of the acute psychosis).

A second view of depressive symptoms was postulated by De Arlacon and Carney (1969) who noted both depressive symptoms and suicide in schizophrenic patients started on long-acting neuroleptics. They postulated that the neuroleptics could induce depressive symptomatology directly. Nitwad and Nicolshi-Oproin (1978) compared stabilized schizophrenics maintained on depot and oral neuroleptics and found no significant difference (21% vs 29%) in depressive symptomatology, thus challenging De Arlacon's theory regarding depot neuroleptics inducing depression and even suicide.

Lambert (1987) in reviewing the possible role of neuroleptics in causing depression, also suggests that the patient's awareness of the chronic nature of schizophrenia may cause the depression. This also recalls Melanie Klein's work suggesting that adult schizophrenia is due to a disturbance of defence mechanisms, and that if resolution of the disturbance occurs the patient may regress to a depressive phase. Thus, both psychodynamic and existentialist theorists claim a possible explanation for the depressive symptoms, experienced by recovering schizophrenics.

Kendell (1983) in considering the concept of schizoaffective disorders questioned whether this could be two independent conditions (depression and schizophrenia) occurring simultaneously.

McGuffin et al. (1989) has shown that this is an unacceptable idea given that the lifetime risk of schizophrenia is about 0.85%, mania about 1%, and depression about 2.7%, and as such the chance co-occurring risk of depression and schizophrenia is less than 3 per 10000. Nearly all studies find depressive symptoms in at least 20% of schizophrenic patients, so could it be that depression is a separate but not independent illness from schizophrenia, that coexists in a suitable biological environment in a similar way cardiac failure developing and coexisting with impaired renal function? To date the best model for this type of coexisting illnesses has been postulated by Flor-Henry (1978). He suggests that the directionality of lateral hemispheric organization determines the form of the consequent psychosis. Disturbance of the dominant left hemisphere results in schizophrenic symptomatology, whilst disturbance of the non-dominant right hemisphere produces depressive symptomatology. Flor-

Henry (1989) has further developed these ideas, based on the underlying organization principle of (a) interhemispheric activation, (b) interhemispheric coupling, and (c) contralateral inhibition. Flor-Henry proposes an elegant theory: that in normal individuals a balanced brain asymmetry occurs in which the right hemisphere controls the inductive influences of signals emitted by the left hemisphere. Hommes and Panhuyssen (1970) had demonstrated that the more depressed an individual was the more their left hemisphere was lateralized for language. Flor-Henry explains this as being due to increasing right hemisphere disorganization with contralateral inhibition of left hemispheric function through disruption of callosal transfer. Flor-Henry et al. (1983) from a study of unmedicated subjects produced further evidence to support his view of lateralization when he found evidence in schizophrenics of greater left-sided asymmetry as detected by psychological testing, whilst in psychotic depressions there were greater right-sided deficits. Flor-Henry (1989) concluded that depression in schizophrenics could occur from two mechanisms: (a) from a primary right hemispheric basis, or (b) in schizophrenics where the "fundamental" deficit is of the dominant hemisphere, from a left hemispheric basis with consequent contralateral disinhibition disrupting the emotionality systems characteristic of the right hemisphere. These complex but elegant theories have not been refuted, and clearly need further investigation as an aetiological explanation of depressive symptoms in schizophrenic patients.

RELATIONSHIP OF DEPRESSION TO OTHER SYMPTOM CLUSTERS IN SCHIZOPHRENIA

Many investigators have been concerned about the possible relationship between positive and negative symptoms of schizophrenia; and depressive symptoms and hopelessness; and extrapyramidal symptoms and the neuroleptic dysphoria syndrome. Hughlings Jackson may have been the first proponent of negative symptoms but it is Crow (1985) and Andreasen (1979, 1982) who have reawakened interest in the dichotomy between positive and negative symptoms and the associated prognostic significance. Crow's initial differentiation between type I (positive symptom complex) and type II (negative symptom) schizophrenia did not ultimately correlate with his proposed view of biochemical and reversible (type I) and organic and irreversible (type II) schizophrenia. However, Kay et al. (1987) and Andreasen (1982) have refined the concept of positive and negative symptom schizophrenia and developed the rating scales PANSS, and SAPS and SANS, respectively. These scales, together with the Present State Examination (PSE), have become the cornerstone of phenomenological research in schizophrenic symptomatology. The PANSS scale was itself derived and expanded from Overall and Gorham's (1962) BPRS scale.

One of the first studies to investigate depression and negative symptoms in schizophrenics was Lindenmayer et al.'s (1986) paper in which, using the BPRS, the authors found that depressive symptoms correlated with negative symptoms in the acute phase of illness and that both symptom complexes predicted favourable outcome at two years follow-up. However, at subsequent follow-up depressive and negative symptom complexes were no longer correlated, suggesting that even if the complexes shared similarities they were not identified.

Pogue-Geile and Harrow (1984) using the PSE had derived a measure of negative symptoms did not correlate with schizophrenic patients' self report of depression.

Later, Liddle (1987) re-examined the positive - negative symptom dichotomy in a study of 40 schizophrenic patients and concluded from statistical analysis of the PSE that there were 3 independent syndromes: (a) psychomotor poverty (poverty of speech, lack of spontaneous movements, plus aspects of blunting of affect), (b) disorganization (inappropriate affect, poverty of content of speech, and disturbances of form of thought), and (c) reality distortion (particular types of delusions and hallucinations).

There is no uniformity of opinion as to the "correct" way of rating negative symptoms, but the main rating scales are summarized in Figure 2. With regard to depressive symptoms the picture is even less clear. All negative symptoms are rated by observers, but in depression Lindenmayer et al. (1992) has pointed out that variability in assessment of depression may partially be accounted for by the fact that depression can be measured in three separate and distinct ways: through patient self rating (subjective mood state), clinician rating (affective state), and observer ratings (behavioural manifestations). In this paper Lindenmayer demonstrated that clinician-rated (Hamilton Rating Scale for Depression-HAM-D), and observer-rated (NOSIE) assessments tended to correlate significantly, whilst in self-rated scales (Plutchik Mood Scale, Psychiatric Symptom Index, and Personality Profile Index), subjective reports were discordant. Previously, Andreasen (1982) had reported discordance between clinician ratings of negative symptoms and patients' subjective accounts.

Figure 2. Comparison of Items Comprising Negative Symptom Complex

BPRS	PANSS	PSE	SANS*
Blunted affect	Blunted affect	Flat affect	Affective flattening or blunting (8)
Emotional withdrawal	Emotional withdrawal	Poverty of speech	Alogia (5)
	Poor rapport	Psychomotor retardation	Avolition and apathy
	Passive/apathetic social withdrawal		Anhedonia - asociality (5)
	Difficulty in abstract thinking		Attention (3)
	Lack of spontaneity		
	Stereotyped thinking		

* Number of subscales in parentheses.

Do negative symptoms overlap with depressive symptoms, and if so is it possible to tease the essential component items apart to provide greater discrimination between these two symptom clusters? Williams and Dalby (1989) found in a study of 60 stabilized schizophrenic outpatients that depression scores assessed by the MMPI-D scores correlated significantly with Beck Depression Rating scores but not with the SANS. Interestingly, we found female patients most frequently endorsed items of subjective depression (from MMPI-D) whilst males tended to focus more on physical complaints.

Our colleagues from Calgary, Addington et al. (1990), determined to develop a specific rating scale for depression to be used in a psychotic population. They assessed 50 acutely ill schizophrenic patients at two points in time using the Hamilton Depression Rating Scale and the Present State Examination. Factor analysis was used to select items from the HAM-D and PSE-D which explained at each of the two points in time the greatest proportions of variance in the ratings of depression; thereby ensuring all items discorrelated between depressed and non-depressed schizophrenics. The new rating scale (Calgary Depression Scale for Schizophrenics) has only 11 items, 5 derived from HAM-D, and 10 from the PSE, with 4 items from each overlapping. This scale has yet to be utilized to its full potential in clinical research.

To add further to the confusion regarding depression in schizophrenics, Rifkin et al. (1975) pointed out that akinesia, an extrapyramidal side effect of antipsychotic medication characterized by lessening of spontaneity, paucity of gestures, diminished conversation and apathy, could be easily confused with depression, demoralization and residual schizophrenia. Van Putten and May (1978) demonstrated that in 94 schizophrenics treated with antipsychotic medication, 28 developed akinesia and whilst becoming less psychotic, experienced an increase in depressive symptoms. Treatment of akinesia with anticholinergics resulted in significant improvement in depression, somatic concern, emotional withdrawal, blunted affect, and motor retardation.

Siris (1987) returned to this theme when he proposed that one could differentiate post-psychotic depression from akinesia in neuroleptic-treated patients not by symptoms but by response to benztropine. Akinesia can occur in parkinsonism, retarded depression, and the negative symptom state of schizophrenia. Bermanzoh and Siris (1992) suggest this occurs through the common pathway of functional reduction in dopaminergic transmission. Chouinard and Jones (1978), flying in the face of conventional wisdom, had proposed that schizophrenia might result from a relative hypodopaminergic state associated with the negative symptoms of schizophrenia. This hypothesis of frontal hypodopaminergia accounting for negative symptoms, and limbic system hyperdopaminergia producing positive symptoms, has found recent support from Meltzer (1985), Meltzer et al. (1986), and Ereshefsky and Lacombe (1993).

There have been a number of studies looking at suicide and attempted suicide in schizophrenics and a possible association with depression. The results have usually supported the view that depression is related to self harm. Roy (1989) in reviewing the situation concluded that 10% of schizophrenics die by suicide, and that risk factors include being young, male, having a relapsing illness, having been depressed in the past, being currently depressed, and being socially isolated in the community. Addington and Addington (1992) in a study of 50 schizophrenics found prior suicide attempts were significantly correlated with current depression, female sex, lower education, and more frequent hospitalization. Dalby and Williams (1987) failed to find current depression in schizophrenics associated with past suicidal behaviour. Possibly the most interesting observation in the prediction of suicidal behaviour in schizophrenics came from Cooper et al. (1992), who in a prospective study had measured 5HIAA in CSF of 30 drug-free schizophrenics. These patients were followed over a period of 11 years; 10 patients made suicide attempts, and these subjects had significantly lower CSF, 5HIAA levels at initial evaluation than non attempters [mean (S.E.): 6.7 (2.2) vs 23.6 (5.6) ng/ml, P<0.05].   Cooper concludes "our findings provide further evidence of the relation between serotoninergic dysfunction and suicide and suggest a role for drugs with serotoninergic effects in schizophrenia."

Drake et al. (1989) and the Dartmouth group have completed extensive research on suicide in schizophrenics, identifying risk factors, considered the influence of depression and hopelessness and examined the differences between suicide attempters and completers.   They stress the importance of identifying high-risk suicidal schizophrenics and discuss treatment approaches including hospitalization, somatic treatments, and psychotherapy for those in which the suicidal urge seems related to awareness of having a devastating mental illness. They also promote the idea of family therapy and psychosocial rehabilitation as components of a comprehensive treatment program.

So far this chapter has reviewed the concept of depressive symptoms in schizophrenia, and examined theories of possible aetiology, then examined the relationship to negative symptoms and clinical phenocopies of depression, including akinesia, akathisia, and demoralization.   Given the plethora of hypotheses, what is the clinician to do in the assessment and treatment of depressive features in schizophrenia?   A good starting point are the reviews of Siris (1989) and Plasky (1991). In Table 3, I have updated their summaries of clinical trials of treatment of depression in schizophrenics, with four trials reported subsequently.

These trials give conflicting evidence as to the efficacy of tricyclics in treating depressive symptoms in schizophrenics.   The majority of trials found no difference between placebo and tricyclic antidepressant; often with both groups showing a decrease of depressive symptoms over time.   Siris et al. (1987) have been the only clinicians to find evidence supporting the use of imipramine, but they have demonstrated that in depressive responders, removal of imipramine has resulted in relapse of depressive symptoms in chronic schizophrenics. Johnson and Malik's (1975) early study, finding in favour of schizophrenic patients on flupenthixol to have less depressive symptoms than those on fluphenazine, may be confounded by the fact that he found that patients on flupenthixol exhibited either no depressive tendencies or an improvement in depressive symptoms, whilst in the fluphenazine group the overall mood was lowered.

Table 1. Treatments of Depression in Schizophrenics

Study	n	Population	Design / ratings	Medications	Time weeks	Results / comments
Waehrens and Gerlach (1980)	20	Chronic inactive schizophrenics	Double-blind crossover /BPRS, NOSIE, activity-Withdrawl scale	Various neuroleptics, and (a) maprotiline (mean 138mg) (b) placebo	8	NS improvement with antidepressant
Kurland and Nagaraju (1981)	28	Schizophrenic, 18+ on HAM-D	Double-blind, placebo-controlled / BPRS, HAM-D,CGI, Zung Depression	CPZ or Haldol, viloxazine 300 mg	4	NS
Johnson (1981)	50	Chronic schizophrenic, 15+ on BDI	Double-blind, placebo-controlled / HAM-D, BPRS, BDI	Depot fluphenazine or flupenthixol, nortriptyline 150 mg	5	NS, anticholinergics allowed; trend in favour of TCA
Becker (1983)	52	RDC criteria for schizophrenia and major depressive syndrome	Double-blind, placebo - controlled / HAM-D, BPRS, CGI	Thiothixene (mean 40mg) with placebo or CPZ (mean 640 mg) with imipramine (mean 150 mg)	4	NS, but both groups improved in depression scores
Siris et al. (1987)	33	RDC schizophrenics, RDC criteria for minor or major depression,	Double-blind / SADS, CGI, HAM-D	Fluphenazine, imipramine	6	all had received benztropine to rule out akinesia, CGI: p=0.02 in favour of imipramine group HAM-D: p=0.018

Study	N	Population	Design / measures	Medication	Weeks	Results
		12+ on HAM-D				Depressive mood: p=0.047
Kramer et al. (1989)	58	Actively psychotic schizophrenics (DSM-III-R)	Double-blind / BPRS, HAM-D	Haldol, benztropine; (a) desipramine (mean 244 mg) or (b) amitriptyline (mean 230 mg) or (c) placebo	4	NS
Siris (1990)	14	Schizophrenic patients; with post-psychotic depression, and responding to imipramine	Placebo-controlled trial of imipramine maintained or discontinued	Fluphenazine, benztropine; (a) imipramine (b) placebo	52*	6 patients tapered relapsed into depressive / negative symptoms; 2 imipramine patients relapse; p=0.009
Siris (1991)	27	Schizophrenics with negative symptoms and post-psychotic depression	Double-blind, placebo-controlled / CGI, SADS, HAM-D, GAS	Fluphenazine, benztropine and (a) imipramine (150 - 200 mg) (b) placebo	6-9	18 patients with 6-week trial; 9 patients with 9 -week trial; CGI: p=0.009 SADS: p=0.027
Siris (1992)	27	Schizophrenic and schizoaffective patients with post-psychotic depression	Open continuation trial for favourable response to imipramine	Fluphenazine decanoate, benztropine and imipramine	26	4 drop-outs, continuation with TCAs is safe
Hillert (1992)	10	3 schizodepressive and 7 major depressive episodes; 20+ on BRMS and 35+ on BPRS	Open / BPRS, BRMS, SAPS, SANS, Raskin Depression GAS	Risperidone 2 - 10 mg daily	6	Only 3 schizophenic patients; all showed improvement in BPRS and SAPS scores

* Or to relapse.

Waehren and Gerlach's (1980) study had found maprotiline to improve depression but not to improve negative symptoms, implying there were different biological mechanisms responsible for the two symptom clusters. However, Siris et al. (1990, 1991) found that imipramine was not only an effective treatment for depressive symptoms (akinetic depression having been excluded by a trial of benztropine), but also for negative symptom items as measured by the SADS in a subset of schizophrenic patients. The mechanism of action of imipramine on either depressive or negative symptoms is unclear, though it is known that imipramine can inhibit presynaptic norepinephrine reuptake and desensitize at least some norepinephrine receptors; it also has anticholinergic properties. Quite what happens to biological systems when TCAs are added to neuroleptics or conversely neuroleptics are added to a system when TCAs are already present in terms of brain functioning is unclear. It is of note that many clinicians anecdotely claim that adjunctive low-dose chlomipramine added to neuroleptics is effective in treating both negative and depressive symptoms, but I can find no clinical double blind trial reported to-date of this combination.

It would thus seem that in depressed schizophrenics in whom akinetic depression has been excluded by a trial of anticholinergics, a trial of tricyclics (with most success to date reported with imipramine) would not be inappropriate.

The Hillert et al. (1992) study quoted is of very poor design, being an open trial of risperidone in 10 patients, three with schizodepressive disorders and seven with major depression with psychotic features. However, what is of significance and of possible clinical importance is that in the three elderly (56 -65 years) schizodepressive patients treated with 6 - 8 mg of risperidone daily, the patients' depression as measured by the Bech Rafaelson Melancholia Score (BRMS) improved from an average score of 27 to 3, whilst the SAPS improved from 39 to 0. It is of course unclear whether the negative symptoms have improved, in acutely psychotic patients (as is usually found), independently of the depressive symptoms. However, it was interesting that in of the psychotically depressed patients the BRMS decreased significantly (as in all the schizophrenic patients) but in three remained virtually unchanged. Risperidone is an atypical neuroleptic (not generally inducing EPS) with mixed $5HT_2$ and D2 antagonist properties. Ereshefsky and Lacombe (1993) in an excellent review of the biology of schizophrenia have summarized the current state of knowledge regarding atypical neuroleptics and their putative mechanism of action. In this model, $5HT_2$ blockade in the prefrontal cortex leads to reversal of prefrontal hypodpaminergia and, through altered modulation by GABA and NMDA pathways to the limbic system, decreases the high dopamine activity then that is associated with delusions and hallucinations. It seems possible that atypical antipsychotics thus act by releasing nigrostriatal dopaminergic neurons from tonic serotonergic inhibition. It is theroetically possible that atypical neuroleptics will be able to reduce negative and/or depressive symptoms in schizophrenics, especially when used in appropriately low doses; however, as of March 1994, no statistics have definitively reported on this. The clinican is left to hop for new breakthroughs in the specific area of treatment of depression in schizophrenic patients and should probably remain guided in his own clinical decisions by the work of Siris and colleagues, quoted earlier.

REFERENCES

Addington, D.E. and Addington, J.M. (1992)."Attempted suicide and depression in schizophrenia", Acta. Psychiatr. Scand., 85, 288 - 291.

Addington, D.E. et al. (1990). "A depression rating scale for schizophrenics", Schizophr. Res., 3, 247 - 251.

Andreasen, N.C. (1979). "Affective flattening and the criteria for schizophrenia", Am. J Psychiatry, 136, 944 - 947.

Andreasen, N.C. (1982). "Negative symptoms in schizophrenia, definition and reliability", Arch. Gen. Psychiatry 39, 784 - 788.

Becker, R.E. (1983). "Implications of the efficacy of thiothixene and a chlorpromazine - imipramine combination for depression in schizophrenia", Am. J. Psychiatry 140, 208 - 211.

Bermanzoh, P.C. and Siris, S.G. (1992) "Akinesi: a syndrome common to Parkinsonism, retarded depression and negative symptoms of schizophrenia", Comp. Psychiatry, 33(4), 221 - 232.

Bleuler, E. (1950). Dementia Praecox or the Group of Schizophrenia International Universities Press, New York.

Chouinard, G. and Jones, B.D. (1978). "Schizophrenia as a depressive deficiency disease", Lancet ii, 99 - 100.

Cooper, S.J. et al. (1992). "5-HIAA in CSF and predictions of suicidal behavior in schizophrenia", Lancet 340, 940 - 941.

Crow, T.J. (1985). "The two-syndrome concept: origins and current status", Schizophr. Bull. 11, 471 - 485.

Dalby, J.T. and Williams, R. (1987). "Depression in schizophrenia, the influence of intelligence", Can. J. Psychiatry 32, 816 - 817.

De Arlacon, R. and Carney, M.P. (1969). "Severe depressive mood changes following slow release intramuscular fluphenazine injections", Br. Med. J., 3, 564 - 567.

Drake, R.E. et al. (1989). "Suicide in schizophrenia: clinical approaches". In Depression in Schizophrenics (ed.R.Williams and J.T. Dalby), Plenum Publishing Corporation, New York.

Ereshefsky, L. and Lacombe, S. (1993). "Pharmacological profile of risperidone", Can. J. Psychiatry, 38 (Suppl.), 3, 580 - 588.

Flor-Henry, P. (1978). "The endogenous psychoses: a reflection of lateralized dysfunction of the anterior limbic system". In Limbic Mechanisms (eds K.E. Livingston and O. Hornykiewica), Plenum Publishing Corporation, New York.

Flor-Henry, P. (1989). "Interhemispheric relations and depression in schizophrenia in the perspective of cerebral laterality". In Depression in Schizophrenics (eds R. Williams and J.T. Dalby), Plenum Publishing Corporation, New York.

Flor-Henry, P., Fromm-Auch, D. and Schopflocher, D. (1983). "Neuropsychological dimensions in psychopathology". in Laterality and Psychopathology (eds P. Flor-Henry and J. Gruzelier), Elsevier Science Publishers, Amsterdam.

Hillert, A. et al. (1992). "Risperidone in the treatment of disorders with a combined psychotic and depressive syndromes", Pharmacopsychiatry,25, 213 - 217.

Hommes, O.R. and Panhuyssen L.H.H.M. (1970). "Bilateral intracarotid amytal injection", Psychiatr. Neurol. Neurochir., 73, 447 - 459.

Johnson, D.A.W. (1981). "Studies of depressive symptoms in schizophrenia", Br. J. Psychiatry, 139, 89 - 101.

Johnson, D. and Malik, N. (1975). "A double blind comparison of fluphenazine decanoate and flupenthixol decanoate in the treatment of acute schizophrenia", Acta Psychiatr. Scand., 51, 257 - 267.

Kay, S.R., Fishzbein, A. and Opler, L.A. (1987). "The positive and negative syndrome scale (PANSS) for schizophrenia", Schizophr. Bull,. 13, 261 - 275.

Kendell, R.E. (1983). "Other functional psychosis". In Companion to Psychiatric Studies (eds R.E. Kendell and A.K. Zealley), Churchill Livingstone, Edinburgh.

Knights, A. and Hirsch S.R. (1981). "Revealed depression and drug treatment for schizophrenia", Arch. Gen. Psychiatry, 38, 806 - 811.

Kraeplin, E. (1917). Dementia Praecox and Paraphrenia Livingstone, Edinburgh.

Kramer, et. al. (1989). "Antidepressants in depressed schizophrenic in-patients", Arch. Gen. Psychiatry, 46, 922 - 928.

Kurland, A.A. and Nagaraju, A. (1981). "Viloxazine and the depressed schizophrenic: methodological issues", J. Clin. Pharmacol 21, 37 - 41.

Lambert, P.A. (1987). "Depression et neuroleptiques à action prolongie" Acta. Psychiatr, 4, 100 - 108.

Liddle, P.F. (1987). "The symptoms of chronic schizophrenia", Br. J. Psychiatry, 151, 145 - 151.

Lindenmayer, J.P., Kay, S.R. and Friedman, C. (1986). "Negative and positive schizophrenic syndromes after the acute phase: a prospective follow-up", Comp. Psychiatry, 27, 276 - 286.

Lindenmayer, J.P. et al. (1992). "Multivantaged assessment of depression in schizophrenia", Psychiatr. Res., 42, 199 - 207.

Mandel, M.R. et al. (1982). "Development and prediction of post psychotic depression in neuroleptic treated schizophrenics", Arch. Gen. Psychiatry,39, 197 - 203.

Martin, R.L. et al. (1985). "Frequency and differential diagnosis of depressive syndromes in schizophrenia" J. Clin. Psychiatry 46(11), 9 - 13.

McGuffin, P. et al. (1989). "Genetics and affective changes in schizophrenia". In Depression in Schizophrenics , (eds R. Williams and J.T. Dalby), Plenum Publishing Corporation, New York.

Meltzer, H.Y. (1985). "Depressive and negative symptoms in schizophrenics", in Controversies in schizophrenia (ed. M. Alpert), pp. 110 - 136. Guilford Press, New York.

Meltzer, H.Y. et al. (1986). "The effect of neuroleptics and other psychotropic drugs on negative symptoms in schizophrenia", J. Clin. Psychopharmacol.,6, 329 - 338.

Nitwad, A. and Nicolshi-Oproin, L. (1978). "Suicidal risk in the treatment of outpatient schizophrenics with long acting neuroleptics", Agressologue, 19c, 145 - 148.

Overall, J. and Gorham, D. (1962). "The brief psychiatric rating scale",Psychol. Rep., 10, 799 - 812.

Plasky, P. (1991). "Antidepressant usage in schizophrenia", Schizophr. Bull. , 17(4), 649 - 657.

Pogue-Geile and M.F., Harrow, M. (1984). "Negative and positive symptoms in schizophrenia and depression: a follow-up", Schizophr. Bull, 10, 371 - 387.

Rifkin, A. et al. (1975). "Akinesia", Arch. Gen. Psychiatry, 32, 672 - 674.

Roy, A. (1989). "Suicidal behavior in schizophrenics". In Depression in Schizophrenics (eds R. Williams and J.T. Dalby), Plenum Publishing Corporation, New York.

Siris, S.G. (1987). "Akinesia and post psychotic depression: a difficult differential diagnosis", J. Clin. Psychiatry, 48(6), 240 - 243.

Siris, S.G. (1989). "Antidepressants in 'depressed' schizophrenics". In Depression in Schizophrenics (eds R. Williams and J.T. Dalby), Plenum Publishing Corporation, New York.

Siris, S.G., Morgan, V., Fagerstrom, R., et al. (1987). "Adjunctive imipramine in the treatment of post-psychotic depression: a controlled trial", Arch. Gen. Psychiatry, 44, 533 - 539.

Siris, S.G. et al. (1990). "Adjunctive imipramine maintenance in post psychotic depression/negative symptoms", Psychopharmacol. Bull, 26(1), 91 - 94.

Siris, S.G. et al. (1991). "The use of anitdepressants for negative symptoms in a subset of schizophrenic patients", Psychopharmacol. Bull, 27(3), 331 - 335.

Siris, S.G. et al. (1992). "Continuation treatment with adjunctive imipramine in schizophrenia", Psychopharmacol. Bull, 28(3), 303 - 307.

Van Putten, T. and May, R.A. (1978). "Akinetic depression in schizophrenia", Arch. Gen. Psychiatry, 35, 1102 - 1107.

Waehrens, J. and Gerlach, J. (1980). "Antidepressant drugs in anergic schizophrenia: a double-blind cross-over study with maprotiline and placebo", Acta Psychiatr. Scand., 61, 438 - 444.

Williams, R. and Dalby, J.T. (1989). "Drug and subject influences on measures of depression and negative symptoms in schizophrenic patients". In Depression in Schizophrenics (eds R. Williams and J.T. Dalby), Plenum Publishing Corporation, New York.

14

EXPLORING HEMISPHERIC FUNCTION USING HIGH FREQUENCY DIGITAL EEG

Michael Gaetz and Raymond J. Ancill

INTRODUCTION

Specific and observable symptoms are widely held to be necessary components of psychiatric diagnosis. However, the specific symptoms that are believed to characterize schizophrenia and other major mental disorders vary, and continue to do so across time and cultures (Andreasen & Flaum, 1991). Recent advances in neuroimaging have allowed researchers to identify biological correlates to at least some of the commonly agreed upon symptoms of major mental illness. The ability to identify structural and functional correlates of specific symptoms or symptom clusters adds power to the diagnostic process while helping to elucidate the nature of the illness. Areas in which neuroimaging have made contributions include disorders whose symptoms fall along the positive/negative symptom continuum, including mood disorder with psychotic symptoms, schizoaffective disorder and schizophrenia. Schizophrenia in particular has been the focus of studies designed to elucidate relationships between symptoms and symptom clusters and structural or functional anomalies. Findings in this area consistently suggest that the brains of individuals exhibiting primarily positive or negative symptoms differ both structurally and functionally. This has led some to suggest that individuals with hallucinations and delusions in the absence of large proportions of negative symptoms, for example, may be suffering from a different disease process than those with primarily mixed or negative symptoms.

Schizophrenia: Exploring the Spectrum of Psychosis. Edited by R. Ancill © 1994
John Wiley & Sons Ltd

Several of the neuro-imaging techniques that have evolved over the past decade and have been used to study schizophrenia. Structural imaging techniques such as computed tomography (CT) and magnetic resonance imaging (MRI) provide information regarding the size, shape and density of neuronal matter and support structures. Functional imaging techniques including positron emission Tomography (PET) and digital electroencephalography (DEEG) measure the brain's metabolic/neurochemical activity and electrical activity respectively. Research using each technique has provided important information as to differences in individuals along the positive and negative symptom continuum in relation to biological markers for various disorders.

POSITIVE AND NEGATIVE SYMPTOMS

Distinguishing between positive and negative symptoms has been a popular method for the classification of mental illness. One of the first articles to revive the positive/negative symptom distinction in schizophrenia was by Andreasen and Olsen (1982a). It was the opinion of the authors that both acute and chronic schizophrenia are heterogeneous in nature, reflecting a domain of related disorders dependent upon underlying neurochemistry and function of various brain systems. Positive and negative symptoms represent opposite poles of this domain. Various positive symptoms described were "delusions, hallucinations, formal thought disorder, and bizarre behaviour" (Andreasen and Olsen, 1982a; p. 790). Negative symptoms were said to include alogia, affective flattening, avolition, apathy, anhedonia, asociality and attentional impairment. Another category, mixed schizophrenia has also been suggested by the authors for individuals who do not meet the above criteria, or meet both (Andreasen and Olsen, 1982a).

Subsequently, several positive and negative symptom rating scales have been developed (SANS, Andreasen, 1983; SAPS, Andreasen, 1984; PANSS, Kay, Opler & Fisbein, 1985). These rating scales have helped to support diagnostic criteria and generally benefitted the development of reliable classification systems for schizophrenia and related disorders. Identifying biological correlates of symptoms can also assist in this process. However, until approximately 20 years ago, there were limited numbers of tools and techniques to study complex systems and structures in the living human. Consequently, attempts to study the biological basis of mental illness were also limited. Over the past two decades, the development and proliferation of a variety of neuroimaging techniques including CT, MRI, PET, SPECT and DEEG has afforded both clinicians and researchers the luxury of studying complex brain function and structure in psychiatric populations.

CT AND MRI

CT and MRI are the most often used structural imaging techniques in schizophrenia research. Several structural anomalies have been discovered using these techniques, some correlated to the patient's positive and/or negative symptoms. Among the first CT studies on schizophrenia was that by Johnstone et al. (1976), who found that in a chronic schizophrenic population a significantly greater proportion of individuals with enlarged ventricles existed than control subjects of a similar age. Since then, several authors have reported similar findings with CT and MRI, some related to the presence of negative symptoms. For instance, Andreasen et al., (1982) found that patients with the largest ventricular enlargements displayed impairment of the sensorium as well as having a preponderance of negative symptoms. The subgroup of patients with small ventricles was characterized by more positive symptoms. MRI studies (Andreasen et al., 1986) also suggest that schizophrenics evidenced significantly smaller frontal lobes as well as smaller cerebrums and craniums associated with negative symptoms, while reduced frontal lobe size was not.

Other CT and MRI studies suggest a left hemisphere involvement related to a higher proportion of positive symptoms. In 1979, Luchins et al. reported that schizophrenics without brain atrophy exhibited larger numbers of reversals of normal cerebral asymmetries. The authors stated that subjects without atrophy and frontal reversals had milder forms of the illness while those with atrophy and occipital reversals tended to require more hospitalizations and spent longer periods in hospital when admitted. Subsequent studies also tend to support apparent left hemisphere involvement in patients exhibiting greater numbers of positive symptoms. For example De Lisi et al. (1992) studied subjects recruited during first admissions for psychosis including hallucinations, delusions and formal thought disorder. These patients exhibited greater right than left hemisphere volumes. In addition, Shenton et al. (1992) reported left hemisphere anomalies in 11 subjects rated high in positive symptoms and four mixed symptom schizophrenics. Planned comparisons between patients and controls revealed that volume of left anterior hippocampus, both parahippocampal gyri and left superior temporal gyrus were significantly smaller in patients than controls. Several correlations among volumetric measurements of these areas were also reported, indicating that various areas may operate as a network for auditory processing. Furthermore, a correlation between thought disorder and absolute volume of the left posterior superior temporal gyrus (r = 0.81) was reported. Thought disorder increased exponentially as a function of volume reduction in this area (Shenton et al., 1992). Recently, further support for MRI abnormalities related to temporal lobe has been provided by Woodruff et al. (1993). The authors report reductions in corpus callosum areas that communicate between temporal lobes in schizophrenic groups when compared with controls.

Hallucinations have received much interest of late in terms of their neural bases. Auditory hallucinations have been the most frequently studied type as they represent the majority of reports of hallucinations in schizophrenia. Auditory hallucinations may occur due to pathology in perception and memory systems in temporal lobe. The auditory association cortex projects widely to other systems, including amygdala and hippocampus; therefore, pathological phenomena could occur due to a disruption in any part of this network of systems.

In 1990, Barta et al. studied hallucinations using MRI to obtain volumetric measurements at superior temporal gyrus and amygdala. The results indicated that although reductions in right superior temporal gyrus volume may be attributable to overall brain volumes, reductions in left amygdala and left superior temporal gyrus volumes were not. Another interesting finding was that auditory hallucinations were highly correlated with reductions in left superior temporal gyrus volumes (Barta et al., 1990). Therefore subjects exhibiting positive symptoms appear to display less global cortical atrophy and more localized structural asymmetries, primarily in the left temporal lobe.

PET AND SPECT

PET studies have generated data in agreement with the aforementioned structural imaging studies. Ingvar and Franzen (1974) were among the first to use PET technology to provide information regarding metabolic correlates of brain function in schizophrenics. The authors describe a phenomenon observed when comparing normals and schizophrenic patients which they termed "hypofrontalis". In normal resting subjects, cerebral blood flow was maximal in frontal lobes, with reduced flow recorded in temporal and parietal areas. The lowest regional cerebral blood flow (rCBF) flows occurred in occipital regions. Conversely, schizophrenic patients exhibited relatively lower levels of frontal lobe cerebral blood flow or hypofrontal activity. Others have replicated hypofrontalis in schizophrenic populations including Buchsbaum et al. (1984), who attempted to verify its presence in a schizophrenic and affective disorder population. Schizophrenic subjects and those with affective disorder showed reduced anterior-posterior gradients bilaterally, especially at the uppermost slice level (Buchsbaum et al., 1984).

Other PET studies appear to indicate left hemisphere pathology in schizophrenics, specifically those with greater proportions of positive symptoms. Gur et al. (1985) suggested that left hemisphere may be more active in specific populations of schizophrenics. Results suggest that for resting rCBF, schizophrenic subjects had higher left than right hemisphere rCBF while controls exhibited no difference between hemispheres. For verbal tasks, schizophrenics showed increased left hemisphere rCBF. In a subsequent study, Gur et al. (1987) replicated the previous findings and, in addition, provided longitudinal data as to the stability of left hemisphere overactivation even when comparing unmedicated first trials to medicated second trials. Liddle et al. (1992), also used PET to study rCFB and its relation to symptoms in schizophrenic patients. A factor analysis produced three syndromes (factors): psychomotor poverty, disorganization, and reality distortion. A correlation between the reality distortion factor and PET data support the left hemisphere overactivation hypothesis. Significant positive correlations between the factor and rCBF were evidenced in left temporal and frontal regions, including the left parahippocampal gyrus region, the left superior temporal pole and the left prefrontal cortex. Negative correlations involving this factor were primarily confined to the right hemisphere (Liddle et al., 1992). Recently, Suzuki et al. (1993), have also presented confirmatory evidence for left hemisphere overactivation using single positron emission computed tomography (SPECT). The authors report that schizophrenic and schizophreniform subjects experiencing prominent auditory hallucinations tended to have increased rCBF in the left superior temporal area. Following clinical improvement, the rCBF distribution had normalized. Following a relapse, one of the patients showed a similar increase in rCBF uptake at left superior temporal sites. MRI data for two of the patients revealed reduced temporal lobe volume, providing further evidence linking cortical atrophy and overactivation in this area (Suzuki et al., 1993).

NEUROCHEMISTRY

Therefore, neuro-imaging results have in the past supported the existence of biological correlates for positive and negative symptoms. Further support can be found in cellular models that include the dopamine (DA) serotonin (5-HT) and gamma amino butyric acid (GABA) systems. Swerdlow and Koob (1987) attempted to develop a model based on the dopamine hypothesis of schizophrenia which suggests an overactivation in the central DA system. Several lines of evidence for overactivation of this system in schizophrenics, especially the meso-limbic DA system, were described. Interestingly, the model was stated to apply primarily to positive symptoms, as individuals with more negative symptoms exhibit tendencies toward having fewer D2 DA cells and most respond poorly to neuroleptics. Also implied were possible modes of activation for over activation, including kindling. The authors review evidence suggesting that epileptoform discharges in limbic cortex have been shown to increase NAC D2 receptor density. Also, psychosis observed in some schizophrenics resembles similar symptoms in temporal lobe epileptics, therefore, hyper-excitability of the limbic system may be present in both disorders (Swerdlow and Koob, 1987).

Another possible mode of onset for DA system overactivation may initially involve 5-HT. In fact, the 5-HT system may play a role in the initiation of kindling phenomena similar to that previously mentioned in hippocampus. Mandel (1980) states that 5-HT inhibitory regulation of hippocampal CA3 cells leads to at least two events. One is cell hyper-excitability and the other is a loss of CA3 cell system 'gating' of emotionally laden matching of internal" versus external events (Mandel, 1980). This can lead to hippocampal synchronous discharges and overwhelming emotional states. The hippocampal cells then die due to their characteristic feed-forward facilitation and hyper-excitation, which can result in a kindling type phenomenon (Mandel, 1980). This is consistent in may ways with the neuro-imaging results discussed previously. A common feature of schizophrenia is gating of internal versus external events, which is a central issue in the facilitation of hippocampal CA3 cell loss. Further support for a DA - 5-HT interaction has been suggested by Meltzer (1992), who believes that an interaction of the two systems may be of importance in the genesis of schizophrenia. Additionally, Meltzer suggests that the interaction of DA and 5-HT is important in the efficacy of antipsychotics such as clozapine.

Other writers have implied further connections between DA activation and subcortical structures in schizophrenics. Reynolds (1983) has provided histological evidence in which schizophrenic brains were analyzed for DA concentrations in various structures bilaterally. The results indicated that significant increases in amygdala DA concentrations were reported with non - significant amounts found in caudate nucleus. Also, asymmetric DA concentrations were evidenced in left amygdala with no evidence of increased caudate DA or amygdala norepinephrine (NE) found. The author notes that the findings are consistent with left dominant temporal lobe dysfunction and its possible connection with temporal lobe epilepsy. In addition, Reynolds reports that certain neuroleptics may act selectively on left hemisphere (Reynolds, 1983). Subsequently, Reynolds et al. (1990), have proposed a link between left amygdala DA, neuropathology and laterality in the GABA system. In the study, histological preparations of schizophrenics, hippocampus and amygdala were obtained to determine whether 3H nicopecotic acid binding to these structures would determine a change in the GABAergic terminals. The authors report that no differences were found between control and schizophrenic samples in amygdala for nicopecotic acid binding. However, a significant deficit in the schizophrenic group in overall GABAergic binding sites in left hemisphere hippocampus was recorded. Coupled with this was a significant increase in DA in left but not right amygdala. Therefore, it appears that a parallel change in neurotransmitter function occurs in the GABAergic system as it occurs in the DA system in left amygdala (Reynolds et al., 1990).

DIGITAL ELECTROENCEPHALOGRAPHY (DEEG)

DEEG research has generally supported the results obtained with the previously mentioned techniques. Flor-Henry was among the first to report that schizophrenics had significantly more EEG power in the left temporal region than normals (Flor-Henry, 1974). Since then, several studies have reported differences in spontaneous EEG activity as well as evoked and event-related potentials (EP and ERP). A study designed to analyze spectral content of spontaneous and task-related EEG in schizophrenics was performed by Morstyn et al. (1983). The authors report asymmetric activation of the left anterior temporal region in schizophrenics in all conditions. The activity recorded was in the fast beta band (24-27.75 Hz), resembling high-frequency low-amplitude activation that occurs during cognitive functioning (Morstyn et al., 1983). Since this study, several other publications have surfaced that report left hemisphere anomalies in positive symptom schizophrenics supporting the overactivation hypothesis. These studies include left hemisphere changes related to spectral alpha intensities (Etevenon, 1984; Gaebel and Ulrich, 1988) and widespread dysfunction in left hemisphere during multi-sensorimotor activation (Guenther and Breitling, 1985).

More recently, EP studies have offered additional information about left hemisphere dysfunction in schizophrenics. P300 studies are probably over used in psychiatric DEEG research and claims regarding their significance overstated. However, when properly used, P300 can be an accurate indicator of information processing in various sense modalities. McCarley et al. (1991), have provided interesting results involving schizophrenia, symptoms and P300 asymmetry independent of reference electrode site, motor vs. auditory paradigms, and in patients withdrawn from medication or medication naive. Additionally, the authors report voltage asymmetries primarily in the presence of left temporal lobe tissue loss and positive symptoms (McCarley et al., 1991). More recent information provided by this group (Faux et al., 1993) has shown that schizophrenics withdrawn from medication for 21 days show statistically significant differences between groups consistent with left < right voltage asymmetries. Since P300 amplitude reductions are believed to represent increased information processing, left temporal lobe, compared to the contralateral sites, appears to be overactive. Guenther and others have also reported in numerous DEEG studies the presence of left hemisphere anomalies in the presence of positive symptoms (Guenther and Breitling, 1985; Guenther et al., 1988; Guenther, 1992).

COHERENCE ANALYSIS

Another analytical technique used in DEEG research is coherence analysis - a measure of the phase relationships found between frequency components at two electrode sites. Cortical electrical activity can be analyzed as a function frequency over a specified period of time using fast Fourier transforms (FFT). Coherence is a useful way to study cortical relationships as it offers information about inter and intra-hemispheric activity. The analysis of coherence as a function of frequency phase relationships is a technique that may be applicable to the delineation of positive and negative symptoms in schizophrenia. In a study that used coherence to observe lateral preference in schizophrenia (Shaw et al. 1983), coherence in the alpha band was measured. The results indicated that alpha band coherence was reduced in the schizophrenic sample in left hemisphere only, indicating that schizophrenics may have a "less lateralized organization than neurotics" (Shaw et al., 1983, p.303).

Recently, we initiated development of a DEEG system capable of detecting inter- and intra-hemispheric differences at high EEG frequencies. Until a short time ago, a significant drawback of DEEG use was availability due to cost. Although the cost of several commercially available systems has decreased in recent years, several additional problems accompany their use. Complaints range from poor technical support to the general frustration of dealing with 'black-box' technology. It is with these issues in mind that we have developed a 'hybrid' DEEG system in attempts to avoid the aforementioned deterrents. One important aspect of the hybrid system is its ability to explore a much wider range of frequencies than possible with traditional EEG. The current frequency range explored with the hybrid system has been from 6 to 242 Hz maximum while maintaining the ability to record lower frequencies (0.5 to 32 Hz) if desired.

Frequencies in the EEG power spectrum above 35 Hz (gamma band activity) are not routinely studied in clinical settings. Reasons for neglect of supra-beta activity are primarily due to limitations of clinical EEG systems such as pen response times and hardware and software limitations. Other limitations of recording high-frequency (HF) cortical activity reliably are attenuation due to intermediary structures and contamination by muscle artefact. Current advancements in DEEG research suggest that some of the previous limitations to recording cortical activity have been overcome.

Recent reports in epilepsy research (Fisher et al., 1992), also indicate that HF activity in the gamma band may be of use in localizing seizure foci. Other researchers (Krieger and Dillbeck, 1987) report the presence of HF EEG activity related to reaction time tasks. HF activity may warrant study in a variety of subject areas.

Our hybrid DEEG system has recently been used to study HF neuronal activity in three subject populations: depressives, psychotics, and normal controls. Due to the lack of published data on HF activity in any population, no a priori hypothesis was proposed. Additionally, much attention was directed toward the reduction of muscle artefact and other signal-processing issues to ensure accurate recordings in HF bands. The primary analytical tool used to study HF activity was inter-hemispheric frequency or phase relationships between homologous electrode sites.

DEEG METHODOLOGY

Normal volunteers were employees from the Department of Psychiatry at St. Vincent's Hospital in Vancouver. Depressed and psychotic inpatients were from the Geriatric or the Adult Psychiatry programs. Two males and two females constituted the controls (n=4), four females comprised the depressed group (n=4) and three females and two males made up the psychotic group (n=5).

Psychiatric subjects did not receive psychoactive substances 24 hours prior to recording. Each subject was fitted with four Ag-Ag Grass electrodes and conductance was effected with electrode paste. The impedances were below 5 Kohms and electrodes were placed at F7, F8, T5 and T6 according to the International 10-20 System. The data was digitized at 1024 Hz and Cz served as a reference. High-pass filters were set at 3 Hz and low pass filters were set at 300 Hz. The recording device was a 486/50 PC with Rhythm V.8 data acquisition software (Stellate Systems Inc., 1992) linked to Grass model 8 amplifiers. The amplifier setting was at a gain of x 30,000 with the notch filter out.

The EEG was recorded during approximately three-minute epochs with the subject's eyes closed. Fourier transforms were completed by selecting no less than 2-second samples of visually inspected artefact-free EEG until 30 seconds cumulative were available for analysis. Phase calculations were then performed using FFT data for F7-F8 and T5-T6 electrode positions for frequencies within the 6-242 Hz range. Data in this range was arbitrarily divided into 18 ten Hz band-widths. Averages of absolute phase difference from zero (i.e. zero = 100% coherence) were calculated within each band width for each subject. The frequency bands 46-74, 116-124 and 176-184 were excluded from the analysis due to the possible presence of 60 Hz artefact and its harmonics. Absolute phase difference from zero within each band width was compared across groups using a factorial design.

DEEG RESULTS

Preliminary results show several differences between groups at the p.<0.05 level between F7-F8 but not T5-T6. As shown in Figure 1, average phase differences from zero between controls and both clinical conditions are numerous between 76-194 Hz. Significant differences at the p.<0.05 level were also noted between depressives and psychotics between 206 and 234 Hz. Bonferroni corrected multiple comparisons were also made, resulting in significant differences in absolute phase between control and clinical groups. FFT values tended to confirm higher left versus right hemisphere activation for psychotics compared to depressed and control subjects.

The preliminary results can be interpreted to mean that group differences in absolute phase across the frequency spectrum result from differences in cortical organization between the groups. Controls tend to be far more in phase than do either depressed or psychotic patients. The psychotic group in particular tends to show increased left hemisphere activation at various frequencies which may be initiating this groups lack of coherence. Since psychotics generally exhibit behaviour more congruent with a positive symptom profile, and likewise, depressed patients with negative symptoms continuum, it was interesting to observe groups differences using this limited number of subjects. Future projects should include assessment of symptoms using one or more of the rating scales in order to derive correlates of maximum phase difference at high frequencies with symptoms.

Figure 1. Absolute Phase Differences Between F7-F8 for Psychotics, Depressives and Controls.

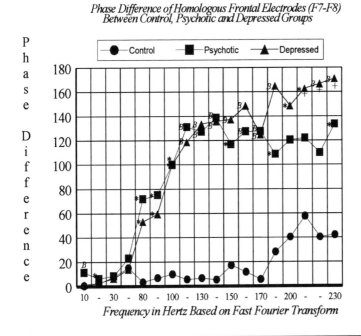

Phase Difference of Homologous Frontal Electrodes (F7-F8) Between Control, Psychotic and Depressed Groups

Factorial design analysis resulted in significant group differences between controls and both clinical groups at the $p. < 0.05$ (*). Significant differences at the $p.<0.05$ between clinical conditions are indicated using (+). Bonferroni corrected comparisons significantly different at the $p.< 0.05$ level are indicated with (B).

DEEG - FUTURE DIRECTIONS

DEEG research offers results consistent with the other imaging studies regarding the positive/negative symptom continuum and biological correlates. Patients with greater numbers of negative symptoms tend toward generalized cortical atrophy with decreased probability of remission or neuroleptic relief. Patients with increased numbers of positive symptoms appear to show anomalies of the left hemisphere; however, this may be a misnomer due to sampling. An equiprobable explanation may be that since right-handers are generally over-represented in the majority of studies, anomalies of dominant hemisphere as opposed to the simple notion of either left or right hemisphere dissimilarity might be behind reports of brain asymmetries. Language studies have repeatedly shown that almost all right handers are dominant for language in left hemisphere, while left handed individuals show approximately 70% left hemisphere dominance based on aphasia studies (Kimura and D'Amico, 1989), Wada testing and cortical stimulation mapping (Ojemann, 1983). Other related studies have shown that the dominant hemisphere may also be more involved in fine motor movements and that sex differences are present for language organization (Kimura and D'Amico, 1989). Support for this hypothesis has recently been published by Holinger et al. (1992), who have reported differences in left versus right hemisphere P300 voltage asymmetries between left and right handed schizophrenic patients. The authors report that right handed schizophrenics showed lower left than right hemisphere P300 amplitude while left handed schizophrenics showed the opposite effect. Therefore, what may be the faulty neural mechanism in sub-populations of schizophrenic subjects is a disruption in the hemisphere dominant for language and fine motor skills rather that simply left hemisphere. Overactivation of a system involving superior temporal, frontal and limbic structures in the dominant hemisphere may be responsible for psychotic language-related symptoms including auditory hallucinations. Further, this may be a process restricted to those who present as psychotic with very few negative symptoms. As previously stated, patients with these symptoms can benefit from neuroleptic treatment whereas primarily negative-symptom patients cannot. Interestingly, patients with mixed positive and negative symptoms often benefit by a reduction of positive symptoms during neuroleptic intervention, with little improvement in negative symptoms. Clinically, it is these subjects as well as those with increased numbers of negative symptoms that have lower expectations for remission and may eventually be classified in the chronic category. Therefore, dichotomous clinical entities may be present based on either positive, mixed or negative symptoms. Positive symptoms may purely reflect psychosis in some cases while negative and mixed symptoms represent schizophrenia proper. This dichotomy appears well represented biologically and clinically.

Accordingly, future studies should be sensitive to controlling for sex, handedness and especially symptoms as these appear to influence research results. Additionally, techniques that detect anomalies between dominant and non-dominant hemisphere will be useful for discovering markers for psychosis as an entity distinct from schizophrenia. HF EEG research may be one such technique as it has successfully shown differential asymmetric electrical activity between controls and patients and between psychotics and depressives.

ACKNOWLEDGEMENT

This work was supported by a Medical Research Council of Canada Studentship Grant # 43012.

REFERENCES

Andreasen, N.C. (1983). "The Scale for the Assessment of Negative Symptoms (SANS). Iowa City, IA: the University of Iowa.

Andreasen, N.C. (1984). "The Scale for the Assessment of Positive Symptoms (SAPS). Iowa City, IA: the University of Iowa.

Andreasen, N.C. & Flaum, M. (1991). "Schizophrenia: the characteristic symptoms", Schiz. Bull., 17, 27 - 49.

Andreasen, N.C., Nasrallah, H.A., Dunn, V., et al., (1986). "Structural abnormalities in the frontal system in schizophrenia: a magnetic resonance imaging study", Arch. Gen. Psychiatry, 43, 136 - 144.

Andreasen, N.C., Olsen, S.A. (1982). "Negative v positive schizophrenia", Arch. Gen. Psychiatry, 39, 136 - 144.

Andreasen, N.C., Olsen, S.A., Dennert, J.W. and Smith, M.R. (1982b). "Ventricular enlargement in schizophrenia: relationship to positive and negative symptoms", Am. J. Psychiatry, 139, 297 - 301.

Barta, P.E., Pearlson, G.D., Powers, R.E., Richards, S.S. and Tune, L.E. (1990). "Auditory hallucinations and smaller superior temporal gyral volume in schizophrenia", Am. J. Psychiatry, 147, 1457 - 1462..

Buchsbaum, M.S., DeLisi, L.E., Holcomb, H.H. et al. (1984). "Anteroposterior gradients in cerebral glucose use in schizophrenia and affective disorders", Arch. Gen. Psychiatry, 41, 1159-1166.

DeLisi, L., Stritzke, P., Riordan, H. et al. (1992). "The timing of brain morphological changes in schizophrenia and their relation to clinical outcome", Biol. Psychiatry, 31, 241 - 254.

Etevenon, P. (1984). "Intra and inter-hemispheric changes in alpha intensities in EEGs of schizophrenic patients versus matched controls", Biol. Psychiatry, 19, 247 - 279.

Faux, S.F., McCarley, R.W., Nestor, P.G. et al. (1993). "P300 topographic asymmetries are present in unmedicated schizophrenics", Electroencephalogr. Clin. Neurophysiol., 88, 32 - 41.

Fischer, R.S., Webber, W.R.S., Lesser, R.P., Arroyo, S., Uematsu, S. (1992). "High-frequency EEG activity at the start of seizures", J. Clin. Neurophysiol., 9, 441 - 448.

Flor-Henry, P. (1969). " Schizophrenia-like reactions and affective psychosis associated with temporal lobe epilepsy: etiological factors", Am. J. Psychiatry, 26, 400 - 403.

Gaebel, W. and Ulrich, G. (1988). "Topographical distribution of absolute alpha-power in the EEG and psychopathology in schizophrenia outpatients",Acta. Psychiatr. Scand., 77, 390 - 397.

Guenther, W. (1992). "MRI-SPECT and PET-EEG findings on brain dysfunction in schizophrenia", Prog. Neuro-Psychopharmacol. & Biol. Psychiatry, 16, 445 - 462.

Guenther, W. & Breitling, D. (1985). "Predominant sensorimotor area left hemisphere dysfunction in schizophrenia measured by electrical activity brain mapping", Biol. Psychiatry, 20, 515 - 532.

Guenther, W., Davous, P., Godet, J., Guillabert, E., Breitling, D., Rondot, P. (1988). "Bilateral brain dysfunction during motor activation intype II schizophrenia measured by EEG mapping", Biol. Psychiatry, 23, 295 - 311.

Gur, R.E., Gur, R.C., Skolnick, B.E. et al. (1985). "Brain function in psychiatric disorders III. Regional cerebral blood flow in unmedicated schizophrenics",Arch. Gen. Psychiatry, 42, 329 - 334.

Gur, R.E., Resnick, S.M., Gur, R.C. et al. (1987) "Regional brain function in schizophrenia II. Repeated evaluation with positron emission tomography", 44, 126 - 129. Arch. Gen. Psychiatry 44, 126-129.

Holinger, D.P., Faux, S.F., Shenton, M.E. et al. (1992). "Reversed temporal region asymmetries of P300 topography in left and right-handed schizophrenic subjects", Electroencephalogr. Clin. Neurophysiol., 84, 532 - 537.

Ingvar, D.H. and Franzen, G. (1974). "Abnormalities of cerebral blood flow distribution in patients with chronic schizophrenia", Acta. Psychiatr. Scand, 50, 425 - 462.

Johnstone, E.C., Crow, T.J., Frith, C.D., et al. (1976). "Cerebral ventricular size and cognitive impairment in chronic schizophrenia", Lancet ii, 924 - 926.

Holinger, D.P., Faux, S.F., Shenton, M.E. et al. (1992). "Reversed temporal region asymmetries of P300 topography in left and right-handed schizophrenic subjects", Electroencephalogr. Clin. Neurophysiol., 84, 532 - 537.

Ingvar, D.H. and Franzen, G. (1974). "Abnormalities of cerebral blood flow distribution in patients with chronic schizophrenia", Acta. Psychiatr. Scand, 50, 425 - 462.

Johnstone, E.C., Crow, T.J., Frith, C.D., et al. (1976). "Cerebral ventricular size and cognitive impairment in chronic schizophrenia", Lancet ii, 924 - 926.

Kay, S.R., Opler, L.A., Fisbein, A. (1985). " Positive and Negative Syndrome Scale (PANSS)", Dept. of Psychiatry, Albert Einstein College of Medicine.

Kimura, D. and D'Amico, C. (1989). "Evidence for subgroups of adextrals based on speech lateralization and cognitive patterns", Neuropsychologia 27, 977 - 986.

Krieger, D. and Dillbeck, M. (1987). "High frequency scalp potentials evoked by a reaction time task", Electroencephalogr. Clin. Neurophysiol.,67, 222 - 230.

Liddle, P.F., Friston, K.J., Frith, C.D., Hirsch, S.R., Jones, T., Frackowiak, R.S.J. (1992). "Patterns of cerebral blood flow in schizophrenia', Brit. J. Psychiatry, 160, 179 -186.

Luchins, D., Weinberger, D. and Wyatt, R. (1979). "Schizophrenia: evidence of a subgroup with reversed cerebral asymmetry", Arch. Gen. Psychiatry 36, 1309 - 1311.

Mandell, A. (1980). "Toward a psychobiology of transcendence: God in the brain", in Psychobiology of Consciousness (eds. J. Davidson & R. Davidson), pp. 379 - 463, New York: Plenum.

McCarley, R.W., Faux, S.F., Shenton, M.E., Nestor, P.G. and Holinger, D. P. (1991)."Is there P300 asymmetry in schizophrenia?' Arch. Gen. Psychiatry, 48, 380 - 381.

Meltzer, H. (1992). "The role of dopamine in schizophrenia". In New Biological Vistas on Schizophrenia (eds. J. Lindemayer & S. Kay), pp. 131-157, New York: Brunner/Mazel.

Morstyn, R., Duffy, F.H. and McCarley, R.W. (1983). "Altered topography of EEG spectral content in schizophrenia", Electroencephalogr. Clin. Neurophysiol.,. 56, 263 - 271.

Ojemann, G.A. (1983). "Brain organization for language from the perspective of electrical stimulation mapping", Behav. Brain Sci., 2, 189 - 230.

Reynolds, G.P. (1983). "Increased concentrations and lateral asymmetry of amygdala dopamine in schizophrenia", Nature, 305, 527 - 528.

Reynolds, G. P., Czudek, C. and Andrews, H.B. (1990). "Deficit and hemispheric asymmetry of GABA uptake sites in the hippocampus in schizophrenia",Biol. Psychiatry 27, 1038 - 1044.

Shaw, J.C., Colter N. and Resek, G. (1983). "EEG coherence, lateral preference and schizophrenia", Psychol. Med 13, 299 - 306.

Shenton, M.E., Kikinis and R., Jolesz, F.A. (1992). "Abnormalities of the left temporal lobe and thought disorder in schizophrenia", N. Engl. J. Med 327, 604 - 612.

Swerdlow, N.R. and Koob, G.F. (1987). "Dopamine, schizophrenia, mania, and depression: toward a unified hypothesis of cortico-striato-pallido-thalamic function", Behav. Brain Sci., 10, 197 - 245.

Suzuki, M., Yuasa, S., Minabe, Y., Murata, M.and Kurachi, M. (1993). "Left superior temporal blood flow increases in schizophrenic and schizophreniform patients with auditory hallucination: a longitudinal case study using 123 I-IMP SPECT, Eur. Arch. Psychiatry Clin. Neurosci, 242, 257 - 261.

Woodruff, P.W.R., Pearlson, G.D., Geer, M.J., Barta, P.E. and Chilcoat, H.D. (1993)."A computerized magnetic resonance imaging study off corpus callosum morphology in schizophrenia", Psychol. Med, 23, 45 - 56.

15

SUBSTANCE ABUSE AND PSYCHOSIS

John R. Steinberg

DRUG-INDUCED PSYCHOSES

Substance abuse and psychosis are associated in two major ways. Psychosis may be seen secondary to drug intoxication or withdrawal. Additionally, patients who are suffering from a major psychiatric diagnosis such as schizophrenia may have second primary diagnoses of drug or alcohol intoxication. They may, as well, intermittently use intoxicants. Either pattern may complicate diagnostic and treatment issues related to their psychosis. Drug-related psychosis will be discussed initially and dual-diagnosis patients will be discussed in the latter part of this presentation.

Most drugs associated with drug-induced psychoses are psychoactive agents commonly used as intoxicants. Their use preceding onset of acute psychosis may be licit or illicit. Presence of drugs on a toxicology screen is only suggestive, not diagnostic, and certainly does not preclude other etiologic explanations for the acute psychotic state. Further complicating the diagnosis is the fact that withdrawal syndromes from sedatives, hypnotics, benzodiazepines, barbiturates and alcohol may produce an acute psychotic state. This withdrawal psychosis may occur at a time when drug screens are negative because of elimination of the substance from the body. It is also necessary to consider that a population involved in illicit drug use may be HIV infected (up to 58% incidence in one series) (Marmor and Costikyan, 1988) or generally immunocompromised and prone to CNS infections. Either of these conditions may independently produce an acute organic psychosis.

Schizophrenia: Exploring the Spectrum of Psychosis. Edited by R. Ancill. © 1994 John Wiley & Sons Ltd.

The temporal course of the psychosis is of diagnostic value. When psychotic symptoms persist beyond three to five days, drug use is unlikely as a cause (Hurlbut, 1991). Management of drug-induced psychoses may require only supportive care in many cases and these psychoses are rarely lethal. Exceptions to this rule are when the intoxicants (particularly cocaine or anticholinergics) may be lethal in and of themselves.

Cocaine is one of the drugs commonly associated with acute psychosis. Cocaine blocks reuptake of dopamine and norepinephrine and intoxicated patients may exhibit mydriasis, partial cycloplegia, tachycardia, hypertension and hyperthermia. Several distinct psychoactive effects are produced upon ingestion and include an initial "rush", a less intense euphoric "high", dysphoria as the initial effects wear off and, with chronic use, a paranoid psychosis which closely resembles paranoid schizophrenia. Chronic cocaine use typically produces psychotic delusions in the presence of a clear sensorium whereas acute intoxication often exhibits associated confusion, disorientation and delirium.

Patients typically exhibit suspicious behavior with associated delusions. These delusions may be vague or they may be systematic and well organized. Intravenous users or those who are compulsively sexually active within the context of their cocaine use (a common phenomenon) are at increased risk of HIV infection (Shaffer and Costikyan, 1988). HIV infection may produce neuropsychiatric symptoms at various points in the course of AIDS and persistence of psychotic symptoms over time increases the likelihood of this etiology.

While overall management of cocaine intoxication and psychosis is beyond the scope of this discussion, two specific issues must be addressed. Beta-blockers leave a state of unopposed alpha-adrenergic activity exacerbated by excess catecholamines. Central alpha agonists such as clonidine or mixed peripheral alpha and beta-blockers such as labetolol are safer to use for cardiovascular problems. For management of associated agitation, benzodiazepines are much safer than phenothiazines which may lower seizure thresholds (Dubin, 1988).

Amphetamines are structurally related to the neurotransmitters dopamine and norepinephrine and produce their effects by inducing release or blocking reuptake of these neurotransmitters. Cardiovascular complications are common and there are other similarities to cocaine. Intoxication produces agitation, jitteriness, and some degree of suspiciousness. Insomnia is common and polydrug use is common secondary to the use of sedatives, hypnotics or alcohol to induce sleep. While insomnia is common, sleep deprivation does not appear to be necessary for amphetamine psychosis to appear (Griffith et al., 1972).

Use of amphetamine produces a "rush", hyperactivity, hyperexcitability and euphoria. Persistent use may continue for a period of days and culminate in fatigue, paranoia and confusion. Depression may follow cessation of use. Suspicious behavior may proceed to psychosis. Apprehension, fear, delusions of persecution and both auditory and visual hallucinations are common. Aggressive and even violent behavior may be exhibited and impaired judgment exacerbates the danger associated with managing these patients.

Psychosis may last from 12 h to as long as seven days after drug withdrawal and typically does not involve impaired consciousness (Bell, 1973). Urinary acidification to enhance drug elimination is controversial. It is not of proven benefit and may have adverse cardiovascular effects. Calm, reassuring approaches and direct communication are helpful. Benzodiazepines are the best agents for rapid tranquilization, but antipsychotics may be necessary.

Lysergic acid diethylamide (LSD) is a common hallucinogen whose use is currently undergoing a resurgence in the United States. Its principal mode of action is believed to be mediated by postsynaptic serotonin receptors (Hurlbut, 1991) Physical effects include prominent mydriasis, slight increases in heart rate, temperature and respiratory rate as well as parasympathomimetic effects such as salivation. For most users, psychotropic effects include vivid visual hallucinations, distortions of body image, synesthesia, hyperacusis and depersonalization .

Three types of adverse events may result from use of LSD. A "bad trip" consists of severely heightened anxiety and confusion. Reassurance is often adequate and restraints should be avoided. A benzodiazepine may be used and re-orientation to the passage of time is helpful. The "flashback" phenomenon refers to the unpredictable recurrence of perceptual changes and other drug effects. Again, reassurance and anxiolytics often provide adequate relief. The etiology of flashbacks is unknown.

Overt psychosis following ingestion has been observed and has persisted in some patients even after single ingestions.(Frosch et al., 1965) Some of these patients had manifested evidence of schizophrenia prior to LSD ingestion and it remains unclear whether LSD can acutely trigger the onset of schizophrenia (Roy, 1981). Suicide and self-inflicted trauma may occur and are a greater risk than assaultive outbursts. Paranoia and bizarre delusions are common. Treatment consists of reassurance, reduction of environmental stimuli and benzodiazepines.

Haloperidol may be used if needed but phenothiazines should be avoided as they may reduce seizure thresholds (seizures have been observed in LSD use), exacerbate extrapyramidal symptoms and cause hypotension.

Mescaline is the active component of hallucinogenic cacti and is rapidly absorbed following oral ingestion. A typical peyote button contains 45 mg of mescaline and the dose used is estimated to be 5 mg/kg. Initial effects include gastrointestinal distress and sympathomimetic effects. Large doses may produce hypertension and bradycardia, but cardiac instability is rare (Mack, 1986). Changes in mood, altered time perception and hallucinations are common. Paranoid ideation may occur and reassurance coupled with a nonthreatening environment are usually sufficient management.

Hallucinogenic mushrooms of the *Psilocybe* genus have psilocin, an indole compound, as their active ingredient. Effects are similar to mescaline but consciousness level usually remains normal. Patients occasionally exhibit paranoid ideation but they generally recover in 6 - 12 hours (Peden et al., 1982). A more serious possible adverse reaction is serious toxicity due to mushroom misidentification where anticholinergic effects predominate and outcomes may be lethal.

Phencyclidine (PCP) was introduced as an analgesic drug and was withdrawn a few years after introduction because of its propensity to produce disturbing hallucinations and bizarre behavior. As an illicit substance, it has been associated with severe psychiatric sequelae and these sequelae, rather than the general management of PCP intoxication, will be the focus of this discussion. PCP is usually ingested by smoking and has a half-life of approximately 20 to 24 hours. PCP has numerous neurotransmitter effects. It stimulates release of dopamine, inhibits accumulation of dopamine uptake into vesicles, non-competitively inhibits nicotinic receptor sites and affects both mu and sigma opioid receptors (Giannini et al., 1984). Agitation and violent behavior, coupled with impaired judgment and diminished pain perception, have resulted in many deaths.

Acute PCP delirium is the most common psychiatric syndrome. Patients have distorted perception, dysarthric ataxia, bursts of aggression and clouded consciousness (Pearlson, 1981). The syndrome may wax and wane over 3 - 8 hours and periods of lucidity and improvement do not imply full resolution. Staff should take adequate precautions as visual hallucinations and threatening delusions may result in unanticipated violent behavior. PCP has also been associated with a prolonged delirium lasting from 24 hours to over one week. Treatment consists of providing a protected environment, avoidance of restraints and benzodiazepines as needed. Neuroleptics may only safely be used in protracted syndromes after all signs of acute PCP intoxication have resolved.

PCP has also been associated with manic and schizophrenic syndromes of far longer duration than drug half-life that do not appear to be dose related. These syndromes are usually associated with a clear consciousness and may occur as relapses unassociated with any further drug use (Pearlson, 1981). Psychotic episodes brought on by PCP use may be quite severe, prolonged and difficult to manage. Depression may follow when the acute psychosis resolves. Inpatient psychiatric care is often necessary.

Cannabis is one of the most widely used illicit substances in North America. The major active ingredient is delta-9-tetrahydrocannabinol (THC). THC slows cognitive processes and reaction times, impairs coordination, produces sensory perception alterations and may produce an effect of depersonalization (Leikin et al., 1989). Several associated psychiatric syndromes have been described including amotivational syndrome, anxiety reactions, dysphoric reactions, disorientation, paranoid delusions and hallucinations. Specific treatment is usually not needed. These effects appear to be dose related and resolve within a few hours (Tunving, 1985). The diagnosis of cannabis psychosis remains controversial. Some authors state that drug induced psychosis is self-limited and resolves in 6 - 12 hours. Others are more skeptical (Thornicroft, 1990). While cannabis can produce psychotic symptoms, precipitation of schizophreniform episodes is most often relapse of known cases of schizophrenia unrelated to drug use. Hallucinations and persecutory delusions may occur in the course of acute intoxication but "there is no convincing support for a separate clinical diagnosis of cannabis psychosis" (Thornicroft, 1990). Whether or not such a syndrome exists, psychiatric syndromes related to THC are usually mild, transient and self-limited, resolving rapidly after drug use ceases.

Recently, minor modifications of the phenylethylamine molecule by "street chemists" have produced a plethora of "designer drugs" known by the initials of the compound, including TMA-2, STP or DOM, PMA, DOB, MDA, MDMA and MDEA. Occasionally referred to as hallucinogenic amphetamines they have actions other than stimulation or hallucination at doses used. Actions include rapid decreases in serotonin and, with prolonged use, depletion of dopamine and norepinephrine. MDMA, known in the illicit drug culture as "ecstasy", is used to achieve a state of euphoria, positive mood changes and an increased feeling of closeness to others. However, agitation, bizarre behavior, depression and flashbacks have occurred. While uncommon, repeated anxiety attacks, chronic insomnia, rage reactions and psychosis may occur. Psychosis, manifesting as paranoia, ideas of reference, and auditory hallucinations, is typically the result of high doses. Though rare, MDMA psychosis may be persistent and refractory to treatment (Hayner and McKinney, 1986). Anxiety, agitation and other symptoms of hyperactivity are best managed with benzodiazepines. Paranoid symptoms and hallucinations may require antipsychotics. As discussed previously, these drugs must be used with caution and are more safely used after acute intoxication has resolved.

A number of prescription drugs, over-the-counter drugs and common plants (e.g. Jimson weed) have pronounced anticholinergic properties. Central effects may include delirium and hallucinations. Tricyclic overdose and other anticholinergic crises are potentially lethal. Differential diagnosis rests on clinical phenomena and for details of management the reader is referred to a manual of clinical toxicology. Psychotic symptoms are not the major concern in this situation although psychiatric symptoms may be present.

Both anabolic steroids and corticosteroids have been associated with affective syndromes of mood swings and other psychiatric syndromes including psychoses. While usually presenting within the first few weeks of treatment, risk of corticosteroid-induced psychiatric symptoms increases with increasing daily doses and most often occurs in patients receiving more than 40 mg of prednisone daily (Lewis and Smith, 1983). Anabolic steroids have been associated with significant increases in aggressive behavior, hostility, anger, depression, anxiety and psychosis (Su et al., 1993). Primary treatment is to reduce the dose or, if possible, eliminate the drug (e.g. anabolics). Mild tranquilizers or neuroleptics may be needed, but the majority of patients recover completely and do not suffer sequelae of steroid-induced psychiatric illness (Hurlbut, 1991). One caveat is that immunosuppression results from chronic glucocorticoid use and, as with intravenous drug users, CNS infections are part of the differential diagnosis in such patients who present with psychiatric illness.

POSTULATED MECHANISMS OF DRUG-INDUCED AND IDIO-PATHIC PSYCHOSIS

Investigation into mechanisms of drug-induced psychosis has yielded not only considerable information in that area but has also shed light on what are, in effect, perhaps the best available models for idiopathic schizophrenic illness. While multiple neurotransmitter systems are implicated in psychotic illness, two of the most well studied models are the dopamine system (stimulant-induced psychosis) and N-methyl-d-aspartate or NMDA (PCP-induced psychosis). Historically, dopaminergic mechanism studies antedate those of NMDA.

Stimulant-related psychosis serves as the genesis of these investigations. While there are major findings not explained by dopaminergic mechanisms, many valid findings have been replicated. "Stimulant loading" with high doses of amphetamine can produce psychosis in non-psychotic subjects (Angrist and Gershon, 1970). Stimulant drugs can provoke or exacerbate psychotic symptoms in many schizophrenic patients (Liberman et al., 1987). Not all schizophrenic patients respond in this manner, however, perhaps reflecting the heterogeneous nature of schizophrenic pathophysiology (van Kammen et al., 1982). Additionally, certain effects of chronic stimulant use may persist long after drug use ceases. Overall, schizophrenic patients show a similar response to normal patients, but at greater stimulant sensitivity; i.e. the dose response curve is shifted significantly to the left (Post, 1975). Possible mechanisms include potentiating presynaptic dopamine release and blocking reuptake, thus enhancing dopaminergic activity. The psychotogenic potency of drugs in this class has been correlated to their dopamine agonist activity (Janowsky and Davis, 1976). Presynaptic dopamine depletion results in upregulation of postsynaptic dopamine receptors which with coincident development of autoreceptor subsensitivity produces a dysregulation of both pre- and postsynaptic mechanisms resulting in increased dopamine neurotransmission believed to play a role in the pathogenesis of psychosis (Liberman et al., 1990).

Stereotyped behaviors triggered by early dopamine enhancement are maintained despite a subsequent decline in dopamine levels which suggests an uncoupling of some post-synaptic effector mechanism. D2 receptors are believed to mediate the effects of neuroleptics (Creese et al., 1976) and are upregulated in psychosis. Stimulant drugs may lead to desensitization of D1 receptors and upregulation of D2 receptors and produce a dysregulation of dopamine homeostasis which may facilitate the onset of psychosis.

One of the areas not well explained in purely dopaminergic terms is the observation that while concomitant neuroleptic administration may block the development of behavioral sensitization to repeated amphetamine administration it will not block the sensitized response that occurs after rechallenge once the initial pattern is established. This implies that persistent behavioral alterations may be perpetuated by non-dopaminergic mechanisms such as kindling (Post, Weiss & Pert, 1988). This may also reflect underlying mechanisms of neuroleptic resistant psychosis (Post et al., 1988).

The ability of neuroleptics to block initial sensitization but not rechallenge responses after heightened dopamine sensitivity is established resembles hypothetical models in the development of schizophrenia. Enhanced dopamine neural activity is postulated, yet no direct evidence of this increase was established in early investigations (Haracz, 1982). Patients may experience relapse or exacerbation after stressful events or use of stimulants despite adequate neuroleptic treatment. This observation of endogenous disease correlates with studies of drug-induced psychosis.

Persistent effects may be mediated by neuronal degeneration which is observed in animal models after prolonged high-dose methamphetamine administration (Ellison and Eison, 1983). Stimulant-induced massive release of dopamine and inhibition of monamine oxidase results in nonenzymatic conversion of dopamine into 6-hydroxydopamine. Uptake of this toxic compound into the presynaptic neuron causes axonal terminal degeneration 30 and provides a substrate for treatment-resistant persistent effects.

More recent research has focused on the use of PCP as a research tool to investigate NMDA receptor-mediated effects. There is a symmetry and completeness to this model which is lacking in purely dopaminergic hypotheses. Both dopamine and NMDA exert GABA-mediated effects which are independent and complementary.

While support for the dopaminergic hypothesis of schizophrenic evolution includes observations of stimulant-augmented dopaminergic activity and induced symptoms resembling acute paranoid schizophrenia (Sayed and Garrison, 1983), many schizophrenic patients do not respond to dopamine antagonists. This implies the involvement of other mechanisms. An alternative model based on effects produced by phencyclidine was proposed in 1962 (Luby et al.. However, the neurochemical mediators of PCP effects were poorly understood at that time. More recent receptor-transmitter investigations have increased our knowledge of PCP effects and shown relevance for a more comprehensive model of schizophrenia.

In non-schizophrenic normal subjects, sub-anesthetic doses of PCP produce psychotic symptoms including concrete, idiosyncratic and bizarre thought patterns (Bakker and Amini, 1961). Autistic withdrawal and impoverished affect are observed. Formal tests of neuropsychological function show a spectrum of findings uniquely similar to schizophrenia and not induced by LSD or amphetamines (Rosenbaum et al., 1959). Selective attention and paired associate learning are most affected (Bakker and Amini, 1961) demonstrating frontal lobe and temporohippocampal dysfunction as seen in schizophrenia (Berman et al., 1988). Administering PCP to schizophrenic subjects exacerbates thought disorder, assertiveness and hostility (Ban et al., 1961). Unlike LSD induced secondary characteristics of schizophrenia, PCP produces primary "pathology-specific" perceptual and cognitive abnormalities (Domino and Luby, 1981).

Relative resistance to the effects of PCP is seen only in prefrontally lobotomized subjects (Itil et al., 1967). Additionally, whereas chronic, stabilized schizophrenics are less affected by amphetamine (Kornetsky, 1976), PCP will exacerbate schizophrenic symptoms in acutely ill or chronically stable schizophrenics (Angrist et al., 1982). This suggests that the neural substrates of schizophrenia are specifically vulnerable to PCP at all times but are only susceptible to amphetamine in an acutely decompensated state. Retrospective studies have demonstrated acute PCP intoxication to be indistinguishable from schizophrenia based solely on observation of presenting symptoms (Erard et al., 1980).

PCP receptors have been located within the N-methyl-d-aspartate receptor complex ion-channel (Javitt & Sukin, 1990). NMDA receptors are a type of receptor for the excitatory neurotransmitter l-glutamate. In drug discrimination studies, PCP-appropriate responses are unique with respect to dopaminergic agents. Dopamine antagonists, such as haloperidol, do not inhibit them and dopamine agonists, such as amphetamine, do not reproduce them (Browne, 1986). Thus, while no unitary dopamine function abnormality hypothesis accounts for a full spectrum of schizophrenic symptoms, primary NMDA receptor dysfunction leading to secondary dopamine dysregulation can account for a full range of symptoms and the observed paucity of neuropathologic correlates of the purported hyperdopaminergic state of schizophrenia (Kleinman et al., 1988).

Amphetamines and PCP are both able to produce psychoses which broadly resemble idiopathic schizophrenia. Amphetamine produces predominantly positive schizophrenic symptoms such as hostility, agitation, paranoia, and paranoid delusions (Kay, 1987). It does not, however, typically produce core schizophrenic symptoms of loose associations, dissolution of ego boundaries, concrete thought and bizarreness of thought patterns (Angrist et al., 1974; Bell, 1965). This implies that non-Schneiderian (Schneider, 1959) symptom generation is not linked to excessive dopamine activity. In contrast to this, PCP produces symptoms that much more closely resemble the core negative symptoms of schizophrenia in addition to producing the positive symptoms of agitation, hallucination, paranoia, and unpredictable violence. The symptoms proposed by Bleuler (1950) to represent the primary symptoms of schizophrenia ("the four A's"): affective blunting, ambivalence, autism and disturbance of association - are thus much more reliably and consistently produced by PCP than by amphetamine administration.

PCP induces a schizophrenia-like psychosis by inhibiting NMDA receptor-mediated effects suggesting (Javitt and Zukin, 1991) that endogenous dysfunction or dysregulation at this locus might also exist in endogenous schizophrenia and contribute to symptom generation. The mechanism by which PCP produces psychotomimetic effects thus provides a neurochemical model of schizophrenia distinct from the dopamine hypothesis (Javitt and Zukin, 1991) and inclusive of a broader range of symptoms which more closely resemble idiopathic schizophrenia.

PSYCHOSIS CO-EXISTING WITH SUBSTANCE ABUSE: DUAL DIAGNOSIS EPIDEMIOLOGY

The association of substance abuse and psychosis has been remarked upon by numerous authors. Incidences of schizophrenia and other psychiatric disorders have been observed at rates greater than that of the general population in individuals with a primary diagnosis of substance abuse. Occurrence of organic psychosis in this population has been reported at rates as high as 33% (McLellan et al., 1980). In another study, 66% of patients seeking treatment for substance abuse or alcohol problems met DSM-III criteria for some other psychiatric disorder (Ross et al., 1988). Anxiety disorders were most common, followed in descending order by phobias, affective disorders and schizophrenia. A 1980 National Center for Health Statistics (McKenna and Paredes, 1992) survey revealed that in the discharge diagnoses of patients in non-federal, short-term general and specialty hospitals, 12% had a dual diagnosis. In 7% the primary diagnosis was substance abuse and in 5% the primary diagnosis was some other mental disorder.

From the perspective of primary non-substance psychiatric disorders, increased incidences of association are also observed. Of individuals on the psychiatric service of one hospital, 50% reported serious alcohol or drug abuse problems. (McLellan et al., 1980). Nineteen per cent of this population had a dual-diagnosis. Where the primary diagnosis was psychiatric, 34% had a depressive neurosis, 24% had a diagnosis of psychosis and 19% had a personality disorder. Of those with any primary psychiatric dual-diagnosis combination, the secondary substance abuse diagnosis was alcohol related in 87% and drug related in the remainder.

In a Veterans Hospital survey of patients admitted to the psychiatric service, 61% had a substance-abuse problem (Crowe et al., 1991). Other investigators also report high incidences of association between substance abuse and other psychiatric disorders. In one series (Caton et al., 1989) where 50% had some dual diagnosis, one-third began drug use before the onset of psychiatric illness, usually schizophrenia. Half of those dually diagnosed used multiple substances.

In a series (Muesser et al., 1990) of patients with schizophrenia, schizoaffective disorders and schizophreniform psychoses, 47% used alcohol, 42% used cannabis, 25% used stimulants, 18% used hallucinogens, 7% used sedatives and 4% used narcotics. Other series (McKenna & Paredes, 1992) have reported that 15 - 60% of schizophrenic patients use psychoactive substances.

There are many conflicting data as to which substances are preferentially used by schizophrenics. Some report a clear preference for alcohol (McLellan and Druely, 1977) while other series show a preference for stimulants and hallucinogens (Schneier and Siris, 1987). The predominant finding seems to be a preference for dopaminergic drugs. These agents may counteract some of the negative symptoms even though they may exacerbate positive symptoms. While there is much speculation as to what substances are used and why, two principles seem well established. Co-occurrence of substance abuse and schizophrenia is widespread (Turner and Tsuang, 1990) and while psychopathologic conditions predispose to drug abuse, drug abuse also predisposes to psychopathologic conditions (Andreasson et al., 1987; Drake et al., 1990).

PHARMACOLOGIC MANAGEMENT

There are three broad areas where pharmacologic intervention is of real or potential benefit in the management of the substance-abusing patient and psychosis. The first area encompasses agents used to treat substance abuse disorders with special considerations engendered when treating these disorders in the presence of psychosis. The second major area is that of substance - related psychoses including intoxication, overdose, withdrawal and acute substance-induced exacerbation of underlying psychosis. The final major area is that of the schizophrenic substance abuser whose illness is complicated by concomitant or secondary mood and affective disorders including anxiety, depression and panic disorder.

A number of pharmacologic interventions for substance abuse have been attempted. Major areas of treatment include substitution therapies, blocking agents and attempts to manipulate the neurotransmitters that mediate a substance's effects. To date, no "magic bullet" exists for the treatment of substance abuse, with or without schizophrenia.

Methadone has been used as a substitution treatment for opiate dependence. Opiates have been found to reduce or diminish some of the dysphoric symptoms of schizophrenia (Zweben et al., 1991) (Comfort, 1977). It may, however, alter the neuroleptic dose needed (Gold et al., 1978). Use of methadone is best reserved for maintenance of those dually diagnosed with primary opiate dependence and schizophrenia and has no place in the primary management of psychosis. Use is best when assessed in individual patients with a goal of achieving maximum stability.

Blocking agents have also been used with varying degrees of success in the management of substance abuse disorders. Naltrexone has not been shown to be of value in an opiate-abusing schizophrenic population. Disulfiram may be considered for use in alcoholic schizophrenics but caution is required in use. Schizophrenic-like psychoses have been reported to be initiated or exacerbated by its use (Ban, 1977).

Attempts to intervene at the level of neurotransmitter effects has principally focused on psychostimulant use and manipulation of dopaminergic and/or cholinergic pathways. Psychostimulants are direct or indirect catecholamine agonists (Gawin and Kleber, 1986). Neuroleptics block dopamine receptors. When given neuroleptics, monkeys demonstrate reduced rates of cocaine self-administration (Woolverton and Balster, 1981). Rats, however, will override this effect with increased doses of cocaine (Roberts and Vickers, 1984). In humans, neuroleptics may reduce paranoia, but not euphoria (Gawin, 1986). Neuroleptics are best used, when appropriate, for schizophrenia, but without expecting any consistently positive additional effects regarding cocaine cravings or use.

It has been postulated that neuroleptic-induced akinesia and related anergia may increase the tendency to self-medicate with psychostimulants (Siris, 1990). As dopamine agonists, there is a pharmacologic basis for cocaine and amphetamine to provide such relief, even though they both ultimately exacerbate the underlying schizophrenia. More appropriate for neuroleptically managed substance abusers would be a trial of an antiparkinsonian anticholinergic agent at full therapeutic doses (Siris, 1990).

These medications themselves are potential drugs of abuse (Zweben et al., 1991; Evans and Sullivan, 1990). Patients who run out of these anticholinergics before their antipsychotic medication supply is exhausted may be abusing them. This may cause further problems as, if overdose occurs, anticholinergic excess may be difficult to distinguish from an exacerbation of underlying psychosis. An EKG showing widened QRS complexes, prolonged QT intervals and tachycardia may help to confirm anticholinergic overdose.

Dopaminergic drugs have also been used in cocaine addicts and some antiparkinsonian agents are dopaminergic agonists as well. Amantadine is a dopamine agonist with nigrostriatal affinity but lacking mesolimbic activity

(Bailey and Stone, 1975; Allen, 1983). Further, amantadine has been shown in some studies (Kosten, 1989) to reduce cocaine cravings. Thus, while safety and efficacy issues remain incompletely studied, amantadine may be of use in schizophrenic stimulant abusers prone to abusing anticholinergic antiparkinsonian agents.

Bromocryptine is another dopaminergic antiparkinsonian used by some (Dackis et al., 1985) to treat cocaine abuse in nonschizophrenic patients. As a postsynaptic dopamine agonist, bromocryptine can result in receptor downregulation and reduced affinity to cocaine. However, unless neuroleptics are being used, bromocryptine can exacerbate psychosis when used alone (King, 1978). To date, bromocryptine has been of minimal use in schizophrenia. It has been used to treat neuroleptic malignant syndrome (Addonizio et al., 1987) and may be of some use in tardive dyskinesia (Roehrick et al., 1987). Benztropine is an anticholinergic antiparkinsonian agent with pronounced intrinsic dopaminergic agonist properties (Coyle and Snyder, 1969) and may be a safer drug when attempts are made to downregulate dopamine receptors in such patients.

Regarding the second mentioned category, psychotic symptoms may occur in the setting of intoxication, withdrawal or overdose. As these syndromes may resemble idiopathic schizophrenia and require specific intervention, accurate diagnosis is essential. Serum and urine toxicology screens are essential. Toxic psychoses require judicious treatment. Neuroleptics may precipitate seizures (Zweben et al., 1991) in stimulant overdoses and if used to control manic patients using stimulants may result in lethal hyperthermic crisis (Kosten and Kleber, 1988). Neuroleptics are not absolutely contraindicated and will effectively manage (Siris, 1990) substance-induced psychoses in non-schizophrenic individuals. High-potency agents such as haloperidol and droperidol (Zweben et al., 1991; Dubin et al., 1986), are preferred as they are less likely to exacerbate substance induced orthostatic hypotension, tachycardia, or anticholinergic effects.

Benzodiazepines may be of use in certain situations and can be used concomitantly with neuroleptics. One of their major uses is in the management of alcohol or minor tranquilizer withdrawal in the schizophrenic patient. Withdrawal itself does not usually produce psychosis and, conversely, in the agitated schizophrenic withdrawing from alcohol or tranquilizers, antipsychotic drugs alone will not suffice. General principles of management include the following (Zweben et al., 1991): if psychotic symptoms are not distressing to the patient, avoid neuroleptics and if multiple drug management is deemed necessary, use the lowest effective antipsychotic dose and full, even sedating, benzodiazepine doses.

Stimulant overdose as well as PCP or hallucinogen overdose present the danger of potential violence in addition to other problems. Observation, capability of using restraints, and judicious use of sedating, potent antipsychotics such as droperidol are a reasonable approach. Other potential diagnostic and management problems include alcoholic hallucinosis and amphetamine-induced organic delusional disorder. Both usually resolve with time and abstinence, but many patients will need antipsychotic medication (Roy, 1981). Protracted psychotic episodes persisting after drug use has ceased have also been reported after chronic cocaine use (Zweben et al., 1991).

The best approach to many of these acute interactions between substance abuse syndromes and psychoses is to use a longitudinal chronologic approach to assessment (Zweben et al., 1991) and to be willing to treat according to provisional diagnoses, re-evaluating patients as time passes.

Anxiety and panic disorder coexisting with substance abuse and psychosis present unique problems. Some of the agents used to treat anxiety are, in and of themselves, abusable drugs. While some experts (Salzman, 1991) do not consider benzodiazepines to be drugs of abuse, experts in addiction medicine (including this author) have strong opinions to the contrary. Schizophrenic patients with panic disorder may self-medicate and even benefit from benzodiazepines (Sandberg and Siris, 1987) although other drugs may be more effective. Anxious patients may also self-medicate with benzodiazepines. This may reduce negative symptoms (Csernansky et al., 1984) and in one study (Kellner et al., 1975) reduce anxiety significantly more than when placebo was added to the neuroleptic. However, not all studies have shown this effect and when substance abuse complicates the clinical picture, these drugs should be avoided. Some authors (McKenna and Paredes, 1992) feel alcoholic schizophrenics should never be treated with benzodiazepines. Buspirone is an excellent alternative for many of these patients. While benzodiazepines are usually drugs of second choice in a substance-abusing population and their use often attends the use of other drugs (e.g. stimulants), there are enough legitimate concerns regarding their actual and potential problems that they should be considered relatively, if not absolutely, contraindicated in this patient group.

Depressive illness is also a significant problem in this population. Substance abuse and post-psychotic depression are both frequently seen in schizophrenic patients. There is an interrelationship between self-medication of depressive symptoms with stimulants and the propensity of these drugs to cause or exacerbate depression when chronically used. Antidepressants are effective in some non-schizophrenic substance abusers (Gawin and Kleber, 1986), particularly in users of psychostimulants. And substance abuse, particularly with psychostimulants (Schneier and Siris, 1987), is common in schizophrenia. Indeed, psychostimulants are preferentially used by schizophrenics (Schneier and Siris, 1987) and among the most common drugs reported (Siris et al., 1988) when there is a history of substance abuse which antedates the onset of schizophrenic illness. Therefore, there exists a potential role for the use of adjunctive antidepressant medication in selected schizophrenic patients (Singh et al., 1978; Siris, 1990).

As depression-like syndromes may occur in as many as 25% of schizophrenics, (McGlashan and Carpenter, 1976) it is important to differentiate among antidepressant drugs as to efficacy in these patients. MAO inhibitors have not been reported (Siris et al., 1978) as effective adjuncts in schizophrenics and may produce hypertensive crisis if stimulants are used concomitantly. Of course, if stimulants are used shortly after beginning tricyclic antidepressants, hypertensive reactions may also occur as catecholamine uptake blockade occurs rapidly and receptor sensitivity downregulation does not occur for several weeks (Kosten, 1989). Lithium may be of use in certain substance-abusing, depressed schizophrenics. It may even counteract the euphoric effects of self-administered cocaine (Gawin and Kleber, 1986). Ideal candidates for treatment with lithium would be those with bipolar symptoms complicating stimulant abuse and schizophrenia (Siris, 1990).

Most efficacy has been shown with cyclic antidepressants. While results are not uniformly positive this may result from differences in study methodology (Siris et al., 1991). A review of nine randomized, double-blind, placebo-controlled studies showed greatest response with imipramine, trazodone and amitriptyline. The most pronounced response was seen with 200 mg./day of imipramine as adjunctive therapy to a stable neuroleptic/benztropine regimen (Siris et al, 1987). Imipramine itself can reduce cocaine cravings (Siris et al., 1991; Gawin and Kleber, 1986).

Therefore, antidepressants may be of use in stable substance-abuse prone schizophrenics and in the treatment of dysphoric schizophrenics who have recently used or are currently using stimulants. Of further interest is the observation that a history of substance abuse does not mitigate against effective response to antidepressant adjunctive therapy in post-psychotically depressed schizophrenics maintained on neuroleptic/antiparkinsonian regimens (Siris et al., 1989, 1991). Once neuroleptic-induced akinesia has been ruled out, a trial of adjunctive tricyclic antidepressant medication in substance-abusing dysphoric schizophrenic patients is clearly warranted (Siris et al., 1991).

BARRIERS TO EFFECTIVE TREATMENT

There are numerous impediments to the effective management of the substance abusing patient who suffers from additional major psychiatric illness. These difficulties include diagnostic dilemmas, structural aspects of facilities and programs, funding issues, staff training and biases, and legal issues. Because the re-occurrence of these disorders is frequent (Boyd et al., 1984) and that in some cases (Ridgely et al., 1986) (Galanter et al., 1988) it has even been reported to be more a rule than an exception to see patients with multiple illnesses, many individuals will have to face some of these barriers when seeking treatment.

Prevalence studies, adjusted for age, race and gender (Regier et al., 1984) have shown the lifetime prevalence of schizophrenia in alcoholics to be 3.8% (Regier et al., 1990) . These studies have also shown the lifetime prevalence of alcoholism in schizophrenics to be 33.7% and the lifetime prevalence of any substance abuse or dependence disorder in schizophrenics to be 47%. Among users of specific drugs, cocaine abusers had the highest rate of schizophrenia at 16.7%. In terms of absolute numbers, as alcoholism has a lifetime community prevalence of 13.5% (Regier, et al., 1990), the combined presence of alcoholism and schizophrenia is the most common dual diagnosis.

Assessment and diagnosis are the first obstacle to effective treatment. Alcoholic delirium tremens may be misdiagnosed as psychosis and result in inappropriate prescription of neuroleptics (Salloum et al., 1991). Alcoholic hallucinosis with auditory hallucinations in the presence of a clear sensorium presents such a diagnostic conundrum that one author (Glass, 1984) noted "the complete absence of a consensus view as to the nature of this problem". Drug induced psychoses are also often confused with schizophrenia.

Not only are substance-related psychotic episodes often misdiagnosed (Surawicz, 1980), but substance abuse is under-recognized (Solomon and Davis, 1986) in psychotic patients. When both disorders are present, the usual (Schwartz and Goldfinger, 1981) diagnosis given is schizophrenia. Part of the problem is that diagnostic instruments of value in non-schizophrenic alcoholics may lose validity in the dually-diagnosed population. Cognitive distortions invalidate many responses to the Michigan Alcoholism Screening Test when used in diagnosing schizophrenics (Toland and Moss, 1989). Here, biochemical measures and toxicology screens may be superior diagnostic tools.

Patients with psychoses and substance abuse disorders usually receive treatment for one or the other problem, but rarely receive specialized services for both disorders (Pinsker, 1983). Individuals who have both problems are often refused admission or prematurely discharged from facilities primarily oriented to either disorder (Galanter et al., 1988). Neuroleptic medication may conflict with "drug-free" programs and in these addiction programs, the behavior of schizophrenic patients is often viewed as disruptive. Few treatment settings explicitly offer programs specifically tailored to address both substance abuse and schizophrenia (McKenna and Paredes, 1992). These challenging patients are now forced (in addition to the primary burden of their illnesses) to contend with the additional burden of dealing with service providers established to address single disabilities (Ridgely et al., 1986). Newer approaches (Ridgely et al., 1987) stress the necessity of providing specific and intensive treatment for both disorders in a single setting which is able to effectively utilize both mental health and substance abuse resources.

Public funding in the United States has been characterized by a pattern of establishing separate systems for each disorder. This further compromises the ability of facilities to provide services effectively or efficiently. Eligibility criteria are typically focused on one, single, primary diagnosis. This can produce two inappropriate outcomes (Ridgely et al., 1990). An individual may be deemed eligible for provided services (but ignoring other needs) or may be denied services as a secondary diagnosis renders the patient ineligible for service. Further, the fact that both substance abuse disorders and schizophrenia are chronic illnesses that present with acute exacerbations means that addressing treatment to emergent crises is likely to result in inappropriate long-term management.

Where private third-party payers are involved, rules on pre-existing conditions often produce insurmountable barriers to accessing treatment. Even when qualified, special services for dual-diagnosis patients may not be deemed eligible for reimbursement. Cost containment efforts may further provide for inadequate lengths of in-patient stays or restrict reimbursement to inadequate or inappropriate out-patient services.

Regardless of the background and training of those involved in the treatment of the duallydiagnosed patient, certain strengths and certain deficits will be apparent. Variations in training mandate that specialists in either area assure that the patient receive an appropriate comprehensive evaluation. Many chemical dependency facilities employ counselors and other non-medical personnel. These clinicians often feel that the management of patients with additional psychiatric diagnoses, particularly schizophrenia, is beyond their ability. Even for physician providers, many in addiction medicine lack formal psychiatric training and many psychiatrists lack in-depth experience with alcoholics and substance abusers.

Attitudes, as well as skills, may vary widely and produce further problems. Those involved with abstinent-model treatment and self-help programs may be extremely reluctant to use pharmacologic treatments. Attitudes toward patients also complicate the situation. Mentally ill substance-abusing patients have been described in the psychiatric literature as "being difficult, manipulative, dangerous, noncompliant with, and abusive of medications (Bachrach, 1987)". Other descriptions (Pepper, 1985) include "attention seeking and help rejecting" and as being in "a chronic state of crisis". Such attitudes and perceptions can only complicate the provision of effective and compassionate treatment.

Despite the prevalence of comorbidity, effective psychotherapeutic approaches are lacking (Tyndal, 1974). For both alcoholism and schizophrenia, group therapy is an essential aspect of treatment (Lowinson, 1982; O'Brien, 1982). However, the approach to the patient with either disorder alone differs considerably. Confrontational approaches are used to penetrate the alcoholic's denial. For schizophrenic patients, a supportive and less demanding approach is called for (Mosher and Keith, 1980). Stressful interpersonal relationships often exacerbate schizophrenic symptoms and these patients may respond poorly to the confrontational techniques used in substance abuse treatment (Salloum et al., 1991). When treating schizophrenic alcoholics there are considerable difficulties in achieving a therapeutic balance between these conflicting approaches. Yet balance is essential as categorical programs designed to treat only one or the other problem have resulted in a needless redundancy of services. Focusing on an assumed "primary" diagnosis fails to provide comprehensive treatment and wastes precious health care resources.

Part of the reluctance to manage dual-diagnosis patients, particularly in primary chemical dependency facilities, is the potential for incurring real or perceived legal risks. Philosophic orientation (i.e. toward abstinent model treatment) does not absolve the treatment team of the responsibility to inform the patient regarding other therapeutic options (Klerman, 1990) based on a comprehensive assessment. Failure to sufficiently consider the psychiatric illness may lead to an inappropriate reluctance to prescribe psychotropic medication. This may lead to a failure to appropriately reduce suicidal risk when this unfortunate outcome may have been eminently preventable. Antipsychotic or antidepressant medications cannot be withheld due to programmatic biases when such medications are warranted.

IMPACT ON COURSE AND OUTCOME

The interrelationship of substance abuse and schizophrenia on the course, outcome and response to treatment of disease is complex, occasionally inconsistent, and often speculative. Nevertheless, observations reveal certain predominant trends. Psychopathologic disorders may predispose (Andreasson, et al., 1987) to and increase the incidence of some types of substance abuse (McLellan and Druely, 1977). Further, drug abuse may predispose toward psychiatric illness (Drake et al., 1990) and may exacerbate psychiatric disorders (Schneier and Siris, 1987) (Turner and Tsuang, 1990). Several scenarios (Pearlson, 1981) are possible and all require that an accurate chronologic history be obtained. Substance abuse may precede psychiatric illness, either precipitating or possibly causing psychopathology. Substance abuse may follow the development of psychiatric illness and represent self-medication or attempts at symptom reduction. And finally, substance abuse may simply accompany some other primary psychiatric illness.

Schizophrenics who used drugs tend to have an earlier age of onset of illness (Tsuang et al., 1982; Breakey et al., 1974) and an earlier age of initial hospitalization (Tsuang et al., 1982). There may be a genetic component to illness in some patients. The relationship between susceptibility to drug-induced psychosis in males and parental psychiatric illness is reciprocal (Bowers and Swigar, 1983). Premorbid personality in LSD psychosis patients did not differ, but extensive family histories of psychosis, suicide, and alcoholism were found (Vardy and Kay, 1983). On admission, substance-abusing schizophrenics as compared with non-substance-abusing schizophrenics had similar scores on global assessments and negative symptom ratings (Dixon et al., 1989). However, the substance-abusers had better scores on sociability, peer relations, and sexual adjustment. The substance-abusers also had better premorbid functioning except for worse scholastic adaptation (McKenna, and Paredes, 1992). It has been speculated that they have to be better adapted in order to function well enough to procure drugs in an illicit drug culture. This may also relate to the increased degree of improvement seen when drug-abusing schizophrenics are hospitalized and remain abstinent from drugs (Dixon et al., 1991).

It is possible that drug use precipitates psychosis in those who otherwise would have been less vulnerable (Breakey et al., 1974). Certainly, there is an increased incidence of psychiatric hospitalization among drug users than in the general population (Tsuang et al., 1982). Those susceptible to drug-induced psychosis do seem to have lower incidences of pre-morbid personality disorders (Glass and Bowers, 1970) (Breakey et al., 1974).

As to specific drugs, in one Veterans Administration study (McClellan et al., 1979) over half those with chronic (six-year) histories of repeated stimulant related admissions ultimately developed a psychosis. Of course, self-selection and predisposition cannot be ruled out. LSD (Hensala et al., 1967) may precipitate psychosis. Cocaine users also have increased rates of psychosis related psychiatric hospitalization (Rounsaville et al., 1991). Alcoholic schizophrenics report increased incidences of hallucinations as well as episodes of mania and depression (Pulver , et al., 1989).

Response to treatment may be affected. Those patients with a history of cannabis use or cocaine use may be less responsive to neuroleptics (Bowers et al., 1990), possibly on the basis of drug-induced alterations of dopaminergic mechanisms. Many patients are left with chronic disability after drug use ceases (Salloum et al., 1991). In a 6 year study (McKenna and Paredes, 1992), 63% of those admitted for use of hallucinogens, stimulants and inhalants had symptoms resembling schizophrenia. In many of these, these symptoms persisted long after detoxification.

Psychiatric patients with comorbid substance abuse disorders have increased rates of use of generalized psychiatric services (Regier et al., 1990), inpatient psychiatric hospitalization (Safer, 1987) community mental health resources (Pepper et al., 1981) and psychiatric emergency services (Schwartz et al., 1972). Outcomes are variable. In one series (Bowers, 1977) of patients hospitalized after psychotic reactions to drug use, half did well and half did not. Those substance-abusing psychotic patients who, at initial presentation, have more severe psychopathology, do less well than those with drug reactions which included psychotic features (Perkins et al., 1986). Overall, there is a sense of worse outcome in dual-diagnosis patients. Drug abusing schizophrenics have been stated to have poorer attitudes to treatment than non-drug-users (Alterman et al., 1982). Substance-abusers also have increased rates of missed appointments, treatment self-discontinuation, and failure to show treatment-related benefits (Hall, et al., 1977). This may be due to increased rates of marked mood changes (Alterman et al., 1982) and increased rates of sociopathology (Geller, 1980) in these patients.

Clearly, if alcoholism or drug abuse patients enrolled in treatment have more severe psychopathology, they have a worse overall outcome (McLellan et al., 1983). Dual-diagnosed patients have increased rates of relapse and re-hospitalization (Schwartz and Goldfinger, 1981). Typically, the shorter the history of drug abuse, the less the associated psychopathology (Tsuang et al., 1982). Compared to non-drug users, drug-abusing schizophrenics had similar lengths of stay, time to first pass and dose of neuroleptic medication, but had higher rates of discharge against medical advice (Miller and Tanenbaum, 1989).

While some feel poorer prognosis in dually-diagnosed patients is not necessarily validated (Stoffelmeyer et al., 1989), most studies show increased rates of treatment failure (LaPorte, et al., 1981) and poorer prognosis regardless of treatment modality (Alterman et al., 1982; La Porte et al., 1981).

CONCLUSION

Psychosis and substance abuse have numerous interrelationships. Some are statistical, some causal, and some mechanistically related. While co-existence has complicated treatment for some patients, psychoactive drugs and their mechanisms of action have also shed light on potential disease pathophysiology. Hopefully, the acquisition of new information will lead to ever more sophisticated interventions allowing us to refine our abilities to treat these devastating illnesses.

REFERENCES

Addonizio, G. Susman, V.L. and Roth, S.D. (1987). "Neuroleptic malignant syndrome: review and analysis of 115 cases", Biol. Psychiatry, 22, 1004 - 1020.

Allen R.M. (1983). "Role of amantadine in the management of neuroleptic-induced extrapyramidal syndromes: overview and pharmacology", Clin. Neuropharmacol., 6 (Suppl. 1), 64 - 73.

Alterman, A.I., Erdlen D.L and Murphy E. (1982). "Effects of illicit drug use in an inpatient psychiatric population", Addict. Disord.,7, 231 - 242.

Andreasson, S., Engtorm A. et al.,. (1987). "Cannabis and schizophrenia: a longitudinal study of Swedish conscripts", Lancet ii, 1483 - 1486.

Angrist, B., Peselow, E., Rubinstein, M. Corwin, J. Rotrosen, J. (1982). "Partial improvement in negative schizophrenic symptoms after amphetamine", Psychopharmacology (Berlin), 78, 128 - 130.

Angrist, B., Sathananthan, G. Wilk S, Gershon S. (1974) "Amphetamine psychosis: behavioral and biochemical aspects", J. Psychiatr. Res., 11, 13 - 23.

Angrist B.M., and Gershon S., "The phenomenology of experimentally induced amphetamine psychosis- Preliminary observations", Biol. Psychiatry, 2, 95 - 107.

Bachrach L.L. (1987). "The context of care for the chronic mental patient with substance abuse", Psychiatr. Q., 58, 1 - 14.

Bailey, E.V. and Stone, J.W. (1975) . "The mechanism of action of amantadine in parkinsonism: a review", Arch. Int. Pharmacodyn. Ther., 216, 246 - 262.

Bakker, C.B. and Amini F.B. (1961). "Observations on the psychotomimetic effects of Sernyl:, Compr. Psychiatry, 2, 269 - 280.

Ban T.A., Lohrenz J.J. and Lehmann H.E. (1961). "Observations on the action of Sernyl - a new psychotropic drug", Can. Psychiatr. Assoc. J., 6, 150 - 156.

Ban, T.A. (1977). "Alcoholism and schizophrenia: diagnostic and therapeutic considerations", Alcohol. Clin. Exp. Res 1, 113 - 117.

Bell, D.S. (1965). "Comparison of amphetamine psychosis and schizophrenia", Br. J. Psychiatry , 701 - 707.

Bell D.S. (1973). "The experimental reproduction of amphetamine psychosis", Arch. Gen. Psychiatry 29, 35 - 40.

Berman, K.F., Illowsky B.P. and Weinberger D.R. (1988). "Physiologic dysfunction of dorsolateral prefrontal cortex in schizophrenia", Arch Gen. Psychiatry, 45, 616 - 622.

Bleuler E.P. (1950). Dementia Praecox or the Group of Schizophrenias (1908). Translated by J. Sinkin, International Universities Press, New York.

Bowers, M.B. Jr. (1977). "Psychoses precipitated by psychotomimetic drugs: a follow-up study", Arch. Gen. Psychiatry. 34, 832 - 835.

Bowers, M.B Jr. and Swigar, M.E. (1983). "Vulnerability to psychosis associated with hallucinogen use", Psychiatry Res., 9, 91 - 97.

Bowers, M.B, Mazure, M.B, et.al. (1990). "Psychotogenic drug use and neuroleptic response", Schizophr. Bull., 16, 81 - 85.

Boyd, J.H, Burke, J.D, Gruenberg E, et al.,. (1984). "Exclusion criteria of DSM-III: a study of co-ocurrence of hierarchy-free syndromes", Arch. Gen. Psychiatry, 41, 983 -989.

Breakey, W.R, Goodell, H, Lorenz, P.C and McHugh, P.R. (1974)"Hallucinogenic drugs as precipitants of schizophrenia", Psychol. Med.,4, 255 - 261.

Browne, R.G. (1986) "Discriminative stimulus properties of PCP mimetics". In Phencyclidine: An Update, NIDA Research Monograph 64, (ed. D. Clouet), National Institute on Drug Abuse, Rockville, MD.

Caton, CL, Gralnick, A, et al.,. (1989). "Young chronic schizophrenics and substance abuse", J. Hosp. Comm. Psychiatry, 40, 1037 - 1040.

Clark, H.W. and Zweben, J.E. (1989). "Legal vulnerabilities in the treatment of chemically dependent dual diagnosis patients", J. Psychoactive Drugs 21, 251 - 257.

Comfort, A. (1977). "Morphine as an antipsychotic", Lancet, I, 443 - 444.

Coyle, J.T. and Snyder, S.H. (1969). "Antiparkinsonian drugs: inhibition of dopamine uptake in the corpus striatum as a possible mechanism of action", Science 166, 899 -901.

Creese D., Burt, D. R. and Snyder, S. H. (1976). "Dopamine receptor binding predicts clinical and pharmacological potencies of antischizophrenic drugs", Science, 192, 481 - 483.

Crowe D.B., Rosse R.B., et al.,. (1991). "Substance use diagnoses and discharge patterns among psychiatric patients", J. Hosp. Comm. Psychiatry, 42, 403 - 405.

Csernansky, J.G., Lombrozo, L., Gulevich, G.D. and Hollister, L.E. (1984). "Treatment of negative schizophrenic symptoms with alprazolam: a preliminary open-label study", J. Clin. Psychopharmacol., 4, 349 - 352.

Dackis, C.A., Gold, M.S., Davies, R.K. and Sweeney, D.R. (1985). "Bromocriptine treatment for cocaine abuse: the dopamine depletion hypothesis", Int. J. Psychiatry Med., 15, 125 - 135.

Dixon, L., Haas, G., Weiden, P., et.al. (1989). "Drug Abuse and Schizophrenia: clinical Correlates", Paper presented at the 142nd annual meeting of the APA, San Francisco, May 8, 1989.

Dixon, L., Haas, G., Weiden, P., et.al. (1991). "Drug abuse in schizophrenic patients: clinical correlates and reasons for use", Am. J. Psychiatry, 148, 224 - 230.

Domino, E.F. and Luby, E. (1981). "Abnormal mental states induced by phencyclidine as a model of schizophrenia". In PCP (Phencyclidine): Historical and Current Perspectives, (ed. E.F. Domino), Ann Arbor, NPP Books.

Drake, R.E., Osher, F.C., et al.,. (1990) "Diagnoses of alcohol use disorder in schizophrenia", Schizophr. Bull., 16, 56 - 57.

Dubin, W.R. (1988) "Rapid tranquilization: antipsychotics or benzodiazepines?", J. Clin Psychiatry, 49, pp 5 - 12.

Dubin, W.R.; Weiss, K.J.; and Dorn, J.M. (1986) "Pharmacotherapy of psychiatric emergencies", Journal of Psychopharmacology, 6, 210-222.

Ellison, G. D. and Eison, M.A. (1983). "Continuous amphetamine intoxication: an animal model of the acute psychotic episode", Psychol. Med, 13, 751 - 762.

Erard, R., Luisada, P.V. and Peele, R. (1980). "The PCP psychosis: prolonged intoxication or drug-precipitated functional illness?", J. Psychedelic Drugs 12, 235 - 245.

Evans, K. and Sullivan, J.M. (1990). "Dual-Diagnosis: counseling the Mentally Ill Substance Abuser", Guilford Press, New York.

Frosch, W.A., Rabbins E.S. and Stern, M. (1965). Untoward reactions to Iysergic acid diethylamide (LSD) resulting in hospitalization. N. Engl. J. Med., 273, 1235 - 1239.

Galanter M., Castaneda R. and Ferman, J. (1988). "Substance abuse among general psychiatric patients: place of presentation, diagnosis and treatment", Am. J. Drug Alcohol Abuse, 14, 211 - 235.

Gawin, F.H. (1986). "Neuroleptic reduction of cocaine-induced paranoia but not euphoria?", Psychopharmacology, 90, 142 - 143, 1986.

Gawin, F.H. and Kleber, H.D. (1986). "Pharmacological treatments of cocaine abuse", Psychiatr. Clin. of N. Am., 9, 573 - 583.

Geller, M.P. (1980). "Sociopathic adaptations in psychiatric patients", Hosp. Community Psychiatry. 31, 108 - 112.

Giannini A.J., Loiselle, R.H., Giannini M.L., et al., (1984). "Phencyclidine and the dissociatives", Psychiatr. Med, 3, 197 - 217.

Glass, B.I. (1989). "Alcoholic hallucinations: a psychiatric enigma - 1. The development of an idea", Br. J. Addict., 84, 29 - 41 (1989).

Glass, G.S. and Bowers M.B. Jr. (1970). "Chronic psychosis associated with long-term psychotornimetic drug abuse", Arch. Gen. Psychiatry, 23, 97 - 103.

Gold, M.S, Redmond, D.E, Donabedian, R.K et al.,.(1978). "Increase in serum prolactin by exogenous and endogenous opiates: evidence for antidopamine and antipsychotic effects", Am. J. Psychiatry, 135, 1415 - 1416.

Griffith, J.D., Cavanaugh, I., Held, J., et al., (1972). "Dextroamphetamine evaluation of psychomimetic properties in man", Arch. Gen. Psychiatry, 26, 97 - 100.

Hall, R.C., Popkin, M.K., DeVaul, R, et.al. (1977). "The effect of unrecognized drug abuse on diagnosis and therapeutic outcome", Am. J. Drug Alcohol Abuse, 4, 455 - 465.

Haracz, J.L. (1982). "The dopamine hypothesis: an overview of studies with schizophrenic patients", Schizophr. Bulletin, 8, 438 - 469.

Hayner G.N., McKinney H. (1986). "MDMA, the dark side of ecstasy", J. Psychoactive Drugs, 18, 341 - 347.

Hensala, J.D., Epstein, L.J. and Blacker, K.H. (1967). LSD and psychiatry, 16, 554 - 559.

Hurlbut, K. M. (1991). "Drug Induced Psychoses", Emergency Medicine Clinics of North America., Vol. 9, No. 1, pp. 31 - 52.

Itil, T., Keskiner, A., Kiremitci, N., Holden J.M.C. (1967). "Effect of phencyclidine in chronic schizophrenics", Can. Psychiatr. Assoc. J., 12, 209 - 212.

Janowsky, D.S., and Davis, J.M. (1976). "Methylphenidate, dextroamphetamine, and levamphetamine: effects on schizophrenic symptoms", Arch. Gen. Psychiatry, 33, 304 -308.

Javitt, D.C. and Sukin S.R (1990). "Role of excitatory amino acids in neuropsychiatric illness", J Neuropsychiatry Clin. Neurosci., 2, 44 - 52.

Javitt, D.C. and Zukin, S.R. (1991). "Recent Advances in the Phencyclidine Model of Schizophrenia", Am. J. Psychiatry, 148, 10, 1301 - 1308.

Kay, S.R., Fiszbein, A. and Opler L.A. (1987). "The positive and negative syndrome scale (PANSS) for schizophrenia", Schizophr. Bull., 13, 261 - 276.

Kellner, R., Wilson, R.M., Muldower, M.D. and Pathak, D. (1975). "Anxiety in schizophrenia: the response to chlordiazepoxide in an intensive design study",Arch. Gen. Psychiatry, 32, 1246 - 1254.

King, D.J. (1978). "Dopamine agonists for negative symptoms in schizophrenia",Br. J. Clin. Pharmacol., 6, 541 - 542.

Kleinman, J.E., Casanova, E.M. and Jaskiv, G.E. (1988). "The neuropathology of schizophrenia. Schizophr. Bull, 14, 209 - 216.

Klerman, G. (1990). "The psychiatric patient's right to effective treatment: implications of the Oshroffversus Chestnut Lodge", Am. J. Psychiatry, 147, 409 - 418.

Kornetsky, C. (1976). "Hyporesponsivity of chronic schizophrenic patients to dextroamphetamine", Arch. Gen. Psychiatry, 33, 1425 - 1428.

Kosten, T. R. (1989). "Pharmacotherapeutic interventions for cocaine abuse: matching patients to treatments", J. Nerv. Ment. Dis., 177, 379 - 389.

Kosten, T. R. and Kleber, H.D. (1988). "Differential diagnosis of psychiatric comorbidity in substance abusers", J. Subst. Abuse Treat., 5, 201 - 206.

La Porte D.J, McLellan A.T, O'Brien C.P, et.al. (1981). "Treatment response in psychiatrically impaired drug abusers", Compr. Psychiatry, 22, 411 - 419.

Leikin, J.B., Krantz, A.J., Zell-Kanter, M. et al., (1989). "Clinical features and management of intoxication due to hallucinogenic drugs", Med. Toxicol. Adverse Drug Exp., 4, 324 - 350.

Lewis, D.A. and Smith R.E. (1983). "Steroid induced psychiatric syndromes", J. Affect. Disord., 5, 319 - 332.

Lieberman, J.A., Kane, J.M. and Alvir, J. (1987). "Provocative tests with psychostimulant drugs in schizophrenia", Psychopharmacology 91, 415 - 433.

Lieberman, J.A., Kinon, F.J., and Loebel, A.D. (1990). "Dopaminergic mechanisms in idiopathic and drug-induced psychoses", Schizophr. Bull, Vol. 16, No. 1, 97 - 110.

Lowinson, J.H. (1982). "Group psychotherapy with substance abusers and alcoholics". In Comprehensive Group Psychotherapy, 2nd ed., (eds. H.I. Kaplan and B.J. Sadock), Williams and Wilkins, Baltimore..

Luby, E.D., Gottlieb, J.S., Cohen, B.D., Rosenbaum, G. and Domino E.F. (1962)."Model psychoses and schizophrenia", Am. J. Psychiatry, 119, 61 - 67.

Mack, R.B. (1986). "Marching to a different cactus: peyote (mescaline) intoxification", N.C. Med. J. 47, 137 - 138.

Marmor, M., Des Jarlais, D.C., Friedman, S.R., Lyden M. and El Sadr, W. (1984)."The epidemic of acquired immunodeficiency syndrome (AIDS) and suggestions for its control in drug abusers", J. Subst. Abuse Treat., 1, 237 - 247.

McGlashan, T.H. and Carpenter, W.T. Jr. (1976). "Postpsychotic depression in schizophrenia", Arch. Gen. Psychiatry, 33, 231 - 239.

McKenna, A.M. and Paredes, A. (1992). "Dual diagnosis: empirical and developmental-humanistic approaches", In Recent Developments in Alcoholism", Vol. 10, (ed. M. Galanter), Plenum Press, New York, 89 - 107.

McLellan, A.T., Luborsky, L. and Woody, G.E. (1983). "Predicting response to alcohol and drug abuse treatments: role of psychiatric severity", Arch. Gen. Psychiatry. 40, 620 - 625.

McLellan, A.T., Mac Gahan, J.A., Druley, K.A. (1980). "Psychopathology and substance abuse". In Substance Abuse and Psychiatric Illness (eds. Gottheil E., McLellan AT, Druley RA), Pergamon Press, New York.

McLellan, A.T. and Druely, K.A. (1977). "Non-random relation between drugs of abuse and psychiatric diagnosis", J. Psychiatric Res., 13, 179 - 184.

McClellan, A.T., Woody, G.E. and O'Brien, C.P. (1979). "Development of psychiatric illness in drug abusers", NEJM. 301, 1310 - 1314.

Miller, F.T. and Tanenbaum, J.H. (1989). "Drug abuse in schizophrenia", Hosp. Comm. Psychiatry, 40, 847 - 849.

Mosher, LR and Keith, S.J. (1980). "Psychosocial treatment: individual, group, family, and community support approaches", Schizophr. Bull, 6, 10 - 41.

Muesser, K.T., Yarnold P.R., Levinson D.F., et al.,. (1990). "Prevalence of substance abuse in schizophrenia, demographic and clinical correlates", Schizophr. Bull.,16, 31-56.

O'Brien, C.P. (1982) "Group psychotherapy with schizophrenia and affective disorders". In Comprehensive Group Psychotherapy, 2nd ed. (eds. H.I. Kaplan and B.J. Sadock), Williams and Wilkins, Baltimore.

Pearlson, G.D. (1981) "Psychiatric and medical syndromes associated with phencyclidine (PCP) abuse", Johns Hopkins Med. J., 148, 25 - 33, 1981.

Peden, N.R., Pringle, S.D. and Crooks, J. (1982). "The problem of psilocybin mushroom abuse", Human Toxicol 1, 417 - 424.

Pepper, B., Kirshner M.C. and Ryglewicz, H. (1981). "The young chronic patient: overview of a population", Hosp. Comm. Psychiatry, 32, 463 - 467.

Pepper, B. (1985). "The young adult chronic patient: population overview", J. Clin. Psychopharmacol. , 5(3) Suppl., 35 - 75.

Perkins, K.A, Simpson, J.C., and Tsuang M.T. (1986). "Ten-year follow-up of drug abusers with acute or chronic psychosis", Hosp. Comm. Psychiatry 37, 481 - 484.

Pinsker, H. (1983). "Addicted patients in hospital psychiatric units", Psychiatr. Ann. 13, 619 - 623.

Post, R.M., Weiss, S.R.B. and Pert, A. (1988). "Cocaine induced behavioral sensitization and kindling: implications for the emergence of psychopathology and seizures", Ann. N.Y. Acad. Sci., 537, 292 - 308.

Post, R.M. (1975) "Cocaine psychosis: a continuum model", Am. J. Psychiatry, 132, 225 - 231.

Pulver A.E, Wolyniec B.S, Wagnser M.G, et.al. (1989). "An epidemiologic investigation of alcohol-dependent schizophrenics", Acta. Psychiatr. Scand..79, 603 - 612.

Regier, D.A., Farmer, M.E., Rae, D.S., et.al. (1990). "Comorbidity of mental disorders with alcohol and other drug abuses", JAMA., 264, 2511 - 2518.

Regier, D.A., Myers, J.K., Kramer, M., et.al. (1984). "The NIMH Epidemiologic Catchment Area Program: historical context, major objectives and study population characteristics", Arch. Gen. Psychiatry, 41, 934 - 941.

Ridgely, M.L.S, Goldman, H.H, and Talbott J.A. (1986). Chronic Mentally Ill Young Adults With Substance Abuse Problems: A Review of the Literature and Creation of a Research Agenda, Mental Health Policy Studies, University of Maryland School of Medicine, Baltimore.

Ridgely, M.S., Osher, F.C. and Talbott, J.A. (1987). Chronically Mentally Ill Young Adults With Substance Abuse Problems: Treatment and Training Issues, Mental Health Policy Studies, University of Maryland School of Medicine, Baltimore.

Ridgely, M.S., Goldman, H.H. and Willenbring, M. (1990). "Barriers to the care of persons with dual diagnoses: Organizational and financing issues",Schizophr. Bull., 16, 123 - 132.

Roberts, D.C.S., and Vickers, G. (1984) "Atypical neuroleptics increase self-admininstration of cocaine: An evaluation of behavioral screen for anti-psychotic activity", Psychopharmacology, 82, 135 - 139.

Roehrick, H., Dackis, C.A., and Gold, M.S. (1987). "Bromocryptine", Medical Research Reviews, 7, 243 - 269.

Rosenbaum, G., Cohen, B.D., Luby, E.D., Gottlieb, J.S. and Yelen, D. (1959). "Comparisons of Sernyl with other drugs", Arch. Gen. Psychiatry, 1, 651 - 656.

Ross, H., Glaser, T. and Germanson, T. (1988). "The prevalence of psychiatric disorders in patients with alcohol and other drug problems", Arch. Gen. Psychiatry, 45, 1023 - 1031.

Rounsaville, B.J., Anton, S.F. and Carroll K, et.al. (1991). "Psychiatric diagnoses of treatmentseeking cocaine abusers", Arch. Gen. Psychiatry, 48, 43-51 .

Roy, A. (1981). "LSD and onset of schizophrenia", Can. J. Psychiatry , 26, 64 - 65.

Safer, D.J. (1987). "Substance abuse by young adult chronic patients", Hosp. Comm. Psychiatry, 38, 511 - 514.

Salloum, I.M, Moss, H.B. and Daley, D.C. (1991). "Substance abuse and schizophrenia: Impediments to optimal care", Am. J. Drug Alcohol Abuse, 17, 321 - 336.

Salzman, C. (1991). "The APA Task Force Report on Benzodiazepine Dependence, Toxicity, and Abuse", Am. J. Psychiatry, 148, 151 - 152, (editorial).

Sandberg, L. and Siris, S.G. (1987). "Panic disorder" in schizophrenia: a case report", J. Nerv. Ment. Dis., 175, 627 - 628.

Sayed, Y. and Garrison, J.M. (1983). "The dopamine hypothesis of schizophrenia and the antagonistic action of neuroleptic drugs-a review", Psychopharmacol. Bull. , 19, 283 - 288.

Schneider, K. (1959). "Clinical Psychopathology", Grune & Stratton, New York.

Schneider, E.F. and Siris S.G. (1987). "A review of psychoactive substance use and abuse in schizophrenia: patterns of drug choice", J.Nerv. Ment. Dis., 175, 641 - 652.

Schwartz, D.A, Weiss, A.T and Miner, J.M. (1972). "Community psychiatry and emergency service", Am. J. Psychiatry, 129, 710 - 714.

Schwartz, S. and Goldfinger, S. (1981). "The new chronic patient: clinical characteristics of an emerging subgroup", Hosp. Comm. Psychiatry, 32, 470 - 474.

Seiden, L.S., and Ricaurte, G.A. (1987). "Neurotoxicity of methamphetamine and related drugs". In Psychopharmacology: The Third Generation of Progress, (ed. H.Y. Meltzer), Raven Press, New York, 359 - 366.

Shaffer, H.J. and Costikyan, N.S. (1988). "Cocaine Psychosis and AIDS: a contemporary Diagnostic Dilemma", J. Subst. Abuse Treat., 5, 9 - 12.

Singh, A.N.; Saxena, B.; and Nelson, H.L.. (1978) "A controlled study of trazodone in chronic schizophrenic patients with pronounced depressive symptomatology",. Curr. Ther. Res., 23, 485 - 501.

Siris, S.G. (1990). "Pharmacological treatment of depression in schizophrenia". In: Depression in Schizophrenia, (ed. L.E. DeLisi), American Psychiatric Press, Washington, D.C., 141 - 162.

Siris, S.G., Bermanzohn, P.C., Mason, S.E. and Shuwall, M.A. (1991) "Antidepressant for substance-abusing schizophrenic patients: a minireview", Prog. Neuropsychopharmacol. Biol. Psychiatry, 15, 1 - 13.

Siris, S.G., Kane, J.M., Frechen, K., Sellew, A., Mandeli J., and Fasanodube, B.. (1988). "Histories of substance abuse in patients with post-psychotic depressions", Compr. Psychiatry 29, 550 - 557.

Siris, S.G., Morgan V., Fagerstrom, R., Rifkin, A. and Cooper, T.B. (1987). "Adjunctive imiprimine in the treatment of post-psychotic depression: a controlled trial", Arch. Gen. Psychiatry, 44, 533 - 539.

Siris, S.G. van Kammen, D.P. and Docherty, J.P. (1978). "Use of antidepressant drugs in schizophrenia", Arch. Gen. Psychiatry, 35, 1368 - 1377.

Siris, S.G. (1990). "Pharmacologic treatment of substance-abusing schizophrenic patients", Schizophr. Bull., 111-122.

Solomon, P. and Davis, J.M. (1986). "The effects of alcohol abuse among the new chronically mentally ill", Social Work and Health Care, 11, 65 - 74 .

Stoffelmeyer, B.E, Benijhek, L.A., et al. (1989). "Substance abuse prognosis with an additional psychiatric diagnosis: understanding of the relationship", J. Psychoactive Drugs, 21, 145 - 152.

Su, T.P., Pagliaro R.N., Schmidt P.J. et al., (1993). "Neuropsychiatric effects of anabolic steroids in male normal volunteers", JAMA , 269, 2760 - 2764.

Surawicz, F.G. (1980). "Alcoholic hallucinosis: a missed diagnosis", Can. J. Psychiatry 25, 57-63.

Thornicroft, Graham (1990). "Cannabis and psychosis: Is there epidemiological evidence for an association?", Br. J. Psychiatry., 157, 25 - 33.

Toland, A.M. and Moss, H.B. (1989). "Identification of the alcoholic schizophrenic: use of clinical laboratory tests and the MAST", J. Stud. Alcohol, 50, 49 - 53.

Tsuang, M.T., Simpson, J.C., and Kronfol, Z. (1982). "Subtypes of drug abuse with psychosis: demographic characteristics, clinical features and family history", Arch. Gen. Psychiatry. 39, 141 - 147.

Tunving, K. (1985) "Psychiatric effects of cannabis use", Acta. Psychiatr. Scand., 72, 209-217.

Turner, W.M. and Tsuang, M.T. (1990). "Impact of substance abuse on the course and outcome of schizophrenia", Schizophr. Bull, 16, 87 - 95.

Tyndal, M. (1974). "Psychiatric study of 1000 alcoholic patients", Can. Psychiatr. Assoc. J. , 19, 21 - 24.

Van Kammen, D.P., Bunney, W.E. Jr., Dochery, J.P. et. al. (1982). "d-Amphetamine-induced heterogeneous changes in psychotic behavior in schizophrenia", Am. J. Psychiatry, 139, 991 - 997.

Vardy, M..M. and Kay S.R. (1983). "LSD psychosis or LSD-induced schizophrenia?: a multimethod inquiry", Arch. Gen. Psychiatry, 40, 877 - 883.

Woolverton, W. L., and Balster, R.L. (1981). "Effects of antipsychotic compounds in rhesus monkeys given a choice between cocaine and food", Drug Alcohol Depend., 8, 69 - 78.

Zweben, J.E., Smith, D.E., and Stewart, P. (1991). "Psychotic conditions and substance use: prescribing guidelines and other treatment issues", J. Psychiatric Drugs, 23, 387 -395.

16

STRESS AND PSYCHOSIS

Michael A. Simpson

How have you been keeping?
How have you been keeping it (noun, adverb)
What have you been keeping?
What is it?
How have you been keeping?
What is it that you have been keeping?
  (Hopes, Hopes)
To see significance in the phrase.
          Rod, 1978; (cited in Simpson,1980).

It would require far more space than is available in this chapter to comprehensively review the literature on stress and schizophrenia, let alone the broader topic of stress and psychosis. These are dealt with more fully in my Conference paper (Simpson, 1994); and there have been several useful recent reviews (Norman and Malla, 1993a and b; Rabkin, 1993; Teague et al, 1989).

A relationship between stress and psychosis has long been assumed, and many authorities consider patients with schizophrenia to be particularly vulnerable to stress; and that stress may play a part in the aetiology, pathogenesis, or the precipitation, of episodes of schizophrenia and other psychoses.

Various authors have suggested that people who develop schizophrenia are especially sensitive to certain stresses such as actual or perceived   threats   to self-esteem or self-image; and that they may respond to events other people

Schizophrenia: Exploring the Spectrum of Psychosis. Edited by R. Ancill. © 1994 John Wiley & Sons Ltd.

wouldn't find distressing. Lehmann (1975, p. 891) wrote: "Those who have worked extensively with schizophrenics know that these patients are very easily hurt by...behaviour that, in most cases, would hardly be noticed by persons of normal sensitivity or, if noticed, certainly would not lead to traumatic experiences."

Yet while research so far has generated too much relevant data to allow us to reject these and related hypotheses, it has not yet produced enough evidence to enable us to fully accept and understand them. As Rabkin (1993) concluded: "Given the discrepancies in design and the unevenness of methodological rigor of these studies, one cannot justifiably conclude that they have disproved the possibility of an association between stressful life events and schizophrenia onset; rather, they have failed to provide positive evidence for such a link." Accordingly, I will concentrate largely on continuing areas of puzzlement within this field; on methodological problems and ways in which current models have limited our ability to comprehend this relationship, and on how insights from other aspects of stress research, including the field of traumatic stress, can open a field that has been obtunded by premature closure. The methods and models chosen, by abridging interactions for the sake of methodological simplicity or elegance, have often obscured vital issues, and may forfeit all real probability of illuminating the questions we are seeking to answer.

Research in recent decades has almost totally ignored all possible relationships between stress and schizophrenia except for two; the relation of recent life events to onset or relapse, and the impact of a specific and laboriously measured aspect of family interactions on relapse. The overwhelming influence of the methodologies of Brown and his colleagues and the concept of xpressed emotion (EE), while shedding some light on some issues, has shed darkness on many others; illustrating clearly the tragic results of the excessive dominance of a field of inquiry by a small number of models and/or methodologies.

The inconsistent results produced so far suggest other possible questions: are some schizophrenics less sensitive to some of the stressors which trouble others, and which seem to precipitate or worsen other psychiatric illnesses? What specific situations are especially stressful to a schizophrenic, which might not stress others? Why does the literature on schizophrenia contain so many descriptions of special vulnerability and sensitivity, yet so little evidence of the usual stress effects? Something is being missed.

STRESS MODELS AND MARKERS OF ONSET

The model of stress and its impacts used in research relating to psychosis is not always clear, but much modern work favours an interactive model. Individuals may, by chance, experience an unusual number or quality of stressors in life. Their own personality, sensitivities, interpersonal and life skills, will influence their ability to forestall the occurrences of avoidable undesirable life events; their provocation of undesirable events that are open to precipitation but not inevitable; their ability to encourage good events to occur; and the availability of and access to mediating factors including social and family supports. When bad events occur (or good events fail to occur) these challenges are met with more or less success.

Some models, like Holmes-Rahe, seem to assume that it's better if nothing happens to you, not even marriage or parenthood; while others seem to admire invulnerability and impassivity in the face of stress, an ideal which may represent massive denial and repression, rather than health. Stress needs to be distressing, to some degree, if one is to handle it effectively. The"brave hero" is often merely stupid or extremely unimaginative; or denying very salient aspects of reality.

Generally, there has been acceptance of a stress-diathesis model. But far more specification of the nature and operational effects of the diathesis is needed. A variety of potential markers of vulnerability have been identified, including deficits in social relatedness, attentional and cognitive processing limitations, autonomic hyperactivity, and changes in brain structure, metabolism and function. We need far more clarity on how such structural and functional anomalies would affect the individual's sensitivity to, and responses to, various types of stress. Does the stressor cause vulnerability as some formative models would require, or do the vulnerabilities engender stressors?

While we are truly interested in factors leading to the development of schizophrenia ab initio, difficulties in establishing when early and prodromal stages of the illness commence, have led many researchers to ignore this question, and to concentrate instead on factors which may precipitate relapses, which are generally easier to recognize and date. When using the onset of florid symptomatology as a convenient marker, earlier and more subtle phases of illness, potentially more affected by stress, are ignored.

Studies often fail to distinguish meaningfully between the onset of even such florid symptoms, and the decision (by the individual or by others) to seek help or to bring matters to the notices of the sort of people who count these things; these are rarely the same event, nor occurring at the same time, and are affected by many factors within other people (family and existing or potential care-givers) and not only the patient. Especially in a condition like schizophrenia, decisions about help-seeking and resuming treatment are often taken by or heavily influenced by others; what may most determine the system's recognition of the existence of a relapse? It is odd that researchers, often so keen to exclude all but "independent" life events, choose to use a highly dependent marker like relapse. We know that many people with diagnosable disorders remain untreated (either they do not seek help or it doesn't pursue them) and treated cases are in significant ways not representative of all cases.

EVENT DEFINITIONS

Much work has used scales listing life events---marriage, birth of a child, loss of a loved one---and added the number of events, with or without weighting. Not only do the data not show equivalence between classes of events (and the basis for ranking or weighting them has never been overwhelmingly convincing) but there is no demonstrated equivalence within classes of event. Marriage and bereavement, for example, vary widely in their impact and potential to cause serious stress. Such summative scores of differing events are not as meaningful as they look.

Another broad problem is that many events on the scales are irrelevant to many sub-groups and age groups in society. At 14 you can't have a divorce; at 78 you won't have a child; if you've never been able to get a job (a chronic situational stress) you cannot lose your job (an event).

CHARACTERISTIC OF STRESSOR EVENTS, THE INDIVIDUAL AND THE CONTEXT

There is no doubt, from research on psychological trauma, that characteristics of events, and personal interpretations of them, are highly relevant to determining their impact, though these are hardly ever considered in schizophrenia research. Was an event expected (happily or with dread?) or surprising? Familiar or novel? Desired or undesired? Of what severity, intensity or trajectory in time? Sudden, gradual or recurrent? Specific or general? Ambiguous and complex or simple and overt? Discrete and individual, or prolonged in time or broad in extent? What losses or threats did it impose on the person, and how did these relate to their realistic and fantasized fears and vulnerabilities? How was it subjectively perceived by the patient? Was it considered controllable or uncontrollable?

Characteristics of the individual are important, including their stage of psychological development, strengths and skills, coping style, resistances, problem-solving expertise, vulnerabilities and sensitivities and how these match characteristics of the stressor; and the results of previous exposure to similar or other stresses. The effects of stress are also affected by the characteristics of the ambient and recovery environment; such as social supports, cultural expectations, acceptance or denial by society of the seriousness of the stresses, and the presence or absence of continuing or new stresses.

Striving to separate person from individual context and environment is folly. Except perhaps in areas of science like astronomy, we rarely study a person-free environment; we never study an environment-free person. By throwing aside those events that are "possibly consequences of the patients; mental states" (but only possibly) - we are tossing away events that are also possibly independent, biasing the results. Even attempts by Brown and others to produce"contextual" measures of life events are not ultimately convincing: the interviewer gathers details of events and their contexts, steadfastly ignoring any of the subject's reactions, then has other people rate how unpleasant they imagine these to be.

PROBLEMS OF COGNITIVE DEFICITS AND INSTABILITY OF CONCEPTUAL STRUCTURES

One should also take into account the evidence (e.g. Bannister & Fransella, 1986) of loose construing and instability of conceptual structures in schizophrenia; these would increase the probability that the experience and interpretation of stressful events in such patients would be unlike those solemnly chosen by researchers deliberately ignoring the individual's views, or by consensus among that popular and atypical experimental animal, the college student.

As Green's (1993) review shows, schizophrenic patients, on average, show deficits on nearly all information-processing measures: in perceptual processes, problem-solving, verbal memory, social perception, and communication. These, and other impairments, would probably seriously impair their capacity to handle stress; and particular kinds of stress, such as interpersonal, could be particularly difficult.

PROBLEMS OF TIME SCALE AND DEFINITIONS

There are numerous problems in the application of standard lists or questionnaires of events; some people, by fate or choice, could not possibly experience some of the events (an unmarried person, for instance, cannot experience divorce) so their opportunities to be stressed by occurrences the study will recognize are more limited than others. Other people are exposed to rare or peculiar stressors, and may risk being very substantially affected by events the study won't recognize. Many studies fail to acknowledge the stress of absence of desired and anticipated events; being jilted, not getting a job or scholarship that was much hoped for, etc. Arbitrary decisions have been made in various studies about the time-scale; how close in time must an event be, to onset of illness, to be considered relevant? There is good reason *not* to expect a simple answer, or a short interval, as so much research assumes. Why should we assume that the relevant interval would be the same for all people, or for all events? Why, any more than for bacteria or viruses, should incubation periods be identical? And incubation periods are highly relevant; certainly the body's response to physical and chemical stress can take decades to produce obvious and perceptible results which are no less caused by these initiating factors. Life experiences also need to be metabolized, rarely exerting or showing their full effects promptly.

Distinctions between, and relevances of, life events, hassles, and problems in living, are not sufficiently clear. Some events, to adapt a pathological term, are "acute on chronic". One or more acute and specific events on a background of chronic problems and challenges may have a degree of impact that neither the acute nor the chronic events themselves would have. With really chronic events like severe illness of a spouse or relative-when do they start, and stop, being a relevant stressor? Duration may be very relevant, and we generally don't know what durations, of what levels of stress, have significant psychopathological impact. So there are many unresolved problems in regard to methods of measurement and validity of stressor mensuration.

Illnesses like schizophrenia have preclinical, subclinical, and prodromal phases, and often very gradual onset of changes in behaviour and of biochemistry. If stress has an effect, where in the natural history is its influence? In practice, in schizophrenia, the easiest point on which to establish timing is the onset of florid symptoms: but the impact of stress may have been far earlier. If we look at onset of visibly and irritatingly bizarre behaviour, it may be relatively easy to identify date of onset. But when does "impaired daily functioning" or "social withdrawal", or "lack of drive" actually begin? Or inappropriate affect impairment in role functioning, impairment in personal hygiene (how many baths must be missed before this symptom is present?) Such symptoms are easy to recognize when they have been present to a marked degree for some time; but very difficult to pinpoint as to date of origin. Patients don't sit up one day, announce: "Gosh, I've lost my drive!" and note it in their diary. Some symptoms need to have been present for an unspecified period before their existence will be recognized. Even delusions and hallucinations may remain unrecognized and undated internal experiences for a variable period before they're formally revealed and recognized, even by the patient.

THE FALLACY OF FATEFULNESS

An inescapable dilemma in research on human beings is that denial of the very essence of their humanity - their individual, complex and quirky appraisal of the world in which they exist - may lead to elegant but meaningless research. Some researchers strive to distinguish fateful events, supposedly unrelated to the patient's behaviour, from nonfateful, possibly influenced by actions or inactions of the patient. There's no reason to believe that such Acts of God or Fate are more likely to be causative of illness. The distinction is often artificial; and there is evidence that "fateful" events are less pathoplastically stressful than those of human agency. By what logic could one argue that only random events can cause stress sufficient to influence the onset or course of illness? Complicity in one's own fate may be a highly relevant part of the pain. Events per se are not relevant influences; it is solely by being perceived and experienced by the individual that events gain relevance. Otherwise this becomes astrological epidemiology, where we can be confident that only the movement of the stars and planets are not themselves affected by the patient's conduct, and are truly fateful.

Concentrating on distilling out "fateful" and chance events greatly reduces the number and variety of possible events anyone could experience within any specific (especially if brief) period of time, and reduces the chance of finding any real differences between groups. Indeed, the more one moves towards attending only to essentially random events, the more likely it is that, being random, they should occur with the same frequency in both experimental and control groups. We know that humans very often regard random events as caused or influenced by them (watch gamblers at work!). And delusions often posit either that you influence events or that events influence you, to a degree with which others disagree. Variables such as locus of control are usually overlooked in this context; but some people feel responsible for, and able to influence, events where objectively, this cannot be so; while others feel no responsibility for, or capacity to influence events which are in their control.

Such attributional styles are highly relevant in influencing impact of events. Numerous studies since Brown and Birley's publications in the 1960s, have found an excess of events in patient's lives, preceding a schizophrenic episode, compared with community controls, but interposing the dubious requirement of "independence" for events reduces this difference, to a smaller effect, mainly within the final three weeks. Independent events may, in the vulnerable, increase the likelihood of "non-independent" events, in a manner similar to the "cascade" effect in blood clotting.

THE FALLACY OF THE GENERIC STRESSOR

Much research assesses generic stressors (the generic marriage, the generic divorce) exerting generic effects on all who experience them; though this is definitively fallacious. There is a lock and key relationship. Hardly anyone is entirely lacking in resilience and capability, wholly hapless and hopeless when faced by stress; and no-one is invulnerable. We vary in our areas of sensitivity/vulnerability and of capability/strength. What is likely to be relevant, both short and long-term, is the match or mismatch between the challenges-physical, emotional, spiritual, economic and social-which life events throw at us, and our capabilities. Where challenge meets ability, it will be dealt with, and the individual may be strengthened and boosted by the success. Where challenge meets vulnerability, the result may be failure to cope, sensitization to the risk of further similar challenges, and harmful impact on health.

THE FALLACY OF TIMING

What is the relevant period between event and illness? Various researchers have assumed six months, others prefer three weeks - essentially arbitrary intervals. Prospective studies of survivors of major trauma (e.g. Ursano, 1981; Ursano et al., 1981) found a significant relationship between the severity of stress experienced and the proportion of survivors with psychiatric diagnoses five years later - an effect not noticeable soon after the trauma. The proportion with psychiatric problems in the group exposed to high stress increased during the intervening five years, while those with less severe stress showed a declining rate of disorder.

THE FALLACY OF CONCENTRATING ON EVENTS, NOT PROCESSES

We also obscure data from ourselves by concentrating on *events* rather than processes. A nagging or cruel spouse, is not an event. Life with them may contain a multitude of individual events; cruelties and hurts, snubs and spites, great and small. One does not and cannot recall each individual component of the enduring stress; it has no date, only duration. As with someone stoned to death, no individual stone may be unmistakeably fatal - only the effects of the cumulation of blows.

OTHER PROBLEMS OF RESEARCH DESIGN

Specific problems of research design, especially of retrospective studies, of recall error and retrospective confabulation, have been reviewed elsewhere. Prospective designs with long intervals between measurements often include the disadvantages of retrospective designs. Problems of sampling can be especially distorting in retrospective studies. In studying schizophrenia, researchers often prefer patients with good premorbid personality (facilitating clearer recognition of onset); and similarly prefer cases with acute clear onset. but acute onset may be more likely to be associated with a precipitating event; while strong premorbid personalities would probably experience less events or lesser impact of events. The effect on the likelihood of identifying precipitating events is unpredictable. Are such patients more able to report, or more interested in reporting, events; maybe more interested in some events than in others? Is it easier for a researcher to probe and persist in seeking events in such patients?

THE FALLACY OF IGNORING EVENT INTERACTIONS

Within the psychotic or pre-psychotic individual, there has been no proper study of the interaction between stressors; what is the effect of repeated exposure to similar or differing stressors; of the pacing and spacing of trauma, stresses and hassles? What are the modes of recovery from significant stressors, and how is recovery affected by re-exposure or further challenge? What is the nature and effect of what Lazarus et al. (1985) and others have called uplifts: the opposite of hassles, sustaining events which can as act anti-stressors?

THE FALLACY OF ASSUMING SIMPLE, LINEAR, UNDIRECTIONAL RELATIONSHIPS

The widespread assumptions that the causal relationship must be linear and simple and unidirectional are without any convincingly demonstrated foundation. Neither is it clear why we should assume that degree of variance explained is the appropriate measure of the extent of such effects: using alternative measures such as population attributable risk, the degree of effect, even when limited to "independent" events, is more substantial, and would be more so if the "independence" assumption were questioned.

Why should we assume a single effect, at a single stage in the evolution of disease, of single cycles and single sequences? Psychosis, and schizophrenia, are not unitary and homogeneous phenomena: stress is likely to have different effects in clinical subtypes, and in different individuals with differing combinations of vulnerabilities, at different stages in the evolution of illness.

THE INTERPLAY OF PSYCHOSOCIAL AND BIOLOGICAL ASPECTS OF SEVERE STRESS

From trauma studies, we know that stress changes both the environment and the biology of individuals. Neurobiological mechanisms including behavioural sensitization have been recognized in post-traumatic stress disorder (PTSD) and affective disorder, and induced by psychomotor stimulants, which would produce lasting alterations in structure and function that fit clinical observations, and broadly similar mechanisms could explain some aspects of schizophrenia.

Marked activation of neurotransmitter pathways leads not only to prompt and brief reactions, but to long-lasting intracellular changes at gene-transcription level (as reviewed in Post, 1992), such as induction of transcription factors like the c-fos proto-oncogene. By binding at DNA sites and inducing mRNAs for other substrates and affecting other neuropeptides, gene expression is changed and effects can last months. Similar long-term changes could be encoded at gene-transcription level in schizophrenia, after an initial episode has been triggered, similarly leading to long-term vulnerability. Vulnerability may precede the initial episode, but may also follow it, and be due to it. Later episodes may be triggered by lesser, perhaps even more broadly symbolic stressors, and these would be more likely to be missed by the relatively crude methods used currently. After a number of repetitions, spontaneous recurrence may occur. The research on cocaine-induced sensitization suggests that conditioned and associative factors, such as the context and environment in which the illness occurred, can influence the later responses. Anatomically encoded memory traces also have been found to migrate over time, involving different structures.

There is a temporal evolution of these disorders, during which the effects of various kinds of stressors will change, as well as the microstructural and neurochemical mechanisms and neuroanatomical substrates. We must accept that the psycho-neurobiology of these conditions form a moving target, changing with the progression of the illness; and affected by the illness itself and by attempts to treat it. Episodes of the illness are not a simple reprise, like the chorus of a song; they may both increase vulnerability to further episodes, and alter the pathological mechanisms in such a way as to render previously effective treatments less effective or ineffective.

PROBLEMS WITH THE DOMINANT EE CONCEPT

The finding of a relationship between EE and relapse seems reasonably robust; but there are serious grounds for concern about this concept and methodology, and especially about the excessive dominance they have enjoyed. It is not firmly established to what extent high EE is causal rather than reactive; and it need not be wholly either. We do know that EE status is not fixed and immutable, and does change: but there are no sound studies of what factors influence such changes. Oddly, the studies showing change have shown mainly declines in EE: the causes of increased EE have not been clarified. The relationships between the dimensions of EE themselves, and between these and characteristics of the patient, are still not clear. Very few relatives are rated high on all three dimensions.

As cut-off scores were decided statistically and not clinically, it is far from clear in what way these constructs are clinically meaningful: and even programs claiming to have demonstrated beneficial changes in EE are likely to have generated other helpful changes by their relatively indirect methods. EE can also be seen as a variant of the earlier family-blaming models, desperate disclaimers.

Is EE stressor, a buffer, or both? How does a patient experience a high-EE relative? Is it the high-EE-ness of the relative that constitutes as relevant stressor, or their lack of low-EE-ness, which could constitute the loss of a buffer against other interpersonal and/or life stressors? What are the effects of stresses and life events (both individual and those shared with the patient) on family members, and their behaviour as regards EE-ness?

TRAUMATIC STRESS AND SCHIZOPHRENIA

There are intriguing possible relations between the results of traumatic stress and schizophrenia, discussed at length elsewhere (Simpson 1993a, 1993b, 1994). There have been reports of PTSD following psychosis (e.g. McGorry et al., 1991, reported it in 46% of patients who had recovered from a psychotic episode). Both PTSD and schizophrenia show positive and negative symptom clusters; and negative symptoms of PTSD (especially emotional numbing, affective constriction and estrangement from others) overlap significantly with schizophrenia. It is possible that part of the negative symptomatology of schizophrenia might be related to a post-traumatic stress element, at least at some phases of the illness. There might also be a similar biological substrate.

Although there are reports of schizophrenia following severe traumatic stress (Simpson, 1994), such as concentration camp or torture experiences, these are surprisingly uncommon. Considering that a relationship has been shown between stress and such other psychiatric disorders as anxiety, PTSD, depression, even organic brains syndromes, it would be very peculiar if Schizophrenia and the psychoses were to be somehow exempt from these ubiquitous effects; indeed, it would raise the question of whether psychosis were somehow protective for the effects of substantial stress. Early workers on battle fatigue agreed with Swank's (1949) conclusion that"all normal men eventually sudden combat exhaustion in prolonged combat. The exceptions to this rule are psychotic (insane) soldiers".

BRIEF REACTIVE PSYCHOSIS

Brief reactive psychosis as defined in DSM-III-R has seriously flawed criteria (see Jauch and Carpenter, 1988, and others). It even, ludicrously, lists schizotypal personality disorder both as excluding the diagnosis, and as a predisposing factor! There have been remarkably few studies of the condition, probably because the untested and invalidated criteria are so restrictive as to have impaired recognition of the condition. Unquestionably, there are conditions which are brief, reactive, and psychotic, but don't meet the present, incompetent, criteria for brief reactive psychosis.

It is said that Pinel's first question to new patients was: "Have you suffered vexation, grief or reverse of fortune?" This is still an excellent opening.

REFERENCES

Bannister D. and Fransella F. (1986). Inquiring Man: The Psychology of Personal Constructs, 2nd Edition, Croom-Helm, London.

Green, M.F. (1993) "Cognitive remediation in schizophrenia: is it time yet?" Am. J. Psychiatry, 150, 2, 178 - 187.

Jauch D.A. and Carpenter W.T. (1988). "Reactive psychosis II: does DSM-III-R define a third psychosis?", J. Nerv. Ment. Dis. 176, 2, 82 - 86.

Lazarus, R.S., De Longis, A., Folkman S. et al. (1985). "Stress and adaptational outcomes: the problem of confounded measures", Am. Psychol, 40, 770 - 779.

McGorry, P.D., Chanen, A., McCarthy, E., et al. (1991). "Posttraumatic stress disorder following recent-onset psychosis: an unrecognized postpsychotic syndrome", J. Nerv. Ment. Dis., 179, 253 - 258.

Norman, R.M.G. and Malla, A.K. (1993a). "Stressful life events and schizophrenia: I. a review of the research", Br. J. Psychiatry, 162, 2, 161 - 166.

Norman R.M.G. and Malla, A.K. (1993b). "Stressful life events and schizophrenia: II. conceptual and methodological issues", Br. J. Psychiatry, 162, 2, 167 - 174.

Post, R.M. (1992). "Transduction of psychosocial stress into the neurobiology of recurrent affective disorder", Am. J. Psychiatry, 149, 8, 999 - 1010.

Rabkin, J.G. (1993). "Stress and psychiatric disorders". In Handbook of Stress: Theoretical & Clinical Aspects, 2nd Edition (eds. L. Goldberger, S. Breznitz), Free Press, New York, pp. 477 - 495.

Simpson, M.A. (1980). "Introduction, and "Language and Communication in Schizophrenia". In Psycholinguistics in Clinical Practice (ed. M.A. Simpson), Irvington, New York.

Simpson, M.A. (1993a). "Bitter waters: effects on children of stresses of unrest and oppression". In International Handbook of Traumatic Stress Syndromes (ed. M.A. Simpson), Plenum, New York, pp 601 - 624.

Simpson, M.A. (1993b). "Traumatic stress and the bruising of the soul: the effects of torture and coercive interrogation". In International Handbook of Traumatic Stress Syndromes (eds J.P. Wilson and B. Raphael), Plenum, New York, pp 666-684.

Simpson, M.A. (1994). "Stress and psychosis", Paper presented to Schizophrenia 1994: Exploring the Spectrum of Psychosis; 3rd International Conference, Vancouver, British Columbia, Canada.

Swank, R.L. (1949). Combat exhaustion", J. Nerv. Ment. Dis., 109, 475.

Teague, G.B., Drake, R.E. and Bartels S.J. (1989). "Stress and schizophrenia: a review of research models and findings", Stress Med., 5, 153 - 165.

Ursano, R. (1981). "The Viet Nam era prisoner of war: precaptivity personality and the development of psychiatric illness", Am. J. Psychiatry, 138, 315 - 318.

Ursano, R., Boydstun, J. and Wheatley R. (1981). "Psychiatric illness in U.S. Air Force Viet Nam prisoners of war, a five-year follow-up", Am. J. Psychiatry, 138, 310 - 314.

17

NEUROLEPTIC -INDUCED DEFICIT SYNDROME: BEHAVIOURAL TOXICITY OF NEUROLEPTICS IN MAN

Ian Hindmarch

There can be few more devastating illnesses, in terms of psychological impairments and deficits, than schizophrenia. It is perhaps the severity of the untreated illness that has clouded medical awareness of the extent and severity of the adverse reactions and the side effects of antipsychotic medications.

TOXICITY OF ANTI PSYCHOTIC MEDICATIONS

Most clinicians are aware of the inherent toxicity of classic antipsychotics, (e.g.) phenothiazines, butyrophenones, thioxanthines, diphenylbutylpiperidines, with extrapyramidal side effects, hepatic abnormalities, sudden death, agranulocytosis, convulsions, tardive dyskinesia, and cardia arrhythmias. However, until the advent of the new generation of neuroleptics (remoxipride, sulpiride, clozapine, risperidone) such adverse effects were necessary sequelae of antipsychotic medications, as there were few, if any, effective and non-toxic compounds available. it was difficult with early phenothiazine derivatives to estimate realistic risk - benefit ratio as the inherent toxicity and adverse reactions associated with the compounds all but overwhelmed any benefit except in the most serious of cases. It should also be remembered that a large percentage of patients would have been hospitalized while under medication with classical neuroleptic agents. It is only in recent years with the move towards the management of schizophrenic patients in the community that issues of toxicity, side effects and adverse events have been raised. Although it seems likely that the newer antipsychotics are clinically efficacious and without the characteristic extrapyramidal side effect of many of the other drugs (Gerlach, 1991), there have been reports of agranulocytosis and/or myocarditis associated with their use. However, in spite of such side effects the newer molecules are still safer as regards their overall physical toxicity (Kerwin, 1993).

As well as physical toxicity and sometimes life-threatening adverse events it is also necessary to investigate behavioural toxicity if the complete impact of a neuroleptic on an ambulant patient is to be assessed. The concept of behavioural toxicity embraces two interrelated aspects of CNS side effects following the administration of a psychoactive drug. The first aspect relates to the"safety", i.e. increased risk of accident, of patients using psychotropics while performing the tasks of everyday living, and the second covers side effects which in themselves are countertherapeutic. Neuroleptics have been shown to produce sedation, cognitive impairment and motor retardation (Baldessarini, 1985) which could well increase the risk of an accident in ambulant patients in domestic or even sheltered workshop environments by simply prolonging the speed of psychomotor response to critical stimuli. It could well be that aspects of cognitive impairment coupled with the emotional withdrawal, blunted affect and dysphoria associated with the use of some neuroleptics (Carpenter et al., 1985; Emerick and Sanberg, 1991) give rise to the symptoms of depressive illness associated with schizophrenia. Patients treated with neuroleptics frequently complain about feeling excessively drugged and having problems with memory, motivation and concentration. Indeed, the major problems of the clinical use of high-dose neuroleptics are an increase in severity of side effects, a greater behavioural disturbance and a deterioration in mental state (Herrera et al., 1988; Solano et al., 1989; Van Puten et al., 1990)

The combined reaction of both objectively determined side effects and those patient reports of untoward neuroleptic activity is a serious limitation to the utility of an antipsychotic medication especially for those patients treated in the community. It is within the community milieu that side effects of neuroleptics or aspects of sexual behaviour, for example, achieve an importance especially as patients begin readjustment to the activities of living. Loss of sexual interest and libido is a reasonably common report from both male and female patients treated with antipsychotic drugs and erectile dysfunction has been associated with the use of a variety of different drugs, including thioridizine, chlorpromazine, haloperidol and fluphenazine (Mitchell and Popkin, 1982; Barnes, 1984). Again, the motor disorders so frequently associated with neuroleptics in clinical use are a major concern in ambulant outpatients as they lower compliance to medication and often cause debilitating and demoralizing side effects which may lead to relapse or exacerbation of the underlying disorder. The side effects of antipsychotic drugs are legion and barely a single physiological system escapes without some impairment or adverse activity observed after both acute and chronic treatment regimens. There are side effects of neuroleptics on CNS, ANS, endocrine, cardiovascular, hepatic, respiratory, gastrointestinal and immune systems. - the net result of which will certainly be countertherapeutic and may well lead to relapse and the need for urgent hospitalization. Recently the notion of neuroleptic-induced deficit syndrome (NIDS) was introduced (Lader, 1993) to describe the countertherapeutic activity of antipsychotic medication. NIDS describes the overall impairment of patient well-being due directly to the side effects of the administration of neuroleptics, whereas behavioural toxicity is a specific reference to CNS side effects of psychoactive drugs. The emphasis in this chapter is on behavioural toxicity which results from a direct interference with psychological behaviour by an antipsychotic medication. Psychomotor speed, memory, information-processing ability, cognitive skills, vigilance, alertness and attentional processes are all aspects of the overall psychological behaviour which can be modified by neuroleptics. Drug effects on motor activity and visual and other sensory systems are also relevant and will be included, but others such as changes in body weight, photosensitivity, gastrointestinal activity, convulsions and agitation, although important determinants of NIDS, will not be discussed unless they are deemed to be a direct cause of a psychological or behavioural deficit. Table 1 compares a cross-section of antipsychotics as regards their intrinsic abilities to produce side effects likely to be associated with NIDS and behavioural toxicity.

Although cognitive impairment seems to be associated with tardive dyskinesia, especially orofacial involuntary movements, it is not clear as to the extent to which the extrapyramidal effects of certain drugs could be said to be causal agents in producing cognitive impairment (Barnes and Edwards, 1993). An assessment of extrapyramidal side effects is given in Table 1, although this should not imply that there is a relationship between such effects and cognitive ability. However, it is clear that extrapyramidal effects of akathesia, dystonia, choreic movements, etc. will contribute greatly to the general NIDS. The most likely source of unwanted CNS effects are sedation, antihistaminic and anticholinergic activity (see Table 1). Sedation, a generic name for tiredness, sleepiness, drowsiness, etc., has a profound and far-reaching effect on the integrity of psychological performance and produces impairments on all systems, particularly those requiring attention, sensori-motor coordination and psychomotor speech.

Table 1. Severity of Side Effects of Selected Antipsychotic Agents Contributing to NIDS and Behavioural Toxicity Index

Classification	Non-specific sedation	Extra-pyramidal effects	Anticho-linergic activity	Antihist-aminic effects	Hypotensive properties
Butyrophenones (e.g.) haloperidol	1 - 2	5	1 - 2	0 - 1	1 - 2
Dibenzoxaxepines (e.g.) clozapine	1 - 2	3 - 4	1 - 2	4 - 5	1 - 2
Diphenylbutyl-piperidines (e.g.) pimozide	1 - 2	5	1 - 2	0	1 - 2
Phenothiozines Alipathic derivatives (a) (e.g.) chlorpromazine	5	3 - 4	3 - 4	3 - 4	3 - 4
Piperidine derivatives (e.g.) thioridazine	3 - 4	1 - 2	5	3 - 4	3 - 4
Piperazine derivatives	1 - 2	5	1 - 2	2 - 3	1 - 2
Substituted Benzamides (e.g.) sulpiride	1 - 2	1 - 2	0	0	0
Thioxanthines (e.g.) flupenthixol	1 - 2	3 - 4	1 - 2	4 - 5	3 - 4

Legend:
0 = no effects
1 = some effects reported
2 = mild effects usually reported
3 = moderate severity
4 = severe side effects, sometimes debilitating
5 = very severe side effects, often debilitating.

Anticholinergic activity is characterized, on CNS functions, by a general sedation and reduced sensori-motor ability and is, moreover, associated with detrimental effects on memory and overall mental ability. The extent of anti-cholinergic activity on intellectual function can be gauged from the initial use of tacrine (recently licensed in the USA as an anti-dementia agent) as an antidote for tricyclic antidepressant overdosing, i.e. cholinergic enhancement has anti-dementia properties, while anti-cholinergic activity can be regarded as promoting a "pseudodementia".

Antihistaminic effects produce sedation and can impair visuo-motor coordination, although the full extent of H1 antihistamine effects on human cognitive behaviour has yet to be fully documented and most evidence for the existence of such effects is derived primarily from animal studies, whereas the anticholinergic activity of many antipsychotic agents is betrayed by dry mouth, blurred vision, urinary retention, etc. However, it is evident from Table 1 that the majority of antipsychotic medications have the intrinsic potential to impair important aspects of CNS function and so contribute to ratings of behavioural toxicity. The exceptions might be sulpiride and, to a lesser extent, diphenylbutylpiperidines where the relatively low level of anticholinergic and antihistaminic activity might imply a low potential to suppress or impair general mental faculties. The existence of low levels of sedation following most neuroleptic pharmacotherapies probably owes more to the nature of the underlying disorder than any specific drug effects. It is generally accepted that with increasing doses there is a corresponding increase in side effects, especially when very high does are used (Hirsch and Barnes, 1994). Neuroleptics in general have inconsistent dose response relationships: some observers find U-shaped relationships between both clinical activities and side effects and dose of drug, while others find no reliable relationship (Curry, 1993). Such inconsistencies clearly make for difficulties in forming any generalizations regarding a particular dose/treatment regimen of neuroleptic and even greater difficulties when the intra-individual variability of patients is taken into account, particularly as some schizophrenics are seemingly less sensitive to sedative side effects and the metabolism of some neuroleptics (notably chlorpromazine) can be enhanced via enzyme induction in cigarette smokers, which will lead to lower sedation in such patients (Barnes and Edwards, 1993).

Hypotension, while not a direct CNS side effect, is directly related to behavioural toxicity due to associated falls, stumbling and poor motor ability. Such detrimental effects impair the performance of the psychomotor tasks of everyday life and an assessment of the potential of various drugs to produce hypotensive effects is therefore included in Table 1. The relation between accidents and hypotensive agents has been well established (Barnes and Edwards, 1993), and, as with other psychoactive drugs, it is the older patient who is at greater risk.

It is not the intention here to argue the extent to which patients with schizophrenia suffer from cognitive impairment; suffice it to say that since Kraeplin first drew attention to the mental impairment associated with "dementia praecox" in the early part of this century there has been little disagreement that cognitive impairment is a feature of psychotic illness, although it might be argued as to the "stable" or "progressive" nature of the disturbance (Hyde et al., 1994). Of particular interest are the findings that schizophrenic patients have a performance deficit on tasks of attention and information processing, including backward masking (Kornetsky and Orzack, 1978); Asarnow and Macrimmon, 1978; Braff, 1981; Braff and Sacuzzo, 1982), which is probably a reflection of the impairment of sustained attention so often seen as a symptom of schizophrenia.

Given there is both clinical and psychometric evidence to show that patients requiring antipsychotic medication have psychological performance deficits, then it is clear that should the prescribed medication augment these pre-existing or illness-related cognitive impairments it will at least be countertherapeutic and at worse make it impossible for a patient to maintain cognitive integrity in an outpatient environment, which could lead to an overall worsening of the underlying psychotic state. In order to establish the extent to which neuroleptics induce cognitive impairment it is necessary to use reliable and valid assessments in methodologically sound protocols.

ASSESSMENT OF NEUROLEPTIC EFFECTS ON COGNITION

King (1990) reviewed the psychomotor and cognitive effects of various antipsychotic medications in both volunteer and schizophrenic patient populations from studies using objective neuropsychological tests. The clinical condition of the individual patients made for difficulties in interpreting the results and deriving generalizations regarding different medications. However, more recent work (Saletu et al., 1994) has shown that appropriate psychometrics can measure neuroleptic side effects in patients. There is a literature on the effects of neuroleptics on psychological performance in normal volunteers, although it is neither extensive nor easy to evaluate as there is no consistency between studies regarding dose treatment regimens or psychometrics. It is possible, however, to gain some idea of the behavioural toxicity of neuroleptics and, although in clinical use there is little to suggest that neuroleptics will always behave in the manner suggested by either experimental psycopharmacology or clinical pharmacology, a review of studies with good methodology and design is presented in Table 2. There are several caveats.

Table 2. Selected Studies of Neuroleptic Effects on Cognition

Drug/dose regimen (mg)	CFF	DSST	CPT[a]/RIP[b]	CRT	VIGIL	Sensori - Motor[a] Ballistic[b]	SPEM[a] SEM[b]	Reference
Butyrophenones								
Haloperidol								
1	W			B		O[a]		Parrott and Hindmarch (1975)
1	W			O		O		Hindmarch and Tiplady (1984)
1				B				Henry (1992)
2						W[b]		Janke andDebus (1972)
2	W	W		B				Saletu et al. (1983a , 1983b)
3			W[b]					McClelland et al. (1987, 1990)
5	O	W	W[b]	O				King and Bell (1990)
>10	O	W		O				Magliozzi et al. (1989)
0.5 b.i.d. * 2	O	W						Saattiachorere (1988)
0.75 i.v.	O					O[b]	O[b]	Frey et al. (1989)
Dibenzoxaxenines								
Clozapine								
50	W	W		W	W[a, b]			Saletu et al. (1987)
Phenothiazines								
Alipathic								
chlorpromazine								
50	W							Besser and Duncan (1967)
50					W			Loeb et al. (1965)
50			W[b]					McClelland et. al (1990)
75								Hartley et al. (1977)
100	W	W	O[a]	W	W		W[b]	King et al. (1990)
200		W	W			W[a]		DiMascio et al. (1957)
200		W				W[a]		Kometsky et al. (1957)
1.0 mg/kg						W[a]		Milner and Landauer (1971)
1.3 mg/kg							O[a]	Holzman et al. (1975)

(Table Continues)

Table 2. Selected Studies of Neuroleptic Effects on Cognition (continued)

Drug/dose regimen (mg)	CFF	DSST	CPT[a]/RIP[b]	VIGIL	CRT	Sensori-Motor[a] Ballistic[b]	SPEM[a] SEM[b]	Reference
Piperidines								
thioridazine								
20 t.i.d. * 14						O[a]		Liljequist et al. (1978)
50	W	W				W[a,b]		Theophilopoulous et al. (1984)
50	W					W[a]		Hindmarch and Tiplady (1994)
50		W/B			W	W[a]		Szabadi et al. (1980)
1.0 mg/kg						W[a]		Milner and Landauer (1971)
10 t.i.d. * 2w						O[a]		Liljequist et al. (1975)
20 t.i.d. * 2w						O[a,b]		Saario (1976)
Piperazines								
perphenazine								
16		B	O			B[a,b]		DiMascio et al. (1963)
prochlorperazine								
50	W	W			W			Isah et al. (1991)
Substituted benzamides								
sulpiride								
100		O			O	O[a]		Bartafi and Wiesel (1986)
400			W[b]					McClelland et al. (1990)
300 * 7							O[b]	Von Aschoff et al. (1974)
50 t.i.d. * 14					O	O[ab]		Lijequist et al. (1975)

Table 2: Legend

CFF = critical flicker fusion threshold (inc. two flash threshold)
DSST = digit symbol subs(substitution test (inc., digit and letter cancellation, Symbol copying)
CPT[a] = continuous performance tests
RIP[b] = rapid information Processing tasks
CRT = choice reaction time (inc. all reaction time tasks)
VIG = sustained attention, tasks (auditory and visual)
SMC[a] = sensori-motor coordination tasks (e.g.) pursuit error
BMT[b] = ballistic movement, tests (e.g.) finger tapping
SPEM[a] = smooth pursuit eye movements

B = performance improved with respect to control/placebo conditions
W = performance impaired with respect to control/placebo conditions
0 = no noticeable effects reported
>10 = doses up to and including
SEM[b] = saccadic eye movements

The studies listed are by no means exhaustive as some with equivocal results or problems with the design have been omitted. More recent studies with remoxipride have not been considered as the substance is no longer available. It did, however, seem that remoxipride at doses between 30 - 100 mg was not without some adverse effects in volunteers on tests of psychomotor performance (Fagan et al., 1988; Mattila et al., 1988) although remoxipride 100 mg was not as impairing as thioridizine 50 mg or to a lesser extent, haloperidol 1 mg, on a battery of tests including 24-hour continuous EEG (Hindmarch and Tiplady, 1994). The lack of data from controlled studies in volunteers is the only reason that certain drugs do not feature in the table. It may seem strange that memory is not included in the psychometrics; this is due mainly to a lack of data, but also to the findings from the few available studies (e.g. Liljequist et al., 1975, 1978) that there are no direct effects of thioridizine or chlorpromazine, for example, on tests of learning and memory. Recently, it was shown (Hindmarch and Tiplady, 1994) that both thioridazine 50 mg and haloperidol 2 mg had no significant effect on impairing memory, yet the test used was sensitive and showed a significant impairment following the administration of the positive internal control (lorazepam 2 mg). It is tempting under such circumstances to claim that there are no amnestic effects of neuroleptics but a reported lack of effect or unavailable data should not, however, be construed as a claim that there are no amnestic effects of neuroleptics, particularly in patient populations where more heroic dose treatment regimens are employed. The impairment produced by some substances is evident on more than one psychometric and in such instances it can be claimed that in patient populations there is at least the potential for that drug to induce behavioural toxicity independent of any illness/individual factors which may also play a part. Chlorpromazine in a range of doses 50-200 mg impairs psychomotor tasks and certain aspects of information processing, while haloperidol 1-10 mg has less cognitive and sensori-motor activity, but is able to impair reaction time and information-processing capacity. The behavioural toxicity of neuroleptics is an area of study that demands more investigation especially when an increasing number of patients are being treated in the community. There are certainly some psychometrics which are useful tools to identify those drugs which impair psychological aspects of behaviour but the advance will be in the development of new test systems which are particularly sensitive to the effects of anti-psychotic agents (King, 1993).

Within the context of community-based treatment it is worth recalling that many patients receive neuroleptics as adjunctive therapy with antidepressants. The behavioural toxicity of a sample of antidepressants is given in Table 3.

Table 3. The Behavioural Toxicity of a Sample of Antidepressants

	CFF	CRT	SMC
TCAs			
amitriptyline	W[a]	W[a]	W[a]
dothiepin	W[a]	W[a]	W[a]
SSRIs			
fluoxetine	O	O	O
fluvoxamine	O	O	O
paroxetine	B	O	W
sertraline	B	O	O
RIMAs			
biofaromine	O	O	O
moclobemide	O	O	O

W = significantly impaired with respect to control conditions;
B = significantly arousing; O = neutral; [a] = severely debilitating.
Other legends as for Table 2.

Tricyclic antidepressants (TCAs) (as can be expected from their general anticholinergic and antihistaminic properties) are seen to be (Table 3) behaviourally toxic and impair psychomotor speed, memory, motor integrity, information processing and visual processes (Hindmarch and Kerr, 1992) and TCAs are also liable to interact with phenothiazines and behavioural impairment will be augmented. A combination of neuroleptic and TCA must, if behavioural toxicity is a concern, be avoided in community based patients without adequate regular monitoring. With SSRIs the overall behavioural toxicity index is low (Kerr et al., 1992). CFF (Kerr et al. 1992), which might pose problems with the more agitated patient. Fluoxetine and fluvoxamine are probably the least behaviourally toxic of the SSRIs and RIMAs to have a virtually neutral profile with respect to psychological, behavioural and cognitive effects (Fairweather et al., 1993) and in this respect would not in themselves pose problems for co-prescribing with neuroleptics.

Perhaps the greatest difficulty in drawing up a "league table" of the potential neuroleptics to cause side effects liable to produce NIDS, or to impair the cognitive behavioural system, is the numerous non-biological factors which operate in both hospitalized and community-based patients. A patient's attitudes, education, sex, personality and expectation will govern compliance to treatment regimens and subjective response to both therapeutic and non-therapeutic side effects (Gaebel, 1993). Certainly, the behaviour and attitudes of relatives, spouses and friends can also modify an individual patient's response to neuroleptic treatment (Gaebel et al., 1986). A supportive therapeutic environment (Carpenter et al., 1977) in a ward or within a community will do much to ensure compliance and tolerance of side effects. On the other hand an off-hand "laissez-faire" milieu could well result in patients suffering or reporting more symptoms (Spadom and Smith, 1969) experience a worse NIDS. Such psychosocial factors are not beyond measurement but little information regarding their impact in increasing or decreasing levels of behavioural toxicity is available and remains still to be identified.

It would appear until such time as attention has been paid to the psychopharmacological assessment of new neuroleptics using appropriate psychometrics, this current information at least reminds the prescribing physician of the need for monitoring the untoward effects of neuroleptics in those ambulant patients at large in the community and using those drug regimens which have not only a low potential for NIDS but also a low rating of behavioural toxicity.

REFERENCES

Asarnow, R.F. and MacCrimmon, D.J. (1978). "Residual performance deficit in clinically remitted schizophrenics: a marker of schizophrenia?", J. Abnorm. Psychol., 87, 1006 -1011.

Baldessarini, R.J. (1985). "Drugs and the treatment of psychiatric disorders". In The Pharmacological Basis of Therapeutics, 7th edition (eds G.A. Goodman, L.S. Goodman, T. Rall, and F. Murad), Macmillan, New York, pp. 387 - 445.

Barnes, T.R.E. (1984). "Drugs and sexual dysfunction". In Current Themes in Psychiatry. (eds. R.N. Gaind, F.L. Fawzy, B.L. Hudson and R.O. Pasnau), pp. 51 - 92. Spectrum, New York, Vol. 3.

Barnes, T.R.E. and Edwards, J.G. (1993). "The side-effects of antipsychotic drugs, 1. CNS and neuromuscular effects". In Antipsychotic Drugs and their Side Effects, (ed. T.R.E. Barnes).

Barfai, T.R.E. and Edwards, J.G. (1986). "Effect of sulpiride on vigilance in healthy subjects", Int. J. Psychophysiol., 4, 1 - 5.

Besser, G.M. and Dunasen, C. (1967). "The time course of action of single doses of diazepam, chlorpromazine and some barbiturates as measured by auditory flutter fusion and visual flicker fusion threshold in man", Br. J. Pharmacol. Chemother, 30, 341- 348.

Braff, D.L. (1981). "Impaired speed of information processing in nonmedicated schizotypal patients", Schizophr. Bulletin, 7, 499 - 508.

Braff, D.L. and Saccuzzo, D.P. (1982). "Effect of antipsychotic medication on speed of information processing in schizophrenic patients", Am. J. Psychiatry 139, 1127 - 1130.

Carpenter, W.T., McGlashan, T. and Strauss, J.S. (1977). "The treatment of acute schizophrenia without drugs: an investigation of some current assumptions", Am. J. Psychiatry, 134, 14 - 20.

Carpenter, W.T., Heinrichs, D.W. and Alphs L.D. (1985). "Treatment of negative symptoms", Schizophr. Bull., 11, 440 - 452.

Curry, S.H. (1993). "Pharmacokinetics of antipsychotic drugs", In Antipsychotic Drugs and their Side Effects (ed. T.R.E. Barnes).

DiMassio, A., Havens, L.L. and Kierman, G.L. (1963). "The psychopharmacology of phenothiazine compounds: a comparative study of the effects of chlorpromazine, promethazine, trifluoperazine, and perphenazine in normal males: II: Results and discussion", J. Nerv. Ment. Disord., 136, 15 - 28.

Emerick, D.F. and Sanberg, P.R. (1991). "Neuroleptic dysphoria", Biol. Psychiatry, 29, 201 - 203.

Fagan, D., Scott, D.B. and Mitchell, M. (1988). "The psychomotor effects of remoxipride in healthy volunteers", Neurose Lett. Suppl., 32, S45.

Fairweather, D.B., Kerr, J.S., Harrison, D.A., Moon, C.A. and Hindmarch, I. (1993). "A double blind comparison of the effects of fluoxetine and amitriptyline on cognitive function in elderly depressed patients", Hum. Psychopharmacol, 8, 41 - 47.

Gaebel, W. (1993). "The importance of non-biological factors in influencing the outcome of clinical trials", Br. J. Psychiatry, 163 (Suppl. 22), 45 - 50.

Gaebel, W., Pietzcker, A. and Barngartner, A. (1986). "3 year follow-up of schizophrenic patients: outcome dimensions and neuroleptic treatment", Pharmacopsychiatry, 19, 208 - 209.

Gerlach, J. (1991). "New antipsychotics: classification, efficacy and adverse effects", Schizophr. Bull., 17, 289 - 309.

Hartley, L., Couper-Smartt, J. and Henry, T. (1977). "Behavioural antagonism between chlorpromazine and noise in man", Psychopharmacology, 55, 97 - 102.

Herrera, J.N., Sramek, J.J. and Costa, J.F. (1988). "High potency neuroleptics and violence in schizophrenia", J. Nerv. Ment. Dis., 176, 558 - 561.

Hindmarch, L. and Kerr, J.S. (1992). "Behavioural toxicity of antidepressants with particular reference to moclobemide", Psychopharmacol, 44, 111 - 115.

Hindmarch, I. and Tiplady, B. (1994). "A comparison of the psychometric effects of remoxipride with those of haloperidol, thioridazine, and lorazepam in healthy volunteers", Hum. Psychopharmacol. (in press).

Hirsch, S.R. and Barnes, T.R.E. (1994). "Clinical use of high-dose neuroleptics", Br. J. Psychiatry, 164, 94 - 96.

Hyde, T.M., Nawroz, S., Goldberg, T.E., Bigelow, L.B., Strong, D., Ostrem, J.L., Weinberger, D.R. and Kleinman, J.E. (1994). "Is there cognitive decline in schizophrenia?: a cross section study", Br. J. Psychiatry, 164, 494 - 500.

Isah, A.O., Rawlins, M.D. and Briteman, D.N. (1991). "Clinical pharmacology of prochloperazine in health young males", Br. J. Psychiatry 32, 677 - 684.

Janke, W. and Debus, G. (1972). "Double blind psychometric evaluation of pimozide and haloperidol versus placebo in emotionally labile volunteers under two different work load conditions", Pharmakopsychiatry, 1, 34 - 51.

Kerr, J.S., Sherwood, N. and Hindmarch, L. (1991). "The comparative psychopharmacology of 5HT reuptake inhibitors", Hum. Psychopharmacol., 6, 313 - 317.

Kerwin, R. (1993). "Adverse reaction reporting and new antipsychotics", Lancet, 342, 1440.

King, D.J. (1990). "The effect of neuroleptics on cognitive and psychomotor function", Br. J. Psychiatry, 157, 799 - 811.

King, D.J. (1993). "Measures of neuroleptic effects on cognition and psychomotor performance in healthy volunteers", In Human Psychopharmacol., Vol. 4 (eds. I. Hindmarch and Stoinier), Wiley, Chichester.

King, D.J. and Bell, P. (1990). "Differential effects of temazepam and haloperidol on saccadic eye movements and psychomotor performance", Br. J. Clin. Pharmacol, 29, 590.

King, D.J. and Henry, G. (1992). "The effect of neuroleptics on cognitive and psychomotor function: a preliminary study in healthy volunteers", Br. J. Psychiatry, 160, 647 - 653.

King, D.J., Bell, P., Best, S.J. and Mannion, M. (1990). "A comparison of the effects of chlorpromazine and temazepam on saccadic eye movements and psychomotor performance", Br. J. Clin. Pharmacol., 30, 309P - 310P.

Kornetsky, C., Humphries, O. and Evarts, E.V. (1957). "Comparison of psychological effects of certain centrally acting drugs in man", AMA Arch. Neurol. Psychiatry, 77, 318 - 324.

Lader, M. (1993). "Neuroleptic-induced deficit syndrome: old problem, new challenge", J. Psychopharmacol.,7 (4), 392 - 393.

Liljequist, R., Linnoila, M., Mattila, M.J., Saario, I., and Seppala, T. (1975). "Effect of two weeks' treatment with thioridazine, chlorpromazine, sulpiride and bromazepam, alone or in combination with alcohol, on learning and memory in man", Psychopharmacol., 44, 205 - 208.

Liljequist, R., Linnoila, M. and Mattila, M.J. (1978). "Effect of diazepam and chlorpromazine on memory functions in man", Eur. J. Clin. Pharmacol, 13, 339 - 343.

Loch, M., Hawkes, J., Evans, P. and Alluisi, E.A. (1965). "Influence of d-amphetamine, benactyzine and chlorpromazine on performances in an auditory vigilance task", Psychonomic Sci., 3, 29 - 30.

Magliozzi, J.R., Mungas, D., Laubly, J.N. and Blunden, D. (1989)."Effect of haloperidol on a symbol digit substitution task in normal adult males",Neuropsychopharmac., 2, 29 - 37.

Mattila, M.J., Mattila, M.E., Komno, K. and Saarialho-Kere, U. (1988). "Objective and subjective effects of remoxipride, alone and in combination with ethanol or diazepam, on performance in health subjects", J. Psychoparmacol, 138 -149.

McClelland, G.R., Cooper, S.M. and Raptopoulos, P. (1987). "Paroxetine and haloperidol: effects on psychomotor performance", Br. J. Clin. Pharmacol., 24, 268P - 269P.

McClelland, G.R., Cooper, S.M. and Pilgrim, A.J. (1990). "A comparison of the central nervous system effects of haloperidol, chlorpromazine and sulpiride in normal volunteers", Br. J. Clin. Pharmacol., 30, 795 - 803.

Milner, G. and Landauer, A.A. (1971). "Alcohol, thioridazine and chlorpromazine effects on skills related to driving behaviour", Br. J. Psychiatry, 118, 351 - 352.

Mitchell, J.E. and Popkin, M.K. (1982). "Antipsychotic drug therapy and sexual dysfunction in men", Am. J. Psychiatry, 39, 633 - 637.

Parrott, A.C. and Hindmarch, I. (1975). "Haloperidol and chlorpromazine: comparative effects upon arousal and performance", Med. Sci, 3, 562.

Saarialho-Kere, U. (1988). "Psychomotor, respiratory and neuroendocrinological effects of nalbuphine and haloperidol, alone and in combination, in healthy subjects", Br. J. Clin. Pharmacol., 26, 79 - 87.

Saario, I. (1976). "Psychomotor skills during subacute treatment with thioridazine and bromazepam, and the combined effects with alcohol", Ann. Clin. Res., 8, 117 - 123.

Saletu, B., Grunberger, J., Linzmayer, L. and Dubini, A. (1983a). "Determination of pharmacodynamics of the new neuroleptic zetidoline by neuroendocrinologic, pharmaco-EEG and psychometric studies", Part I, Int. J. Clin. Pharmacol. Ther. Toxicol., 21, 489 - 495.

Saletu, B., Grunberger, J., Linzmayer, L. and Dubini, A. (1983b). "Determination of pharmacodynamics of the new neuroleptic zetidoline by neuroendocrinologic, pharmaco-EEG, and psychometric studies", Part II Int. J. Clin. Pharmacol. Ther. Toxicol., 21, 544 - 551.

Saletu, B., Grunberger, J., Lintzmayer, L. and Anderer P. (1987). Comparative placebo-controlled pharmacodynamic studies with zoetpine and clozapine utilizing pharmaco-EEG and psychometry", Pharmacopsychiatry, 20, 12 - 27.

Saletu, B., Kufferle, B., Grunberger, J., Foldes, P., Topitz, A. and Anderer, P. (1994). "Clinical, EEG mapping psychometric studies in negative schizophrenia: comparative trials with amisulpride and fluphenazine", Neuropsychobiology, 125 - 135.

Solano, D.A., Sadow, T. and Anseth, (1989). "Rapid tranquilization: a reevaluation", Neuropsychobiology, 90 - 96.

Spadoni, A.J. and Smith, J.A. (1969). "Milieu therapy in schizophrenia", Arch. Gen. Psychiatry, 20, 547 - 551.

Szabadi, E., Bradshaw, C.M. and Gaszner, P. (1980). "The comparison of the effects of Dl-308, a potential neuroleptic agent, and thioridazine on some psychological and psychological functions in healthy volunteers", Psychopharmacology 68, 125 -134.

Theofilopoulos, N., Szabadi, E. and Bradshaw, C.M. (1984). "Comparison of the effects of ranitidine, cimetidine and thioridazine on psychomotor functions in healthy volunteers", Br. J. Clin. Pharmacol., 18, 135 - 144.

Van Putten, T., Marder, S.R. and Julintz, J. (1990). "A controlled dose comparison of haloperidol in newly admitted schizophrenic patients", Arch. Gen. Psychiatry, 47, 754 - 758.

Von Aschoff, J.C., Becker, W., and Weinert, D. (1974) "Computer-nystagmographic alsneuc Bestimmungsmethode von Vigilanz und Reaktionsverhalten unter Psychopharmaka", <u>Arzneim-Forsch. (Drug Res.)</u>, 24, 1085 - 1087.

18

IMPLICATIONS OF LATE-LIFE ONSET SCHIZOPHRENIA:

A NEW HYPOTHESIS

Peter V. Rabins

Bleuler (1950) entitled his classic monograph *The Group of Schizophrenias*, indicating by this title that he did not believe schizophrenia was a single condition. Although this hypothesis cannot be confirmed until specific neuropathologies and etiologies are identified, current thinking supports this view. While there is evidence of heterogeneity in schizophrenia, a large body of evidence, including signs, symptoms, course, biological markers and response to treatment, suggests that it remains worthwhile to consider schizophrenia a single syndrome with multiple etiologies (Carpenter and Buchanan, 1994). The purpose of this chapter is to integrate data suggesting that schizophrenia can begin throughout the lifespan with theories about the etiology of idiopathic schizophrenia.

Even in the young the evidence suggests that a variety of brain insults can cause schizophrenia. This implies that several causal agents affect a single site, that varying lesions throughout a brain system can lead to a similar set of symptoms or that the brain's response to injury can lead to these symptoms. It is this latter hypothesis that will be proposed here: the schizophrenia syndrome can be caused by aberrant connectivity established either during development or in response to injury.

Schizophrenia: Exploring the Spectrum of Psychosis. Edited by R. Ancill . © 1994   John Wiley & Sons Ltd

The contention that schizophrenia can begin across the lifespan remains controversial especially in North America. There is consensus that the majority of cases of schizophrenia begin in early life, with the modal onset in males in the late teenage years and in females about a decade later. However, European researchers and clinicians (Post, 1966) have built upon the observations of Kraeplin (1915) that some individuals who present with a schizophrenia-like condition but have intact personality and lack of social decline (which Kraeplin called paraphrenia) develop a chronic disorder with later dilapidation in personality, cognition and social function.

Work over the past 40 years demonstrates that there are phenomenologic, neuroimaging, treatment response, and genetic similarities between individuals who develop schizophrenia-like conditions in early and later life. Data includes findings that, in both groups, hallucinations and delusions, including the so-called first rank symptoms of Schneider (Kay, 1972, Kay et al., 1976; Rabins et al., 1984; Pearlson et al., 1989) are prominent. Furthermore, both the early and late-onset conditions lack prominent changes in mood (Kay et al., 1976). The evidence regarding similarities in cognitive performance are less well established but the lack of dramatic cognitive decline in late-onset cases over short follow-up (Hymas et al.,1989) and some similarities in cognitive patterns (Heaton et Drexler, 1987) also suggest a single syndrome. Neuroimaging studies have found non-specific ventricular dilatation in early and late-onset cases (Rabins et al., 1984) and more recent work has demonstrated focal abnormalities in the planum temporali and elevation in D2 receptor numbers in some individuals from both groups (Pearlson et al., 1989).

There are few adequately designed treatment studies of late-life onset schizophreniform illness but the evidence to date suggests that the response to neuroleptics in the late onset group is similar to that in the young (Rabins et al., 1984). Genetic analyses suggest some familial clustering in late-onset cases but the evidence of familial/genetic contribution is weaker than among early onset cases (Kay et al., 1976; Rabins et al., 1984).

There are several notable differences between the schizophrenia-like illnesses that begins in early and late life. Most prominent are the dramatically lower rates of thought disorder and personality deterioration in the late-life onset cases. Because these are often seen by some, particularly by those who adhere to the Bleulerian concept, as central to the definition of schizophrenia, these phenomenologic differences provide significant counter-evidence to the contention that the early and late-onset conditions are a single syndrome.

Nonetheless, we believe it is beneficial to begin with the point of view that the similarities between early and late-onset cases might provide insight into potential pathogenic mechanisms. While no single etiologic theory of schizophrenia has withstood the challenge of hypothesis testing, several lines of evidence require inclusion in any theory. Family and adoption studies demonstrate a genetic contribution to vulnerability. Early brain injury and exposure to infectious agents in utero are risk factors in some studies. Imaging studies suggest impairment in the left temporal and dorsal frontal regions; findings of nonspecific pathologic changes in these areas, a higher frequency of schizophreniform psychosis following left hemisphere trauma and left side complex partial seizure disorder lends further credence to their involvement. The fact that dopaminergic blockade is the single neurochemical function shared by all effective therapeutic agents suggests that dopaminergic pathways are involved in some fashion.

What might late-onset cases add to these clues? First, a significant body of evidence suggests that sensory impairment, particularly hearing impairment, is associated with the development of schizophrenia-like psychoses in mid and late-life (Cooper et al., 1974; Pearlson et al., 1989). This finding is of particular interest given the recent evidence that working in noisome occupations prior to the development of symptoms is a risk factor for developing schizophrenia in young individuals (Link, 1994). Indeed, Link (1994) has even suggested that this might explain the higher occurrence of schizophrenia in individuals with lower socioeconomic status.

The developmental hypothesis of Weinberger (1989) is one theory that has attempted to link the timing of injury with the development of schizophrenia. Observations that brain plasticity is present through the adult years in insects (Cayre et al., 1994), non-human primates (Merzenich et al., 1990) and humans (Ramachandran, 1993) suggests that changes in neuronal linkages can occur throughout adulthood. The demonstration of planum temporali atrophy and the correlation between the extent of atrophy and severity of both auditory hallucinations and thought disorder, the involvement of this area in hearing and language comprehension and the finding that impaired hearing is a risk factor among later-onset cases suggest that injury to this area, whether during or after neural development, alters the usual function of circuits that involve hearing and language comprehension.

We propose that the "positive" symptoms of schizophrenia (such as hallucinations and delusions) result from an aberrant rewiring of the sensory apparatus in the brain. The genesis of these changes would vary across the life-span; in the young, the injury could be due to environmental events, such as infection or injury, which appear at crucial junctures during nervous system development or to abnormalities in the genetic control of brain organization, circuit selection and intercellular connectivity. Late-onset cases, in contrast, would more likely be caused (or predisposed to) by brain injury to the circuits of the sensory or language systems.

Thus, this hypothesis proposes that the schizophrenic syndrome in younger individuals results from developmentally induced aberrant neuronal connectivity while later-onset cases result from abnormalities in connectivity that result from the reparative response to neuraxis injury.

This hypothesis does not account for the lower rates of thought disorder and negative symptoms seen in late-onset cases. Among the plausible explanations are relative imperviousness of "personality" to change once its neuronal development is complete because its neural basis is widely distributed. The hypothesis also predicts that thought disorder requires that the language system still be developing, perhaps akin to the ability of the child to develop language in the opposite hemisphere after an injury. There is no data to support this suggestion. Thus, the theory predicts that "reconnection" is less likely to occur in systems underlying personality, initiative and language than in systems subserving the sensory system.

The emergence of schizophrenia in late life also suggests that there may be factors delaying its onset. Knowledge that schizophrenia has a lifetime prevalence equal in men and woman, begins on average 10 years later in females and after age 45 almost exclusively in women has led to speculation (Seeman, 1981) that estrogens might be protective in early life. The differential rates by gender of dopamine receptor loss across the age span (Wong et al., 1984), interactions between estrogens and the dopamine receptor, and the possible neuroprotective effects of estrogens (Schrabji, 1994) suggest that high estrogen may delay onset.

In conclusion, the broad skepticisim that a schizophrenia-like condition can begin in mid and late-life should be reconsidered. There are clear differences between early and late-onset cases but science often benefits from studying exceptions as well as usual cases. Appreciating the similarities and differences between early and late onset cases has the potential of identifying pathogenic mechanisms for this scourge of mankind. The evidence continues to suggest that Bleuler was right: schizophrenia is a syndrome that will likely have multiple etiologies.

REFERENCES

Bleuler, E. (1950). Dementia Praecox; or, The Group of Schizophrenias, (Translated by J. Zinkin), International Universities Press, New York.

Carpenter, W.T. and Buchanan, R.W. (1994). Schizophrenia", N. Engl. J. Med., 10, 681 - 690.

Cayre, M., Strambi, C. and Strambi, A. (1994). "Neurogenesis in an adult insect brain and its hormonal control", Nature, 368, 57 - 59.

Cooper, A.F., Curry, A.R., Kay, D.W.K., Garside, R.F. and Roth, M. (1974). "Hearing loss in paranoid and affective psychoses of the elderly", Lancet, 12, 851 - 854.

Goldberg, T.E., Hyde, T.M., Kleinman, J.E. and Weinberger, D.R. (1993). "Course of schizophrenia: neuropsychological evidence for a static encephalopathy", Schizophr. Bull., 19, 797 - 804.

Heaton, R.K. and Drexler, M. (1987). "Clinical neuropsychological findings in schizophrenia and aging". In Schizophrenia and Aging (Eds N.E. Miller and G.D. Cohen), The Guilford Press, New York, pp. 145 - 161.

Hymas, N., Naguib, M. and Levy, R. (1989). "Late paraphrenia: a follow-up study", Int. J. Geriatr. Psychiatry, 4, 23 - 29.

Kay, D.W.K. (1972). "Schizophrenia and schizophrenia-like states in the elderly", Br. J. Hosp. Med., 8, 369 - 376.

Kay, D.W.K., Cooper, A.F., Garside, R.F. and Roth, M. (1976). "The differentiation of paranoid from affective psychoses by patients' premorbid characteristics", Br. J. Psychiatry, 129, 297 - 215.

Kraeplin, R. (1915). Clinical Psychiatry (Edited and translated by A.R. Diefendor)., Macmillan, New York.

Link, B. (1994). "Occupational characteristics", Paper presented March 4, 1994, American Psychopathological Association, New York.

Merzenich, M.M., Recanzone, G.H. Jenkins, W.M. and Grajski, K.A. (1990). "Adaptive mechanisms in cortical networks underlying cortical contributions to learning and nondeclarative memory", Cold Spring Harbor Sympos. Quant. Biol, 60, 873 - 887.

Pearlson, G., Kreger, L., Rabins, P.V., Chase, G.H., Cohen, B., Wirth, J.B., Schlaepfer, T.B. and Tune, L.E. (1989). "A chart review of late-onset schizophrenia", Am. J. of Psychiatry, 146, 1568 - 1574.

Pearlson, G.D., Tune, L.E. Wong, D.F. Aylward, E.H., Barta, P.E., Powers, R.E., Tien, A.Y., Chase, G.A., Harris, G.J. and Rabins, P.V. (1993). "Quantitative D2 dopamine receptor PET and structural MRI changes inlate-onset schizophrenia", Schizophr. Bull., 19, 783 - 795.

Post, F. (1966) Persistent Persecutory States of the Elderly, Pergamon Press, Oxford.

Rabins, P.V., Pauker, S., and Thomas, J. (1984). "Can schizophrenia begin after age 44?", Compr. Psychiatry, 25, 290 - 293.

Ramachandran, V.S. (1993). "Behavioural and magnetoencephalographic correlates of plasticity in the adult human brain", Proc. Natl Acad. Sci, 90, 10413 - 10420.

Schneider, K. (1959). Clinical Psychopathology, (translated by M.W. Hamilton), Grune & Stratton, New York.

Seeman, M.V. (1981). "Gender and the onset of schizophrenia: neurohumoral influences", Psychiatr. J. Univ. Ottawa, 6, 136 - 138.

Sohrabji, F., Miranda, R.C. and Toran-Allerand, C.D. (1994). "Estrogen differentially regulates estrogen and nerve growth factor receptor mRNAs in adult sensory neurons",J. Neurosci., 14, 459 - 471.

Weinberger, D.R. (1989). "Implications of normal brain development for the pathogenesis of schizophrenia", Arch. Gen. Psychiatry, 44, 660 - 669.

Wong D.F., Wagner, H.N., Dannals, R.F., Links, J.M., Frost, J.J., Ravert, H.T., Wilson, A.A., Rosenbaum, A.E., Gjedde, A., Douglass, K.H., Petronis, J.D., Folstein, M.D., Toung, J.K.T., Burns, D. and Kuhas, M.J. (1984). "Effects of age on dopamine and serotonin receptors as measured by positron tomography in the living human brain", Science, 226, 1393 - 1396.

19

LATE ONSET SCHIZOPHRENIA CURRENT STATUS AND FUTURE DEVELOPMENTS

Robert Howard and Raymond Levy

INTRODUCTION

Schizophrenia researchers, particularly those in North America, appear to have been late themselves in showing interest in those cases of schizophrenia which arise late in life. Within the European psychiatric tradition, the concept of late-onset schizophrenia is as old as that of schizophrenia itself and a number of distinguished psychiatrists have been involved in a long-running debate regarding the relationship between the conditions. Initially regarded as a rare, extreme and delayed variant of an illness that more typically began in early adult life, such cases have come to be viewed as part of a spectrum of heterogeneous conditions characterized by the emergence in an elderly person of paranoid delusions, hallucinations and schizophrenic core symptomatology. Variation in the aetiological contributions of organic brain changes, sensory impairment, genetic, personality and social factors appear to reflect this heterogeneity.

For the past thirty years, the diagnosis of late paraphrenia has been in widespread use in Britain to describe patients with a schizophrenia-like illness that arises after the age of 60 in the absence of gross organic brain disease. Whilst the term late paraphrenia has been criticized and has disappeared from the latest edition of the International Classification of Diseases, the spirit of the term lives on, if only in the form of an implied awareness that such cases differ from those schizophrenias that arise earlier in life. This would certainly be the position adopted by the authors and we have elsewhere bemoaned the fact that the

Schizophrenia: Exploring the Spectrum of Psychosis. Edited by R. Ancill © 1994
John Wiley & Sons Ltd

disappearance of late paraphrenia, and indeed late-onset schizophrenia, from contemporary classificatory systems may inhibit what promises to be an emerging global research interest in these conditions (Quintal et al. 1991 Naguib and Levy 1991).

In this chapter, we briefly review selected highlights of the late paraphrenia/schizophrenia literature with reference to clinical heterogeneity and present some of our own neuropsychological and imaging investigations into the nature of the heterogeneity that we believe exists among this group of patients.

EUROPEAN CLINICAL STUDIES

In the first two decades of the present century, E. Bleuler (1911), Kraepelin (1913) and Kleist (1913) all concluded that cases of schizophrenia which had their onset late in life (after the age of 40 or 50 years) were essentially no different in terms of phenomenology and clinical courses from those cases of schizophrenia that had arisen in early adulthood. Manfred Bleuler (1943), who specifically collected and studied patients with late-onset schizophrenia, came to the same conclusion and this was confirmed for an English-speaking audience by Fish (1960) .

The description of a schizophrenia-like syndrome (Roth and Morrissey, 1952) that arose after the age of 55 or 60 years and was paraphrenic in character revived interest and controversy in this group of patients. Although Kay and Roth (1961) believed late paraphrenia to be the expression of schizophrenia in old age, they recognized heterogeneity within such patients which they believed reflected the differing aetiological contributions of premorbid personality, social isolation, sensory impairment and constitutional (presumably genetic) factors. This heterogeneous view was reflected by the three clinical subgroups of late paraphrenics that they described. Group 1 were individuals with abnormal personalities who had a paranoid psychosis but no hallucinosis and constituted 20% of the patients. Group 2 were paraphrenias which had arisen under unusual circumstances or following prolonged periods of isolation (25%) and Group 3 were so-called endogenous paraphrenias (55%). Whilst acknowledging that a degree of overlap often occurred between functional and organic psychoses in old age, Kay and Roth (1961) believed that the late paraphrenia syndrome could be attributed to frank cerebral disease in only a small minority of patients. To support this conclusion, they cited their observation that only 12% of 57 Swedish late paraphrenics followed up for ten years ultimately went on to develop dementia (Kay and Roth 1961).

Felix Post (1966), working in our hospital, believed that patients with late paraphrenia represented a heterogeneous mixture of diagnoses and preferred to avoid diagnostic controversy by terming such cases "persistent persecutory states". Within this broad category he recognized three clinical syndromes: a "true" schizophrenia (37%), a schizophreniform syndrome (38%) and a "paranoid hallucinosis" group (25%). Post regarded organic cerebral changes as being more aetiologically important than Kay and Roth. He was able to identify proven organic factors in 16 of his 93 patients with persistent persecutory states. Post (1980) however believed that in such "organic" cases, disturbed memory and concentration could be clearly seen to have preceded the first emergence of persecutory delusions.

With the benefit of a retrospective follow-up, Holden (1987) also working at the Maudsley Hospital, examined the 10-year clinical course of 47 cases of paranoid psychosis identified from the Camberwell Case Register. He was able to exclude immediately 10 cases as misdiagnosed affective or clearly organic psychoses. Of the 37 patients who remained, 13 had progressed to dementia within three years. Those patients who were older, experienced visual hallucinations and were mildly cognitively impaired at presentation, had a worse outcome.

From the results of a three year prospective follow-up of late paraphrenic patients, Naguib (1993) , using cluster analysis, identified two main sub-types of late paraphrenia amongst a group of 43 patients. The first group he called "hallucinatory paraphrenia" (66%) with prominent auditory hallucinations and first rank symptoms in about 50%. These patients were characterized by the very high psychiatric morbidity at presentation and later follow-up. Naguib's second sub-type he chose to call "delusional paraphrenia". Such patients had rather limited psychopathology, a high mortality at follow-up but only limited cognitive deterioration.

The advent of ICD-10 (WHO 1992) has removed the diagnostic category of late paraphrenia and such patients will in future be ascribed to the diagnoses of schizophrenia and delusional disorder (Quintal et al. 1991). Around 60% of patients previously diagnosed as late paraphrenic fit ICD-10 criteria for schizophrenia (Quintal et al. 1991; Howard et al. 1994a) , the majority of the remainder; delusional disorder with a few cases of schizoaffective disorders. Unfortunately, under this classification, the mere presence of prominent auditory hallucinations is sufficient to warrant a diagnosis of schizophrenia and to exclude any other. We have recently collected a large prospective sample of 101 patients with late paraphrenia, all of whom were examined using the Present State Examination. These late paraphrenics were ascribed ICD-10 diagnoses and the clinical and demographic features associated with these diagnoses are shown in Table 1. The observed differences between diagnostic groups in terms of number of PSE psychotic symptoms and systematization of and preoccupation with delusions are to be expected. After all, patients who fulfill diagnostic criteria for schizophrenia rather than delusional disorder are obviously more likely to have more widespread and florid psychopathology. The lack of any significant differences between these groups in terms of age at illness onset, ratio of males to females, proportion of patients who never married (although the trend for this is in the anticipated direction) and response to treatment, are perhaps disappointing given the postulated differences in the contributions of various aetiological and risk factors that may underlie these diagnostic groups. Of some interest, however, are the differences in mean mini Mental State Examination Score achieved by the patients in the different diagnostic groups. While the MMSE is only a very superficial test of cognitive function, which is used as a screening instrument at the time of subject recruitment (a score of less than 24 out of 30 or clinical evidence of an emerging dementia syndrome were exclusion criteria) , the difference of two points between the mean scores of the schizophrenic and delusional disorder groups is highly significant and probably reflects a greater organic contribution to the delusional disorder of patients and symptomatology. As we shall see later, this conclusion is supported by neuroimaging data from the same patients. Nevertheless, a 3-year cognitive follow-up of a similar group of patients did not suggest that they eventually developed overt dementia (Hymas et al. 1989), their cognitive changes remaining subtle in nature.

NORTH AMERICAN CLINICAL STUDIES

The North American view, until the revision of DSM-III (APA 1987) was that onset after the age of 44 precluded a diagnosis of schizophrenia (APA 1980). Repeated reports of patients who were clinically indistinguishable from individuals with schizophrenia, but whose age at onset had been greater than the arbitrary limit of 45 years set by DSM-III, led to a call for the diagnostic criteria to be changed so as to accommodate such patients within schizophrenia (Gold, 1984, Harris and Jeste, 1988, Rabins et al. 1984, Volavka, 1985). After 1987, the view appeared to be that the similarities between early-onset and late-onset cases of schizophrenia outweighed any phenomenological differences (Pearlson et al. 1989). Combined with ventricular brain ratios (VBR) estimation from CT studies of late-onset schizophrenics (Pearlson et al. 1987; Rabins et al. 1987), which revealed differences between patients and healthy age-matched controls that appeared to mirror those found in early-onset cases, an equivalence, or at least some continuity, between late and early-onset cases was suggested. In a clear reflection of this view, the current draft of DSM IV (APA 1993) does not include a "late onset" category for schizophrenia.

Table 1. Clinical and Demographic Features Associated with ICD-10 Diagnoses in Patients with Late Paraphrenia

Variables	Schizophrenia (n=62)	Delusional Disorder (n=31)	Schizoaffective Disorder (n=8)	p
Age (mean)	79.6	80.3	81.7	0.646
(SD)	(6.1)	(7.1)	(4.3)	
Age at onset (mean)	73.7	75.6	72.2	0.442
(SD)	(8.1)	(8.5)	(7.4)	
MMSE (mean)	27.6†	25.6†	26.6	<0.001
(SD)	(2.2)	(2.1)	(2.3)	
Number of PSE psychotic symptoms (mean)	9.4†‡	7.1†	5.0‡	0.008
(SD)	(4.7)	(4.1)	(3.6)	
Systematization of delusions (mean)	2.1	1.5	1.3	0.005
(SD)	(0.7)	(0.8)	(0.9)	
Preoccupation with delusions (mean)	3.1†‡	2.5†	2.0‡	0.007
(SD)	(1.0)	(1.0)	(1.4)	
Female sex	83.9%	90.3%	87.5%	0.681
Never married	35.5%	38.7%	25.0%	0.762
Partial or full response to medication	66.1%	64.5%	75.0%	0.333

† Schizophrenia ≠ delusional disorder, p<0.05.
‡ Schizophrenia ≠ schizoaffective disorder, p<0.05.

NEUROPSYCHOLOGICAL TESTING

Hopkins and Roth (1953) gave the Vocabulary Subtest from the Wechsler-Bellevue Scale, a shortened form of Raven's Progressive Matrices and a general test of orientation and information to 12 patients with late paraphrenia who performed as well as elderly depressed patients on these tests. This result provided further support for a distinction between late paraphrenia and those psychoses that could be attributed to organic factors.

Naguib and Levy (1987) evaluated 43 late paraphrenics with the Mental Test Score, a Digit Copying Test and the Digit Symbol Substitution Test and found that patients performed less well than age-matched controls on both the Mental

Test Score and Digit Copying Test. Patients showed a mild deterioration in their Mental Test Scores at 3.7 years follow-up (Hymas et al. 1989) but tended to remain above the cut-off point for a diagnosis of dementia.

The most detailed published neuropsychological investigation of patients with onset of psychosis late in life has been by Miller et al. (1991) who assessed 24 patients with an illness onset after the age of 45. These authors used a comprehensive battery of tests including the MMSE, the WAIS, the Wisconsin Card Sort Test, logical memory and visual reproduction subtests from the Wechsler Memory Scale, a test of verbal fluency, the Stroop Test and the Warrington Recognition Memory Test. Patients performed less well than controls on all tests.

In an as yet unpublished study from our own department, Almeida (1993) has been able to identify two separate subgroups of late paraphrenic patients, based on cluster analysis of clinical data and the results of neuropsychological testing. From a group of 40 patients, Almeida was able to recognize a "functional group" which was characterized by neuropsychological impairment restricted to executive functions, in particular on performance of a computerized test assessing a shift in extra-and intradimensional attention set and a test of planning. Such patients had both a high frequency and severity of positive psychotic symptoms and were unlikely to have abnormalities on neurological examination. Almeida also recognized a second organic group; characterized by a widespread impairment of cognitive functions, a lower frequency of positive psychotic symptoms and a higher prevalence of abnormalities detected on neurological examination.

BRAIN IMAGING STUDIES

The first X-ray CT study specifically to examine patients with schizophrenic symptoms with an onset in late life was by Miller et al. (1986). Five female patients were scanned and three of these were found to have extensive cortical and subcortical areas of infarction and one had normal pressure hydrocephalus. The scan appearances were so abnormal that the authors titled their paper "Late life paraphrenia: an organic delusional syndrome". Better selection of patients, scrupulous exclusion of those with a history or clinical signs of neurological disease or dementia has not tended to confirm this conclusion. Rabins et al. (1987) determined ventricle to brain ratios (VBRs) with CT in 29 patients whose onset of schizophrenia had been after the age of 44 years. Mean VBR was 13.3% in patients and 8.6% in age-matched controls. Naguib and Levy (1987) reported a strikingly similar result for 45 cases of late paraphrenia. Mean VBR in patients was 13.09% compared with 9.75% in controls. Larger values of VBR were not associated with length of illness or any measured cognitive parameters.

We have explored the brain imaging correlates of clinical heterogeneity in late paraphrenia. Re-examination of the scans of Naguib and Levy's series together with planimetric measurements made on the CT scans of 14 prospectively recruited late paraphrenics demonstrated that those patients who had not experienced Schneiderian first-rank symptoms of schizophrenia had less well preserved cerebral cortices (Howard et al. 1992a and 1992b) . The view that those patients with an onset late in life of a less schizophrenic syndrome in which delusions represent the most prominent aspects of psychopathology tend to have brains that are more structurally abnormal than late onset schizophrenics is supported by the observations of Flint et al. (1991). These authors found areas of unsuspected cerebral infarction generally subcortical or frontal to be significantly commoner in late paraphrenic patients who had delusions but no hallucinations.

Pearlson et al. (1993) have recently reported quantitative volumetric measurements of the third ventricle and estimations of VBR from the MR images of 11 patients with late-onset schizophrenia (mean age at onset 70 years) and 18 healthy elderly control subjects. Third ventricle volumes were raised by 45% and VBR by 30% in late-onset schizophrenics compared with controls.

We (Howard et al. 1994b) have recently reported the results of MR volumetric measurements of brain and extra- and intracerebral CSF volumes from 47 patients with late paraphrenia and 33 age-matched healthy control subjects. We have described the criteria for entry to our late paraphrenia studies in detail elsewhere (Howard et al. 1994a), but briefly these are:

> Onset of persecutory, fantastic, referential or grandiose delusions with, or without, hallucinations after the age of 60.

> Intellectual capacity consistent with normal ageing: MMSE score of 24 or greater and no clinical evidence of dementia.

> Absence of a primary affective disorder.

> Psychotic phenomena always occur in setting of clear consciousness.

> Absence of history or clinical signs of stroke, neurological illness, alcohol or drug abuse.

In our study, volumes of the lateral and third ventricles were significantly greater in patients than in age-matched healthy controls. When the late paraphrenics were divided into the alternative ICD-10 (WHO 1992) diagnoses of schizophrenia (n=31) and delusional disorder (n=16) that will replace late paraphrenia (Quintal et al. 1991), some interesting differences between these subgroups of patients emerged. Delusional disorder patients were older (mean 83.2 years) than schizophrenics (mean 78.1 years) and had lower scores on the MMSE (mean 27.5) than schizophrenics (mean 28.6), although both had scores appreciably above those generally seen in Alzheimer's disease and other dementias. Schizophrenics tended to have larger right (6.6%) and left (12.1%) lateral and third (27%) ventricles than control subjects, but these differences were modest in comparison with the increases in right (74.6%) and left (93.5%) lateral and third (55%) ventricle volumes measured in patients with delusional disorder. These large differences between patients with delusional disorder and schizophrenia cannot be accounted for by differences in the ages of the diagnostic groups alone and most probably indicate some increased organic contribution to the aetiology of delusional disorder. We are currently carrying out a follow-up of the cognitive performance of the patients who underwent scanning, but since measurements of total brain and hippocampal volumes were not reduced in delusional disorder patients we are fairly confident that this group do not represent misdiagnosed cases of Alzheimer's disease whose marked cognitive decline will later become apparent.

These brain-imaging findings, taken together with the results of our neuropsychological studies of late paraphrenics (Almeida 1993), provide further evidence for the heterogeneity of such patients that has been indicated byearlier clinical studies.

SHOULD WE PRESERVE LATE-ONSET SCHIZOPHRENIA AND WHAT SHOULD THE CUT-OFF AGE BE?

We have argued for the retention of some indication of the lateness in life of onset of a schizophrenia-like illness for a number of reasons (Almeida et al. 1992; Howard et al. 1993; Quintal et al. 1991). In terms of the phenomenology, associated neuropsychological impairment and implicated risk factors for these psychoses they seem to be essentially different from schizophrenia that arises in early adulthood. It should be stressed, however, that there have been very few studies specifically comparing the features of early and late-onset schizophrenia and these have not always been in agreement. What does seem clear is that some important schizophrenic symptoms, in particular negative symptoms and formal thought disorder, are unusual in late life schizophrenia (Howard et al. 1993 and

1994a; Pearlson et al. 1989). The dramatic excess of females over males is also beyond dispute and cannot be explained by a simple "shift to the right" of the age-related prevalence curve for schizophrenia which has a tendency to arise slightly later in females than males anyway (Castle and Murray 1991).

Retention of a late-onset category undoubtedly aids case-retrieval and hence makes research easier. These cases are comparatively rare and would be easy to lose within the great body of patients with schizophrenia. We are dismayed by the failure of both ICD-10 and DSM-IV to recognize this, although encouraged by informal suggestions from WHO (Sartorius personal communication) that, this may be corrected when ICD-10 is revised in 1998.

The issue of exactly where the cut-off for cases to be considered late-onset should be is a complicated one. DSM-III-R chose 45 years for arbitrary reasons, but perhaps reflecting Manfred Bleuler's original notion that onset after the age of 40 marked the divide between late and early cases. We, of course, are proud to be Old Age Psychiatrists and hence have our own reasons for preferring to use 60 as our cut-off age. What is clear is that, not unexpectedly, the later the cut-off point is set then the greater the apparent differences between early and late-onset cases become (Howard et al. 1993).

Whatever age cut-off is adopted, it seems ill-conceived to choose on a purely arbitrary basis and preferable to do so by means of a more sophisticated mathematical analysis of the data (Levy and Almeida 1994).

In conclusion, we would argue that whatever these conditions are called, and at whatever age they are deemed to have their onset, it is premature to write them out of existence. The debate concerning late-onset schizophrenia has dogged psychiatry for many years and should not be brought to an abrupt end, particularly now that it is becoming amenable to objective examination.

REFERENCES

Almeida 0. (1993). "Clinical and cognitive diversity of psychotic states arising in late life (late paraphrenia)", PhD Thesis. University of London.

Almeida O., Howard R., Fbrstl H. and Levy R. (1992). "Should the diagnosis of late paraphrenia be abandoned?", Psychol. Med.,22, 11 - 14.

American Psychiatric Association (1980). "Diagnostic and Statistical Manual of Mental Disorder", Third Edition (DSM-III), A.P.A. Washington.

American Psychiatric Association (1987). "Diagnostic and Statistical Manual of Mental Disorders", Third Edition Revised. A.P.A. Washington.

American Psychiatric Association (1993). "Diagnostic and Statistical Manual of Mental Disorders", Draft of Fourth Edition. DSM-IV Draft Task Working Party. A.P.A. Washington.

Bleuler E. P. (1911). "Dementia Praecox or the Group of Schizophrenias", (Translated by J. Zinkin, International Universities Press, New York, 1950). Leipzig. Deuticke.

Bleuler M. (1943). "Die spatschizophrenen krankheitsbilder (Late schizophrenia clinical picture)", Fortschritte der Neurologie Psychiatrie, 15, 259-290.

Castle D. and Murray R. (1991). "The neurodevelopmental basis of sex differences in schizophrenia", Psychol. Med., 21, 565 - 575.

Fish F. (1960). "Senile schizophrenia", J. Ment. Science, 106, 938 - 946.

Flint A., Rifat S. and Eastwood M. (1991). "Late-onset paranoia: distinct from paraphrenia?", Int. J. Geri. Psychiatry, 6, 103 - 109.

Gold D.G. (1984). "Late age of onset of schizophrenia: present but unaccounted for", Comp. Psychiatry, 25, 225 - 237.

Harris M.J. and Jeste D.V. (1988). "Late-onset schizophrenia: an overview", Schizophr. Bull., 14, 39 - 45.

Herbert M.E. and Jacobson S. (1967). "Late paraphrenia", Br. J. Psychiatry, 113, 461 - 469.

Holden N.L. (1987). "Late paraphrenia or the paraphrenias? A descriptive study with a 10-year follow-up", Br. J. Psychiatry, 150, 635 - 639.

Hopkins B. and Roth M. (1953). "Psychological test performance in patients over 60. Paraphrenia, arteriosclerotic psychosis and 14 acute confusion", J. Ment. Science, 99, 451 - 463.

Howard R., Almeida 0. and Levy R. (1994a). "Phenomenology, demography and diagnosis in late paraphrenia", Psychol. Med.

Howard R., Almeida O., Levy R., Graves P. and Graves M. (1994b). "Quantitative magnetic resonance imaging volumetry of the brain, third and lateral ventricles in late paraphrenia distinguishes delusional disorder from late-onset schizophrenia", Br. J. Psychiatry.

Howard R., Castle D., Wessely S. and Murray R. (1993). "A comparative study of 470 cases of early and late-onset schizophrenia", Br. J. Psychiatry 163, 352 - 357.

Howard R., Forstl H., Almeida O., Burns A. and Levy R. (1992a). "Computer assisted CT measurements in late paraphrenics with and without Schneiderian first rank symptoms - a preliminary report", Int. J. Geri. Psychiatry, 7, 35 - 38.

Howard R., Forstl H., Naguib M., Burns A. and Levy R. (1992b). "First rank symptoms in late paraphrenia: cortical structural correlates", Br. J. Psychiatry, 160, 108 - 109.

Hymas N., Naguib M. and Levy R. (1989) "Late paraphrenia. A follow-up study", Int. J. Geri. Psychiatry, 4, 23 - 29.

Kay D. and Roth M. (1961). "Environmental and hereditary factors in the schizohrenias of old age ("late paraphrenia") and their bearing on the general problem of causation in schizophrenia", J. Ment. Science, 107, 649 - 686.

Kleist K. (1913) "Die Involutionsparanoia (involutional paranoia)", Allgemeine Zeitschrift fur Psychiatrie, 70, 1 - 134.

Kraepelin E. (1913). "Psychiatrie, ein Lehrbuch fur Studierende und Artze (Psychiatry, a Text for Students and Practitioners)", Eighth Edition. Barth. Leipzig.

Kraepelin E. (1950). "Dementia Praecox and Paraphrenia" (Translated by R.M. Barclay). Livingstone. Edinburgh.

Levy R. and Almeida 0. (1994). "Late-onset schizophrenia versus late paraphrenia", Br. J. Psychiatry, 164, 127 - 128.

Miller B., Benson F., Cummings J.L. and Neshkes R. (1986). "Late-life paraphrenia: an organic delusional syndrome", J. Clin. Psychiatry, 47, 204 - 207.

Miller B.L., Lesser I.M., Boone K., Goldberg M., Hill E., Miller M.H., Benson D.F. and Mehringer M. (1989). "Brain white-matter lesions and psychosis", Br. J. Psychiatry, 155, 7378.

Miller B., Lesser I., Boone K., Hill E., Mehringer C. and Wong K. (1991). "Brain lesions and cognitive function in late-life psychosis", Br. J. Psychiatry 158, 76 - 82.

Miller B.L., Lesser I.M., Mena I., Villanueva-Meyer J., HillGutierrez E., Boone K. and Mehringer C.M. (1992). "Regional cerebral blood flow in late-life-onset psychosis", Neuropsychiatry, Neuropsychology and Behavioural Neurology 5, 132 - 137.

Naguib M. (1993). "Late paraphrenia: phenomenology, classification and risk factors implicated in its causation", Unpublished PhD thesis. University of London.

Naguib M. and Levy R. (1987). "Late paraphrenia: neuropsychological impairment and structural brain abnormalities on computed tomography", Int. J. Geri. Psychiatry, 2, 83 -90.

Naguib M. and Levy R. (1991). "Paranoid states in the elderly and late paraphrenia". In: Psychiatry in the Elderly (Eds. R. Jacoby and C. Oppenheimer). Oxford University Press. Oxford.

Pearlson G.D., Garbacz D., Tompkins R.H., Ahn H.O., and Rabins P.V. (1987). "Lateral cerebral ventricular size in late-onset schizophrenia". In: Schizophrenia and Aging (N.E. Miller and G.E. Cohen, Eds.). Guildford Press. New York.

Pearlson G.D., Kreger L., Rabins P., Chase G.A., Cohen B., Wirth J., Schlaepfer T. and Tune L. (1989). "A chart review study of late-onset and early-onset schizophrenia", Am. J. Psychiatry, 146, 1568 - 1574.

Pearlson G.D., Tune L.E., Wong D.F., Aylward E.H., Barta P.E., Powers R.E., Tien A.Y., Chase G.A., Harris G.J. and Rabins P.V. (1993). "Quantitative D2 dopamine receptor PET and structural MRI changes in late-onset schizophrenia", Schizophr. Bull., 19, 783 - 795.

Post F. (1966) "Persistent Persecutory States of the Elderly", Pergamon. Oxford.

Post F. (1980). "Paranoid, schizophrenia-like and schizophrenic states in the aged". In: Handbook of Mental Health and Ageing (Eds. J.E. Brien and R.B. Sloane) Prentice Hall. Englewood Cliffs.

Quintal M., Day-Cody D. and Levy R. (1991). "Late paraphrenia and ICD-10", Int. J. Geri. Psychiatry, 6, 111 - 116.

Rabins P.V., Pauker S. and Thomas J. (1984). "Can schizophrenia begin after age 44?", Comp. Psychiatry, 25, 290 - 293.

Rabins P., Pearlson G., Jayaram G., Steele C. and Tune L. (1987) "Ventricle-to-brain ratio in late-onset schizophrenia", Am. J. Psychiatry 144, 1216 - 1218.

Roth M. and Morrisey J. (1952). "Problems in the diagnosis and classification of mental disorders in old age", J. Ment. Science, 98, 66 - 80.
Volavka J. (1985) "Later-onset schizophrenia: a review", Comp. Psychiatry, 26, 148 -156.

World Health Organization (1992). "The ICD-10 Classification of Mental and Behavioural Disorders", Clinical Descriptions and Diagnostic Guidelines. W.H.O. Geneva.

20

RECOGNIZING PSYCHOSIS IN PERSONS WITH DEVELOPMENTAL DISABILITES WHO DO NOT USE SPOKEN COMMUNICATION

Ruth M. Ryan

It is well established that persons with developmental disabilities are vulnerable to the full range of psychiatric illnesses (Sovner and DesNoyers Hurley, 1989; Szymanski, 1977; Ryan, 1993). It is also observed that persons who do not speak may still suffer with schizophrenia (Eaton and Menolascino, 1982; Matson, et al, 1991; Ryan, 1993). Schizophrenia in persons with mild mental retardation (who use spoken communication) is felt to be clinically similar to schizophrenia in persons with normal intelligence (Meadows et al. 1991). Some screening tools which examine for psychosis in nonverbal persons appear to equate the presence of psychosis with a diagnosis of schizophrenia (Matson et al. 1991), whereas some suggest that it is nearly impossible to assess the presence or absence of psychotic symptoms in persons with moderate or greater impairments (Sovner and DesNoyers Hurley, 1989). It has also been noted that when a person cannot speak, the first symptom of any psychiatric or other medical/situational stress may be a change in behavior, and automatically equating unusual behavior with psychosis will lead to overdiagnosis of psychosis and underrecognition of anxiety and depression (Sovner and DesNoyers Hurley, 1989; Sovner and DesNoyers Hurley, 1994; Reiss, 1993).

In a sample of 569 persons with developmental disabilities who were referred for comprehensive evaluation by the Behavior Pharmacology Clinics of Colorado (Ryan et al., 1991) approximately 1% were found to meet criteria for schizophrenia or schizoaffective disorder. A much larger percentage were found

Schizophrenia: Exploring the Spectrum of Psychosis. Edited by R. Ancill © 1994
John Wiley & Sons Ltd.

to have apparent psychotic symptoms. The majority of people in this sample met criteria for major depression (32%), various anxiety disorders (including post-traumatic stress disorder, 40%), and other affective disorders (20%), often with complicating comorbid medical illness which intensified the psychiatric symptoms (70% or more). There were no differences between the verbal and nonverbal individuals with respect to psychiatric epidemiology. Through the process described below it was possible to determine when these symptoms were actually a purely medically driven delirium, psychosis associated with mood disorders, volitionally enacted conditioned behaviors, a response to medical illness, or dissociative symptoms of PTSD.

This methodology was useful for all individuals, and allowed assessment of individuals who were nonverbal for specific diagnoses. Though treatment outcome does not confirm diagnosis, it was observed that use of this methodology to arrive at more specific diagnoses was associated with outcomes that included reduction of symptoms, increased alertness, increased occupational functioning, improved relationship participation, and optimization of cognitive skills. Medication simplification was a feature in these clinical outcomes as well.

One of the goals of the team was to be able to accurately recognize the presence of hallucinations (auditory, visual, tactile, olfactory, gustatory), delusions (false beliefs), and paranoia, then to complete an inventory of background information and other symptoms to determine whether the symptom represented hallucination of a thought disorder, affective disorder, or delirium, or if the symptom was a conditioned behavior or a dissociative event.

Psychosis might be suspected when the person:

1. stares to the side or into corners and nods, as though involved in a conversation. This may be suggestive of auditory hallucinations, such as hearing voices. If the person's response to the imaginary voices appears to be entirely fearful or sad, and there is an association with vegetative signs and symptoms of depression, major depression with psychotic features might be suspected, especially if staff can document that the sadness and vegetative signs and symptoms preceded the onset of the "voices". The "voices" and the vegetative signs and symptoms will not resolve with treatment with an antipsychotic medications alone. If the person has been living in settings where there is very little stimulation or human interaction, is in control of these "conversations", and is not otherwise depressed, anxious, hypervigilant, eccentric, euphoric (as in mania), or confused (as in delirium), one might suspect this is a nonverbal version of "self-talk", where

the person has learned to compensate for an otherwise excessively low stimulation environment. If it can be established that the person has experienced abuse or other trauma, the response to the "voices" is almost always fearful or self-protective, and the person demonstrates symptoms of anxiety, avoidance, hypervigilance, interrupted sleep/nightmares, then a flashback type of experience of posttraumatic stress disorder might be considered.

2. seems to be shadow boxing with unseen others. When the person was seen to be fighting with unseen others, this was much more commonly part of a dissociative experience. The presence of criteria of a previous traumatic abuse experience, hypervigilance, avoidance, and nightmares was suggestive. The absence of persistent gating deficits, bizarre or eccentric behavior would further rule out schizophrenia. The absence of disorientation or confusion would possibly rule out delirium.

3. keeps brushing unseen material off the body. This can be a clue to tactile hallucinations. The other possibilities to be aware of are paresthesias/pain due to a medical condition, obsessive compulsive disorder (Gedye, 1992), or partial flashback type experiences of PTSD.

4. wears multiple layers of clothing. This can be a direct response to some of the physiologic changes as well as the sense of disintegration of a person with schizophrenia. However individuals who have street skill (savvy enough to carry all important items with them) and do not have other symptoms, persons with endocrine disorders which make them feel cold (such as hypothyroidism, which was seen in 15% of the people in this sample), or individuals with sensorimotor integration deficits (more commonly seen in persons with genetic syndromes), or experiencing certain medication effects may demonstrate this symptom without also having a thought disorder.

5. covers eyes or ears. This can be a clue to auditory or visual hallucinations. This can also be seen in persons with hyperacute senses, infections of the eyes or ears, migraine headaches (especially when accompanied by nausea or avoidance of light), or a strong sense of preferences. A careful inventory of other symptoms can establish whether a thought disorder, anxiety disorder (such as PTSD) or a mood disorder is the underlying cause of the symptom.

6. places wrappings around the ankles, collars, sleeves, ears, or other "openings". This can be a clue that the person is avoiding imaginary

dangerous forces entering, or preventing parts of the individual slipping away. Other possibilities might include hypersensitive senses, sensorimotor integration deficits, pain or paresthesia, or repetition phenomena associated with previous trauma (an example would be someone who wraps multiple layers around the genital area as a way of preventing recurrent sexual assault).

7. glares with intensely angry facial expression at strangers or previously liked others. This can be a clue to paranoia. This can also be a clue to dissociative states (particularly if the "look" is not persistent, or has an abrupt onset/discontinuation), or can be part of the aura of temporal lobe epilepsy. The person may have also learned this as a survival skill in placements.

8. displays the "bandana sign". When a person wraps their head with scarves or a bandana, and this does not really go with the rest of the outfit or the weather needs, one might suspect the person is trying to "keep in" voices. Most of the time, however, this is nothing more than a fashion statement.

9. wears costumes. This can be a clue to delusions, which can, of course, be grandiose, hyperreligious, or bizarre, providing clues to diagnosis. Alternative possibilities may include repetition phenomena, transsexualism, or expressions of intense wishes, rather than false beliefs.

10. inspects or refuses food with fear or other intensity. This can be a clue to paranoia, delusions that the person is being poisoned, or olfactory/gustatory hallucinations. Other possibilities are that the person has allergies, or has been trained to be cautious in settings where drugs were hidden in foods.

11. grimaces or winces as though smelling or tasting something foul. This can be suggestive of gustatory or olfactory hallucinations. It is important to note that gustatory and olfactory phenomena are very commonly associated with temporal lobe epilepsy or other irritative temporal lobe phenomena. Other common associations may include migraine headaches, auras of other types of seizures, infections, or dissociative phenomena.

The diagnosis of schizophrenia not only requires exclusion of other possibilities that may be more likely, but also requires the presence of certain symptoms as well. Indeed, the presence of another comorbid condition, such as post-traumatic stress disorder, does not preclude the presence of schizophrenia. Other symptoms which would need to be present for the person to meet criteria for schizophrenia include social withdrawal, inability to initiate activities, bizarre delusions or other psychotic symptoms, isolativeness when stressed/stimulated, persistent sensory gating deficits, and gradual onset of deterioration. All of these symptoms except persistent sensory gating deficits can be seen in other conditions, however, so the meticulous review for vegetative signs and symptoms, family, trauma, and other background history must be done regardless of the firmness of the suspicion of schizophrenia. If a person is able to function just as well in a high-stimulation/chaotic environment as they are in a quiet environment, the likelihood that there are persistent gating deficits is reduced. Also, if the content of a person's psychotic symptoms appears to be (at times) neutral or even positive/encouraging, this may further suggest the presence of a thought disorder.

There are a number of symptoms which, although unusual, are usually not later determined to be psychosis, and do not respond well to treatment geared toward thought disorders:

- Imaginary friends.

- Speaking in altered voices.

- Experiencing the presence of dead or absent ill family or friends.

- Phenomena the person can start or stop at will.

In conclusion, it has been recognized for many years that people with developmental disabilities do suffer with the full range of psychiatric conditions, and that many authorities have described exceptional difficulties in identifying and diagnosing psychosis in persons who do not use spoken communication. An assessment team working in collaboration with individuals and the people who know them best has utilized observation of nonverbal communications with extensive background review and staff interviews to arrive at a consensus regarding the presence (or absence) of psychosis, as well as differential diagnosis, in a large number of nonverbal people. It is recommended that if the clinician is feeling unable to make this determination in a specific individual (despite adequate background information) the clinican should spend an increased amount of unstructured time observing the individual and the people who know the person best. Specific goals would be to learn the person's communication methods, observe the response to stimulation, relatedness to others, degree of bizarreness, strengths, and level of consciousness with behavior changes. This can allow a process leading to more specific diagnosis and a more positive therapeutic outcome.

REFERENCES

Gedye, A. (1992). "Recognizing obsessive-compulsive disorder in clients with developmental disabilities" Habilitative Mental Healthcare Newsletter, 11, (11), 73 - 77.

Eaton, L.F. and Menolascino, F.J. (1982) "Psychiatric disorders in the mentally retarded: types, problems, and challenges", Am. J. Psychiatr, 139, 1297 - 1303.

Matson, J.L., Gardner, W.I., Coe, D.A., Sovner, R.A. (1991). "Scale for evaluating emotional disorders in severely and profoundly mentally retarded persons (the DASH scale)", Br. J. Psychiatr, 159, 404 - 409.

Meadows, G., Turner, T., Campbell, L., Lewis, S.W., Revely, M.A. and Murray R.M. (1991). "Assessing schizophrenia in adults with mental retardation", Br. J. Psychiatry, 158, 103 - 105.

Reiss, S. (1993). "Assessment of psychopathology in persons with mental retardation". In Psychopathology in the Mentally Retarded (eds J.I. Matson and R.P. Barrett), Allyn and Bacon, Needham Heights, MA.

Ryan, R.M., Rodden, R., and Sunada, K. (1991). "A model for interdisciplinary on-site evaluation of people who have "Dual Diagnosis", NADD Newsletter, 8.

Sovner R. and DesNoyers Hurley, A. (1989) "Ten diagnostic principles for recognizing psychiatric disorders in mentally retarded persons", Psychiatr. Aspects Ment. Retard. Rev. 8, (2).

Sovner, R., DesNoyers Hurley, A. (1990). "Assessment tools which facilitate psychiatric evaluations and treatment", Habilitative Mental Healthcare Newsletter, 9, (11).

Sovner, R. and DesNoyers Hurley, A. (1994). "A false negative strategy for dealing with the difficulty in diagnosing psychosis in persons with developmental disabilities", Habilitative Mental Healthcare Newsletter, 13, (1), 17-18.

Szymanski L.S. (1977). "Psychiatric diagnostic evaluation of mentally retarded individuals", J. Am. Acad. Child Psychiatry, 16, 67 - 87.

21

SEX, SCHIZOPHRENIA AND THE CEREBRAL CORTEX

Godfrey D. Pearlson and Ann E. Pulver

The major hypotheses to be explored in this chapter are: (a) that schizophrenia is etiologically heterogeneous; (b) that men and women have different risks for developing different subtypes of this disorder; and that (c) in male and female schizophrenics there is differential involvement of an important system of parallel distributed cortical networks within the brain, an integrated, phylogenetically recent development of the cerebral cortex, the heteromodal association cortical system (HASC). In turn, this differential HASC pathology is linked to differential symptom expression in male versus female schizophrenics.

HETEROGENEITY AND SCHIZOPHRENIA IS A DISPUTED TOPIC

The issue of heterogeneity in schizophrenia is a disputed topic. Opposing views range from that of Weinberger (1987), "no subtypes...only graded differences in pathology" to that of Mesulam (1985), "an umbrella term for several diseases". Carpenter et al. (1993) have usefully conceived of heterogeneity as covered by three broad models. The first model proceeds from pathoplastic explanation in which differences in schizophrenia subtypes are due to the biological system in which the illness appears, (for example older vs younger, or male vs female brains). An analogy here would be Huntington's chorea, in which changes in a single gene are expressed at variable onset times and with a variety of clinical features. A second model posits clinical differences as being due to heterogeneity of etiology and pathophysiology. Here schizophrenia is conceived

Schizophrenia: Exploring the Spectrum of Psychosis. Edited by R. Ancill © 1994
John Wiley & Sons Ltd

of as several different disease entities converging on a similar clinical endpoint (the paradigm being mental retardation). A third model posits each symptom complex as an independent disease entity (for example negative symptoms, positive symptoms, and cognitive deficits might each represent separate etio-pathologies).

Recent reviews suggest that schizophrenia is heterogenous and that heterogeneity is closely intertwined with the issue of sex. For examples, etiologically, men and women may be at different risks for developing different subtypes of the disorder (see review by Goldstein, 1990; Wolyniec et al., 1992). Evidence supporting this general hypothesis is based on the observation that gender appears to influence schizophrenia in a variety of ways including differences in etiology, clinical picture and biologic markers of the disease. Some examples are: (1) the clinical expression of the disease, (e.g., age at onset, pre-morbid history, symptoms, course and outcome); (2) the association between obstetrical complications and the risk for schizophrenia; (3) response to pharmacologic treatment; (4) familial risk for schizophrenia; (5) the probability of having neurologic deficits (Manschreck and Ames, 1984); (6) inter-hemispheric differences in cerebral blood flow; (7) olfactory agnosia; (8) corpus callosum reduction; 9) lateral ventricular enlargement (Andreasen 1990); and (10) density of dopamine D_2 receptors in basal ganglia, assessed by positron emission tomography (PET) scanning, (Tune, et al., 1994).

Structural neuroimaging techniques provide a powerful tool to increase our understanding of the pathophysiology of schizophrenia. In particular, knowledge of usual brain development and normal male/female brain differences allows inferences to be made from identification of specific disease-related regional brain anomalies about the timing of developmental abnormalities associated with the disorder.

This chapter is organized as follows: (a) a review of gender differences in schizophrenia; (b) a discussion of normal gender differences in brain organization; (c) reviews of schizophrenia, etiology and male - female brain differences; and (d) of cerebral structural changes in schizophrenia.

In outline, our argument is as follows. Schizophrenia is likely an etiologically heterogeneous disorder. Sex is closely related to the issue of heterogeneity. Men and women differ in their clinical expression of schizophrenia (symptom predominance, age of onset, treatment response), in the association between risk factors (e.g., genetic versus obstetric risk) and in putative biologic disease markers (e.g., neurologic deficits, cerebral structural and functional changes). Possible explanations are that (a) men and women represent different distributions of etiologic subtypes; (b) that a disorder with the same etiology is expressed differently in brains which normally differ in distribution of cortical regions affected by the disease as well as differential response to cerebral injury. (A third hypothesis combines (a) and (b)).

GENDER DIFFERENCES IN SCHIZOPHRENIA

Differences between the sexes in age at onset, premorbid adjustment, clinical expression, course of illness, response to treatment and familial risk suggest that gender is an important differentiator in schizophrenia, (Goldstein, 1988; Goldstein and Link, 1988; Goldstein et al., 1990; Wolyniec et al., 1992; Hafner, 1992). To summarize some of the differences noted, males are more likely to have earlier onset of their disease (e.g. Lewine, 1981); to have poor premorbid histories (Eaton, 1991; Walker and Lewine, 1993); more deficit symptoms (Lewine, 1981); and poorer outcome (Seeman, 1986; Nicole et al., 1992; Haas et al.,1990). On the other hand, female schizophrenics are more likely to have relatives with schizophrenia (Goldstein 1988; Wolyniec et al., 1992), are less likely to have had a history of obstetrical complications (Goldstein et al. 1990), and are less likely to manifest abnormal neurological signs.

Despite relative neglect of female subjects in schizophrenia research (e.g. Wahl and Hunter, 1992), and possibly a non-equal sex incidence of the illness (Iacono and Beiser, 1992; Nicole et al., 1992), it is feasible that clinical differences in female vs male schizophrenics reflect differing balances of etiologies, or prevalence of subtypes (i.e., more genetic contribution in females, more environmental determinants in males). We hypothesize that these etiologic differences in turn interact with the structural and functional sex differences normally found in male and female brains.

Gender Differences in Brain Organization

There is now preliminary evidence that male and female brains are normally organized differently, and differ in the distribution of cortical regions affected by the disease, as well as differential response to the cerebral injury. Sexually dimorphic behaviors include both reproductive and cognitive elements. Neuropathological studies report sex differences in several human brain regions related to reproductive behavior. At least two hypothalamic nuclei are known to be smaller in women. There are subtle sexual differences in human cognitive functions (Maccoby and Jacklin, 1974). A consistent finding is that males tend to perform slightly but significantly better in tasks requiring the mental ability to retain and manipulate spatial and numeric data that cannot be solved verbally

(Benbow and Stanley, 1980), whereas females generally have greater verbal abilities (Gladue et al., 1990; Bakan, 1974). One would expect that this cognitive dimorphism would also be reflected in functional and/or structural brain differences between the sexes, analogous to the neuroanatomic dimorphism related to reproductive behavior.

Several such structural differences have been established in quantitative post-mortem neuropathology studies. One recent study reported that handedness correlated with anatomy of the Sylvian fissure in men but not in women (Witelson and Kigar, 1992). A similar study suggested that the anterior commissure is also larger in women (Allen and Gorski, 1992). New brain imaging methods are shedding light on these differences. Functionally, a cerebral flow study found higher cortical blood flow in women than in men (Gur, et al., 1982), which the investigators hypothesized was related to increased gray matter volume in women. Structural brain differences, if they exist, may well play an important role in mediating the cognitive differences. However, to date there are few post-mortem or in vivo volumetric studies directly comparing regional cortical volumes in healthy women and men.

Heteromodal association cortex, the most evolutionary advanced part of the cerebral cortex, appears to be structurally differentially distributed in men and women (Schlaepfer et al., submitted).

These authors recently showed that despite female brains being smaller in volume, they contain relatively more gray matter, with significantly more gray matter being found in heteromodal association cortical regions. For example in the dorsolateral prefrontal cortex, females had 23 % more gray matter than males. Given the role of dorsolateral prefrontal cortex abnormalities in mediating negative symptoms (see review of Berman and Weinberger, 1990), this relative normal female excess of dorsal lateral prefrontal cortical gray might offer some "buffering" against negative symptoms in women.

The etiology of sexually dimorphic brain differences remains unknown. Suggested factors include the role of androgen exposure in utero (Geschwind & Levitsky, 1968; Seeman smf Lang, 1990); that structurally, female brains are smaller secondary to the smaller female body mass, height, muscle mass and consequently the cerebral mechanisms for muscle coordination. Finally, the effects of genetic (especially sex-chromosomal) influences on brain development remain relatively unexplored.

Schizophrenia, Etiology and Male-Female Brain Differences

We think it probable that environmental interactions such as obstetric complications, which some have claimed are are seen more frequently in male schizophrenics, are associated with widespread and etiologically nonspecific brain changes such as enlarged ventricles and cerebral sulcal enlargement. As argued by us previously (Pearlson et al., 1989b) adulthood ventriculomegaly is a common consequence of perinatal intracerebral bleeding. Male brains in general are more vulnerable or less plastic, in their ability to respond to environmental insults of all sorts (e.g., Lansdell, 1962). Brain-based disorders such as learning disabilities and mental retardation are commoner in men. The cause of this greater vulnerability of the male CNS is unknown, but roles have been suggested for fetal brain exposure to testosterone, and cerebral developmental effects of the Y-chromosome. It is logical that genetic abnormalities are one cause of the observed specific disturbances in localized regional volumes and asymmetry patterns visible on MRI scans in schizophrenia (and perhaps the cellular disorder seen neuropathologically). Such specific changes are more crucially dependent on disruption of timed developmental sequences than the more general abnormalities described above (and, in fact, provide a means of dating the disruption as much is known about timetables of normal brain development).

It is notable that sex interacts significantly with most, if not all, conventional subtypes (e.g., paranoid, hebephrenic) used to classify schizophrenia as heterogeneous (e.g., Seeman, 1981, 1982, 1985). As explained in detail below, two major models can account for this sex-related heterogeneity. The first explains the difference as due to the biological system (the male versus the female brain) in which the illness manifests, i.e., a pathoplastic explanation. This derives support from studies (reviewed above) which show that normal female and male brains differ structurally and functionally (sexual dimorphism). A second and unrelated explanation is that the balance of etiologies, or prevalence of subtypes, differs between the sexes for schizophrenia. As noted above, evidence suggests that females have more genetic contribution and males more environmental determinants. A combined model (e.g., Lewine et al., 1990; Castle and Murray, 1991) posits that such etiologic differences interact with normal sexually dimorphic structural/functional brain differences.

These arguments lead us to a *sex-specific threshold model*. As noted above, male brains are more vulnerable to environmental insults of all sorts as well as less plastic in response to injury (Lansdell, 1962). An analogy here is the male cardiovascular system, which responds to risk factors such as hypertension or increased cholesterol with greater pathological change than in (pre-menopausal) females. The etiology of this male cerebral vulnerability is unknown; however, it has been hypothesized to be related to the male brain being perhaps more lateralized and specialized in certain respects. The role of fetal brain exposure to testosterone in determining this underlying differentiation has been mentioned above. "Cerebral maleness" may therefore normally consist of having more structural asymmetries, stronger hand dominance, somewhat slower neural development, and thus more chances to be injured or "pruned".

This brings us to a "two-hit" model of schizophrenia, requiring both genetic liability plus a second, environmental, "hit". The female brain is less likely to be injured by environmental events, and thus more genetic loading is necessary in the case of a female schizophrenic.

Known Cerebral Structural Involvement in Schizophrenia

Structural brain studies in schizophrenia have rapidly evolved from a stage of no known regional involvement to demonstration that multiple regions are affected. Evidence (e.g., recent reviews of Pearlson and Marsh, 1993; Gur and Pearlson, 1993), suggests two major processes, (a) generalized cerebral involvement (consisting of reduced total brain volume, sulcal atrophy and ventriculomegaly) and, (b) more specific instances of regional involvement. We suggest that these processes vary with etiology and sex.

Generalized Changes

As summarized by Nasrallah (1992) over 75% of 60 CT studies, that included 1600 patients, revealed pathological ventricular dilatation, (mostly lateral and third), in schizophrenic patients, primarily in males (e.g., Andreasen et al. 1992) although not all studies agree on this, (e.g., Zigun et al. 1992). We hypothesize that these more generalized (e.g., modest ventricular and sulcal changes) most likely result from perinatal and postnatal complications, perhaps acting via sub-ependymal and intraventricular hemorrhage, or hypoxia, as argued by Pearlson et al. (1989a) and Murray et al. (1985). Pearlson et al. (1989) showed a history of abnormal delivery to be a significant predictor of lateral ventricular enlargement. Similarly, cortical sulcal enlargement seen in 70% of over 20 studies of > 900 patients (Nasrallah, 1992), is common in men (e.g., Gur et al. 1991). These generalized changes are not specific to schizophrenia, are likely static, and are present at or before the onset of clinical illness (e.g., Nasrallah, 1992). Like the smaller (on CT and MRI), lighter (on neuropathology) brains seen in schizophrenia (by 2 - 8%) and the overall reductions in gray matter of similar magnitude, (e.g., Zipursky et al. 1992; Schlaepfer. et al., in press), these generalized changes tend to be exceeded in extent by specific regional (e.g., limbic and heteromodal cortical) changes in schizophrenia. The magnitude of the latter has been reported to be 15 - 25% (e.g., Barta et al., 1990; McGilchrist et al., 1993; Degreef et al., 1992; Schlaepfer, et al., in press).

Regional Abnormalities

Specific regional changes in schizophrenia affecting predominantly mesial temporal regions (e.g., Roberts, 1991), basal ganglia (e.g., Jernigan, 1992) and association cortex (e.g., Barta, 1992) have been reported from MRI and neuropathologic studies. Neurodevelopmental disruptions of processes such as neuronal migration, proliferation and pruning in fetal development are most convincingly associated with the pathogenesis of these regional abnormalities, (e.g., Nasrallah, 1992; Waddington, 1993; DeLisi and Lieberman, 1991). We are currently investigating if gender has a differentiated impact on regional structural changes, especially those occurring in cortical regions. We wish to document whether or not specific brain changes are more likely to occur or are more severe in extent in male versus female schizophrenic patients and their association with genetic and obstetric risks. Few, if any, prior studies have included sufficiently large samples of female schizophrenics to attempt to answer these questions definitively.

Are regional cortical changes in schizophrenia organized into systems? We have collected evidence suggesting the especial involvement of heteromodal association cortex (HASC), a sexually dimorphic brain system, in schizophrenia (Pearlson et al., submitted; Gur and Pearlson, 1993).

There are numerous approaches for classifying human cerebral cortex. Mesulam (1985) used a scheme organized by regions with shared characteristics, and classified heteromodal association isocortex (HASC) as the most advanced and complex type of association cortex. HASC is an integrated, phylogenetically recent development of the neocortex. From anatomic double labeling experiments primarily carried out in non-human primates by Goldman-Rakic and co-workers (Goldman-Rakic, 1990; Selemon and Goldman-Rakic, 1988), and by others (Pandya et al. 1985) it consists of multiple parallel neural circuits. Three important neural components of HASC are (a) dorsolateral prefrontal cortex (DLPFC), (b) superior temporal gyrus (STG) (which posteriorly includes Wernicke's area, the L planum temporale), and (c) inferior parietal lobule (IPL), which includes the supramarginal and angular gyri. We have hypothesized elsewhere (e.g. Gur and Pearlson, 1993), that heteromodal association cortex is especially affected in patients with schizophrenia, and especially so in women. Preliminary data (Schalaepfer et al., in press) also suggest HASC is normally prominently sexual dimorphic. Evidence also suggests that HASC regions are also normally highly asymmetrical and Crow (1990, 1992) has suggested that schizophrenia is characterized by disturbances in cerebral asymmetry.

Temporal Lobe Findings in Schizophrenia

A series of both post-mortem and neuroimaging studies have demonstrated abnormalities of the temporal lobe in schizophrenia (Brown et. al., 1986; Bogerts, 1984, 1985). Several limbic temporal lobe structures have been shown to be smaller in patients with schizophrenia, including the amygdala, hippocampus and parahippocampal gyrus (e.g., Roberts, 1991). Until recently, less attention was paid to temporal cortex. However, post-mortem (Jakob and Beckman, 1986), MRI and functional imaging studies (DeLisi et al., 1988; Cleghorn, 1992; Andreasen et al., 1992) implicate this region, as do earlier cerebral stimulation studies (Penfield and Perot, 1963).

Evidence is emerging that lateral temporal lobe abnormalities may be related to positive symptoms of schizophrenia (see Gur and Pearlson, 1993, for review), and that the superior temporal gyrus in particular may thus be particularly relevant to the study of the biological underpinnings of schizophrenia. Changes in lateral temporal structures seem strongly associated with two important primary symptoms of schizophrenia: hallucinations (especially auditory) and thought disorder.

PET and SPECT data demonstrate that some positive symptoms of schizophrenia correlate with increased glucose metabolism or blood flow in the temporal lobe in the region of the superior temporal gyrus, especially on the left side (e.g., McGuire et al., 1993; Suzuki et al., 1993). Gender differences in this finding should be studied with adequate power, but to date relatively few studies have attempted this, and data are absent or inconclusive.

Volume reduction in STG has now been shown to be associated with positive schizophrenic symptoms by three independent groups. These associations include auditory hallucinations (Barta et al., 1990; Flaum et al., 1992), as well as with thought disorder and posterior STG gray matter reductions (Shenton, et al., 1992), logically implicating the planum temporale and Wernicke's area. Recent studies from our group (Schlaepfer et al., in press) reveal significant sexual dimorphism in STG, with females having relatively increased local gray matter, even after accounting for generalized differences.

Dorso-Lateral Prefrontal Cortex

Dorso-lateral prefrontal cortex (DLPFC), is another major HASC region. Berman and Weinberger (1990) recently summarized data from many studies pointing to DLPFC involvement in schizophrenia, especially those involving measurement of regional blood flow during locally dependent cognitive tasks. Regional dysfunction seems linked to "negative" or "deficit" symptoms of the disease. Research into the non-human primate analog of DLPFC reveals anatomic connections to multiple other HASC areas, especially IPL (Selemon and Goldman-Rakic, 1988), as well as to limbic regions and to basal ganglia. Our group has recently demonstrated striking sexual dimorphism in DLPFC, with normal females showing a >20% excess in relative regional gray-matter volume, compared to normal males.

Inferior Parietal Lobule

Many investigators (e.g., Mesulam and Geschwind, 1983; Manschreck and Ames, 1984) have suggested parietal lobe involvement in schizophrenia based on localized deficits in selective attention, localizing neurologic signs, and impairment of facial recognition seen in schizophrenic patients. Both Cleghorn and co-workers (1989) and Tamminga et al. (1992) have documented reduced inferior parietal glucose metabolism in both treated and untreated schizophrenic patients, associated in the latter study with deficit symptoms of schizophrenia.

HASC: Are Heteromodal Association Cortex Gray Matter Deficits Out of Proportion to More Widely Distributed Gray Matter Deficits?

We have preliminary data to support the view that cortical gray matter volume decreases in schizophrenia are greatest in heteromodal association cortex areas. Schlaepfer et al. (in press) measured total brain and regional gray matter volumes in 46 schizophrenic patients and 60 age and sex-matched controls, using a "cortical peel" analysis of segmented dual-echo 5 mm magnetic resonance images. Approximations to dorsolateral prefrontal, inferior parietal, and superior temporal cortex were selected as regions of interest for HASC, and occipital and sensori-motor areas were used as control regions. As predicted by others (e.g., Zipurski et al., 1992), overall, gray matter volume was reduced in schizophrenics. However, gray matter volume was notably reduced in schizophrenic patients in HASC regions even when covaried for overall brain volume, sex, and age ($p<0.03$), accounting for which removed significance from the finding of mild overall gray matter reductions. The most significant patient/control HASC differences were seen in female schizophrenics. The diagnostic specificity of this finding was examined by assessing 27 patients with a mixture of psychotic and non-psychotic bipolar disorder; these did not show heteromodal gray matter reduction compared to normals. After covariance, control regions and global gray did not differ between the three groups. Individual regional post-hoc analysis found no additional gray matter differences in non-HASC regions in schizophrenia. These findings offer preliminary support for a hypothesis of disproportionate and rather specific reduction of heteromodal association cortex in schizophrenia (although in this pilot study, regions could be only approximately defined).

HASC gender differences in normals

A second finding to emerge from a related study of normals (Schlaepfer et al., (submitted) was the difference in DLPFC volume between screened healthy control men (N=43) and women (N=17), of comparable age. Even after correction for generalized cortical gray matter volume (since women had smaller bodies of brain volume (p<0.001)), women had 23% more gray matter in DLPFC than men (P<0.0001), and a 13% increase in STG gray (p<0.001). There thus appear to be localized structural sex-related differences in the cerebral cortex. This finding has especially interesting implications. Compared to male schizophrenics, women with schizophrenia tend to have significantly fewer deficit symptoms. If women on average normally have significantly greater relative DLPFC gray volumes, then this may act as a "cortical reserve", and offer some protection from schizophrenia-associated HASC reductions, even in the face of proportionately greater losses in female schizophrenics.

Data from several groups show involvement of medial temporal and basal ganglia regions in schizophrenia but it is clear that these changes are neither universal in nor specific to schizophrenia. Our preliminary data on heteromodal association cortex indicate changes in schizophrenia that appear to be of a greater magnitude than those found elsewhere, with at least some suggestions that these changes may perhaps be specific to schizophrenia. Given the relatively small samples studied, it has not yet been possible to test for gender differences with adequate power.

Other regions

Corpus Callosum

Because mid-sagittal MRI studies yield excellent delineation of corpus callosum, and many conflicting reports of altered callosal size or morphology in males vs females (e.g., DeLacoste, 1982) and in schizophrenic vs controls, we measured corpus callosum area, width and length, on mid-sagittal MRI scans, using a computer outlining method, in 30 schizophrenic and 44 matched normal controls (Woodruff et al., 1993). Mid-sagittal corpus callosum area, length and anterior widths were reduced in schizophrenia, not accounted for by cortical area shrinkage. The largest schizophrenic area difference was seen in the portion of the corpus callosum believed to communicate between the two superior temporal gyri. Interestingly, patient/control group differences were accounted for by comparisons between males only (although the female N was low). Total brain area, although significantly different between male and female normals, was not different between male and female schizophrenia. We concluded that "if ... the process of schizophrenia results in a pattern of structural abnormalities that evens out any pre-existing sex differences, it may mean that males are more vulnerable to the structural effects of this process".

SUMMARY

As we have noted elsewhere (Gur and Pearlson, 1993) it is unlikely that a disorder as complex as schizophrenia is associated with a single structural or functional lesion in a single neuroanatomical location. Indeed, no such lesion has been identified. Many regions are implicated, but the nature of the abnormalities appears both non-uniform and sexually dimorphic (although few studies have examined possible heterogeneity). It is clear that schizophrenic disease expression differs clinically in men and women. These differences may be due to interaction of pathologic changes with the innately different structure and function normally seen in male vs female brains (that is, an interaction of pathoplasticity with sexual dimorphism). It is also possible that etiologic factors themselves differ in men and women, with women having a form of schizophrenia with a relatively more robust genetic etiology and men having a form in which "brain injury" is more predominant. We further hypothesize that "male" schizophrenia is therefore more associated with generalized brain changes (such as reductions in total brain volume and ventricular enlargement) while "female" schizophrenia is more likely to be confined to neocortical polymodal association cortical regions. In addition, similar sex-related heterogeneity is likely to affect other key regions known to be implicated in the neuropathology of schizophrenia, including temporal limbic areas and basal ganglia. In summary, we believe that the clinical features and findings from pathological and neuroimaging studies in schizophrenia suggest prominent heteromodal association cortical involvement in the disease. We believe that this hypothesis has heuristic value, and elsewhere have presented preliminary evidence showing striking MRI findings in two portions of the heteromodal system (planum temporale and inferior parietal lobule) in patients with schizophrenia compared to controls (Petty et al., 1993; McGilchrist et al., 1993), as well as significant sexual dimorphism in normals in DLPFC and STG (Schlaepfer et al., submitted).

ACKNOWLEDGEMENTS

Funded in part by the following NIH grants:
To GDP: MH43775, MH43326, and OP GCRC RR00722
ToAEP: MH45588

REFERENCES

Allen, L.S. and Gorski, R.A. (1992). "Sexual orientation and the size of the anterior commissure in the human brain", Proc. Natl. Acad. Sci. USA, 89, 7199 - 7202.

Andreasen, N.C., Swayze, V.W. II, Flaum. M., Yates, W.R., Arndt, S. and McChesney, C. (1990). "Ventricular enlargement in schizophrenia evaluated with computed tomographic scanning effects of gender, age and stage of illncss", Arch. Gen. Psychiatry, 47, 1008 - 1015.

Andreasen, N.C., Ehrhardt, J.C., Swayze, V.W., Alliger, R.J., Yuh, W.T.C., Cohen, G. and Ziebell, S. (1992). "Magnetic resonance imaging of the brain in schizophrenia", Arch. Gen. Psychiatry, 47, 35 - 44.

Barta, P.E., Pearlson, G.D., Richards, S.S., Powers, R.E. and Tune, L.E. (1990). "Reduced superior temporal gyrus volume in schizophrenia: relationship to hallucinations", Am. J. Psychiatry, 147, 1457 - 1462.

Benbow, C.P. and Stanley, J.C. (1980). "Sex differences in mathematical ability: fact or artifact?", Science, 210, 1262 - 1264.

Berman, K.F. and Weinberger, D.R. (1990). "The prefrontal cortex in schizophrenia and other neuropsychiatric diseases". In: Progress in Brain Research (eds. H. Uylings and C.G. Van Eden), Vol. 85: The Prefrontal Cortex, pp. 521 - 537, Elsevier, Amsterdam.

Bogerts, B. (1984)."Zur neuropathologie der schizophrenien", Fortschr. Neurol. Psychiatr., 52, 428 - 437.

Bogerts. B., Meertz, E. and Schonfeldt-Bausch, R. (1985). "Basal ganglia and limbic system pathology in schizophrenia: a morphometric study of brain volume and shrinkage", Arch. Gen. Psychiatry, 42, 784 - 791.

Brown, R., Colter, N., Corsellis, J.A.N., Crow, T.J., Frith, C.D. Jagoe, R., Johnstone, E.C., and Marsh, L. (1986). "Postmortem evidence of structural brain changes in schizophrenia. Differences in brain weight, temporal horn area, and parahippocampal gyrus compared with affective disorder", Arch. Gen. Psychiatry, 43, 36 - 42.

Carpenter, W.T., Buchanan, R.W., Kirkpatrick, B., Tamminga, C. and Wood, F. (1993). "Strong inference, theory testing, and the neuroanatomy of schizophrenia", Arch. Gen. Psychiatry, 50, 825 - 831.

Castle, D. and Murray, R.M. (1991). "The neurodevelopmental basis of sex differences in schizophrenia", Psychol. Med, 21, 565 - 575.

Chapman, L. J. and Chapman, J.P. (1987). "The measurement of handedness", Brain Cogn., 6, 175 - 183.

Crow, T.J. (1990). "Strategies for biological research: psychosis as an anomaly of the cerebral dominance gene", In Search for the Causes of Schizophrenia (eds H. Hafner and W.F. Gattaz), Vol 1. Springer-Verlag, Berlin, pp. 383 - 396.

Crow, T.J., Brown, R., Bruton, C.J., Frith, C.D. and Gray, V. (1992). "Loss of sylvian fissure asymmetry in schizophrenia: findings in the Runwell 2 series of brains" (abstract), Schizophr. Res.

Degreef, G., Ashtari, M., Bogerts, B., Bilder, R.M., Jody, D.N., Alvir, J.M.J. and Lieberman, J.A. (1992). "Volumes of ventricular system subdivisions measured from magnetic resonance images in first-episode schizophrenic patients", Arch. Gen. Psychiatry, 49, 531 - 537.

deLacoste-Utamsing, C. and Holloway, R.L. (1982). "Sexual dimorphism in the human corpus callosum", Science, 216, 1431 - 1432.

DeLisi, L.E., Dauphinais, I.D. and Gershon, E.S. (1988). "Perinatal complications and reduced size of brain limbic structures in familial schizophrenia", Schizophr. Bull., 14, 185 - 191.

DeLisi, L.E. and Lieberman, J. (1991). American College of Neuropsychophamacology Satellite Meeting. "Longitudinal perspectives on the pathophysiology of schizophrenia. examining the neurodevelopmental versus neurodegenerative hypotheses", Schizophr. Res., 5, 183 - 210.

Eaton, W.W. (1991). "The update on epidemiology of schizophrenia", Epidemiol. Rev., 3, 1-13.

Falkai, P., Bogerts, B., Benno, G., Pfeiffer, U., Machus, B., Folsch-Reetz, B., Majtenyi, C. and Ovary, I. (in press). "Loss of sylvian fissure asymmetry in schizophrenia: a quantitative post-mortem study", Schizophr. Res.(in press).

Flaum, M.A., Swayze, V.W., Gupta, S., O'Leary, D.S. and Andreasen, N.C. (1992). "Symptom domains and neural substrates of schizophrenia: An MRI study", ACNP New Research Abstracts.

Geschwind, N. and Levitsky, W. (1968). "Human brain: left right asymmetries in temporal speech region", Science, 161, 186 - 187.

Gladue, B.A., Beatty, W.W., Larson, J. and Staton, R.D. (1990). "Sexual orientation and spatial ability in men and women", Psychobiology, 18, 101 - 108.

Goldman-Rakic, P.S. (1990) "Cellular and circuit basis of working memory in prefrontal cortex of nonhuman primates", In Progress in Brain Research (eds H.B.M. Uylings, C. G. Van Eden, J.P.C. De Bruin, M.A. Corner and M.G.P. Feensta), Vol. 85: "The Prefrontal Cortex - Its Structure, Function and Pathology". Elsevier, New York.

Goldstein, J.M. (1988). "Gender differences in the course of schizophrenia", Am. J. Psychiatry, 145, 684 - 689.

Goldstein, J.M. and Link, B.G. (1988). "Gender and the expression of schizophrenia", Am. J. Psychiatry Res., 22, 141 - 155.

Goldstein, J.M., Faraone, S.V., Chen, W.J., Tolomiczencko, G.S. and Tsuang, M.T. (1990). "Sex differences in the familial transmission of schizophrenia", Br. J. Psychiatry, 156, 819 - 826.

Gur, R.E. and Pearlson, G.D. (1993). "Brain imaging in schizophrenia: a review", Schizophr. Bull., 19, 337 - 354.

Gur, R.C., Gur, R.E., Obrist, W.D., Hungerbuhler, J.P., Younkin, D., Rosen, A.D., Skolnick, B.E. and Reivich, M. (1982). "Sex and handedness differences in cerebral blood flow during rest and cognitive activity", Science, 217, 659 - 661.

Gur, R.E., Mozley, D., Resnick, S.M., Shtasel, D., Kohn, M., Zimmerman, R., Herman, G., Atlas, S., Grossman, R., Erwin, R. and Gur, R.C. (1991). "Magnetic resonance imaging in schizophrenia I. Volumetric analysis of brain and cerebrospinal fluid", Arch. Gen. Psychiatry, 48, 407 - 412.

Haas, G.L., Glick, I.D., Clarkin, J.F., Spencer, J.H. and Lewis, A.B. (1990). "Gender and schizophrenia outcome: a clinical trial of an inpatient family intervention", Schizophr. Bull., 16, 277 - 292.

Hafner, H. (1992). "Iraos: an instrument for the assessment of onset course of schizophrenia", Schizophr. Res., 6, 209 - 223.

Iacono, W.G. and Beiser, M. (1992a). "Where are the women in first-episode studies of schizophrenia?" Schizophr. Bull., 18, 471 - 480.

Iacono, W.G. and Beiser, M. (1990). "Are males more likely than females to develop schizophrenia?", Am. J. Psychiatry, 149, 1070 - 1074.

Jakob, J. and Beckmann, H. (1986). "Prenatal developmental disturbances in limbic allocortex in schizophrenics", J. Neural Transm., 65, 303 - 326.

Jernigan, T.L., Zisook, S., Heaton, R.K., Moranville, J.T., Hesselink, J.R. and Braff, D.L. (1991). "Magnetic resonance imaging abnormalities in lenticular nuclei and cerebral cortex in schizophrenia", Arch. Gen. Psychiatry 48, 881 - 890.

Lansdell, H. (1962). "A sex difference in effect of temporal lobe neurosurgery on design preference" Nature, 194, 852 - 854.

Lewine, R.R.J. (1981)."Sex differences in schizophrenia: timing or subtypes?", Psychol. Bull., 90, 432 - 444.

Lewine, R.R.J., Gulley, L.R., Risch, S.C., Jewart, R. and Houpt, J.L. (1990). "Sexual dimorphism, brain morphology and schizophrenia", Schizophr. Bull., 16, 195 - 203.

Maccoby, E. and Jacklin, C. (1974). The Psychology of Sex Differences. Stanford University Press, Stanford, CA.

Manschreck, T.C. and Ames, D. (1984). "Neurologic features and psychopathology in schizophrenic disorders", Biol. Psychiatry, 19, 703 - 719.

McGilchrist, I., Pearlson, G.D., Barta, P.E., Harris, G.J., Tien, A.Y. and Tune, L.E. (1993). "Inferior parietal gray matter loss in schizophrenia", New Res. Abstr., 146th Annual Meeting of the American Psychiatric Association, San Francisco, California, May 22 - 27, 230, 117.

McGuire, P.K., Shah, G.M. and Murray, R.M. (1993). "Increased blood flow in Broca's area during auditory hallucinations in schizophrenia", Lancet, 342, 703 - 706.

Mesulam, M.M. (1985). Principles of Behavioral Neurology, F.A. Davis, Philadelphia.

Mesulam, M.M. and Geschwind, N. (1983). "On the possible role of neocortex and its limbic connections in the process of attention and schizophrenia", J. Psychiatr. Res., 14, 249 - 261.

Murray, R.M., Lewis, S. and Reveley, A.M. (1985). "Towards an aetiological classification of schizophrenia", Lancet ii, 1023 - 1026.

Nasrallah, H.A. (1992). "The neuropsychiatry of schizophrenia". In The APA Textbook of Neuropsychiatry, (eds S.C. Yudofsky, and R.E. Hales), APA Press, Washington, DC, pp. 621 - 638.

Nicole, L., Lesage, A. and Lalonde, P. (1992). "Lower incidence and increased male : female ratio in schizophrenia", Br. J. Psychiatry, 161, 556 - 557.

Pandya, D.N. and Yeterian, E.H. (1985). "Architecture and connections of cortical association areas". In Cerebral Cortex (eds A. Peters and E.G. Jones), Vol. 4. Plenum, New York, pp. 3 - 61.

Pearlson, G.D., Garbacz, D.J., Moberg, P.J., Jayaram, G., Heyler, G., Goldfinger, A.D. and Tune, L.E. (1989a). "Symptomatic familial, perinatal and social correlates of CT changes in schizophrenics and bipolars", Arch. Gen. Psychiatry 46, 690 - 697.

Pearlson, G.D., Kim, W.S., Kubos, K.L., Moberg, P.J. Jayaram, G., Bascom, M.J., Chase, G.A., Goldfinger, A.D. and Tune, L.E. (1989b). "Ventricle-brain ratio, computed tomographic density and brain area in 50 schizophrenics", Arch. Gen. Psychiatry, 46, 690 - 697.

Pearlson, G.D. and Marsh, L.M. (1993). Magnetic resonance imaging, APA Annu. Rev. Psychiatry, 12, 347 - 382.

Pearlson, G.D., Petty, R.G. and Tien, A.Y. (Submitted). "Schizophrenia: a disease of heteromodal association cortex?" (1963).

Penfield, W. and Perot, P. (1963). "The brain's record of auditory and visual experience", Brain, 86, 595 - 696.

Petty, R. Barta, P.E., McGilchrist, I. and Pearlson, G.D. (1993). "Loss of planum temporal asymmetry in schizophrenia", New Res. Abstr., 146th Annual Meeting of the American Psychiatric Association, San Francisco, California, May 22 - 27, 10, 61.

Pulver, A.E. and Bale, S.J. (1989). "Availability of schizophrenic patients and their families for genetic linkage studies: findings from the Maryland epidemiology sample", Gene. Epidemiol., 6, 671 - 780.

Rossi, A., Stratta, P., Mattei, P., Cupillari, M., Bozzao, A., Gallucci, M. and Casacchia, M. (19xx). "Planum temporale in schizophrenia: a magnetic resonance imaging study", Schizophr. Res.

Schlaepfer, T.E., Harris, G.J., Tien, A.Y., Federman, E.B., Peng, L.W., Lee, S. and Pearlson, G.D. (in press). "Pattern of decreased regional cortical grey matter volume using magnetic resonance imaging in schizophrenia", Am. J. Psychiatry

Schlaepfer, T.E., Harris, G.J., Peng, L., Lee, S. and Pearlson, G.D. (submitted). "Structural differences in the cerebral cortex or healthy female and male subjects : an MRI study", Cerebral Cortex.

Seeman, M.V. (1981). "Gender and the onset of schizophrenia : neurohumoral influences", Psychiatry J., 6, 136 - 137.

Seeman, M.V. (1982). "Gender differences in schizophrenia", Can. J. Psychiatry, 27, 107 - 112.

Seeman, M.V. (1986). "Sex and schizophrenia", Can. J. Psychiatry, 30, 313 - 315.

Seeman, M.V. (1986). "Current outcome in schizophrenia: women vs. men", Acta Psychiatr. Scand, 73, 609 - 617.

Seeman, M.V. and Lang, M. (1990). "The role of estrogens in schizophrenia gender differences", Schizophr. Bull., 16, 185 - 194.

Selemon, L.D. and Goldman-Rakic, P.S. (1988). "Common cortical and subcortical targets of the dorsolateral prefrontal and posterior parietal cortices in the rhesus monkey: evidence for a distributed neural network subserving spatially guided behavior", J. Neurosci., 8, 4049 - 4068.

Shenton, M.E., Kikinis, R., Joleschizophrenic, F.A., Pollak, S., LeMay, M. and McCarley, R.W. (1992). "Temporal lobe abnormalities in schizophrenia: an MRI study", APA New Res. Abstr., No. 243, p.107, 145th Annual Meeting, Washington, DC.

Suzuki, M., Yuasa, S., Minabe, Y., Murata, M. and Kurachi, M. (1993). "Left superior temporal blood flow increases in schizophrenic and schizophrenia form patients with auditory hallucinations: a longitudinal case study using 123I-IMP SPECT", Eur. Arch. Psychiatry Clin. Neurosci., 242, 257 - 261.

Tamminga, C.A., Thaker, G.K. and Buchanan, R. (1992). "Limbic system abnormalities identified in schizophrenia using positron emission tomography with fluorodeoxygluxose and neocortical alterations with deficit syndrome", Arch. Gen. Psychiatry 49, 522 - 530.

Tune, L.E., Wong, D.F., Pearlson, G.D., Strauss, M.E. and Wagner, H.N. (in press). "Elevated dopamine D2 receptor density in 25 schizophrenic patients: a PET study with C-11 NMSP", Psychiatry Res. Neuroimaging.

Waddington, J.L. (1993). "Schizophrenia: developmental neurosciences and pathobiology", Lancet, 341.

Wahl, O.F. and Hunter, J. (1992). "Are gender effects being neglected in schizophrenia research?", Schizophr. Bull., 18, 313 - 318.

Walker, E.F. and Lewine, R.R.J. (1993). "Sampling biases in studies of gender and schizophrenia", Schizophr. Bull, 19, 1 - 7.

Weinberger, D.R. (1987). "Implications of normal brain development for the pathogenesis of schizophrenia", Arch. Gen. Psychiatry, 44, 660 - 669.

Witelson, S.F., Kigar, D.L. (1992). "Sylvian fissure morphology and asymmetry in men and women: bilateral differences in relation to handedness in men", J Comp. Neurol., 323, 326 - 340.

Wolyniec, P.S., Pulver, A.E., McGrath, J.A. and Tam, D. (1992). "Schizophrenia: gender and familial risk", J. Psychiatr. Res., 26, 17 - 27.

Woodruff, P., Pearlson, G.D., Barta, P.E. and Chilcoat, H. "Corpus callosum MRI measures in schizophrenia", Psychol. Med, 23, 45 - 56.

Zigun, J.R., Daniel, D.G., Kleinman, J.E. and Weinberger, D.R. (1992). "Ventricular enlargement in schizophrenia: is there really a gender effect?" (letter), Arch. Gen. Psychiatry, 49, 995.

Zipursky, R.B., Lim, K.O., Sullivan, E.V., Brown, B.W. and Pfefferbaum, A. (1992). "Widespread cerebral gray matter volume deficits in schizophrenia", Arch. Gen. Psychiatry, 49, 195 - 205.

Index

Index compiled by Jill Halliday

DRAKE MEMORIAL LIBRARY

WITHDRAWN

THE COLLEGE AT BROCKPORT